Britain since 1700

Second edition

R.J. Cootes

Longman

LONGMAN GROUP LIMITED
Longman House
Burnt Mill, Harlow, Essex CM20 2JE, England
and Associated Companies throughout the World

First published 1968
Second edition 1982
ISBN 0 582 22303 2

Set in 10/12pt Times Roman, Linotron 202

Printed in Great Britain
by Jarrold and Sons Ltd., Norwich

Contents

24   War and the Welfare State

The Second World War and the New Social Services

288

25   Sunset on the Empire

The Commonwealth, Ireland and the EEC

307

26   Towards Automation

Modern Industry, Agriculture, Transport and Communications

325

27   Elizabethan Britain

Social and Political Changes from the 1950s

344

Preface to the Second Edition

Like the First Edition (1968), this book aims to provide a clear and readable account of modern British history for the majority of 14–16 year-olds working towards their first public examinations. Great care has been taken to avoid elaborate language, obscure references and unexplained technical terms. However the text does not 'talk down' and readers are given something substantial to get their teeth into, in the hope that they will develop a genuine interest in and understanding of the period. This is essentially an economic and social history, but enough political material is included to make the account a coherent whole.

New perspectives from recent research have been incorporated, there are many fresh illustrations and some topics are given a more detailed treatment, notably population changes and parliamentary reforms. Above all, the post-Second World War chapters have been entirely recast and rewritten at considerably greater length. The development of the British economy since the war now calls for a less optimistic tone than that struck in the 1960s. Moreover its study is undoubtedly enhanced by a rudimentary understanding of economic theory. To this end, some basic ideas of 'Keynesian' economics are outlined in Chapter 22 and referred to subsequently.

Before this new edition was prepared, the views of teachers familiar with the book were sought. I should like to thank all those who completed the questionnaire sent out in 1979. My revisions are un-likely to satisfy everyone, largely because limitations of space made it impossible to act upon all the suggestions made. Many teachers asked for the replacement of the old *Further Study* sections with questions of the kind found in examinations nowadays. This has been done, and it is hoped that the new *Questions* sections, which draw upon contemporary sources, will prove helpful both in improving pupils' examination technique and in consolidating their learning.

The adoption of a partly thematic approach within a broadly chronological framework necessitates a very thorough contents list and index. Readers should be encouraged to make full use of both in finding their way about the book. To allow for differences in the maturity of pupils at the beginning and end of their course, the book is to some extent 'age graded' – particularly in terms of chapter length.

Thanks are due to Mr L.E. Snellgrove, Dr W.A. Armstrong, Mrs M. Gunny, Mr P. Isaac, Mrs S. Musselwhite, my wife and sons for their help and advice, and, not least, those members of Longman's staff whose dedicated hard work has done much to lighten my task.

RICHARD COOTES, Fareham, 1982

1
Villagers and Townsmen
England in the Early Eighteenth Century

Population density
(per square kilometre)

- 80 or above
- 60–80
- 40–60
- below 40

England in the early eighteenth century

If we travelled back in time to the England of nearly three centuries ago, we would find none of the familiar features of late twentieth-century life. It was like a different world. There were few towns, and, by our standards, these were very small and quiet. There were no mechanical forms of transport and hardly any proper roads. Factories were almost unheard of. The people dressed altogether differently, ate different kinds of food and lived in homes which we would regard as rough, dirty and smelly. Even their favourite sports and pastimes would be almost totally foreign to us. The great majority of people lived in remote villages or small market towns, farming the land or working in the village trades. It was a way of life more like that of the later Middle Ages than our own day.

Population

England and Wales at the beginning of the eighteenth century were inhabited by about 5½ million people – far fewer than the population of present day London. We have no exact figures because the first official *census* (count) was not carried out until 1801, but we can guess fairly accurately on the basis of parish registers and other surviving documents. Roughly a third of the total population lived in south-eastern England. The most densely inhabited area stretched roughly from the mouth of the Severn to below the Thames estuary in the south and the Wash in the north (see map). This is understandable in an age when agriculture was the chief occupation, for these lands are among the most fertile in the British Isles. They also have a relatively warm climate and are not excessively hilly, like much of the North and West.

Parents in the eighteenth century normally had many more children than is usual today. But many died young, especially in infancy. It was estimated that in many towns in the early eighteenth century half the children born died before they were five. Consequently the total population increased only slowly – especially up to about 1750. **Killing diseases** such as smallpox, dysentery, consumption and typhus were widespread. They did most damage among the poor, whose defences against illness were weakened by shortage of food, inadequate shelter and, in some cases, **excessive drinking**. In the period 1720–50 cheap gin was consumed in great quantities, especially in the London area. However in 1751 Parliament greatly increased the tax on spirits, and strictly controlled their sale by distillers and shopkeepers.

Although the poor were most exposed to disease, the general lack of sanitation and medical knowledge meant that even the wealthiest citizens were quite likely to suffer sudden and early death. Queen Anne (1702–14) had seventeen children, yet none reached maturity. However the *death-rate* (the number of deaths per thousand per year) fell in the second half of the eighteenth century. Consequently the population of England and Wales reached 9 million by 1801. This rapid increase was mainly the result of **better diet and living conditions**, which strengthened people's resistance to disease. More food was produced, including potatoes, cheese and fresh meat; more plentiful coal kept homes warmer in winter; soap and clothing were cheaper, as were iron pots and pans – all of which made for greater cleanliness. There were no great improvements in medical treatment, although inoculation against smallpox and the isolation of people with infectious diseases had some effect. Lives were also saved as a result of improvements in the practice of midwifery introduced by a Scotsman, Dr William Smellie.

The village community

The village was still the main centre of English life. Most of the population were engaged in agriculture or rural crafts, like those of the blacksmith, carpenter, wheelwright, thatcher and miller. The village community was very self-sufficient. Few of its inhabitants ever had cause to travel beyond the nearest market town, where they sold their surplus produce and bought shoes, clothes, or anything which might be difficult to obtain in the village. All the most important items in the villager's diet were produced locally. Cereals were the chief crop – wheat, rye, barley or oats – from which bread was baked

A gathering of poor people. About 80 per cent of the population were poor, downtrodden and overworked in this period. Many tried to forget their cares by excessive drinking of strong ale in the local tavern

A group of wealthy people enjoying a supper party

and ale brewed. The other main products of agriculture, apart from wool, were meat and dairy produce and, in some areas, fruit and vegetables. However meat was something of a luxury among ordinary folk, unless they were fortunate enough to own a cow or a pig.

Most farmers were **smallholders**, with anything up to 8 hectares of land. Some of them, together with their families, combined farming with other employment in the home, especially the making of woollen cloth. They lived in roughly built houses of timber, brick or stone according to which building materials were readily available in the area. Most houses in a village were clustered together round the parish church and village inn, along the main highway. Inside they were simply furnished, with strong tables, chairs and stools. Smallholders did without carpets, curtains, upholstered furniture and many other things which we would regard as necessities in our own homes. In the evening, light was provided by dimly burning candles. **Labourers**, working for wages, were normally found on the larger farms, where there was too much work for one family to cope with. They usually lived in squalid wooden or mud-walled shacks, where the whole family slept in one room. The landless labourer could make a satisfactory living at harvest time, but in the winter would be out of work for long periods.

Very little of the land was actually owned by those who farmed it. Most smallholders and larger tenant farmers rented their land from members of the nobility and gentry, though there was, in addition, quite a large class of **freeholders**. Because they had property of their own, most yeoman freeholders were socially superior to tenant farmers. It was an age when a family's position in society depended largely on ownership of land. Consequently the **nobility** dominated the highest political offices and held the top positions in the Church and in the army and navy. It was not unusual for a nobleman's park to measure 80 kilometres round the perimeter. Such families spent tens of thousands of pounds every year on their houses and gardens, and on furniture and works of art. Successful merchants and business-men were keen to invest their wealth in land, for this was the only sure way of gaining acceptance in the higher ranks of society.

Next to the nobility in the social scale came the **gentry** – the major landowners in each county who were not of noble birth. In the vill-age, the chief landowner was called the **squire**. Although he was a Justice of the Peace and often active in politics, he was usually like an ordinary villager in his speech and manners. Much of a squire's life was devoted to fox-hunting, good food and strong ale. His home – the hall – probably seemed like a palace to most of the villagers, but it was bare and uncomfortable by modern standards. Only the best rooms had carpets and few, if any, had curtains. Seats were usually straight-backed chairs, stools and benches. Such houses were so draughty that the family slept in box-beds with built-up sides. Outside there were stables and farm buildings and possibly a coach-house – but coaches could only be used in fine weather, because of the poor state of the roads.

After the squire, the most important individual in the village was the **parson**. Although many people attended church more from habit than religious belief it was still a far more religious age than our own. The parish church was at the very centre of village life. When he was not attending to the needs of his parishioners, the parson usually farmed his own small plot of land, called the glebe. In addition, he received a *tithe* (tenth) of the produce of all the other farms in the parish. Frequently the parson's income from the Church was so small that he relied on the glebe and the tithe to make ends meet.

The parson might give some children of the village a little basic in-struction in reading and writing. However the great majority of people at this time were uneducated. Village records show that even local officials such as churchwardens were often unable to write their own names. Those who did receive some schooling were taught not to have ideas 'above their station'. They were fitted for the place in society to which they had been born, and taught to obey their social superiors. This was believed to be God's will. As the Rev. Isaac Watts put it in 1728, 'The Great God has wisely ordained . . . that among mankind there should be some rich and some poor. And the same Providence hath allotted to the poor the meaner services, and hath given to the rich the superior and more honourable business of life'.

Towns and town life

Towns were few and far between and very small by present day stan-dards, except for **London**. With a population of over half a million, it was more than ten times larger than any other town in Britain and it dominated English life even more than it does today. In London all degrees of splendour and squalor were to be found.

View of London in the 1780s. At that time there were only two bridges across the River Thames

In the fashionable streets and squares to the **west** of the City lived those engaged in business and government, the professions and the arts. Merchants, bankers, lawyers, doctors, writers and politicians rubbed shoulders with the wealthier country gentry, who normally took up residence in their town-houses during the 'social season'. The main centres of social life were the **coffee-houses** where everything from business to political gossip was carried on, amid clouds of tobacco smoke. Political and religious groups each had their favourite coffee-houses, and these later grew into exclusive clubs. Edward **Lloyd's** coffee-house in Lombard Street was the meeting-place for merchants and sea-captains. There they heard shipping news and arranged insurance on cargo and vessels. So much business was done at Lloyd's that before long it became the centre of the world's shipping insurance.

In contrast, the narrow streets, courts and alleys of the **East End** were the home of London's poor. Dockers, seamen and all kinds of other workers lived in filthy, overcrowded dwellings, surrounded by open sewers and back-garden cesspools. The streets overflowed with the rubbish that was thrown into them from every house, shop and workplace. Vice and crime flourished, for there was no police force. No-one went out after dark except on very urgent business, for daytime pickpockets became thieves and murderers at nightfall. Disease was even more common than crime. Probably half the children born in the East End died under the age of two. Those who survived lived in constant fear of the epidemics which swept through the poorer districts from time to time.

London's most crowded highway was the **River Thames**. Passenger traffic jostled with the cargo boats, for, until Westminster Bridge was opened (1750), London Bridge provided the only road over the river. The Pool of London was the centre of the nation's shipping. It handled most of the European, Mediterranean and African trade, some of the sugar and tobacco from the American and West Indian colonies, and practically all the trade with India and the Far East. In addition, almost every English county supplied London with food and raw materials, mostly by sea. In return, London sent foreign imports all over the kingdom and also the products of its own industries, for it was not only a port but an important manufacturing centre. Some of the most skilled workers in Britain were employed in the capital, in the manufacture of a wide range of luxury goods and in shipbuilding, sugar-refining, calico-printing and furniture-making.

The largest **towns outside London** were Norwich (a market town and the centre of the East Anglian cloth trade) and Bristol (the major western port). North of the Border, Edinburgh, the seat of Scottish government and the centre of the country's social life, was almost the same size. However, important as these towns were, it is unlikely that any of them contained as many as 50,000 inhabitants. Other towns were a great deal smaller. Some that are among the biggest today were then either small ports or centres of small-scale domestic industry – for example, Birmingham (metal trades); Newcastle (coal and the Baltic trade); Liverpool (transatlantic trade); Hull (Baltic trade and shipbuilding); Leeds and Manchester (centres of the textile trades of Yorkshire and South Lancashire). It is doubtful if any had a population exceeding 10,000 in 1700.

Some of the largest towns had little or no connection with industry or overseas trade. Places like York, Exeter and Chester were important regional centres of social life as well as being markets for the surrounding countryside. They attracted many of the 'lesser gentry' who could not afford to keep town-houses in London. When the Assizes and Quarter Sessions were held, these towns enjoyed a brief 'season', during which numerous social functions took place – balls, musical recitals, card parties and even plays performed by travelling theatrical companies. But the main centre of fashionable living, outside London, was **Bath**. It was a small, unattractive town before

Bath – centre of fashionable living. Wealthy residents are being carried in sedan chairs to save them the trouble of walking

A public execution at Tyburn. At this time the drop was not used, so the victim was strangled to death in a slow agony. Relatives and friends sometimes pulled the legs of a hanging man to end his torment

Richard Nash went there (1705) and began to organise it as a pleasure resort. His insistence on the highest standards of dress and manners earned him the name of 'Beau' (French for fine or handsome). As Master of Ceremonies, Nash engaged an orchestra and arranged plays, balls, parties and gambling sessions. He even had the streets paved so they would not be out of keeping with the terraces of stately houses, which were fast replacing the shambles of the old town.

Despite their outward show of gracefulness and refinement, the upper classes had many coarse and unpleasant habits. They spat, swore, picked their teeth in public, washed infrequently and ate and drank far too much. They gambled for high stakes, usually for want of anything better to do; and the violent arguments that often resulted could lead to deadly duels with swords and pistols. It was an age of violence and also of brutality. All classes of the population revelled in **bloodthirsty sports and spectacles**. The sufferings of animals were regarded as great entertainment, especially bull- and bear-baiting and cock-fighting. In London large crowds followed the procession of condemned criminals from Newgate Gaol to the gallows at **Tyburn** (along present day Oxford Street). The well-to-do hired rooms in houses overlooking the scaffold to give them a better view of the hangings. Equally popular were visits to watch the antics of the chained lunatics at Bethlem Hospital – usually shortened to 'Bedlam', a word we still use today.

The extremes of poverty and riches were more apparent in the town than in the village. The poorer quarters of the larger provincial towns were as wretched as the East End of London. People lived in waterlogged cellars, crowded into ramshackle wooden huts, or over-ran large houses together with several other families. Well-to-do townspeople, on the other hand, enjoyed more luxuries and comforts than their counterparts in the countryside, as well as a more varied social life. Through their closer contact with London and the other centres of trade and fashionable living, they found it easier to get lux-uries like imported spices, tea and sugar, and domestic items such as china plates and silver cutlery which were rarely seen on the wealth-iest village table.

An age of craftsmanship

The village rather than the town was the centre of English industry in the early eighteenth century. Mining and quarrying, timber-cutting, iron-smelting and a wide range of manufacturing industries were scat-tered around the countryside. Most trades were carried on in the home, and children as young as four or five worked long hours. With-out child labour, many families would not have made ends meet. There were a few examples of large-scale industry, such as the naval dockyards on the Thames and the south coast, where the Admiralty employed hundreds of shipwrights, carpenters, smiths and nail-makers. Even in 1700 the industries of England and Wales were probably more advanced than those of any other country in the world. Very few manufactured goods needed to be imported, while large quantities were sold abroad.

Woollen cloth manufacture had been England's chief industry since the early Middle Ages, and the main source of exports. English cloth was sold all over Europe, and in India, Africa and America. As a

Stonemasons at work

sign of its great importance in English history, the Lord Chancellor still sits on a woolsack in the House of Lords. Cloth was made in almost every county where sheep were reared, but there were three main areas. In West Yorkshire, where the work was mainly done in sheds attached to farms, much of the cheaper, coarser cloth was made. Most of the fine cloth came from the West Country and East Anglia, where the industry was organised on a larger scale. Clothiers often employed their own salesmen, clerks and craftsmen, though the main processes of spinning and weaving were usually carried out in the nearby villages.

Iron was mined and smelted in areas where timber was readily available, for charcoal was used as fuel in the blast-furnace. The manufacture of **metal goods** was centred around Birmingham and the West Midlands, as it is today, and Sheffield was already well known for its cutlery. **Coal-mining** was a long-established industry in the north-east of England, particularly in the Newcastle area. Other mining districts, like South Wales (coal), Cornwall (tin, lead and copper) and Cheshire (salt) were less developed, partly because of the lack of suitable **transport** facilities. There were few navigable rivers, and it was difficult to move bulky goods overland because of the lack of proper roads. This was one of the reasons why practically all industry in the early eighteenth century was on a small scale. Until methods of transport were improved, it would remain very difficult to sell goods in large quantities outside the locality in which they were produced.

In the early years of the century, steam engines began to be used for pumping water out of mines. But, apart from this, and a limited use of water-wheels driven by fast-flowing streams, all forms of industry depended largely upon human strength and skill. A young man who wanted to enter a trade usually had to serve a long and thorough apprenticeship. The apprentice became part of his master's 'family' and, if he was lucky, he would be given some general education in addition to skilled training. It was an age of craftsmanship, when art was still an essential part of industry. Many goods made in this period are highly valued today for their quality of workmanship; especially china and glassware, silver plate and furniture.

Questions

1. Look carefully at the two pictures of rich and poor people on pages 3 and 2. What is the evidence of riches in one picture and poverty in the other?

2. Look at the picture of London in the 1780s (page 5).
   a) What evidence is there to suggest that this was a more religious age than our own?
   b) Name the tallest building (in the centre of the picture).
   c) What were many of the buildings along the riverside used for?
   d) Name the smaller bridge in the background. When was it built?
   e) Nowadays a city with over half a million inhabitants would cover

a much wider area. Why do you think eighteenth-century London was so tightly packed in a small area close to the River?

3. In 1800 an Act of Parliament was passed 'for taking an account of the population of Great Britain, and of the increase or diminution thereof'.
   a) When was the first official count of the population made?
   b) What is such a population survey called?
   c) At what yearly intervals has it been repeated ever since (apart from during the Second World War)?
   d) Most of the early *enumerators* (counters) were schoolmasters and clergymen. Can you give a reason for this?
   e) Name *one* kind of documentary evidence that historians use to estimate the total population before the nineteenth century.

4. 'The boy generally came a week or two on trial, or as they called it "a liking", during which time he ran about the workshop or smithy as he pleased, and amused himself with hammering, filing, boring at his pleasure...He was then taken to the Cutler's Hall to be bound until he reached the age of twenty-one, and now his misery begins and he finds what it is to be a *'prentice*. As the youngest boy he becomes a slave to all above him...and they cuff him and beat him...In the house the apprentices were considered of a different species from the master and his family; their living was mean and coarse and frequently very insufficient.'
   (Arthur Jewitt, a schoolmaster, describing his father's apprenticeship in the mid eighteenth century)

   a) What trade was Arthur Jewitt's father apprenticed into?
   b) He lived in a Yorkshire town which was the main centre of this trade. Name the town.
   c) Why do you think the boy was first given 'a liking'?
   d) What is the meaning of the term 'to be bound'?
   e) Jewitt says elsewhere that masters preferred to take apprentices rather than employ workmen. Can you explain why?

5. Write a paragraph on each of the following:
   a) the village parson (see also page 30)
   b) population increase in the eighteenth century
   c) Bath in the days of Beau Nash
   d) eighteenth-century sports and public entertainments

2

Partners in Power

Crown, Parliament and the Union with Scotland

Queen Anne – the last of the Stuart monarchs

Nowadays the Queen reigns, but she does not *rule*. The important decisions of government are made by Members of Parliament – the people's elected representatives. In the early eighteenth century, however, the **monarch** was far from being a mere figurehead. The Crown and the Houses of Parliament were *partners in power*. Monarchs were expected to give real leadership; to choose their own ministers and to pursue their own policy, especially in foreign affairs. But there were important restrictions on royal power. The greatest of these was the Crown's dependence on **Parliament** for its income. This 'power of the purse' gave MPs an opportunity to resist the policy of the monarch if they considered it unjustified. The day-to-day expenditure of the sovereign was covered by the Civil List, which was granted annually. Extra money for things like the upkeep of the army and navy had to be voted separately by the Commons.

Although monarchs could appoint what **ministers** they liked, in practice their choice was often limited by the need to select men who could command the support of Parliament. The three most important ministers were the First Lord of the Treasury (Chancellor of the Exchequer) who controlled finance, and the two Secretaries of State in charge of foreign and home affairs. The amount of personal influence enjoyed by monarchs varied considerably from one reign to the next – depending on their ability and their relations with ministers and with Parliament. **William III** (1688–1702) was an experienced statesman and, throughout his reign, he was firmly in command of the government. He controlled foreign affairs in particular with little reference to Parliament. But **Queen Anne** (1702–14) found there was a great deal of government business that she was unable to handle personally. She was forced to rely on her ministers more than William had done.

The Hanoverian succession

All of Anne's seventeen children died before she became Queen. So she was the last in the line of Stuart monarchs who had reigned both in England and Scotland since 1603. She had a half-brother, James Edward Stuart, but he was barred from the throne because he was a Catholic. Her father, James II, had been deposed in the Revolution of 1688 for the same religious beliefs. On Anne's death, the succession fell upon a German prince, George of Hanover. **George I** (1714–27) had two important points in his favour. He was a Protestant and a great-grandson of James I, which made him next in line to the throne. But in almost every other respect he was unsuited to his new position.

He was already fifty-four years old, could not speak English, and knew little about the government, laws and customs of his new kingdom.

During the reigns of William and Anne, a kind of **cabinet** of about a dozen important ministers had met two or three times a week to discuss the affairs of government with the sovereign. George I was unable to enter into such discussions, partly because he could not speak the language. Within three years he stopped attending altogether and a different kind of 'inner cabinet' began to develop. It consisted of six or seven of the most powerful ministers, and met in private. Although the King was not included, his permission was required before any topic could be discussed and no decisions were final without his consent. By the reign of George II (1727–60) the inner cabinet was in command of most of the important affairs of government. This was the forerunner of the modern Cabinet.

When the King gave up attending meetings of his ministers, it was natural that one of the inner cabinet should take the lead in discussion and act as the main link with the Crown. As time went on, he became the first or **'prime' minister** – although the title was not an official one until 1905. The first real prime minister was **Sir Robert Walpole**, who was leader of the government from 1721 to 1742, although he never used the title himself. Walpole, a Norfolk landowner, had a great gift for managing people and getting them to do his will. For the best part of twenty years he carried out a policy of peace abroad and financial reform at home which was rarely challenged by the Crown, Parliament or his fellow ministers.

Sir Robert Walpole

Parliament and the people

Ever since the Middle Ages, Parliament had consisted of two separate Houses – the Lords and the Commons. In the early eighteenth century, the membership of the **House of Lords** (under 200) was about a fifth of its present size, yet it had much more power and influence than it has today. Most of the important ministers were peers. The 513 members of the **Commons** (558 after 1707) were elected – but by a very small proportion of the population. Britain was far from being a 'democracy', where voting rights are distributed equally among the adult population. The right to vote was a privilege enjoyed by about 250,000 of the most influential male citizens. No women were allowed to vote before 1918.

Members of Parliament were not paid. They had to have a private income from their property. So the Commons, as well as the Lords, was dominated by landowners – although many MPs had other interests, in trade, banking and the like. At first sight it may seem strange that they were prepared to devote their time to politics without being paid, but this is what local government councillors do today. They want their interests and opinions to be considered before any decisions are taken. In an age when the great majority of the people had no proper schooling, many MPs felt it was their duty, as educated and responsible citizens, to play a part in governing the country. Besides, the wealthier they were the more they had to lose if the nation was

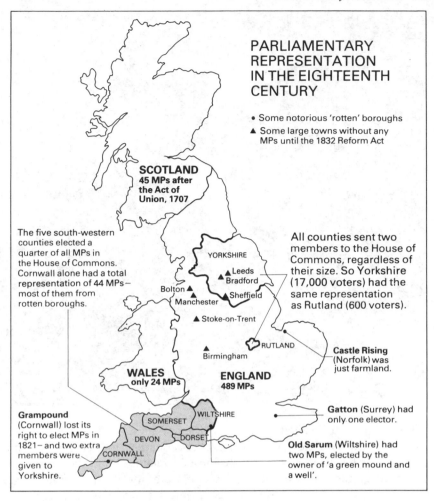

PARLIAMENTARY
REPRESENTATION
IN THE EIGHTEENTH
CENTURY

• Some notorious 'rotten' boroughs

▲ Some large towns without any
  MPs until the 1832 Reform Act

SCOTLAND
45 MPs after
the Act of
Union, 1707

The five south-western
counties elected a
quarter of all MPs in
the House of Commons.
Cornwall alone had a total
representation of 44 MPs –
most of them from
rotten boroughs.

All counties sent two
members to the House of
Commons, regardless of
their size. So Yorkshire
(17,000 voters) had the
same representation
as Rutland (600 voters).

YORKSHIRE

▲ Leeds
Bradford
Bolton ▲
▲ Sheffield
Manchester

▲ Stoke-on-Trent

RUTLAND

▲
Birmingham

Castle Rising
(Norfolk) was
just farmland.

WALES
only 24 MPs

ENGLAND
489 MPs

WILTSHIRE
SOMERSET
DEVON   DORSET
CORNWALL

Gatton (Surrey) had
only one elector.

Grampound
(Cornwall) lost its
right to elect MPs in
1821 – and two extra
members were
given to
Yorkshire.

Old Sarum (Wiltshire) had
two MPs, elected by the
owner of 'a green mound and
a well'.

governed badly and taxes were unwisely spent.

In present day parliamentary **elections**, the country is divided into roughly equal portions (constituencies), each of which returns one MP. In this period, however, members stood for either counties or boroughs. In each county, all freeholders with property worth at least forty shillings (£2) a year could vote, and two members were elected. The remaining seats – well over 400 of them – belonged to the boroughs. Their distribution was not based on the density of population. While places like Leeds, Manchester, Birmingham and Sheffield had no seats at all, scores of hamlets and villages, mostly in the South, returned one or two members each. The boroughs in the five south-western counties together accounted for a quarter of all MPs. **'Rotten'** (decayed) **boroughs** like Old Sarum in Wiltshire and Castle Rising in Norfolk – once busy with markets and local trades – had declined and become farmland. Nevertheless, they continued to return their MPs. Voting rights varied enormously from one borough to the next. In about a dozen, including Westminster, almost every man voted; in others, only the 'freemen' of the trade guilds were the electors.

Most candidates called themselves either 'Whigs' or 'Tories', to indicate their attitudes towards religion, the monarchy and so forth. But **political parties** in this period were loosely organised and did not control politics like they do today. Elections were not decided by making speeches but by wealth and influence. There was no secret ballot. So it was easy for candidates to bribe or bully the electors, for they could check the poll books afterwards to see how the votes were cast. Vast sums of money were spent on buying votes, and the result of an election often depended on which candidates could offer the biggest bribes. Many boroughs were 'in the pocket' of a local landowner (usually called **pocket boroughs**). In other words, one man owned enough property to be able to control the votes of the majority of the electorate. He could often 'arrange' the election without anyone daring to oppose him or the candidates of his choice. When this happened there was no need for any voting, since the number of candidates did not exceed the number of seats available.

No reform of this corrupt electoral system was achieved before 1832 (see page 117). The nobility and gentry had a monopoly of political power and saw no reason why they should risk losing it.

'The Election' by William Hogarth. It shows open voting in an eighteenth-century election. Only about a twentieth of the adult population had the right to vote

Scotland in the early eighteenth century

At the beginning of our period, the English and Scots generally regarded each other as foreigners. They had been ruled by the same monarch since 1603, when James VI of Scotland became James I of England, but they had little else in common. They had separate parliaments and different systems of religion, law and education. The appalling condition of the Great North Road, which was often impassable in winter, meant London and Edinburgh were, at the very best, almost a week's journey apart. This further reduced contact between the two peoples who were generally suspicious and ignorant of each other.

Scotland was much poorer than her southern neighbour. Her **agriculture** was very backward, and frequently unable to support the small population of about 1 million. Thousands died of starvation if the harvest failed, as it did each year from 1696 to 1702, when the crops were continually spoiled by bad weather. Oats were the basic crop, along with barley for making scones and ale. Though many animals were reared, the people ate very little meat. Most of their sheep and cattle had to be sold over the Border to pay for essential imports. Scottish **industry** was as backward as her agriculture in this period. Very few manufactured goods were home-produced, apart from woollen cloth. **Overseas trade** was confined to Ireland and the Continent, especially Norway and the Netherlands, which took small quantities of salmon, coal, salt and lead. It was all on a very small scale. The merchants of Glasgow, the largest port, had only fifteen trading vessels between them in 1700.

Most **peasant farmers** lived in extreme poverty. Their clothes were rough, their children often barefooted, and their tiny homes of turf or stone lacked floors, chimneys and glass windows. The **lairds** (landowners) reflected the poverty of their tenants. Their houses were usually bare and cheerless, and their whole way of life was devoid of luxury, unlike that of the English gentry. The extravagant social life in some English towns had no parallel in Scotland – with the possible exception of Edinburgh, the headquarters of Scottish government, law and religion. Yet even in the capital the strict religious code forbade all dances and theatrical shows.

The port of Glasgow in the early eighteenth century

The Act of Union and the Jacobites

The eighteenth century began with England and Scotland on bad terms. The dethroning of James II (1688) had been bitterly opposed by many Scots, especially the Catholics in the Highlands. It therefore came as no surprise when, in 1703, the Scottish Parliament declared that it would choose its own monarch when Anne died. Continued hostility and complete separation were not, however, in the best interests of either country. If they could settle their quarrels they would have much to gain from closer co-operation. England was at war with France, whose long-standing friendship with Scotland (the 'auld alliance') made possible an invasion of French troops across the Border. If Scotland agreed to a closer connection with England, which would safeguard the English from overland attack, she might, in return, be allowed a share in the valuable English colonial trade.

Representatives of both governments met to discuss their differences, and wisely decided that the two countries would benefit if their parliaments were united. By the **Act of Union (1707)** England and Scotland became Great Britain. From then on they used the same currency and paid the same taxes. The Scots sent forty-five MPs to the Commons and sixteen peers to the Lords. Most important of all for Scotland, her merchants enjoyed free trade with England and the English colonies. The Churches and legal systems of the two countries were so different that it was thought best to let them remain separate, as they still are today. It took some years for the two peoples to learn to trust and understand each other. In the meantime some hostility continued. News of the Union was greeted in Glasgow and Edinburgh with riots and demonstrations, and, before long, Scotsmen were involved in two rebellions against the Crown.

Many Highlanders remained loyal to the descendants of the deposed James II. They were called **Jacobites**, from the Latin word *Jacobus*, meaning James. In 1715 they rose in rebellion, hoping to make James II's son, James Edward Stuart, king. But even before he arrived from the Continent to lead them, they began to drift back to the hills after an indecisive battle at **Sheriff Muir**, near Stirling.

Thirty years later, another Jacobite rebellion proved more serious. James Edward's son, **Bonnie Prince Charlie**, landed on the west coast of Scotland (July 1745) and quickly gathered support on his march to Edinburgh. He proclaimed his father king, defeated a government army at the Battle of Prestonpans and marched into England with 5,000 men. But he failed to rally support among English Catholics. By the time he reached **Derby** (December) only 300 new recruits had joined him. Reluctantly, he turned back, soon to be pursued by the army of the Duke of Cumberland – George II's son. The last remnants of the Jacobite army were massacred at the Battle of **Culloden Moor** (April 1746), a few kilometres from Inverness. Although Charles escaped to France at the end of the year, the Stuart cause was finally dead.

Culloden was the last real battle to be fought on British soil. The rebels who escaped from the field were ruthlessly tracked down and put to the sword or hanged. Nevertheless, when all the bitterness of the rebellion had died down, Scotland entered upon a happier and

Scotland in the Age of the Jacobites

Fierce fighting during the Battle of Prestonpans, near Edinburgh (September 1745)

more prosperous age. The Government broke up the clan system in the Highlands, but raised Highland regiments for the British army, to divert the energies of the clansmen. These did great service in future wars. The building of the first roads through the Highlands, which began after the 1715 Rebellion, brought the spread of Lowland influence into areas which had previously been isolated from the mainstream of civilisation. Agriculture was greatly improved, partly through the enclosing of farms with walls and hedges. Before the end of the century, Scottish farmers, engineers, doctors, painters and writers were making their mark in England.

Above all, the opening of the English **colonial trade** to Scottish merchants after 1707 was, by the middle of the century, helping to raise living standards north of the Border. Many of the imported cargoes of cotton, sugar and tobacco from America and the West Indies were re-exported to the Continent, at considerable profit. This transatlantic trade led to the rapid growth of **Glasgow** and the western ports and the development of industry on Clydeside. Glasgow began to rival Liverpool in size and in the richness of its trade. Its tiny merchant fleet of 15 ships in 1700 had risen to 400 in the last years of the century. Meanwhile, cotton manufacture was developing rapidly in the villages of Lanark, Renfrew and Ayr (west of Glasgow); and in the east, around Perth and Dundee, the linen industry was also growing, to supply the new overseas markets. Not surprisingly, Scottish opposition to the Union had almost disappeared by the late eighteenth century.

Timeline

1688	Revolution. James II deposed.
1688–1702	William III.
1702–14	Queen Anne.
1707	Act of Union.
1714–27	George I.
1715	First Jacobite Rebellion.
1721–42	Walpole leader of the government.
1727–60	George II.
1745	Second Jacobite Rebellion.

Questions

1. Look at the picture of 'open voting' in an election (page 14).
   a) Why was this method of voting open to bribery and corruption?
   b) Can you see any signs of corruption in the picture?
   c) Why were candidates willing to spend large sums of money on getting into Parliament – to do work which was not paid?
   d) Why are there no women in the picture?
   e) How does voting today differ from that shown here?

2. Explain why a prince from Hanover who could not speak English came to rule over the United Kingdom in 1714.

3. Explain the following terms or descriptions.
   a) Parliament's 'power of the purse'
   b) the 'auld alliance'
   c) Jacobites
   d) pocket borough
   e) rotten borough

4. 'Sir, let me tell you, the noblest prospect which a Scotchman ever sees is the high road that leads him to England.' (Dr Samuel Johnson, 1709–84)

   a) At the start of our period very few Scotsmen were inclined to take that 'high road'. Why?
   b) Why did the Scots agree to the Union with England?
   c) What were the terms of the Act of Union (1707)?
   d) In what ways did Scotland benefit from the Union?
   e) What did England gain from the Scottish connection in the eighteenth century?

5. Write a paragraph on each of the following:
   a) Sir Robert Walpole
   b) cabinet government
   c) 'Bonnie Prince Charlie'
   d) Scottish farming in the early eighteenth century

3
Wealth across the Seas
Colonies and Trade

'Trade is the wealth of the world', said the novelist Daniel Defoe in 1728. 'Trade makes the difference as to rich and poor, between one nation and another.' Defoe was right, for trade with the colonies was a vital factor in England's growing prosperity during this period. But although English merchants were among the wealthiest in Europe, they did not have things all their own way. The other seafaring nations of Western Europe, especially France, the Netherlands, Spain and Portugal, had long been rivals in the building up of trading empires in Asia, Africa and the Americas. Each country looked upon its colonies and trading posts as its own property, and foreign merchants were kept out. This explains the willingness of the Scots to unite with England (1707) for they had no colonies of their own and could only be admitted to the rich English trade if the two countries joined together as Great Britain.

The British Empire in 1713

The colonial nations of Western Europe were frequently at war with each other in the eighteenth century, especially the two greatest rivals – Britain and France. Hostilities were not confined to land battles. The side with the greatest **naval strength** usually tried to capture the colonies of the enemy, in the hope of retaining some in the peace treaty. Britain was in a good position because, from the beginning of the century, her navy was the most powerful of all. As a result, when George I came from Hanover (1714) his new kingdom was already the foremost colonial power. A series of land and sea wars against Louis XIV of France had just been concluded by the **Treaty of Utrecht (1713)** which greatly increased Britain's overseas possessions and trading rights, at the expense of France and Spain.

The centre of British colonising activity was North America and the Caribbean. Since the early seventeenth century, increasing numbers of English people had emigrated to make new homes on the east coast of North America. Twelve of the famous **Thirteen Colonies** were already established there before 1700. The thirteenth, Georgia, was founded early in George II's reign (1733) and named after the King. Many of the early American settlers had been escaping from religious persecution at home – like the Pilgrim Fathers (1621) – but they maintained links with 'the mother country'. The governor and certain other officials in each colony were appointed by the Crown. In addition, each colony had its own elected assembly, which voted taxes. Whatever the reason for their original foundation, all the Thirteen

An early eighteenth-century English warship: the 'Royal Sovereign'

The Thirteen Colonies and other British territories in North America

Colonies were looked upon in Britain as actual or possible sources of wealth. They provided markets for the sale of British manufactures, and sent in return tobacco, dyestuffs, coffee and rice (from the south) and pig iron, timber and tar (from the north).

North of the Thirteen Colonies, in present day Canada, lay the territories surrendered by France at the Treaty of Utrecht (see map above). **Newfoundland** and **Nova Scotia** were centres of fishing, and the area around **Hudson Bay** supported a valuable fur trade. These lands were, for the most part, too bleak and uninviting to attract much settlement; but fishermen and fur-trappers put up with the harsh climate because trading prospects were good. Some 2500 kilometres and more to the south were the **West Indies**. Barbados, Jamaica, the Leeward Islands and the Bahamas, together with some of the islands in the later Windward group, and Bermuda in the Atlantic, made up 'the brightest jewel in the British Crown'. They were particularly valuable to Britain because they produced crops which would not grow in a European climate. Vast quantities of sugar (some made into rum and molasses) and raw cotton, were shipped to Britain from slave-worked plantations in the Caribbean.

The British empire in the New World (the Americas) was mainly one of settlement and plantation. Here *colonisation* (the setting up of communities dependent on the mother country) was necessary to create trade where previously there had been none. However, in many other parts of the world, it was sufficient merely to establish **trading**

Surat: an early trading post of the East India Company

posts. For example, in India and the Far East valuable goods were already being produced by the local inhabitants long before European traders arrived on the scene. The **East India Company**, which was founded in England (1600) to trade with this area, did not establish colonies. It contented itself with 'factories' (trading stations) on the Indian coast at Calcutta, Madras, Bombay and Surat. From these bases, the Company's ships brought back silk and printed cottons, coffee, pepper and spices, indigo and saltpetre. By 1700 the Company had a foothold in China, at Canton, from which increasing quantities of tea were imported into Britain.

A number of other British trading companies had bases overseas – including the Hudson's Bay Company (1690), the short-lived South Sea Company (1711) which collapsed in a financial crisis known as the 'South Sea Bubble' (1720–1) and the Royal African Company. The last, which played an important part in the English slave trade, had forts and trading posts along the west coast of Africa – especially in the Gold Coast (present day Ghana). There were also British territories which served as naval bases and so helped in the protection of the Empire. The two most recently acquired were **Gibraltar** (1704) and **Minorca** (1708) in the Mediterranean – both won from Spain and retained in the Treaty of Utrecht.

The slave trade

Slavery is as old as civilisation itself. The pharaohs of Ancient Egypt used slave labour to build the pyramids, and the great empires of Greece and Rome were built on slavery. But the slave trade in our period was of a very special kind. It involved the shipping of Negroes from West Africa across the Atlantic to the New World, where they were sold to the owners of plantations. This trade was started in the early sixteenth century by the Spanish and Portuguese. They were the first to establish colonies in the New World, but, in the process, they almost exterminated the native populations, especially in the West Indies, by their brutality and the diseases they passed on. Consequently they began to import Negroes to work for them in their new colonies.

Realising that sizeable profits could be made from selling shiploads of Negroes, English seamen soon broke the Spanish and Portuguese monopoly of the slave traffic. One of the earliest was Sir John Hawkins, whose first slaving voyage was in 1562. From then on England's share of the slave trade increased rapidly, assisted by the declining power of Spain and Portugal in the seventeenth century. Eventually, as part of the Treaty of Utrecht, Spain sold England a monopoly of the slave trade with the Spanish colonies in the New World. In the next twenty years 150,000 Negroes were shipped to the English and Spanish colonies. Still the demand went on increasing, so that by 1770 more than 100,000 slaves were traded *each year*, half of them in British ships. Bristol had profited most from the British slave traffic in the early eighteenth century, but by about 1800 the merchants of Liverpool controlled six-sevenths of the trade and were among the richest in the kingdom.

The early slave traders worked on a small scale, gaining the protection and assistance of the 'head men' in the African villages by giving them presents. Before long, however, the volume of trade was so great that European agents built coastal forts from which the collection of slaves from the interior could be supervised. Many of the slaves

Negroes being chained on board a slaving ship

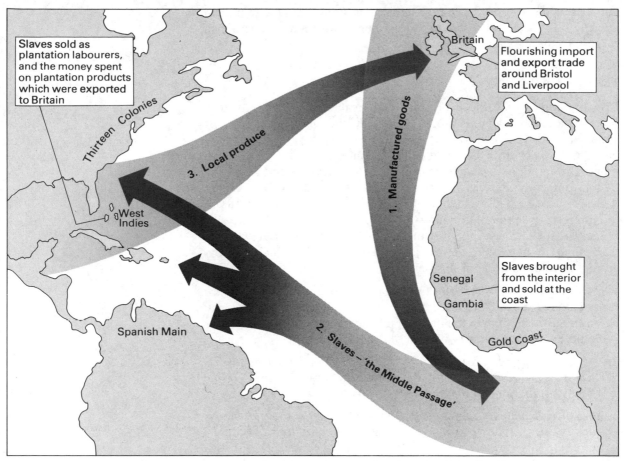

Slaves sold as plantation labourers, and the money spent on plantation products which were exported to Britain

Thirteen Colonies

West Indies

Spanish Main

3. Local produce

1. Manufactured goods

2. Slaves – 'the Middle Passage'

Britain

Flourishing import and export trade around Bristol and Liverpool

Senegal

Gambia

Slaves brought from the interior and sold at the coast

Gold Coast

The Triangular Trade in the eighteenth century

were criminals or prisoners from the numerous tribal wars. The chieftains would probably have cut their throats if they had not been able to trade them. The slave traders offered this as an excuse whenever they were accused of cruelty. But before the Anti-Slavery Movement of the late eighteenth century (see page 119) remarkably few voices were raised in protest against the slave traffic. Many traders sincerely believed that they were helping the Negroes by giving them a chance to become Christians and to escape from the 'primitive' life in the 'dark continent' of Africa.

The slave traffic was part of a larger enterprise – the **Triangular Trade** – so called because it involved three connected voyages. On the first of these, manufactured goods were taken to Africa. Cargoes of cloth, guns, hardware – especially pots and pans – beads, rings and ornaments, spirits and tobacco were exchanged for slaves. Then followed the second or 'Middle Passage' across the Atlantic. The wretched slaves, chained below deck, were often packed shoulder-to-shoulder to fill every available space, so in the likely event of epidemic disease breaking out they died by the score. Unless great care was taken, up to a quarter of the precious cargo might be dead before the three months' passage was over. On arrival in the New World, the slaves were sold, usually by auction, and the ships were reloaded with local produce. Barring accidents, all that now remained was the third stage – the return voyage home, with money and a rich cargo into the bargain.

The 'Laws of Trade'

British colonies, like those of other European nations, were *possessions*, not independent territories. Their defence and much of their administration was paid for out of British taxes. So Parliament felt it had a right to control the trade of the colonies to ensure that Britain – and Britain alone – gained maximum benefit from them. Since the mid seventeenth century, a series of **Navigation Acts**, known as the 'Laws of Trade', had regulated British shipping and colonial trade in the interests of the mother country.

The original Navigation Acts of 1651, 1660 and 1663 were altered from time to time, but there remained three basic principles governing all colonial trade in this period:

1. *All trade to and from British colonies had to be carried in British or colonial ships*. This was intended to encourage both the growth of the British shipping industry and the training of seamen who could defend the country in time of war.

2. *British colonies had to purchase all their manufactured goods via Britain*. The development of British industry was thereby assisted by having guaranteed markets overseas.

3. *British colonies were prevented from sending certain commodities, such as sugar, tobacco, cotton and rice, to any countries outside the Empire. This resulted in a valuable* **re-export** **trade**. The British people could consume only a small proportion of the produce of the colonies. Large surpluses were therefore available for re-export to the Continent, at a handsome profit.

The Laws of Trade gave the colonies the task of supplying commodities which could not be produced in Britain – for example, sugar, cotton and tobacco, all of which required a warm climate. In addition, the colonies were forbidden from competing with the mother country in the production of manufactured goods. Britain's industries served the whole Empire. Woollen cloth was the chief export, followed by all kinds of metal goods, hardware and cutlery. Small quantities of coal, lead, tin and copper were also exported to the colonies. The government further encouraged the growth of British industry through its financial policies. Sir Robert Walpole, for example, in the 1720s and 1730s, removed customs duties on British exports and on imported raw materials, such as cotton, which were necessary to supply manufacturing industries. At the same time, he discouraged imports of foreign manufactures by keeping high duties on them which artificially raised their price to the British buyer.

Despite the growing volume of trade with the colonies, more than half of all British exports in the eighteenth century went to the Continent. Re-exports of colonial commodities were an important part of

William Pitt, Earl of Chatham. He made skilful use of British sea power to defeat France in the Seven Years' War (see page 26)

this trade – much of it concentrated on the ports of Antwerp, Amsterdam, Rotterdam and Hamburg. The Portuguese ports of Lisbon and Oporto also handled much British trade, especially after the Methuen Treaty (1703) with Portugal. This led to increased sales of British cloth to Portugal, in return for a reduction in the British import duty on Portuguese wines. Generally, however, Britain tried to avoid importing goods from Europe, especially if the colonies were capable of producing them. Nevertheless, most of the essential naval supplies – pitch, tar, hemp, timber and bar iron – came from Scandinavia and the Baltic ports. The northern colonies of America sent some timber, tar and pig iron, but not enough to meet Britain's needs.

Large quantities of goods from Europe and elsewhere entered Britain illegally. There were so many complicated trade regulations that they could not be enforced effectively. In any case, customs duties on imported luxury articles were so high that **smuggling** was exceptionally profitable. In 1733 it was estimated that as much as a third of the total trade with France and the Netherlands was smuggled. French wine and brandy, tea from China and tobacco from America were the main items in this illegal trade. The understaffed revenue authorities found it very difficult to catch the culprits, for smugglers were very popular and protected by the public. Smuggling went on almost unchecked until customs duties were reduced to a level which made it no longer a profitable risk. William Pitt's Ministry made an important start in this direction after 1784 (see page 152).

War and discovery, 1739–1783

The peace of 1713 was little more than a pause in the colonial rivalries of the European sea powers. Between 1739 and 1783, Britain was involved in three major wars on land and sea. Her main opponent in each case was France. So many colonies changed hands in these years that the British empire of the late eighteenth century was vastly different from that of 1713. Walpole, for most of the 1720s and 1730s, kept Britain out of expensive foreign wars. He believed peace was essential for prosperity. Many City merchants and businessmen disagreed. They saw no reason to avoid war, for they were confident that British naval superiority would lead to the capture of valuable overseas territories. Their views were strongly represented in Parliament, and they further influenced government policy through close contacts with several of the King's ministers.

In 1739, the 'commercial interest' had its way. Britain went to war with Spain over trading disputes in the Caribbean. Hostility towards Spain had been aroused by a certain Captain Jenkins, who showed MPs an ear which he claimed had been torn off him by Spaniards. In this situation, Walpole's pleas for peace were ignored. Within a year a full-scale European war had broken out over the disputed succession to the Austrian throne. The **War of Austrian Succession (1740–8)** spread to India, North America and the high seas, where the main struggle was between Britain and France. No clear victor emerged from the Anglo-French contest, however, until the **Seven Years' War**

(**1756–63**). It saw the rise to power of one of the greatest war statesmen in British history – **William Pitt**, later Earl of Chatham. From 1757 to 1761 he dominated the Government, in spite of George II's dislike of him, and saw much of the French empire destroyed.

Britain dominated the seas and captured West Indian islands and West African trading posts from France. Even more important, through the efforts of **Robert Clive**, an East India Company clerk who became a general, French power in south-east India was broken. Clive's great victory at Plassey (1757) laid the foundations for future British supremacy over the whole of India. In North America, France controlled the great fertile plain of the interior, from which she planned to keep the Thirteen Colonies penned into the coastlands. Pitt had other ideas, and ordered an all-out attack on Canada (1758). It was a brilliant success for the skilful young generals he put in command. **James Wolfe's** capture of Quebec (1759), which cost him his life, led to the collapse of the French empire in North America. In the **Treaty of Paris (1763)** Britain kept, among other territories, Canada and all of North America down to the Mississippi.

Britain was riding on the crest of a wave – but a shock was in store. The **Thirteen Colonies**, the backbone of her American empire, were becoming increasingly restless under British rule. They objected to being taxed by a Parliament in London in which they were not represented, and complained of the restrictions put upon them by the Laws of Trade. Before 1763 they had needed British military protection against the French, but now they could stand on their own feet. George III and his ministers foolishly ignored mounting opposition in the Colonies. They continued to keep a British army in North America, even though the colonists thought it unnecessary and hated paying taxes to support it. What began as a quarrel soon grew into a full-scale revolutionary war. The Thirteen Colonies banded together and made a **Declaration of Independence** on 4 July 1776. Helped by France and Spain, who joined the rebels to gain revenge on Britain, they forced the Crown to recognise their independence as the United States of America (1783).

Together with the loss of the Thirteen Colonies, Britain was forced to return some of her previous gains from France and Spain, including Florida, Minorca and the West African trading centre of Senegal (won in the Seven Years' War). Nevertheless, in spite of this setback, trade with the new United States of America was soon greater than ever before, and important additions to the Empire were made elsewhere. Since the Seven Years' War, Britain had established many new trading posts and naval stations, taken firm control of India and, above all, brought a whole new continent under the Crown. **Captain James Cook** claimed both **Australia** and **New Zealand** for Britain in 1770. A Spaniard and a Dutchman had sailed there in the seventeenth century, but their coasts had never been fully explored by Europeans before Cook's voyage. At first Britain only seemed interested in Australia· as a place to send convicts. But in the nineteenth century (see page 216) the British realised the great value of the new continent for settlement and trade.

'Clive of India'. At the Battle of Plassey in 1757 his army of less than 3,000 men scattered a French-led force of 50,000

General James Wolfe. His capture of Quebec in 1759 involved a daring assault up the cliffs to the west of the City, under cover of a British naval bombardment

Timeline

1651, 1660, 1663	Navigation Acts.
1713	Treaty of Utrecht.
1739	'War of Jenkins' Ear'.
1740–8	War of Austrian Succession.
1756–63	Seven Years' War.
1757	Battle of Plassey (Clive).
1759	Battle of Quebec (Wolfe).
1763	Treaty of Paris.
1770	Captain Cook claims Australia and New Zealand.
1776–83	American Revolution.

Questions

1. Look at the picture of slaves being put in chains (page 22).
   a) Although vastly outnumbered in a foreign land, the white traders are lightly armed and in no apparent danger. Why?
   b) What was the voyage from Africa to the New World called?
   c) Why was there a need for slaves in the New World?
   d) Name two British ports which were centres of the slave trade.
   e) What 'excuse' did slave traders make whenever they were accused of inhuman behaviour?

2. 'Mr Banister having lately taken from the smugglers a freight of brandy, entertained Mr C, Mr F and myself, in the even, with a bowl of punch.' (Diary of Thomas Turner, a Sussex shopkeeper, 1763)

   a) Apart from brandy, name *three* other articles commonly smuggled at this time.
   b) Why was smuggling so common in the eighteenth century?
   c) Why did the authorities find it so difficult to bring smugglers to justice?
   d) What change in government policy eventually made smuggling no longer worth the risk?

3. On two blank outline maps of the world, show the extent of Britain's overseas possessions
   a) in 1713, after the Treaty of Utrecht
   b) in 1783, after the American Revolution.
   Then summarise, in one paragraph, the main changes that occurred in the space of seventy years.

4. 'Colonies are like fruit which drops from the tree when ripe', said a French statesman in the late eighteenth century. What factors made the American colonists 'ripe' for revolution?

5. Write a paragraph on each of the following:
   a) British naval power in the eighteenth century
   b) the East India Company
   c) the re-export trade
   d) the Seven Years' War

4

Faith and Charity
Religion and Social Improvement

In 1700 the British people could look back on almost 200 years of great religious activity and enthusiasm. But this, in turn, had resulted in much cruelty and bitterness. The period of religious conflict really began when Henry VIII (1509–47) broke away from the Roman Catholic Church and declared himself head of a separate **Church of England**. Before long, the new English (or Anglican) Church found itself opposed not only to the Catholics but also other groups of Protestants called Puritans. These rejected many of its doctrines and practices and established separate **Nonconformist Churches**. Both the Catholic and Nonconformist minorities were persecuted by the Anglicans. Some were fined, imprisoned or put to death for their beliefs. When they gained the upper hand, as the Catholics did in the reign of Mary (1553–8) or the Puritans at the end of the great Civil War (1642–9) they retaliated by persecuting Anglicans. Instead of uniting people in love, religion seemed to be dividing them in hate.

An assembly of Quakers in London. Along with other kinds of Nonconformists, they were free to meet and worship after the Toleration Act of 1689

An Anglican service in the eighteenth century

The Church of England in the eighteenth century

In 1688 James II was deposed, mainly because of his Catholic beliefs. But instead of leading to more religious upheaval, the 1688 Revolution proved to be a turning-point. It was followed by a **Toleration Act (1689)** which allowed Nonconformists to worship freely in their own meeting houses and chapels. Although Catholics were not included in the Act, in practice they too had freedom of worship so long as they did not try to convert others. So the eighteenth century saw an end to the religious conflicts of the past.

Not only were people more tolerant of each other's beliefs, many of them also felt that to be openly *enthusiastic* about religion was dangerous for the peace and harmony of the kingdom. The Church of England in particular became a less powerful force in people's daily lives. The aristocracy and the gentry, who were mostly Anglicans, continued to accept the teachings of their Church and attended its services every Sunday. But they were more casual than they had been in the past. Few made any serious attempt to live strictly according to the principles of the Church. Sir Robert Walpole really spoke for them all when he said 'I am no saint'.

The same was true of many Church leaders. The highest positions in the Anglican Church frequently depended upon party politics. Because archbishops and bishops sat in the House of Lords, the government tried to appoint men whose support could be relied upon. Competition for powerful and well-paid positions became the main interest of many churchmen. **Pluralists**, with more than one appointment, were common. They drew incomes from several parishes, which they rarely visited, and paid curates small salaries to administer them in their absence. Standards of conduct among the clergy were falling. Even parsons who lived in their parishes might devote much of their lives to fox-hunting, drinking and other worldly pleasures. Such slackness was partly the fault of the universities, whose main task was to train the clergy. Oxford and Cambridge had become centres of corruption and laziness. Degrees were awarded almost automatically – often to ignorant men of bad character.

Not all clergymen neglected their religious duties. Some **village parsons** were devoted to their parishioners and led virtuous and useful lives. Nevertheless, for all their good intentions, few had any real understanding of the needs of ordinary people. They were mainly aristocratic in outlook, many being younger sons of landowning families. They mixed with the gentry on equal terms but taught their humble parishioners that it was their Christian duty to know their place and respect their betters. Religion in this form had little appeal in the growing manufacturing communities of Britain. These areas were usually ignored by the Church in any case because they mostly fell outside the traditional parish boundaries. By the middle of the century there were scores of growing industrial villages and towns without any church or priest. Their inhabitants needed a new Christian crusade if religion was to have any meaning in their lives.

John Wesley and the Methodists

The much-needed religious revival was linked with the life of **John Wesley** (1703–91), a clergyman's son from Epworth in Lincolnshire. Wesley had a rare combination of talents. He was a great preacher, capable of reducing the most hostile audience to tears and tremblings, and also a gifted organiser who set on foot a new religious movement and personally supervised every detail of its administration.

After a strict religious upbringing, in which his mother set out to 'break his will' and teach him regular habits of hard work and prayer, he went to Oxford University to prepare to become a clergyman. It was there that he and his brother Charles formed a **Holy Club**, together with George Whitfield, later a famous preacher, and thirteen others. Members cut themselves off from the pleasure-seeking activities of other students and devoted themselves to study, prayer and charitable deeds. They also indulged in periods of 'self-sacrifice' which were so demanding that one member actually died. For example, some nights they laid down in the winter frost for hours on end. All the Club's activities were strictly timetabled. It was this methodical routine which caused fellow students to refer to them as 'Methodists', a nickname which was revived in later years.

Like most great religious leaders, John Wesley continually felt dissatisfied with himself. He failed to settle down as an Anglican minister, and in 1736 he went to the new American colony of Georgia. There he met a group of German Protestants called **Moravians**. Their beliefs and practices, which were like those of the early Christians, greatly impressed him. After returning to England he attended the Moravian meeting house in London where, in May 1738, he went through a strange experience which altered the course of his life. He described his 'conversion', as it is often called, in these words: 'I felt my heart strangely warmed. I felt that I did trust in Christ . . . and an assurance was given me that He had taken *my* sins, even *mine*, and saved me from the law of sin and death.'

From that moment on, Wesley dedicated his life to spreading his

Wesley meets an unfriendly reception at Wednesbury, near Birmingham

belief in personal salvation through Christ. He spent the next fifty-three years travelling, and preached over 40,000 sermons – an average of more than two a day. Wesley had no desire to form a separate church. He accepted Anglican doctrines and always regarded his efforts as an extra activity *within* the Church. But he soon found that very few of his fellow clergymen were willing to let him speak from their pulpits. They distrusted his great fire and enthusiasm. He had no alternative but to preach in the open air, even though the Church of England forbade the holding of services other than in properly consecrated buildings.

Wesley went mainly into areas neglected by the Church and spoke to tradesmen, miners, factory hands and agricultural labourers, many of whom had never before heard the Christian message. He was not always well received. Indeed, on occasions he was attacked with stones and almost lynched by mobs. But the power of his sermons usually won over the most aggressive audiences. Wesley appealed directly to the emotions. He called upon his hearers to repent and begin a new life, and he often spoke of death and the torments of Hell. The effect was sometimes frightening. Wesley recorded that one of his audiences 'exceedingly trembled and quaked... and began to call upon God with strong cries and tears'. The emotional impact of Methodist meetings was increased by the mass singing of hymns. Most were written by **Charles Wesley**, who is said to have composed more than 6,500 altogether. Many are still firm favourites today, such as 'Hark, the herald angels sing!' and 'Rejoice, the Lord is King'.

As well as inspiring people John Wesley could organise them. All converts were formed into permanent congregations with clearly defined rules. The basic unit was the local 'class', consisting of about a dozen members from the same neighbourhood. They met weekly to pray and help each other to overcome temptation. A number of classes made up a 'society'. The eventual aim of each society was to build a chapel where services could be held. By 1784 there were 356 Methodist chapels – mostly in areas where there were no churches, to avoid competition with the Church of England. Preachers were appointed to look after each society and to give sermons and lead the hymn-singing. Most came from the same social background as the people they served. What they lacked in education they tried to make up for in the strength of their religious devotion.

Wesley expected his followers to be Anglicans and attend normal church services in addition to their Methodist meetings. But most Church of England leaders would not co-operate with him. In 1784 the Bishop of London refused Wesley's request that two ministers should be specially ordained to lead the Methodists in America. Wesley ordained them himself, an act which led to a complete break with the Church of England and the formation of a separate **Methodist Church** soon after his death. By 1815 there were nearly a quarter of a million Methodists in Britain, and almost as many in the USA. Today it is one of the largest Protestant Churches, with millions of members scattered throughout every English-speaking country. It has certainly lived up to Wesley's famous motto: 'The world is my parish.'

Opposite: *John Wesley in his later years*

The importance of Wesley

The Methodist movement drew its main support from the 'common people'. It gave a new self-respect to hundreds of thousands of under-privileged citizens and made them thrifty, sober and hardworking. In fact, these 'Methodist virtues' became more widely accepted and played an important part in Britain's growing prosperity. Wesley's work had important **political effects**. Many of the working people who led the early trade unions and fought for parliamentary reform in the nineteenth century gained valuable experience of public speaking in Methodist chapels. Also, by giving the poor hope of a better life in the world to come, Wesley encouraged them to put up with their hardships and reject violence or revolution as a way out. So, indirectly, the Methodist movement may have reduced the possibility of the British people following the example of the French in the Revolution of 1789 (see Chapter 10).

Wesley's teaching not only helped to prevent revolution, it **encouraged peaceful reform**. He was one of the first to organise Sunday schools for poor children – although he had a very narrow view of what should be taught in them. He considered knowledge of the Bible to be sufficient for such children and insisted that they should never be idle. His rather narrow-minded views and superstitious beliefs came out in books he wrote to provide money to support his religious activities. They were priced within the reach of ordinary people and covered a wide range of subjects, including religion, history, grammar, physics and medicine. About medicine he was particularly ignorant. Most of his remedies for ailments were just folklore, like swallowing three pounds (almost 1½ kilograms) of mercury to 'untwist a gut'!

Nevertheless, Wesley did give great encouragement to charitable works and social improvements in general. He was one of the first public figures to speak out against the evils of the slave trade. He strongly supported the campaign for reforming the prisons, led by his friend John Howard. At his London headquarters he opened a dispensary where the poor could get free medicine and medical advice. By the end of his life, his attitude to religion was shared by a large group of clergy and laymen *within* the Church of England. The **Evangelicals**, as they were called, firmly believed that it was a Christian's duty to help the less fortunate. They included such people as William Wilberforce, leader of the movement to abolish slavery. The Evangelicals played a major part in the social reforms of the first half of the nineteenth century (see Chapter 11).

Charity schools and the Foundling Hospital

Methodists claimed the Church of England was 'out of touch' with the common people. Although this was true of the majority of Anglicans, there were important exceptions. Throughout this period, *all* kinds of Christians, working individually and in groups, tried to bring about improvements in social conditions. A good example was the provision of schools for children from poor families. There was no

state system of free education in the eighteenth century – nor, in-deed, before the last quarter of the nineteenth century (see Chapter 18). Consequently most children from families that could not afford the fees of private or grammar schools never learned to read or write. Usually, their only hope was to get a place in a **charity school**.

Charity schools existed in some areas in the seventeenth century, but progress was slow before the foundation of the **Society for the Promotion of Christian Knowledge (1699)**. Through this society the Church of England encouraged parishes to collect local subscriptions towards building and maintaining schools for the poor. Financial sup-port came mostly from the clergy and wealthy landowners, but many tradesmen and others contributed as well. By the end of George I's reign (1727) there were over 20,000 children attending charity schools. Most of the teachers were clergymen and the curriculum was based on Scripture. However the pupils were also taught reading and writing and were sometimes given a grounding in a useful trade. The Charity Schools Movement was the first organised attempt to provide education for the poor. By the 1780s, it was reinforced by the build-ing of **Sunday schools** – especially in growing manufacturing areas such as Lancashire. For children working six days a week, Sunday was the only time available for schooling.

Thomas Coram was a wealthy sea-captain and a deeply religious man who devoted much of his life to helping the poor. Walking through the docklands of East London, he was shocked by the sight of dead children lying by the roadside. He decided to do something about it and began to raise funds to build a hospital for 'foundling'

The bare interior of a charity school. Such schools did not attempt to widen the horizons of the young. They set out to prepare their pupils 'for service or the meaner trades and labours of life'

(deserted) children. There they could be restored to health and given a basic education before being apprenticed to a trade. Some of the greatest people of the time helped him, including the composer Handel, who donated an organ, and the artist Hogarth, who gave paintings to be sold. In 1741 the **Foundling Hospital** was opened – and soon overcrowded, so great was the need for it.

Captain Thomas Coram, 1668–1751

The state of the prisons

The appalling conditions of prison life began to attract the attention of social reformers in this period. Eighteenth-century prisons were not normally used as places of punishment. They were supposed to be temporary lodgings, where suspects awaited trial, debtors were detained until they settled their debts, and convicts were held before going to the gallows or the ships which transported them to the colonies. There were no separate cells. All prisoners, from innocent suspects to the most desperate criminals, were herded together in filthy, overcrowded buildings which were themselves breeding grounds of crime. Gaolers were not paid – they lived on money and goods extracted from the inmates. Wealthy prisoners could get almost anything they wanted, including liquor, if they were prepared to pay inflated prices. On the other hand, the penniless were roughly treated. Gaolers often stole their clothes and left them just a blanket with which to cover themselves.

Debtors' prisons were the greatest scandal of all. Inmates were detained until they paid their debts in full – yet they had no chance of earning money. If friends could not help them, they had to beg from strangers. For this purpose, they were sometimes led in chains through the streets or put in barred cages built into the outside walls of the prison. Even then, much of what they received found its way into the pockets of the gaolers.

In 1729, largely through the efforts of **General James Oglethorpe**, a distinguished soldier, a special Commons Committee investigated two of the most notorious debtors' prisons – the Fleet and Marshalsea – where torture of prisoners had been reported. Some amazingly corrupt practices were revealed. For example, the Warden of the Fleet Prison, who paid £5,000 to get the appointment, made a large income from selling prisoners their freedom. When no direct action resulted from the Inquiry, Oglethorpe pursued a scheme of his own. With the aid of a parliamentary grant, he established the new American colony of **Georgia** (1733) and arranged for many of the early settlers to be debtors straight from gaol.

The most famous prison reformer of the eighteenth century was **John Howard** (1726–90), a Bedfordshire magistrate. In the 1770s, at a personal cost of £30,000, he carried out a detailed investigation of a number of English prisons, including the notorious Newgate Gaol in London. When it was published, in 1777, under the title *The State of the Prisons in England and Wales*, its evidence of appalling corruption and misery shocked public opinion. Howard's recommendations included regular payment of gaolers, better sanitation and ventilation,

clean clothing and bedding, and provision of workshops and chapels for the prisoners. These things are taken for granted today, but in Howard's lifetime they were revolutionary suggestions. It was not until after his death that Parliament even began the task of reforming prisons and prison life.

Humanitarians like Coram, Oglethorpe and Howard only scratched the surface of poverty, misery and neglect. In this period it was not considered the duty of the government to interfere in social life, even to prevent suffering. Nevertheless, their pioneering work helped to make the public more aware of social evils. It paved the way for an 'Age of Reform' in the nineteenth century, when later generations of humanitarians such as William Wilberforce, Elizabeth Fry and Lord Shaftesbury got Parliament to intervene and tackle some of the worst social abuses (see Chapter 11). Like the reformers who followed them, the 'pioneers' of the eighteenth century were all people of strong religious conviction. They, together with John Wesley and the Methodists, brought the Church and its teachings much more into the lives of the poorest and most unfortunate people.

Inquiry into the Fleet Prison, 1729. A notorious gaoler, Bambridge, is being questioned about the reported murder of prisoners. His instruments of torture are on view

Timeline

1689   Toleration Act.
1699   Society for the Promotion of Christian Knowledge.
1738   John Wesley's 'conversion'.
1741   Foundling Hospital opened.
1777   John Howard's *The State of the Prisons in England and Wales*.
1784   Wesley ordains his own ministers.

Questions

1. Look at the picture of John Wesley meeting an unfriendly reception (page 31).
   a) What sorts of people are pictured here?
   b) Why did Wesley deliberately preach to such hostile audiences?
   c) How did he win them over to the Christian message?
   d) What effect did the Methodist Movement have upon many of the people it converted to Christianity?

2. Although it was not his intention, John Wesley's work led to the formation of a Methodist Church, separate from the Church of England. Give reasons why this happened.

3. 'In three or four rooms there were near 150 women crowded together, many young creatures with the old and hardened . . . on the men's side, likewise there were many boys of twelve or fourteen years of age; some almost naked. In the men's infirmary there were only seven iron bedsteads, and there being twenty sick, some of them, naked with sores, in a miserable condition, lay on the floor with only a rag.'
   (John Howard's description of Newgate Gaol, London)

   a) Who was John Howard? Name the book he published in 1777.
   b) What improvements in prison conditions did Howard suggest?
   c) Why were some prisoners short of clothing?
   d) What was the infirmary? Why do you think it was overcrowded?
   e) Why would a prison like this be a breeding ground of crime?

4. 'Men who are to remain and end their days in a Laborious, Tiresome and Painful Station of Life, the sooner they are put upon it at first, the more patiently they'll submit to it for ever after.'
   (B. Mandeville, *Essay on Charity Schools*, 1723)

   a) How does this view of schooling differ from present day educational aims?
   b) What was the main subject taught in a charity school?
   c) Name the Church Society (founded in 1699) which encouraged the provision of charity schools for poor children.
   d) Why were Sunday schools found mainly in manufacturing areas?
   e) Why were most teachers at this time clergymen?

5. Write a paragraph on each of the following:
   a) the Toleration Act (1689)
   b) Evangelicals
   c) Thomas Coram
   d) General James Oglethorpe

5

The Changing Face of the Countryside
Agricultural Improvements

Many pages of history books are filled with the deeds of a few politicians, soldiers, sailors and the like – but the lives of the remainder of the population, though not so glamorous, were devoted to no less important matters. Farming was the main occupation of the British in the eighteenth century, and the same was true of all the peoples of the world at that time. The village and its agriculture was the backbone of the nation. Therefore changes in farming methods could, if widely adopted, affect the lives of millions. In the seventeenth century, before the beginning of our period, there were agricultural changes in plenty. For example, much extra land was brought into cultivation by draining marshes and fenland, new root crops and artificial grasses were introduced, and pasture was improved by flooding water-meadows in the springtime – which helped to increase the number and quality of livestock. Such improvements were taken further and added to in the eighteenth century.

The 'open field' village

Around 1700 most of the cultivated land in the Midlands and South was still being farmed in 'open fields', as it had been since the Middle Ages. Numerous villages in these regions were surrounded by three great, hedgeless fields which contained all the arable (plough) land. The fields were divided into separate **strips**, which were shared out among the villagers – like present day allotments – according to the amount of land they owned or rented. Traditional methods of ploughing had fixed the size of strips. A 'furrow long' or *furlong* of 220 yards (roughly 200 metres) was about as far as a team of oxen could plough before resting and turning round. The width of the average strip was about as long as a cricket pitch (22 yards or approximately 20 metres), which gave it an area of an *acre* (0.4 of a hectare). The separate strips making up each family's total holding were scattered about the fields so that good soil could be evenly distributed.

Each family cultivated its own land, but some of the work was best done on a community basis. Families ploughed the fields in groups, each contributing a share to the ploughing team – usually one of the oxen. Two of the fields were normally devoted to corn crops – rye, barley, oats or wheat. The third normally remained **fallow** (left unsown after ploughing) so that the soil could recover its richness after two consecutive years of cultivation. The fallow period therefore came to each field in rotation, one year out of three, which meant

Plan of an open field village. This was still a common method of farming in the Midlands and South in the early eighteenth century, but it was rarely found in the more rugged countryside of Wales, south-western and northern England

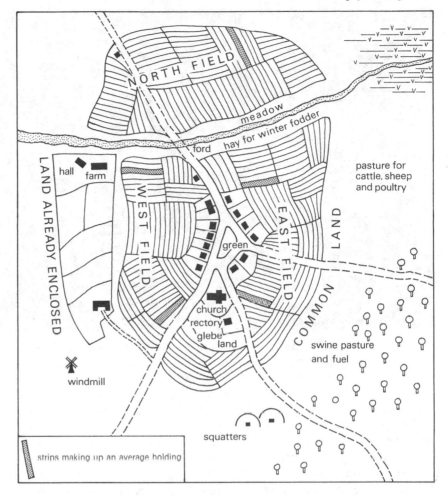

that only two-thirds of the arable land was cultivated at any time. In addition to the three fields, there were commons and wastelands, on which the villagers' livestock grazed in the summer, and meadows, which provided hay for their winter feed.

The open field method of farming was probably started in Britain by the Anglo-Saxon settlers in the fifth century, but we cannot be sure. Some historians think it existed in Britain before the time of Christ. It was still common in many parts of Europe in the eighteenth century, by which time it had also been introduced into the New World by the early colonists. Its long history is understandable, because it was ideally suited to the simple community life of the countryside before the modern industrial age. It made possible the sharing out of each new piece of land as it was brought into cultivation. Above all, it allowed for co-operative ploughing, which was necessary in an age when few families owned either a plough or sufficient oxen to make up a ploughing team.

Nevertheless, open field farming had its drawbacks. It was wasteful of land. The fallow field produced nothing, and, even in the other fields, land was wasted on numerous paths and cart tracks and often

by grass spaces or 'balks' which separated one strip from another. It was wasteful of labour, for the fallow field had to be ploughed even though it was not sown. It was also wasteful of time. Families continually travelled from one part of the village to another to cultivate their scattered strips. The raising of livestock was often handicapped by the open field system. Animals mingled together on the commons and wasteland, spreading diseases and making selective breeding very difficult. There was often insufficient hay to feed all the animals in winter, so some had to be killed off in the autumn and their meat salted. Those that were carried through to the spring were frequently so weak and undersized on their scanty diet of hay that they had to be carried into the fields when grazing was resumed.

The village of Laxton in Nottinghamshire, where open field cultivation is still carried on as a memorial to the past

The open field system was no longer as rigid as it had been in the Middle Ages. In some areas manures were used to enrich the soil and make the fallow period unnecessary. Some farmers managed to introduce new crops on their strips, and even selective breeding of livestock was practised in fenced-off portions of pasture. Nevertheless it was not easy to introduce new methods, because it was usually necessary for the whole village to agree to them. For example, one family could not grow turnips while all the others were growing barley because, after the grain was harvested, cattle were allowed to graze on the stubble and they would eat the growing turnips.

The difficulty of experimenting with new methods had not mattered so much in previous centuries. Then the main concern of the people had been to produce enough for their *own* needs ('subsistence' farming). However, by the eighteenth century, the old methods were unsuited to producing large surpluses of food for the rapidly growing towns. The decline of the open field village, which began long before 1700, was therefore accelerated.

New methods and 'improving landlords'

Interest in experimental farming had been aroused by seventeenth-century travellers to the Continent. They had been impressed by the advances made in countries like the Netherlands, where good agricultural land was too scarce to be wasted by inefficient methods of cultivation. By the mid eighteenth century, the search for better farming techniques in Britain was further encouraged by the need to feed a quickly growing population – although an important reason for the population increase in the first place was the improved diet made possible by earlier agricultural advances (see page 2). The population almost *doubled* in the reign of George III (1760–1820). Most of the increase was in the towns, which depended on the surplus produce of the countryside. Landlords saw that they could make handsome profits if they could find ways of producing a greater surplus for sale. To help increase the productivity of their land they converted open fields into separate, *enclosed* units (if this had not already been done) so that the latest farming techniques could be freely used.

Many 'improvers' (mainly country gentry) published accounts of their experiments. One of the best known of the earlier writers was **Jethro Tull** (1674–1741). On his Berkshire estates he applied some of the methods he had observed abroad, especially in the French vineyards, and described them in *The New Horse-Hoeing Husbandry* (1731). Tull believed that fallow periods could be cut out altogether if the soil was properly ploughed and then regularly hoed while the crops were growing. He invented a **horse-drawn hoe** which penetrated deeper into the ground than the old-fashioned harrow, so that the roots were kept moist and harmful weeds cleared.

Jethro Tull pictured with his seed-drill (see page 42). The drill did not gain popularity in Tull's lifetime. Hand sowing continued on most farms throughout the eighteenth century

Tull, along with many other farmers, was very critical of the old-fashioned method of sowing seed by *broadcasting* (throwing it in handfuls on to the ploughed land). The wastefulness of broadcasting is well summed up in the following little verse:

> Sow four grains in a row,
> One for the pigeon, one for the crow,
> One to rot and one to grow.

Tull's answer was to invent a horse-drawn **seed-drill**, which sowed seeds in rows at a regular depth. With the aid of his new implements, he claimed he could double his crops using only a third of the previous quantity of seed. However Tull's ideas, attractive as they seemed, had no lasting effect on British agriculture. His seed-drill never worked properly, and many of his theories were unsound, including his opposition to the use of manure. His importance was exaggerated by later agricultural writers.

There were other ways of avoiding wasteful fallows, apart from those suggested by Tull. Some enterprising farmers, in the seventeenth century, had copied the Dutch method of growing corn and root crops alternately on the same land. **Roots**, such as turnips and swedes, take their nourishment from the soil at a deeper level than grain crops. Therefore, they can be grown straight after corn and still leave the upper soil refreshed for another corn crop in the following year. Turnips had for centuries only been thought of as a garden crop for human beings, but some continental farmers had begun to grow them for cattle fodder. This greatly interested **Sir Richard Weston**, a Royalist refugee in the Netherlands during the period of Cromwell's republic in the 1650s. On his return to England, Weston developed a *four*-course rotation, including turnips and clover, which made the fallow year unnecessary. Clover enriched the soil while at the same time providing a valuable addition to the diet of livestock.

The growing of roots and artificial grasses such as clover between years of corn crops was well established in some parts of Britain before 1700, usually on enclosed farms. But the idea was popularised by Charles, **Lord Townshend** (1674–1738), a diplomat turned farmer. 'Turnip' Townshend, as he was called in his later years, had a long and distinguished career in politics. As a Minister of State he played a vital part in negotiating both the Union with Scotland (1707) and the Treaty of Utrecht (1713). But he retired suddenly from political life in 1730, after a quarrel with Walpole, and concentrated on farming his estates at Raynham in Norfolk.

Bakewell's 'New Leicester' sheep

Townshend copied the practices of some of his more go-ahead neighbours on the great estates of Norfolk. But because he was a well-known public figure he attracted widespread interest and influenced other farmers. He began by improving the quality of the soil, much of which was sandy swamp. By draining it and adding manure and marl (a mixture of clay and lime) he turned it into rich, cultivable land. Instead of the old 'three-course rotation' of autumn corn, spring corn and fallow, he alternated turnips and clover with corn crops, as Weston had done. This **Norfolk four-course rotation** of turnips, barley

Leicestershire rams, painted shortly after Robert Bakewell's death

or oats, clover and wheat made the production of cattle fodder an important part of arable farming. Farmers using these methods had already found that they produced so much animal feed that their livestock no longer had to be slaughtered in the autumn. Fresh meat could be eaten all the year round, replacing salted meat during the winter months.

A more plentiful supply of winter feed made it possible to breed better quality **livestock**. But a good diet could never be sufficient in itself. Separate enclosed pastures were required so that different breeds of animals could be isolated from each other. In enclosures, breeding could be carefully controlled and the spread of disease greatly reduced. The stock would also be prevented from taking the flesh off their bones by wandering all over the commons. Improvements along these lines spread rapidly in the eighteenth and early nineteenth centuries, and stock-breeding became a specialised art. The greatest improver in this branch of agriculture was **Robert Bakewell** (1725–95) of Dishley in Leicestershire, who took over his father's 180-hectare farm in 1760.

Sheep- and cattle-farmers had previously concentrated on producing wool and milk, but Bakewell aimed to produce high quality meat as well. He selected the finest existing types of livestock and experimented with cross-breeding. Before long he succeeded in greatly increasing the amount of flesh on those parts of the animals which yielded the best cuts. His most famous breed was the **New Leicester** sheep, but he also produced new breeds of longhorn cattle and farm horses. Visitors came from all over Britain and the Continent to see his model farm. They admired the cleanliness of the stalls and sheds and the excellence of Bakewell's feeding methods. In 1700 most animals were small and stringy, but by 1800 better care and selective breeding sometimes produced beasts which weighed from two to three times heavier than those a century earlier.

Average weight of stock at Smithfield Market (London)

	1710	1795
Oxen	168 kilos	363 kilos
Calves	23 kilos	69 kilos
Sheep	17 kilos	36 kilos

The reign of George III (1760–1820) saw the experimental approach to farming well established. The King himself played a part in popularising new methods. He turned part of Windsor Park into a model farm, and his enthusiasm for agricultural improvement earned him the nickname of **Farmer George**. Much depended upon the spread of good example from landlords to their own tenants. This was the policy of **Thomas Coke** (pronounced Cook) of Holkham in Norfolk. Coke (1750–1842) followed in Townshend's footsteps, using marl, manure and clay to increase the fertility of the soil. Then he set out to educate his tenants in the new methods of cultivation. By the terms of their leases they were obliged to use certain crop rotations and were strictly forbidden from growing two successive corn crops on the same soil. Every year Coke held a sheep-shearing festival and awarded prizes to farmers who demonstrated new ideas. As his influence spread, his 'sheep-shearings' attracted visitors from many parts of Europe and set the pattern for future agricultural shows.

King George III. His active interest in experimental farming earned him the nickname of 'Farmer George'

The spread of enclosure

Improvements in soil preparation, crop rotation and stock-breeding usually required the **enclosure** of farmland. When land was enclosed, open fields, commons and wastelands were converted into a number of separate compact farms by means of fences, hedges and ditches. Ever since the Middle Ages various kinds of enclosures had been carried out, often for the purpose of sheep-farming. Occasionally some farmers in open field villages exchanged strips in order to get all their land in one place and then enclosed it. But not until the seventeenth and eighteenth centuries did enclosure of arable land become standard farming practice. It changed the face of the countryside in the Midlands and South, from hedgeless expanses of farmland to the now familiar 'patchwork quilt' of smaller hedged and fenced fields.

Up to about 1740 enclosure normally took place as a result of general agreement among the villagers. If the whole village was owned by one landlord it was even simpler. However, as the century progressed, there remained many landlords who were keen to enclose their land but were prevented from doing so by the opposition of smallholders. The latter feared they would not be able to farm their land on their own, and they were reluctant to give up their right to use the common pasture. Landlords sometimes overcame stubborn smallholders by buying up their land, but this could be a long and expensive process. They grew impatient and began to seek private **Acts of Parliament** which made enclosure compulsory, so long as a sufficient proportion of the landowners were in favour.

To obtain an Enclosure Act, the owners of at least four-fifths of the

Opposite: Farm workers in the early nineteenth century

land of the village had to send a petition to Parliament. The squire, the parson and three or four others often made up the necessary proportion of landowners, even though they were a tiny fraction of the village population. When the Bill had been passed by Parliament – usually a formality – a group of **Parliamentary Commissioners** visited the village. They investigated all claims to a share of the land, settled disputes, and eventually produced a map showing each land-owner's allocation and the position of roads and paths. It seemed a fair procedure, but it worked to the advantage of wealthy landlords and often ignored the wishes of scores of smallholders. Many villagers had no legal documents to prove their ownership of land and their claims were ignored by the Commissioners as a result. Even if they could prove ownership, they were often unable to afford the expense of hedging and ditching and their share of the Commissioners' fees. They were forced to sell out to the highest bidder.

As the following table shows, the pace of parliamentary enclosure quickened after 1760. It reached its peak during the long wars against France (1793–1815) when high food prices encouraged landlords to produce more from their lands (see Chapter 10).

Parliamentary Enclosure Acts

1751–60	156	1781–90	287
1761–70	424	1791–1800	506
1771–80	642	1801–10	906

After about 1810 much of the work was done and the number of Enclosure Acts began to fall. By the mid nineteenth century, open field villages had become a rarity – a picturesque survival from the past.

Some results of enclosure

Enclosure did not automatically lead to better farming. It had been common for centuries in much of the North and West, yet these parts of the country were relatively backward in their farming methods. However in the flatter, more fertile regions of the South and Midlands most agricultural improvements were introduced on enclosed farms. They brought about great changes in the **diet** of the average family. Not only was a greater quantity of food produced, but also a wider variety. More vegetables were grown, including potatoes, which became a basic part of the diet in this period. Improvements in the care of livestock resulted in more milk and dairy produce and fresh instead of salted meat in winter.

By the end of the eighteenth century, the **growth of industrial towns** made it necessary for agriculture to be run more on 'business' lines – in the same way as iron, coal or textiles. Even after the land was enclosed, the bigger landlords still tried to buy out the smaller ones so as to increase the scale of their farming. As often happens when traditional ways of life are upset, many poor people suffered. Those who had no land or were forced to sell out had lost their 'little piece of England', and with it much of their security and self-respect.

There were **anti-enclosure riots** among the landless poor, in spite of the harsh punishments, such as death or transportation, inflicted on the ringleaders.

This conflict between agricultural improvement and social distress can be seen in the works of **Arthur Young**, the leading agricultural writer and journalist of the period. From 1767 onwards, he travelled widely in England and on the Continent, noting improvements and their effects. He edited a journal, *The Annals of Agriculture*, from 1784, and helped to set up the Board of Agriculture (1793) of which he became Secretary. 'The first business of all improvement is enclosure', he said, and he did all he could to encourage it. But he had to admit that enclosures also brought much hardship. 'By nineteen out of twenty enclosure bills the poor are injured', he said. He was critical of the way great landowners used their power in Parliament to force enclosure on the poor, and thought greater efforts should have been made to look after the dispossessed.

The loss of grazing rights on the commons and wastelands was a severe blow to the poorer villagers. These pastures, where they often kept a cow and a few geese or poultry, were almost as valuable to them as the strips they cultivated. They were sometimes given tiny plots of land in return, but these were too small to be of much value. Their plight is neatly summed up in the following verse (quoted by Arthur Young):

Arthur Young, 1741–1820

> 'Tis bad enough in man or woman to steal a goose from off a common. But surely he's without excuse who steals the common from the goose .

Enclosure, by concentrating the ownership of land into fewer hands, added to the class of **landless labourers**. Their numbers were already increasing in any case as a result of the rapid growth of population after about 1750. Where industrial towns were within easy reach, some labourers left the countryside and went to work in factories; but most of them, especially in the South, stayed on the land to work for wages. There was plenty of work on enclosed estates, and as the amount of land under cultivation increased more families earned their living from farming. But despite the growing prosperity of landowners, the wages paid to labourers were pitifully low and often had to be made up to the necessary minimum level out of the parish rates (see page 108).

Timeline

1730–8	'Turnip' Townshend at Raynham.
1731	Jethro Tull's *The New Horse-Hoeing Husbandry*.
1760–95	Robert Bakewell at Dishley.
1760–1820	'Farmer George' III.
1767	Arthur Young begins his tours.
1793	Board of Agriculture established.
1801–10	Peak period of Parliamentary Enclosure.

Questions

1. '...it is found, by long experience, that common or open fields, wherever they are suffered or continued, are great hindrances to a public good...the common objections hitherto raised against enclosures are founded on mistakes...it is plain that (when an enclosure is once resolved on) the poor will be employed for many years, in planting and preserving the hedges, and afterwards will be set to work both in the tillage and pasture.'
(E. Lawrence, *The Duty and Office of a Land Steward*, 1731)

   a) What were open fields? In what ways might they have been 'great hindrances to a public good'?
   b) List some *advantages* of open field farming.
   c) What was enclosure? What 'common objections' were raised against it, and by whom?
   d) What is the difference between tillage and pasture? Which would require the larger number of labourers?
   e) Which point of view does the writer support – that of the large landowner or the smallholder? Give reasons for your answer.

2. Explain the meanings of the following terms:
   a) fallow field
   b) balks
   c) arable farming
   d) subsistence agriculture
   e) landless labourer

3. 'No fortune will be made in Norfolk by farming, unless a judicious course of crops be pursued. That which has been chiefly adopted by the Norfolk farmers is, 1. Turnips, 2. Barley, 3. Clover, 4. Wheat.'
(Arthur Young, *The Farmer's Tour*, 1771)

   a) What were the advantages of this system of crop rotation?
   b) Who developed this idea in the seventeenth century after observing Dutch farming methods?
   c) Who helped to popularise the idea in the 1730s?
   d) Why did the 'Norfolk rotation' lead to better livestock?
   e) Who was Arthur Young, and what was his importance in the development of English farming?

4. Why were private Acts of Parliament required for much of the enclosure carried out after about 1740? Describe the normal procedure involved in parliamentary enclosure. Was it fair to everyone?

5. Outline the contribution of each of the following to agricultural improvement in the eighteenth century:
   a) Jethro Tull
   b) Robert Bakewell
   c) King George III
   d) Thomas Coke

6

Textiles and the Coming of Factories
Industrial Revolution (I)

At the beginning of our period most industries were centred round the home – in villages or small towns. Families usually owned their own tools (such as hammers and files in the metal trades) or simple, hand-worked machines (for example spinning-wheels and hand looms in cloth-making). However, before the end of the eighteenth century all this had begun to change. New techniques of manufacture and the use of machines powered by water-wheels and steam-engines resulted in the organisation of industry on a big scale – in 'factories', where many workers could be collected together in one place. As the Machine Age advanced, the population became increasingly concentrated in towns, especially in the coalfield areas of the Midlands and the North of England, South Wales and the Scottish Lowlands.

These changes came earliest and quickest in certain branches of the textile industry – especially cotton and silk – and in hardware, pottery and chemical manufacture. Nevertheless, factory industry did not become widespread, even in textiles, before the mid nineteenth century. This chapter and the two following are devoted to some of the major developments in British industry before 1850. So great was their effect that historians apply to them the term 'revolution' – a word normally used to describe events as dramatic as the overthrow of governments. But first of all we must try to discover why it was *Britain*, rather than any other country, which had the world's first 'Industrial Revolution'.

Britain leads the way

Conditions in the United Kingdom were especially suitable for the rapid growth of industry in the eighteenth century. There were large deposits of coal and iron ore, and plenty of fast-flowing streams for

'The Industrial Revolution'

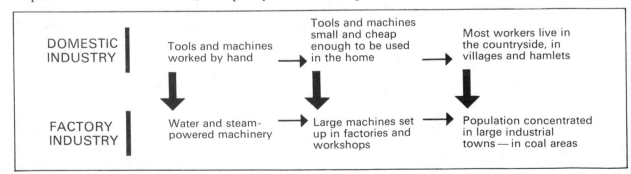

water power. No part of Britain is very far from either the sea or a navigable river – an important factor before transport was mechanised. Moreover, the effect of the warm Atlantic sea currents on the climate means that these vital trade routes do not freeze in winter.

Since the end of the Civil War (1649) Britain has enjoyed almost uninterrupted **peace at home**, and has suffered less from political and religious disputes than any other European country. The last major battle to be fought on British soil (Culloden, 1746) saw the end of the last full-scale political rebellion (see page 16). The rapid expansion of **trade**, from the mid seventeenth century onwards, was assisted by the absence of internal customs duties. In continental countries, like France, each separate province taxed goods passing across its frontiers – which increased their price even before they reached market. In Britain, on the other hand, goods travelling *within* the kingdom could not be taxed. England, Wales and Scotland (after 1707) together made up probably the largest 'free trade' area in Europe.

The growth of the overseas trading empire in this period brought much **wealth** into Britain (see Chapter 3). As a result, merchants were able to influence industry. They wanted more goods to sell and were often prepared to find the money to finance new manufacturing processes. The Bank of England (established 1694) and hundreds of country banks, which sprang up during the eighteenth century, brought together people's savings and made some of them available for industrial development. The colonies provided additional customers for the expanding output of manufactured goods.

The rapid **rise in population** was another important factor. It meant a steadily increasing labour force and, at the same time, more customers to absorb the rising output of manufactured goods.

Population of Britain (excluding Ireland)

1760 (estimated)	8	million
1801	10.5	million
1821	14	million
1861	23	million

As the table shows, the population almost *trebled* in the century after 1760 – when the Industrial Revolution was at its height. There was a rapid fall in the death-rate, particularly among infants and children under five. Cleaner water, a better diet, greater medical skill and improved methods of midwifery were probably the most important reasons. However, cheaper fuel for domestic heating, the spread of cheap cotton clothing (easier to wash and therefore healthier) and the increase in brick-built houses all played a part.

Textiles before the 'Factory Age'

The manufacture of **woollen cloth** had long been Britain's chief industry, and remained so until the end of the eighteenth century. The cloth trade was usually organised by wealthy merchant 'clothiers'. They bought the raw wool, supervised every stage of manufacture

and then sold the finished material. Some skilled tasks, like the finishing processes of fulling and bleaching, required equipment which was too big for the house. These had to be performed in special workshops, often in the towns. Some of the larger ones were already half way to being factories.

However spinning and weaving – the two most important processes – were carried on domestically. **Spinning** involved joining the short 'staples' of wool (previously separated from the mass by a process called carding) into a continuous thread or yarn. It was mostly done by women and girls, often part-time. **Weaving**, on the other hand, was normally a full-time occupation for a man. The loom, on which yarn was woven into cloth, was frequently owned and hired out by the clothier.

Although the woollen cloth trade was Britain's major industry, it was not the first to develop factory methods of production. The newer textile trades, especially silk and cotton, were quicker to introduce technical changes. The woollen cloth industry was held back by a number of factors. The use of new processes was restricted by old-fashioned rules and regulations; it was difficult to increase the supply of raw wool before the development of Australian sheep-farming in the nineteenth century, and wool was more difficult to twist and stretch on a machine than a fibre like cotton.

Hand wheel spinning in the days of 'domestic industry'

The first genuine factory for the production of textile goods was in the **silk** industry. It was built by two brothers, **John and Thomas Lombe**, on an island in the River Derwent at Derby (1721). Silk does not require spinning – this has already been done by the silk-worms. To produce a thread for weaving it has to be unwound and twisted ('thrown'). The silk-throwing machines used by the Lombe brothers were based on designs obtained secretly from Italy. Their five-storeyed mill, over 100 metres long, was driven by a huge water-wheel and employed 300 workers. Other silk manufacturers followed their example, so that, by about 1760, silk-throwing was well established as a factory industry, in North Cheshire, around Stockport and Macclesfield. Nevertheless, it would be wrong to regard these developments as the start of the 'Factory Age' in textiles. Silk remained a minor industry in Britain, unable to rival the products of France and Italy, where raw silk was in abundant supply. It was not until the successful introduction of power-driven machinery into the cotton industry, around 1770, that the 'revolution' in textiles really began.

The **cotton** industry was slow to develop in Britain, mainly because the raw material has to be imported. Cotton was expensive and difficult to obtain before the setting up of plantations in the West Indies and the American mainland. In the early eighteenth century, the art of spinning strong cotton yarn had not yet been learned. It was usually mixed with wool or linen to produce fustian. **South Lancashire** was already the centre of the cotton trade, and it remained so, for several good reasons. It had a first-rate port in Liverpool, which became the main centre of the Atlantic trade by the end of the eighteenth century. Each year Liverpool handled thousands of tonnes of cotton from the New World. The swift-flowing Pennine streams provided water power before the age of steam, and later on Lancashire's coal was well able to satisfy the demands of the steam-engine. In addition, the mild, damp climate is ideal for handling cotton thread, which breaks easily in a dry atmosphere.

At the start of our period, manufacturing processes in all the textile trades were slow and laborious. But improvements were gradually being made in the weaving and finishing stages. The hand loom in particular was becoming more efficient, so that each weaver required five or six spinners to keep him supplied with yarn. This disproportion was greatly increased by the invention of the **flying shuttle** (1733). It was the work of **John Kay** (1704–79), a weaver from Lancashire who was working for a Colchester clothier. Previously, the shuttle (containing the 'weft' or cross-thread) had been thrown *by hand* across the loom, on which the 'warp' (longways thread) was stretched. This meant the width of cloth one man could weave, without an assistant, was limited by the length of his arms. Kay found a way of striking the shuttle to and fro with two wooden hammers which were attached by cords to a lever. In the words of his patent: 'The weaver . . . by a small pull at the cord . . . moves the said new invented shuttle from side to side to pleasure.'

Broadcloth could now be woven without the help of an assistant to catch and return the shuttle, and the whole weaving process was

John Kay

greatly speeded up. But Kay made little money out of his idea. Many manufacturers were glad to use his invention but refused to pay him for it. Worse still, he suffered the bitter hostility of his fellow weavers. They claimed he was trying to put them out of business, and went so far as to wreck his house (1753). He fled to France, where he died in poverty. The flying shuttle was not widely used until after 1760, when it was improved with a device called a **drop-box**, invented by Kay's son **Robert Kay**. The original invention only wove plain cloth, but the drop-box held several shuttles, loaded with yarns of different colours. By bringing the box to different levels, simple pattern-weaving could be done without having to fit different shuttles by hand each time a change of colour was needed.

The mechanisation of cotton-spinning

The flying shuttle, by speeding up weaving, further increased the shortage of yarn. Unless a quicker method of spinning could be found many weavers would have little or no work to do. However, as the old saying goes, '*necessity is the mother of invention*'. The problem of the shortage of yarn soon produced a crop of spinning-machines and, with them, the beginnings of a large-scale factory industry.

The first, a 'roller-spinning' device, patented by **Lewis Paul** in 1738, was a near miss. It had two sets of rollers which travelled at different speeds and so drew out the thread to the right thickness before it was wound off on spindles. Five of these machines were installed in the first cotton-spinning mill in history – at Northampton in the 1740s – but they proved to be frail and unreliable. It was not until the main principles of Paul's machine were taken up by later inventors that roller-spinning became profitable.

In the 1760s, when the flying shuttle became widely used, two highly successful spinning-machines were produced within the space of three years. The first, known as the **spinning-jenny**, was the work of **James Hargreaves**, a carpenter and weaver from Blackburn. It was a straightforward development of the principle of the spinning-wheel, except that one worker could spin several threads at once, simply by turning a handle. The first models had eight spindles, operated by a single wheel. But before long water-powered jennies with eighty spindles or more were built and housed in factories and large workshops. Within thirty years over 20,000 jennies were in use, practically all of them in the cotton industry. Hargreaves suffered the fate of several early textile inventors when his house and machinery were smashed by angry handspinners (1767). But he enjoyed better fortune after moving to Nottingham.

At the time Hargreaves left Blackburn, 16 kilometres away in Preston **Richard Arkwright** (1732–92) was beginning a career in textiles that would make him famous in the history of British industry. He was not really an inventor. He was a clever businessman who rearranged and combined the inventions of others. When he heard of the great need for a spinning-machine, he was a hair-dealer and ex-barber with no mechanical training. But that did not stop him. In

Sir Richard Arkwright

Replica of James Hargreaves's 'spinning-jenny', invented in 1765

Replica of James Hargreaves's 'spinning-jenny', invented in 1765

1768, with the help of a clock-maker, he supervised the construction of a spinning-machine called the **water frame**. It closely resembled Paul's unsuccessful machine, except that it had four pairs of rollers instead of two to stretch the thread and press the fibres together. Probably the main difference between the two machines was that Arkwright's gave the yarn a firmer twist as it was wound off the rollers.

Unlike the jenny, the water frame could not be operated by hand. It needed the power of a water-wheel. So it led directly to the setting up of factories. Because Arkwright's machine led the breakaway from domestic spinning, he is usually regarded as 'the founder of the modern factory system'. With his gift for organisation and his tremendous drive and energy, he was not content simply to take out a patent for the water frame. He wanted his own factories. Arkwright went to Nottingham to raise money, and eventually got the support of a wealthy stocking-manufacturer, Jedediah Strutt. In 1771 he set up his first successful mill, at **Cromford**, near Derby. More mills followed, not only in Derbyshire but also in Lancashire, where the largest employed 600 workers. Arkwright eventually collected a knighthood and half a million pounds in profits.

The jenny and the water frame revolutionised cotton-spinning. But both had limitations. Jenny-spun yarn was fine in texture but too weak to make satisfactory warp (longways thread). The water frame produced yarn which was strong but rather too coarse to make cloth

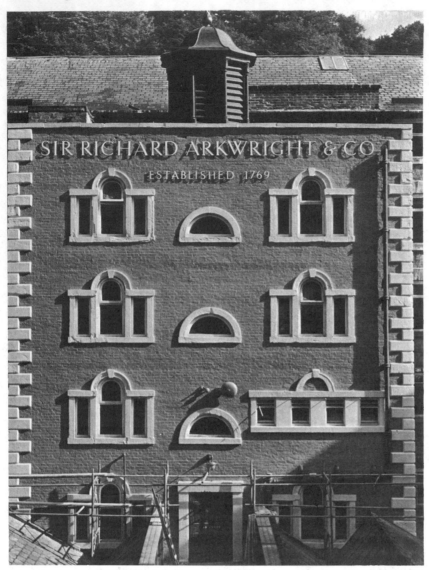

SIR RICHARD ARKWRIGHT & CO

ESTABLISHED 1769

of the highest quality. **Samuel Crompton** (1753–1827), a weaver and spinner from Bolton, overcame this problem with his **spinning-mule** (1779). Just as an ordinary mule is a cross between a horse and a donkey, so Crompton's mule combined features of both the jenny and the water frame to produce strong yarn of fine quality.

Crompton was the opposite of Arkwright. He was an inventor of great skill, but lacking in business ability. While others made fortunes out of his invention, he died a poor man, in spite of a parliamentary grant of £5,000 in 1812, most of which he used to pay off debts. The first mules were hand-operated and could be used at home. By the 1790s large water- and steam-powered versions were built, with as many as 400 spindles. These gradually replaced the jennies and water frames. British cotton cloth, made of mass-produced yarn, now rivalled in quality the best calicoes and muslins of the East. Both the

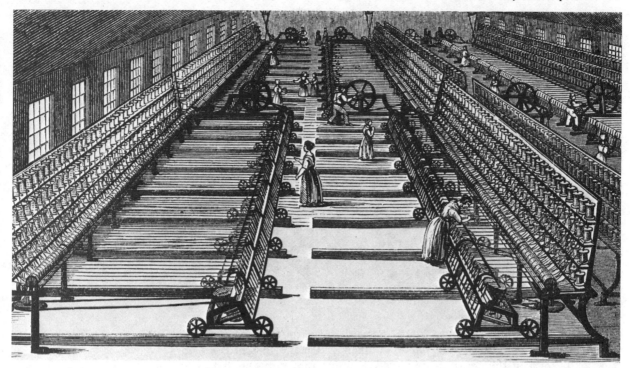

A mule spinning factory in the nineteenth century

name 'mule' and its basic principles are still found in spinning machinery today.

The transfer of cotton-spinning from the home to the factory was almost complete by 1800, much to the regret of country folk who had previously relied on part-time domestic spinning as a source of income. There were two main stages in the growth of the industry. During the first or 'water power' stage mills were set up in the Lancashire and Derbyshire hills, where rushing streams could easily be dammed to create artificial waterfalls. In the second stage, beginning with the introduction of **steam power** in 1785, the industry became concentrated in the coalfield towns of Lancashire and the Scottish Lowlands. Lancashire was by far the more important. By 1800 it was the second richest and most populated county in the kingdom, after Middlesex. Great quantities of cotton goods were now being used by all classes. 'As for the ladies', said a pamphlet of 1782, 'they wear scarcely anything now but cotton, calicoes, muslin or silks.... We have scarcely any woollens now about our beds but blankets.'

The power loom

While spinning was being revolutionised, weaving continued to be a domestic handicraft. It was more difficult to apply water or steam power to the hand loom because of its complicated movements. Machines introduced from the Continent, like the Dutch 'swivel loom', were only satisfactory for the weaving of ribbons; and attempts to apply stocking-knitting machines to cloth-weaving all failed. Meanwhile the weavers prospered. Whereas previously there

had not been enough yarn to keep them all busy, now there was more than they could use. They were so much in demand that in Bolton, at the end of the century, they walked about the streets with £5 notes stuck in their hat-bands.

The great prosperity of the hand loom weavers was short-lived. A talented clergyman named **Edmund Cartwright** (1743–1823) became interested in the idea of a **power loom**, following a conversation with some Manchester manufacturers. They told him of the great need for a mechanical loom but claimed it was impossible to make one. Cartwright decided to try to prove them wrong and paid a blacksmith and a carpenter to help him. His first machine (patented in 1785) was very clumsy and needed two strong men to work it; but he was on the right track. By 1789 he had produced a loom driven by a Watt steam-engine (see Chapter 8) which could weave any kind of plain cloth. All operations previously done by hand or foot could now be performed mechanically and the weaver's task was reduced to that of repairing broken threads. Cartwright, like others before him, made little profit from his invention. Therefore, in recognition of his services to industry, Parliament granted him £10,000 in 1809 and he retired to a farm in Kent.

The **hand loom weavers** realised that their high standard of living was threatened by the power loom and banded together to resist its introduction. Cartwright's attempt at partnership with a Manchester firm (1791) failed when their factory was deliberately burned down. Threatening letters from weavers left no doubt as to the culprits. One said: 'We have sworn together to destroy your factory . . . and to have your lives for ruining our trade.' But the weavers were fighting a losing battle. In the early years of the nineteenth century, an improved, all metal power loom was produced. The competition was too severe for hand-weavers and they were gradually reduced to starvation wages. In 1830 hand looms still outnumbered power looms by three to one, but by the 1840s the power loom was supreme in the cotton industry.

The inventions which made possible the 'revolution' in the cotton industry were not all the work of Englishmen. The American plantations could not have kept up with the rapidly increasing demand for raw cotton without the aid of **Elias Whitney's 'gin'** (engin') invented in 1793. This greatly speeded up the tedious process of 'cleaning' the cotton (separating the little black seeds from the fibre). One horse-worked gin could clean as much cotton as fifty slaves working by hand. The need for such an invention can be seen from the figures for British imports of raw cotton. These alone tell the story of the revolution in cotton manufacture:

British imports of raw cotton (in tonnes)

1760	1800	1830
8000	25,000	100,000

Across the Pennines

Most of the great inventions in cotton-spinning and weaving were later applied to woollen cloth manufacture. But they took an average of thirty years longer to make their impact. By about 1800 the ancient woollen cloth trade had been surpassed in importance by the cotton industry. Two of the three traditional woollen cloth areas were in decline – East Anglia and the West Country. The third, **West Yorkshire**, especially Leeds and Bradford, had already become the centre of the industry.

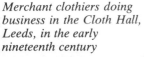

Merchant clothiers doing business in the Cloth Hall, Leeds, in the early nineteenth century

The supremacy of West Yorkshire depended on many factors, including the presence of fast-flowing streams for water power and, later on, plentiful supplies of coal to feed steam-driven machinery. Even so, thousands of small clothiers still worked at home in the Yorkshire villages until well into the nineteenth century. Although machine-spinning of wool began in Yorkshire in the 1780s, it spread slowly. The power loom, which came much later, was not in widespread use until the 1860s.

Businesses were normally smaller east of the Pennines. An exception was **Benjamin Gott**'s large factory in Leeds, which used machines for the spinning and finishing processes from the time it was established in 1793. Britain went to war with France in the same year, and Gott received so many government contracts for army clothing that he ran night shifts to keep his machines at full stretch. He was the first of the great factory-masters in the woollen industry, but he could not rival the wealth of the Lancashire 'Cotton Kings'.

Workers in the mills

In their haste to make profits, most factory-owners gave little thought to the welfare of their workers. Consequently conditions in the early mills were often exceedingly harsh. Working hours were very long, especially in the 'brisk time', when trade was good. Twelve to fourteen hours, with brief periods of rest, was a common working day. Occasionally men, women and children worked as long as nineteen hours a day, Monday to Saturday. Many children were employed in spinning-mills, where the work was easily learned and needed little strength. Their delicate touch was an advantage in jobs like 'piecing' (joining broken threads). Some infants began work at four or five years of age, crawling under the machines to collect fluff from the floor. Children were usually paid between a third and a sixth of the adult wage, which was, in turn, worth less than a sixth of a present day labourer's wage. Payment was often made partly or wholly in 'truck' tickets, which had to be exchanged in the employer's own shop for goods such as flour, sugar and clothing, frequently at inflated prices.

At first, most factory workers were **orphan children**, obtained by employers from parish Poor Law authorities who were glad to be rid of the responsibility of caring for them. They were supposed to be apprentices but, instead of learning a trade, they were given monotonous and unskilled tasks. Long hours in a hot, stuffy mill and little sleep soon ruined their health and deformed their bodies. They were often underfed. In one mill, apprentices struggled with pigs in the yard to get some of the food in the troughs. As machinery became more complicated and steam-engines were used for power, more adults were needed. But child labour continued, for parents could rarely support a family on their wages alone.

Nevertheless most workers enjoyed a higher standard of living in the new factory towns than they had been used to previously. Many of them – men, women and children alike – had worked equally long

Children at work winding cotton (about 1820)

hours at home or in a small workshop, probably for lower wages. Certainly the earnings of agricultural labourers were well below those of factory hands. Before long **hand-workers** such as cottage spinners and weavers were either put out of work by the competition of the new machines, or forced to toil night and day to make a bare living, in conditions that would have shocked a factory inspector. Their only real advantage was independence. They were free to start and stop when they chose. It was the *discipline* in the factories that the town workers hated most of all: the regular hours and strict rules and regulations laid down by the employers. Heavy fines were imposed for trivial offences, such as whistling or 'leaving an oil can out of place'.

Not all the early **factory-masters** were hard on their workers. Some of them, like Robert Peel (senior) and Robert Owen (see pages 120 and 128), showed that it was possible to make good profits while, at the same time, considering the welfare of the people they employed. Benjamin Gott even set up his own scheme of social insurance. Old employees were retained as pensioners and part- or full-time wages were paid to workers absent through sickness or injury. Gott encouraged the regular attendance of children at Sunday school and even prohibited the use of the cane or whip. But employers like Peel, Owen and Gott were few and far between. In most cases there was an urgent need for new laws to control factory conditions and hours of work. The Factory Acts, by which Parliament gradually took on these responsibilities, are dealt with in Chapter 11.

Timeline

1721	John and Thomas Lombe's silk-throwing mill.
1733	John Kay's 'flying shuttle'.
1738	Lewis Paul's roller-spinning machine.
1765	James Hargreaves's 'spinning-jenny'.
1768	Richard Arkwright's 'water frame'.
1771	Arkwright's first factory at Cromford.
1779	Samuel Crompton's 'mule'.
1785	Steam power first used in spinning.
1785–9	Reverend Edmund Cartwright's 'power loom'.
1793	Elias Whitney's 'gin'. Benjamin Gott's factory in Leeds.

Questions

1. 'Necessity is the mother of invention.' How far does the history of the cotton industry between 1760 and 1790 illustrate the truth of this saying?

2. 'Below Matlock a new creation of SR. RD. ARKWRIGHT's is started up, which has crowded the village of Cromford with cottages, supported by his three magnificent cotton mills.' (Entry in the diary of Lord Torrington, 1789)

   a) Why did Arkwright choose the Derbyshire hills for some of his early factories?
   b) At the time this was written Arkwright had already begun to establish mills in coalfield areas. Why?
   c) With what famous spinning invention is Arkwright associated?
   d) Arkwright's machine resembled which earlier, unsuccessful invention?
   e) Why has Arkwright been called 'the founder of the modern factory system'?

3. Explain the following terms or descriptions:
   a) silk-throwing   b) 'flying' shuttle   c) spinning 'mule'
   d) brisk time   e) 'truck' tickets

4. Look at the picture of children winding cotton (page 59).
   a) Why were children employed in the early textile factories?
   b) What advantages did employers find in organising their workers into factories?
   c) Why was cotton manufacture mechanised before the woollen industry?
   d) Many factory children would not have looked as well fed and cared for as those in the picture. Can you think of any reason why an artist might avoid making such a picture realistic?
   e) Describe the main effects the coming of factories had upon the lives of those who worked in them.

5. Write a paragraph on each of the following:
   a) 'domestic' industry   b) John and Thomas Lombe
   c) the cotton 'gin'   d) Benjamin Gott

7

The New Iron Age
Industrial Revolution (II)

Iron was the key to the whole Industrial Revolution. Without great advances in both the quality and quantity of iron, mechanisation in other industries would have been severely restricted. At the beginning of our period the British iron industry was relatively backward, well behind that of countries such as Sweden and Germany. Yet, as a result of a series of technical improvements, Britain soon led the world in the *mass production* of iron and iron goods.

The stages in production and the problem of fuel

There were two main branches of the industry. The first consisted of **mining** and **smelting** (melting, to separate the metal from the ore). These were usually carried out close together, to avoid transport difficulties. The ore was smelted in an open-topped blast-furnace, built of brick or stone. Charcoal was used for fuel, mixed with limestone or clay to help remove the impurities. The molten iron was then run off into sandy moulds called 'pigs' (their shape resembled a sow feeding her piglets).

The stages in iron production

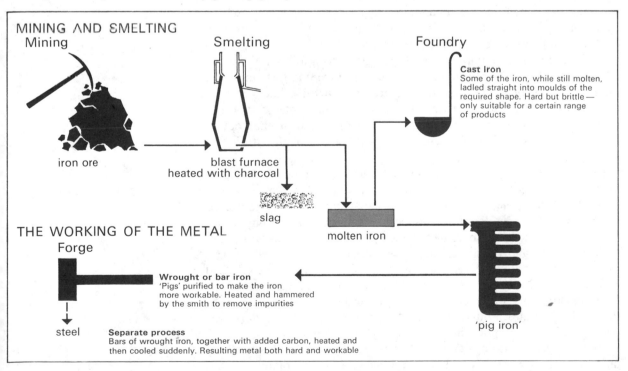

MINING AND SMELTING

Mining

Smelting

Foundry

iron ore

blast furnace
heated with charcoal

slag

molten iron

Cast Iron
Some of the iron, while still molten, ladled straight into moulds of the required shape. Hard but brittle — only suitable for a certain range of products

THE WORKING OF THE METAL

Forge

steel

Wrought or bar iron
'Pigs' purified to make the iron more workable. Heated and hammered by the smith to remove impurities

'pig iron'

Separate process
Bars of wrought iron, together with added carbon, heated and then cooled suddenly. Resulting metal both hard and workable

The main areas of mining and smelting were where the necessary raw materials could all be found fairly close together – iron ore, timber (for converting into charcoal fuel), and swift-flowing streams (water power was often used to drive the bellows which stirred up the flames in the furnace). Around 1700 the main iron-smelting areas were Sussex, the Forest of Dean (Gloucestershire and Herefordshire), the West Midlands, South Wales and the district round Sheffield. Some goods were made of **cast iron**, a process which was really a continuation of smelting and therefore carried on in foundries next to the blast-furnaces. The pigs were simply re-melted and ladled into moulds of the required shape. But cast iron contained a lot of carbon and other impurities which made it very brittle. It could only be used for a limited range of manufactures, such as cannon, cooking-pots, stoves and grates.

The second branch of the industry was the working of the metal. This was done by **smiths** at their forges. By continued hammering and re-heating they removed impurities in the pigs and produced bar or **wrought iron**. This was less hard than cast iron but much more supple and workable. It was made into tools, weapons and a whole range of hardware, including nails – millions of which were made annually at a time when ships, many houses, and even machines were almost entirely made of wood. Water power was often employed for lifting hammers in the larger forges, and coal was used for heating the metal, as well as charcoal. Therefore the smithing trades were already becoming located near fast-flowing rivers and coal-mines at the beginning of our period.

The two main metal-working centres were the districts round Birmingham and Sheffield. **Birmingham** was already well known for its ironmongery. Great quantities of locks, bolts, pins, buttons, nails and the like were produced in backyard workshops by skilled craftsmen with the aid of a few simple tools. Frequently the whole family worked together. Children of five or six were not too young to help in the family trade, even if they mostly ran errands. **Sheffield** had gained a reputation for fine **steel** cutlery, scissors, hammers, files and other tools. Steel was made from bar iron by heating it with charcoal to add a little carbon. (It was a separate process, and is dealt with in the last section of this chapter.)

By 1700 Britain's iron industry faced a serious difficulty. The production of pig iron was diminishing every year. The reason was a grave **shortage of charcoal**, which was at that time the only fuel used in the blast-furnace. Timber was scarce and used for many other things besides making charcoal, including shipbuilding, on which the nation's safety and prosperity depended. Parliament had passed laws to restrict the felling of trees for charcoal-burning ever since the end of the sixteenth century. By 1720 there were only about sixty blast-furnaces still working in England, where before there had been hundreds. Their total output was much less than that of *one* modern furnace, and barely supplied half the country's requirements.

Britain's great natural deposits of iron ore remained almost entirely unworked. Many had been abandoned because the woodlands around

Abraham Darby's ironworks at Coalbrookdale

them had been felled. With the demand for iron goods increasing rapidly, smiths had no alternative but to import large quantities of pig and bar iron from Sweden and Russia. Unless a new fuel for smelting could be found, Britain's hardware industry might have to rely entirely on imported pig iron. The obvious answer to the problem seemed to lie in the use of 'pit coal' instead of charcoal. After all, Britain was rich in deposits of coal and it was already widely used by smiths, as well as by glass-makers, brewers, brick-makers and others. Unfortunately, countless attempts to smelt with coal had failed. Its sulphur compounds made the pig iron brittle and unworkable.

The Darby family and coke-smelting

In 1708 **Abraham Darby** (1677–1717), a Quaker ironmaster, moved to Coalbrookdale in Shropshire and took over an old ironworks there. In the following year he tried, like many others before him, to find a new fuel for smelting. His efforts were described, many years later, in a letter written by his daughter-in-law: 'He first try'd with raw coal as it came out of the mines, but it did not answer. He not discouraged, had the coal coak'd into cynder, as is done for drying malt, and it then succeeded to his satisfaction.' **Coke**, which finally solved the problem, is almost pure carbon, like charcoal. But, *un*like charcoal, it could be produced cheaply and in great quantities. It became the basis for a new Iron Age, but not for another half century.

The pigs produced in Darby's coke furnace were only suitable for casting. This made his discovery less useful because the most urgent need was for pig iron of a kind which could easily be converted into wrought iron. It was really the work of his son, another **Abraham Darby** (1711–63), that opened the way for a great expansion of iron-smelting in the second half of the eighteenth century. Abraham Darby II was not satisfied with his father's method of coking the coal in heaps (like charcoal-burning). He used coking-*ovens*, which produced a superior form of coke. He also strengthened the bellows, to give a stronger blast during smelting. The resulting pig iron was of sufficient quality for refining into bar iron at the forge.

From about 1760 onwards, mining and smelting became located in areas where good supplies of both coal and iron ore were available – South Wales, the West Midlands, South Yorkshire, the North-East of England and Central Scotland. With the exception of the Midlands, all these areas had the advantage of being near the sea, which made transportation easier. The Darby family's business continued to flourish under **the third Abraham Darby** (1750–91). He built the world's first iron bridge (1779) across the River Severn, south of Coalbrookdale. It was 8 metres wide and nearly 100 metres long, made entirely of cast iron. A small town grew up close by it and was appropriately named Ironbridge.

The world's first iron bridge (1779). It still stands across the River Severn at Ironbridge, Shropshire

The importance of coke-smelting to the British iron industry can be seen in the following figures:

British output of pig iron (approximate figures)

1750	30,000 tonnes
1788	68,000 tonnes
1804	250,000 tonnes

'Puddling' and 'rolling'

Once the advances in coke-smelting had made possible the mass production of pig iron a new problem arose. The next stage in the process – the conversion of pigs into bar iron – was now slow by comparison. In other words, the 'bottleneck' which had previously existed at the smelting stage was now transferred to the process of forging wrought iron. A solution was found by **Henry Cort** (1740–1800), who had set up a forge near Portsmouth and was under contract to the Admiralty to supply wrought iron goods to the Royal Navy. In 1783 and 1784 he took out patents for two inventions which together could turn large quantities of pig iron into good quality bar iron, without the need for heating and hammering at the forge.

Puddling, the first of Cort's processes, required a 'reverberatory' furnace, with two main sections separated by a bridge (see diagram below). On one side was a fireplace and on the other a sandy hearth where the pigs were placed. By keeping the fire and the metal separate, Cort found he could use raw coal without any risk of spoiling the iron. The flames swept over the bridge on their way to the outlet (flue) and melted the pigs by striking down (reverberating) from the roof of the chamber. To help drive off the remaining impurities, workers stirred ('puddled') the molten iron with long bars (rabbles) through an opening in the front of the furnace.

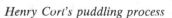
Henry Cort's puddling process

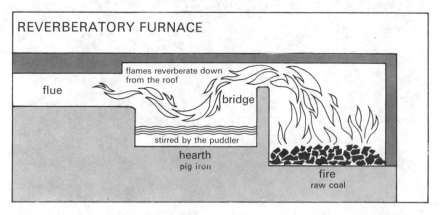

When purified, the iron became spongy and was formed into balls (loops) by the puddler. These were taken out with tongs and, after the slag had been separated, the loops went to the **rolling-mill** – the second of Cort's processes. Here the iron, still hot, was passed between grooved rollers. The rollers were formed in such a way that the iron took the shape of the space left between them, for example that of a rail. So by a single operation an iron bar or sheet, depending on what was required, could be produced quickly and cheaply from a mass of iron. It had previously taken about twelve hours to forge one tonne of bar iron by heating and hammering. Now the same amount was rolled in three-quarters of an hour.

Cort's mass-production methods were quickly taken up by other forge-masters, and, before long, the output of bar iron kept pace with pig iron production. Puddling and rolling enabled the iron industry to cope with the increasing demands being put upon it by the end of the eighteenth century. There was hardly an industry, from farming to shipbuilding, that did not benefit from cheap mass-produced wrought iron. For example, the early machines in textiles had been made almost entirely of wood, but the later iron ones were much longer wearing and far more accurate. Forge-masters no longer needed charcoal fuel, so the production of finished iron goods became entirely based in the coalfield areas, alongside the blast-furnaces. Large-scale businesses developed, with one company often controlling all the stages of production and situating them next to each other.

Puddlers at work. Notice the hot rabbles cooling in trays of water

*John Wilkinson's own coinage
(front and back)*

The great ironmasters

Just as the textile inventions produced great mill-owners, so the new techniques in iron-making saw the rise of rich and powerful ironmasters – men like **John Wilkinson** (1728–1805). He was not an inventor, but, like Richard Arkwright, he was quick to take note of new ideas and use them for profit. Wilkinson was the first to exploit Abraham Darby II's improved coke-smelting process on a large scale. He was also one of the first to employ a Watt steam-engine, instead of a water-wheel, for working the bellows of the blast-furnace (1775). He and his brother William controlled three large ironworks at **Bersham**, near Chester, **Broseley** in Shropshire, and **Bradley** in Staffordshire. The last two were established during the Seven Years' War (1756–63) largely as a result of government contracts for weapons, especially cannon.

Throughout his remarkable career, Wilkinson's industrial 'empire' went on growing. Apart from his ironworks, he controlled coal-mines and had financial interests in Welsh foundries and Cornish tin-mines. He even owned two farms, on which he introduced the first steam threshing-machines. Like some other important businessmen of the period, he issued his own coinage in areas where he was an employer. Copper and silver 'tokens' and guinea notes, stamped with his profile and inscribed 'JOHN WILKINSON, IRON MASTER', were in use in several Midland and Western counties between 1787 and 1808. It was the great business skill and tireless energy of men like Wilkinson that put Britain ahead of her industrial rivals by the early nineteenth century.

'Iron-mad' Wilkinson believed that iron would eventually replace most other materials. He personally did much to extend its range of uses. He helped Abraham Darby III to build the first iron bridge (1779) and, eight years later, he successfully launched a boat made of bolted iron plates. Most people had thought this impossible but, as Wilkinson later wrote: 'It answers all my expectations, and has convinced the unbelievers, who were nine hundred and ninety-nine in a thousand'. He followed this by making 65 kilometres of cast iron pipes for the water supply of Paris (1788). Even then he had not exhausted his ideas for new uses of iron. He built a cast iron chapel for the Methodists at Bradley and, when he died, he was buried in an iron coffin.

Each of the main centres of iron production could boast of at least one great ironmaster, although none could rival the wealth of John Wilkinson of the West Midlands. In South Yorkshire there was **Samuel Walker** of **Rotherham**, famous as a manufacturer of 'cast steel'. He began with a small forge 'in an old nail-shop' in 1741, yet, by persistent hard work, left a small fortune to his sons forty years later. He greatly helped the progress of agriculture in the Midlands with his 'Rotherham plough', which had a cast iron coulter (cutting-piece).

Meanwhile, South Wales was becoming one of the great iron centres, with plentiful resources of coal and iron ore and easy access to the sea. Its greatest ironmaster was **Richard Crawshay**, often called 'the Iron King'. At his **Cyfarthfa** works in Merthyr Tydfil, he was one of the first to use Cort's puddling process in the 1780s. Less than twenty years later he was employing 2,000 workers at Cyfarthfa, and Merthyr Tydfil had grown from a village to an industrial town. In 1840 the Crawshays' business was described as 'the largest in the kingdom'.

Scotland's modern iron industry was founded in 1760 at **Carron**, near Falkirk, by **John Roebuck**. Like Wilkinson, Roebuck saw the opportunity to profit from the demand for munitions during the Seven Years' War. The site for the Carron works was well chosen. There were great quantities of coal and iron ore on the spot and the Firth of Forth nearby. Roebuck went bankrupt in 1773, having taken on too many projects at once, but the works continued to prosper under the Carron Company. It soon became famous all over Europe for its manufacture of weapons, especially naval guns called carron-ades. A French visitor to Carron (1784) was greatly impressed by 'huge cranes, every kind of windlass, lever and tackle for moving heavy loads...darting flames leaping from the blast-furnaces... heavy hammers striking the echoing anvils and the shrill whistling of the air pumps', and likened it to 'a volcano in eruption'.

Hot blast and steam hammer

By the end of the eighteenth century, Britain's iron industry was second to none. The mass-production methods of Abraham Darby and Henry Cort were the basis for the 'revolution in iron'. But there was still plenty of room for further improvements, two of which de-serve special mention.

The first concerned the smelting process. As blast-furnaces got big-ger, the strength of the air blast from the bellows was often insuf-ficient. Water-powered bellows were replaced by steam-driven blow-ing engines from the 1770s onwards, yet this was not a complete answer to the problem. It was not until 1828 that **James Neilson**, Manager of Glasgow Gas Works, hit upon the idea of heating the air *before* it entered the furnace. It had always been believed that a very cool blast was essential for making good quality iron. Neilson, how-ever, pre-heated the air to several hundred degrees centigrade – with the result that it expanded and greatly increased the force of the blast. The **hot blast** had the extra advantage of saving fuel. *Cold* air from the bellows lowered the temperature inside the furnace, but Neilson's blast, which was so hot it could melt lead, made it possible to use far less coke. Moreover, raw coal of the cheapest quality could be used for heating the air because it did not come into contact with the iron. Previously 7 or 8 tonnes of coal had been used to produce a tonne of pig iron; now only 5 tonnes of coal were needed.

Meanwhile, the forging branch of the industry could not afford to stand still. By the 1830s, developments like iron bridges and the building of the first ocean-going steamships (see Chapter 13) meant there was a demand for iron bars of increasing size and weight. In response to this, a Manchester engineer, **James Nasmyth**, invented

James Nasmyth photographed in the 1850s with one of his steam hammers. Its power could be adjusted so accurately that it was possible to make the hammer-head descend with just enough force to break an egg-shell

a **steam hammer** (1839) which could make forgings of greater size than ever before. A heavy iron hammer-head was driven downwards by steam which, added to the force of gravity, enabled blows of great force to be delivered. The gap between the raised hammer-head and the anvil was large enough to take a paddle-wheel shaft for a steamship.

Cast steel

Steel is bar iron blended with a little carbon to make it harder yet still flexible. Nowadays it has largely replaced iron, but before the

Workers preparing crucibles for casting steel

1850s it was too costly for general use. At the beginning of the eighteenth century the average steel furnace, where bar iron and charcoal were heated together in clay pots, took nearly three weeks to produce 10 tonnes of 'blister steel'. This was uneven in quality, being harder on its blistered surface than it was nearer the centre.

Benjamin Huntsman, a Yorkshire clock-maker, was not satisfied with the quality of most of the steel he had to use. He decided to look for a better way of making it, and, after many experiments, he succeeded some time in the 1740s. Huntsman put pieces of blister steel and a little charcoal in closed fireclay pots or *crucibles*. He then burned away all the impurities at a very high temperature in a coke-fired furnace. The resulting **cast steel** was of exceptionally high quality, suitable for articles such as clock springs and razor blades as well as cutlery and edge tools.

Early British advances in factory engineering, which followed some years later, owed much to Huntsman's discovery. The quality of cast steel has never been bettered since, and a few Sheffield firms still make it today. But, because it could only be produced in small quantities and was therefore costly, the steel trade continued on a small scale in comparison with iron. It was not until the 1850s, a century after Huntsman's process was perfected, that further invention led to the mass production of cheap steel (see Chapter 15).

Timeline

1709	Abraham Darby I's coke-smelting process.
1740s	Benjamin Huntsman's 'crucible casting process'.
1779	The first iron bridge (Abraham Darby III).
1783–4	Henry Cort's puddling and rolling.
1787	The first iron boat (John Wilkinson).
1828	James Neilson's hot blast.
1839	James Nasmyth's steam hammer.

Questions

1. Explain how each of the following was produced:
   a) cast iron
   b) pig iron
   c) wrought or bar iron (before the invention of 'puddling')
   d) blister steel
   e) cast steel

2. 'Had not these discoveries been made the iron trade of our own produce would have dwindled away, for woods for charcoal became very scarce...But from pit coal being introduced in its stead the demand for wood charcoal is much lessen'd, and in a few years I apprehend will set the use of that article aside.'
   (Letter of Abiah Darby, wife of Abraham Darby II, 1775)

   a) What were the 'discoveries' referred to (made by Abiah's husband and father-in-law)?
   b) Why would the trade in British-made iron have 'dwindled away' without these discoveries?
   c) Why were countries such as Sweden and Russia able to export iron at the beginning of our period?
   d) Where was the Darby family's ironworks situated?
   e) What was the best known achievement of Abraham Darby III?

3. Look at the picture of 'puddling' (page 66).
   a) What is the man on the right doing with the pair of tongs?
   b) What is the man on the left doing?
   c) Who invented this process?
   d) What further process did he invent at about the same time?
   e) How did these two processes affect the iron industry?

4. In what ways did John Wilkinson occupy a place in the iron industry similar to that of Richard Arkwright in the cotton industry? For what reasons was Wilkinson called 'Iron-mad'?

5. Write a paragraph on each of the following:
   a) Richard Crawshay
   b) the Carron Company
   c) the Hot Blast
   d) James Nasmyth (see also page 168)

8

The Triumph of Steam
Industrial Revolution (III)

Water-wheels powered factories in the early stages of the Industrial Revolution. They had been in use for centuries, first to grind corn in flour-mills, later to drive the mallets of fulling-mills (where cloth was beaten to thicken and cleanse it), and then to work the bellows and hammers of furnaces and forges. By the second half of the eighteenth century, wheelwrights were making huge water-wheels for cotton-mills and ironworks. The one that worked the forge-bellows at the Cyfarthfa works was 16 metres in diameter. Wheels of this size could power large factories, but only where there were good streams of swiftly flowing water. Manufacturers needed a new kind of power if they were to have greater freedom in choosing sites for factories. Steam was the answer. The development of steam-driven machinery was the greatest single achievement of the Industrial Revolution.

Thomas Savery, c. 1650–1715

Raising water by fire

The possibility of using the expanding force of steam had been realised nearly 2,000 years earlier by the Greeks. But not until the seventeenth century did experiments with steam begin to lead to a practical invention. In 1690, a Frenchman named Denis Papin produced a 'steam-atmospheric engine'. It was the first to have a cylinder (combined with a boiler) and a piston which was driven up by steam pressure and down by the force of the atmosphere after the steam in the cylinder was condensed. Eight years later an Englishman, **Thomas Savery**, used the same principles to construct the first 'fire'- or steam-engine to be used for industrial purposes. Savery came from Cornwall, where flooding in the tin- and copper-mines was a serious problem, and his invention was a simple pump designed to overcome this difficulty. However, in practice, his 'Engine to raise Water by Fire' was not powerful enough to drain the deeper mines.

It was left to **Thomas Newcomen**, a locksmith and blacksmith from nearby Dartmouth, to improve on Savery's pump in 1705–6. His **steam-atmospheric engine** was the first to be widely used in industry. Steam from the boiler was fed into an open-topped cylinder through a valve. Meanwhile the piston rose, under the weight of the pump-rods, until a jet of cold water from a cistern caused the steam in the cylinder to condense. A vacuum, or absence of air, was created underneath the piston which caused the atmospheric pressure above to force it back to the bottom of the cylinder. As it sank it pulled its end of the beam down and the pump-handle up. The repetition of this see-saw motion sucked the water from the mine-shaft. In the

*Thomas Newcomen's
steam-atmospheric engine*

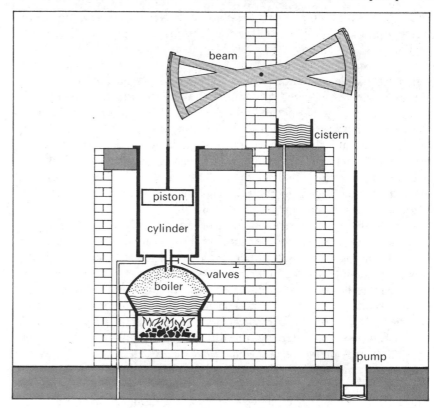

original design, the steam was condensed by the application of cold water *outside* the cylinder, but in later models condensation was speeded up by injecting the water *inside* so that it came into direct contact with the steam.

Newcomen's first models were clumsy and inefficient. It was not yet possible to manufacture the parts with precision, so power was lost through inaccurately bored cylinders and ill-fitting valves. Nevertheless, soon after 1711, when a company was formed to build and sell the engines, their most serious faults were corrected and they came into fairly general use. They were most popular in the coal-mines of the Midlands and the North-East, but some sold as far afield as the Continent. They could pump water from a considerable depth, and so made possible the working of deeper mines. By the 1770s, there were about 100 Newcomen engines in the Northumberland and Durham coalfield alone. They were also used for supplying water to London and other large towns, and, indirectly, for blowing blast-furnaces by raising water to drive a wheel. Abraham Darby II installed one for this purpose at Coalbrookdale.

The career of James Watt

It is often said that **James Watt** invented the steam-engine. This is partly true, since he was the first to design an engine driven entirely by steam, without the aid of atmospheric pressure. But a statement like this is misleading, because Watt took Newcomen's pump as his starting-point and built upon the foundations of a century of research. Much more misleading, however, is Watt's own story that his first invention resulted from a sudden flash of inspiration. He knew very well that his ideas stemmed from long study and careful experiment. He could have achieved nothing without a thorough grounding in mechanics and scientific theory. Born in 1736 at Greenock, near Glasgow, he was the grandson of a mathematics teacher. His father, an architect and shipbuilder, made sure James had a sound education, which enabled him to set up in business at the age of twenty-one as a scientific instrument maker. His workshop was in the grounds of Glasgow University, from which he kept in touch with the main scientific developments of the time.

James Watt, 1736–1819. Unlike most inventors of his day, Watt had some scientific training

Among the apparatus belonging to the University was a demonstration model of a Newcomen engine. In 1763 Watt was asked to repair it. While doing so he was struck by its inefficiency. Each time water was injected into the cylinder much of the next intake of steam was wasted in re-heating the cylinder to the necessary 100 degrees centigrade. Watt's solution was a **separate condenser** (1765) into which steam could be drawn from the cylinder after each upward thrust of the piston. He explained his reasoning as follows: 'To avoid useless condensation, *the vessel in which the steam acted upon the piston ought always to be as hot as the steam itself* . . . [therefore] the steam must be condensed in a *separate* vessel, which might be cooled [with water] to as low a degree as was necessary without affecting the cylinder'. The result was a great saving of steam, so less fuel was needed.

This first improvement led to an even more important one. Watt thought of fixing an airtight cover on the cylinder and using steam 'to act upon the piston in place of the atmosphere'. He therefore began to experiment with a **valve-box**, which could inject steam into the cylinder on *both* sides of the piston alternately.

Watt required financial support to manufacture his improved steam pump and continue with his experiments. In 1768 he was taken into partnership by **John Roebuck**, founder of the Carron ironworks (see page 68). Watt's first engine, called *Beelzebub*, was patented and set up near Edinburgh in 1769. Its production raised many problems. The engineers at Carron were unable to make sufficiently accurate cylinders and closely fitting pistons. It would take time to develop the necessary skills. Meanwhile, *Beelzebub* never worked properly and had to be given up. To make matters worse, Roebuck was soon in great financial difficulties and went bankrupt in 1773.

Watt's invention, still far from complete, was rescued by the foresight of **Matthew Boulton** (1728–1809), a successful hardware manufacturer from Birmingham. He was a friend of both Watt and Roebuck, and had taken a close interest in Watt's work. Roebuck owed Boulton £1,200. Boulton offered to let him off the debt in exchange for his two-thirds share in the partnership with Watt. Therefore, in 1774, Watt came down from Scotland to settle near Boulton's **Soho** factory, north of Birmingham. The Soho works already had a high reputation for quality, using only the best materials and the most

Matthew Boulton's Soho works, near Birmingham

skilled workers. This accuracy of workmanship, combined with Watt's inventive genius, soon made the firm of Boulton and Watt one of the most famous in the history of engineering. Able assistance was given by John Wilkinson (see page 67), who had just patented a new method of boring cannon (1774). This he used to manufacture precision-bored cylinders for Watt's engines.

The trial engine was rebuilt, with more accurate parts. Soon afterwards, Watt wrote to his father, in a hopeful mood: 'The fire engine I have invented is now going and answers much better than any other that has yet been made.' In 1775 his patent was renewed for twenty-five years, and the first Soho engines were delivered to customers, one of them to Wilkinson's Broseley works. Forty engines were erected in the next five years, most of them in the Cornish tin- and copper-mines. Owners of coal-mines had less to gain from changing to Watt's engine, because the saving of fuel was not so important where there was plenty of it on the spot.

At this stage Watt's engine was still only a pump. If it had not been developed further its influence on British industry would have been relatively slight. It was the invention of **rotary motion** (1781) which really began the Age of Steam. This was based on the simple principle of fixing the beam to a connecting rod which turned a fly-wheel. By attaching a belt to the wheel, steam power could be used to work all kinds of machinery. In the early models, the connecting

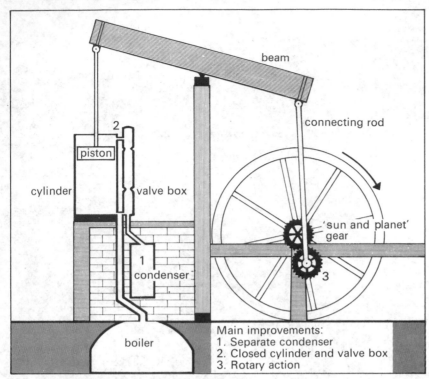

James Watt's rotative steam engine

beam

connecting rod

2

piston

cylinder | valve box

'sun and planet' gear

1 condenser

3

boiler

Main improvements:
1. Separate condenser
2. Closed cylinder and valve box
3. Rotary action

rod had a cogwheel at the end. It was geared to another cogwheel, which was attached to the flywheel itself (see diagram above). This part of the invention – the 'sun and planet gear' – was suggested by **William Murdock**, foreman at Soho. Murdock, a self-taught engineer from Scotland, played a major part in the success of the firm and made some important discoveries of his own. He was the first Briton to build a steam locomotive (1784) and the first to use coal-gas for lighting. (The Soho works was lit by gas as early as 1798.)

The 'rotative engine' greatly extended the range of uses of steam. It was first employed to drive bellows, rollers and hammers in the making of iron. Shortly afterwards, the first steam spinning-mill was set up in Nottinghamshire (1785). By 1800 Boulton and Watt had also erected engines in sugar-refineries, waterworks, flour-mills and breweries. Their patent allowed them a monopoly in the years 1775–1800 and they took full advantage of it, erecting well over 300 engines in Britain, most of them of the rotary type. When the patent expired, they handed over the business to their sons and spent their last years in ease and comfort. It was just a matter of time before rotative engines replaced water-wheels in most industries. Although water power was still supreme in 1800, by the 1830s the Steam Age was in full swing. Large-scale industry, freed from its dependence on rivers, was becoming concentrated in coalfield towns.

Changes in the coal industry

The development of the steam-engine, together with the new methods

A Boulton and Watt rotative engine, built in 1788. On view in London's Science Museum

of mass production in the iron industry, meant the supply of coal had to be greatly increased. The central importance of coal in the Industrial Revolution can be seen geographically. Almost without exception, the new manufacturing towns grew up in areas where large deposits of coal lay under the surface.

In 1700 small quantities of coal were already being mined in most of the present day coalfields. Deposits could still be found on the surface in many areas. Because of transport difficulties, most of the output was used in or near the mining districts for domestic fires, but coal fuel was also used in brewing, soap- and brick-making, forging and sugar-refining. **North-East England**, around the valleys of the rivers Tyne and Wear, was the chief coal-mining area. Since the sixteenth century most of its output had been shipped to London, where it was known as 'sea coal'. By 1705 the north-eastern coal trade employed over 1,200 ships of various kinds and was looked upon as 'the nursery of the English navy'. This same coalfield saw the first 'railways' in Britain. They were wooden wagon-ways, along which horses pulled trucks of coal to the loading quays (staiths) on the rivers. At the staiths, the coal was loaded into riverboats (keels) and carried to the main ports, notably Newcastle and Sunderland, where it was transferred into coastal vessels called 'colliers'.

Very few mine-shafts went down beyond 100 metres in the early eighteenth century, and it was rare for more than forty or fifty miners to be employed in one pit. However, as time went by, shafts had to be sunk deeper to keep pace with the rising demand for coal. This, in turn, increased the **hazards of mining** – floods, fire and poisonous air. Attempts to reduce these dangers and difficulties in the eighteenth and early nineteenth centuries met with varying degrees of success.

Drainage was the first problem to be tackled seriously. In 1700 the usual method was to use a chain of buckets, often worked by a horse.

The pithead of a Staffordshire coal-mine

But this was very slow, and only suitable for shallow workings. It was Newcomen's steam-atmospheric engine which made possible the drainage of deep mines, not only for coal but also tin and copper.

Most mines contain harmful **gases**, notably 'fire damp' (methane). These are liable to explode if they are not dispersed by currents of fresh air. In the eighteenth century, explosions were so frequent and the loss of life so great that it was not usual for inquests to be held on the victims of pit disasters. For example, at Chester-le-Street, County Durham, in 1708, a particularly violent explosion killed a hundred miners and did ' . . . great damage to many houses and persons for several miles around. One man was blown quite out of the mouth of the shaft . . . and found at a prodigious [great] distance from the place'. Such disasters made mining by far the most dangerous way of earning a living.

The traditional method of **ventilation** was to sink two shafts at different levels and draw fresh air down one while foul air was forced up the other. The draught was often drawn through the mine by a series of trapdoors, operated by small children crouching in the darkness. Alternatively, a brazier full of burning coals could be hung in the 'up' shaft to create rising convection currents. But such methods were not satisfactory in deep mines. At the end of the eighteenth century **John Buddle**, a mining engineer from Wallsend, near Newcastle, invented an **exhaust fan** to ventilate larger pits. It drew the bad

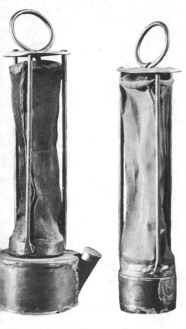

Two original Davy safety lamps. On view in London's Science Museum

air out of the 'up' shaft by suction, and this, in turn, caused a current of fresh air to descend down the other shaft.

To see their way, miners took candles underground. But a naked flame could explode 'fire damp' without any warning. Early in the nineteenth century several **safety lamps** were invented which greatly reduced this hazard. The most famous was that of **Sir Humphrey Davy** (1815) which won a prize from the Royal Society. It shielded the flame with a fine metal gauze, which allowed enough air to get in yet so reduced the heat of the flame that it could not explode any gas outside. If gas were present the flame merely turned blue, which gave a useful warning. The miners' safety lamp helped to increase the output of coal because it made possible the working of pits which had previously been thought too dangerous. Davy could have made a fortune if he had taken out a patent, but he refused, saying: 'I am only too happy to have been able to help our miners. That is my reward'.

Several other improvements helped to increase coal production, even though the actual cutting of the coal was still done by pick and shovel. Instead of leaving pillars of coal uncut in order to support the ceilings of the galleries, wooden **pit-props** began to be used in the late eighteenth century. By this time pit ponies hauled trucks along some of the main underground passages, although in the smaller galleries women and children still had to get down on all fours and harness trucks to their waists. Watt's rotative engine was ideal for hauling coal to the surface – a great improvement on the traditional method whereby women and girls carried baskets up a series of ladders. In one mine they had to climb a distance equal to the height of St Paul's Cathedral. **Steam haulage** did not, however, come into general use until the introduction of wire cables in the 1840s – after which shafts of up to 300 metres could be worked.

A steady increase in the size and number of pits, together with technical improvements, enabled the coal industry to keep up with the new demands put upon it. Coal output increased by 400 per cent in the eighteenth century, and by a further 250 per cent in the next thirty years.

British coal production (*approximate figures*)

1700	2.5 million tonnes
1800	10 million tonnes
1830	25 million tonnes

Josiah Wedgwood and 'The Potteries'

In general, it was the major industries – especially iron and textiles – which were the first to be revolutionised. But an important exception was the pottery industry of North Staffordshire, which earned a worldwide reputation well before 1800.

The making of earthenware pots and jars had been a cottage industry for centuries in **The Potteries** – the district round Stoke-on-Trent – where turf ovens were fed with local clay mixed with charcoal fuel. In the mid eighteenth century, however, the pottery industry began to undergo a series of rapid changes. There were three main reasons for this. First, there was a new demand for fine quality earthenware, because of the growing popularity of tea and coffee drinking. By 1765 nine families out of ten drank tea at least twice a day. Second, it was discovered in the 1760s that white Cornish clay (kaolin) could be mixed with china stone to produce porcelain – a highly valued, fine earthenware. Third, the industry was transformed by the inventiveness and business skill of **Josiah Wedgwood** (1730–95), the most famous potter in British history.

A Wedgwood tea service

The modern pottery industry really dates from 1769, when Wedgwood opened his new **Etruria** works, near Burslem. (It was named after the ancient Etruscans, whose vases and urns inspired many of his own designs.) At Etruria, Wedgwood greatly increased the output per worker by means of a *division of labour*. In other words, he subdivided all the skills of the potter – mixing, shaping, firing and glazing – and allocated each to specialist workers, who concentrated on the one operation. Although he later introduced steam-engines for mixing clay and grinding flints, most processes in his factory continued to be done by hand. Wedgwood's superior production methods, together with new designs, colours and glazes, enabled him to improve the quality not only of fine, ornamental china, but also the ordinary earthenware in everyday use. Even the simplest articles were attractive and well finished – like his famous 'willow pattern', used in hundreds of thousands of British homes.

Few industries have owed so much to one man. Wedgwood was one of the keenest supporters of the Grand Trunk Canal (see page 94), which linked the River Trent with the west coast via the Mersey (1777). He put a great deal of his own money into the scheme, for he realised how much it would benefit the pottery trade.

'The Potteries'

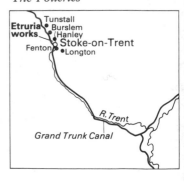

Survival of the old handicrafts

By the early nineteenth century Britain was the world's leading

A traditional nail forge. Such workshops continued to play an important part in British industry long after the introduction of mass-production methods

industrial country. But the speed of change should not be exaggerated. As a writer of the time, William Eden, said in 1797: 'With regard to mechanical knowledge, it is probable that we are still in our infancy ... fifty years hence some new contrivance may be thought of in comparison with which the steam-engine and spinning-jennies ... will be considered as slight and insignificant discoveries.' Although we could not regard the steam-engine as an 'insignificant' discovery, Eden was correct in thinking that the industrial advances of his lifetime were only a beginning. Even in 1830, when the use of steam power was well established, machines had replaced skilled hands in only a few industries. Half the population still lived in the countryside, where life was often much the same as it had been a century or more before.

Handicrafts continued to flourish. For example **shipbuilding**, one of the most vital industries in the early nineteenth century, was only just beginning to feel the effects of the Industrial Revolution. Shipwrights and sail-makers still worked in small yards, and most boats were made of wood before 1850. Even in the regions round Birmingham, Manchester and Glasgow, where the most advanced industries were centralised, **small workshops** predominated until well into the nineteenth century. While hand loom weavers resisted the introduction of the power loom until the 1840s (see pages 56–7) thousands of blacksmiths, nail-makers, cutlers and other metalworkers earned a living at the forge, using anvil, hammer, chisel and file like their grandparents.

The Industrial Revolution set the pattern for the future, but in the early nineteenth century factory workers and machine-minders were only a small proportion of Britain's total working population.

The industrial towns

In areas where the growth of factory industry was most rapid, villages and hamlets became manufacturing towns almost overnight. The earliest and most dramatic changes came in Lancashire. Bolton, which

Nineteenth-century slums

in the 1750s consisted of 'a single rough and ill-paved street, with thatched cottages', had a population of 17,000 by the end of the century. In the same period Oldham grew from a village of about 300 inhabitants to a town of 12,000. Above all, **Manchester** became one of the world's greatest industrial and commercial centres. Manchester's population in 1700 was below 10,000, yet in the first Census (1801) it was the largest British town outside London, with 95,000 inhabitants. The introduction of steam-powered machinery was the chief factor in this remarkable growth. In 1786 only one factory chimney rose above the town – that of Arkwright's mill. Just fifteen years later there were fifty mills in Manchester. In the next twenty years, while Manchester's population exceeded 150,000, those of Glasgow, Liverpool and Birmingham rose above the 100,000 mark. None of these had been of any great size or importance a century before.

In the rush to put up factories and rows of workers' dwellings, many important services were neglected. There were hardly any building regulations and no sanitary inspectors. Consequently houses were often damp, streets unpaved and full of holes, and proper sewers were almost unheard of. There was no collection of refuse, and drinking-water was so scarce that it often had to be bought from street traders. Not surprisingly, epidemic diseases such as cholera and typhoid frequently swept through these towns. As soon as new houses were built, the overflowing population reduced them to crowded, disease-ridden **slums**. Seeing the chance to make quick profits, builders put up as many houses as space would permit, using materials of the cheapest quality. Rows of dwellings were often built 'back-to-back', which meant that through ventilation was impossible and parts of the houses received no direct light. In the older towns, including Manchester and Liverpool, the larger tenement houses were each crammed with several families, and even waterlogged cellars were let as separate dwellings.

Much of the reforming activity of Parliament in the years to come was concerned with social problems created by the new industrial towns. The first attempts to control public health and housing are dealt with in Chapter 16.

Timeline

1698	Thomas Savery's 'fire engine'.
1705–6	Thomas Newcomen's steam-atmospheric engine.
1765	James Watt invents the separate condenser.
1769	Josiah Wedgwood's Etruria works opened.
1774	Watt begins his partnership with Matthew Boulton.
1781	Watt invents the rotative engine.
1815	Humphrey Davy's miners' safety lamp.

Questions

1. 'On Friday last, a steam engine constructed upon Mr Watt's new principles was set to work at Bloomfield Colliery, near Dudley . . . All the iron foundry parts (which are unparalleled for truth) were executed by Mr Wilkinson; the condenser with the valves, pistons and all the small work, at Soho. It made about 14 to 15 strokes per minute and is capable of working with one-fourth of the fuel that a common engine would require to produce the same quantity of power.' (*Birmingham Gazette*, 1776)

   a) What 'new principles' had James Watt introduced by this time to improve the steam pumping engine?
   b) How did these improvements lead to the saving of fuel?

   c) Name one of the 'iron foundry parts' which John Wilkinson had recently improved in quality. What does 'unparalleled for truth' mean?

   d) Who was Watt's business partner and where was 'Soho'?

   e) Why did owners of tin- and copper-mines gain even more than coal-owners from using Watt's engine?

2. Look at the picture of a Staffordshire coal-mine (page 78).
   a) How can we be sure that this picture was painted after 1781?
   b) What tasks are being performed by the steam engine?
   c) Explain why these uses of steam power made possible the sinking of deeper mine-shafts.
   d) Why was mining the most dangerous way to earn a living?
   e) How did Sir Humphrey Davy help to make mining safer?

3. 'Few industries have owed so much to one man.' Outline the contribution of Josiah Wedgwood to the pottery industry.

4. 'New cottages, with or without cellars, huddled together row behind row, may be seen springing up in many parts, but especially in the township of Manchester, where the land is higher in price than the land for cottage sites in other townships.' (*Report of the Committee on the Health of Towns*, 1840)

   a) Why did Manchester grow so rapidly from the 1780s?
   b) Why do you think land was more expensive in Manchester than in other towns? How would this affect building developments?
   c) Name *three* other towns (apart from London) which expanded on a similar scale in this period. In each case, state the main reasons for rapid growth.
   d) What kinds of health hazards resulted from the very fast expansion of industrial towns in this period?

5. Write a paragraph on each of the following:
   a) the uses and limitations of water-wheels
   b) Thomas Newcomen
   c) 'sea-coal'
   d) William Murdock (see also page 137)

9

Turnpikes and Canals
Transport and Communications (I)

There were no mechanical forms of transport in the eighteenth century. The fastest method of travel was on horseback and the quickest way of moving bulky goods was by sailing ship. Similarly, news could not out-speed the swiftest horseman (unless the message was pre-arranged and fires lighted on hilltops) for there was no wireless or telephone. It was a far cry from our Space Age of satellites and rockets. Nevertheless, the eighteenth century was a time of rapid change in transport. The increase in traffic resulting from a rising population and the developments in industry and agriculture made improved roads and waterways essential. In fact, the Industrial Revolution was only made possible by quicker and cheaper transportation to and from the ports and the main centres of population.

Roads, rivers and coastal traffic

In the early eighteenth century, most of Britain's **roads** were little more than paths or rough tracks across the countryside. They were usually impassable in winter, when they were flooded or churned into

A gentleman's carriage jolted to pieces by the rough road

thick mud by horse-drawn vehicles and herds of cattle. In some places the highway was full of holes so deep that travellers had been known to drown in times of heavy rain. Even in dry weather, coaches and wagons were frequently overturned in the ruts left by previous traffic. Some of the roads connecting the main towns of southern England were in a reasonable state of repair, but, these apart, there had been little attempt to build proper roads with hard surfaces and solid foundations since the Romans left Britain 1,300 years before. The original Roman paving was still used in some places; for example on parts of the Great North Road and on Watling Street, which remained the best overland route from London to Chester.

Horses and farm-carts were used for most local journeys. Longer distances were sometimes travelled by **stage-coaches**, but these ran infrequently and were uncomfortable and very expensive. In addition, they were often held up at gunpoint by highwaymen. 'Outsiders', who travelled at a reduced rate on the roof of the coach or on the luggage at the rear, were called upon to keep a lookout, and also to get down occasionally and push up hills. There were few carriages in the streets of most towns because the surfaces, although usually cobbled, were likely to be as uneven and dangerous as country roads. Sedan-chairs became the fashion for town ladies attending balls and dinner-parties and for town doctors on their rounds. Goods and luggage were carried on the better roads in huge **wagons**, drawn by teams of six or eight horses. But **packhorses** were more common. Merchants sometimes employed trains of thirty or forty of them.

A packhorse

The backward state of road transport in the early eighteenth century was reflected in the heavy volume of river and coastal traffic. Britain's natural waterways provided the best means of transporting bulky goods like coal, iron, clay and timber. **The sea** had been an important highway for centuries because, added to the advantage of being an island, Britain has a coastline indented with long estuaries which bring many inland areas within easy reach of open water. Ocean-going vessels were very small by modern standards, but they were capable of carrying much greater loads than wagons or packhorse trains. It was cheaper and often quicker to make long detours by sea rather than carry goods overland. London not only received its coal by sea; corn from Sussex and Hampshire and cheese from Cheshire were also brought round the coast in preference to the overland routes.

Most of Britain's industries and almost all the major towns were located on six main river systems – the Thames, Severn, Trent, Mersey, Humber and Great Ouse. The improvement and extension of these **river navigations** was the most important development in inland transport up to the mid eighteenth century. 'Cuts' (artificial river-beds) were made to straighten bends, and rivers were deepened and supplied with locks to make them navigable in their shallower reaches. The rivers of Yorkshire were improved in this way, as were the Trent and Derwent, to assist the industrial development of Nottingham and Derby. In Lancashire, the improved navigation of the Mersey and its tributaries helped the growth of the port of Liverpool.

Nevertheless, in spite of improvement schemes, few of Britain's rivers could be navigated far inland without becoming too shallow or being obstructed by low bridges. Even the sea had drawbacks, for fragile cargoes were easily broken or spoilt by salt water, and enemy 'privateers' were a serious threat in war-time. If Britain's industries were to develop and expand into new areas, a lot would depend on the roads. Something had to be done to improve them.

'Turnpike fever'

Since the sixteenth century, the people of each parish had been required by law to devote six days a year to repairing the roads. But in practice parish responsibility was an obstacle to progress. Villagers, who were not paid for their labour, worked only on local roads. They neglected *main* roads passing through the parish because these were mostly used by strangers. Much-needed improvements in Britain's trunk roads were unlikely to be carried out until the costs of building and maintenance were put upon the people who used them.

It was for this reason that **turnpike trusts** came into being in the eighteenth century. These were groups of landowners and businessmen who got Parliament to pass private Acts authorising them to take over and rebuild stretches of road. To recover the money invested and to pay for repairs, the trustees were permitted to erect barriers at both ends of the road and make travellers stop and pay a fee or **toll** for using it. Most of the early toll-bars had pikes (spikes) on them, and it was from these that the roads got their name. Tolls ranged from a penny (½p) to as much as two shillings (10p – worth

Toll gates at Hyde Park, London

several pounds today) depending on the length of the road and the nature of the traffic. Different rates were charged for horse and rider, wagon, coach, livestock and so on.

The earliest Turnpike Acts, dating back to 1663, concerned road improvements carried out by county magistrates. It was not until 1706 that Parliament first made a group of local gentry trustees of a turnpike road. From then on rapid progress was made. In the next fifty years, over 400 Acts dealing with the construction and upkeep of roads were passed by Parliament. In some areas the erection of turnpikes was bitterly opposed by the local inhabitants. They protested against having to pay for what they regarded as their own. Riots broke out, and severe penalties were imposed on 'disorderly persons' who 'cut down, pulled down, burnt and otherwise destroyed... turnpike gates and houses'. But such opposition was short-lived. In the period 1750–91, no fewer than 1,600 Turnpike Acts were passed and a kind of *turnpike fever* took hold of the business community.

Better road surfaces made passenger transport swifter and safer and reduced the cost of carrying goods. Horses could draw heavier loads at higher speeds and cattle could be driven to market quicker yet arrive in better condition. But turnpikes had their shortcomings too. There was no overall authority to see that equal attention was given to the whole road. Most turnpike trusts controlled only short stretches of about 15 or 20 kilometres, and these were frequently followed by long sections where no attempt had been made to improve the surface. So travellers might pay several tolls yet still find their route impassable at some point. Only a truly national system could overcome such difficulties, but this did not happen until the Age of the Motor Car. Meanwhile, perhaps the greatest problem was the shortage of skilled engineers. Roadmaking was a lost art in Britain and it took time for it to be rediscovered.

The great roadbuilders

The first of Britain's great road engineers was **General George Wade** (1673–1748) who built 400 kilometres of roads and forty bridges in Scotland in the 1720s and 1730s. Like the Romans, he considered firm foundations to be the first essential of roadbuilding, and he *cambered* (curved) the surface so that water drained off into ditches on each side. Wade's work was financed by the government, which wanted roads good enough to carry an army into the Highlands in case the Jacobites rose again after the 1715 Rebellion (see page 16).

One of the most remarkable surveyors and roadbuilders was **John Metcalfe** (1717–1810) from Knaresborough in Yorkshire. Although totally blind from the age of six, following an attack of smallpox, he led a long and active life. 'Blind Jack', as he was called, was nearly fifty years old when he built his first turnpike road (1765) but in the next twenty-seven years he supervised the construction of nearly 300 kilometres of turnpikes, mostly in Yorkshire and Lancashire. He paid special attention to the bed of the road, and where the soil was soft he laid great quantities of heather as a foundation for layers of stone

Thomas Telford (1757–1834) built some of the finest roads, bridges and canals of his time, even though he was largely self-taught

and gravel. Metcalfe realised that smooth, hard-wearing surfaces could not be made with rounded stones, for these were pushed aside by the traffic. He used jagged broken stones which, in time, bound together under the pressure of wheeled vehicles.

Road construction was only one of the activities of **Thomas Telford**, a Scottish shepherd's son who rose from being a humble stonemason to one of the greatest civil engineers in British history. In addition to surveying and building roads, he designed and constructed bridges, canals, lighthouses, harbours and docks. Much of his early experience was gained as Surveyor of Roads in Shropshire in the 1780s and 1790s. He first came into prominence when he was put in charge of a government scheme of road-, bridge- and canal-building in Scotland (1803). In the next eighteen years he built nearly 1,600 kilometres of road, over 1,000 bridges and the great Caledonian Canal, which made a continuous waterway cutting across northern Scotland from coast to coast. The overall effect of his work was to revolutionise trade and travel north of the Border and quicken communications between England and Scotland.

The work for which Telford is most famous was the **London–Holyhead road**, which took over ten years to build, starting in 1815. The old road had become increasingly unsatisfactory after the Act of Union with Ireland in 1801 (see page 104) for it was one of the main overland routes from London to the Irish Sea. Telford was instructed by Parliament to make it as near perfect for coach traffic as he could. Therefore he set out to achieve gentle gradients and moderate curves,

Part of Thomas Telford's Menai Suspension Bridge. Built in 1826, it is still in use today

which often meant leaving the line of the old road and building entirely new sections. Bangor, on the mainland, was linked with the Isle of Anglesey and Holyhead by a new stretch of road 35 kilometres long. It crossed the Menai Straits by means of a magnificent 520-metre suspension bridge, designed and built by Telford and opened in 1826.

Telford believed that the surest way of keeping a road hard and smooth was to have solid foundations of hand-laid stone blocks. He also provided proper drainage, so that the heaviest rain could not wash away the surface. These techniques were successful but very expensive. Turnpike trusts, with limited money to spend, normally preferred quicker and cheaper methods – like those of another Scotsman, **John Macadam**. He showed that if the subsoil was well drained and the surface of the road slightly raised, it would carry heavy traffic all the year round without the need for costly foundations. Like Metcalfe, Macadam covered the road's surface with a carpet of fine, chipped stones which packed tightly together under the weight of traffic. 'Every piece of stone put into a road which exceeds one inch in any of its dimensions is mischievous,' he said. His methods are still used, but nowadays Macadamised roads are sprayed with tar to give a waterproof 'tarmac' surface.

John Loudon Macadam, 1756–1836

In common with other great roadbuilders of the period, Macadam had no special training. Roads were merely his hobby for many years. It was not until 1815, when he was made Surveyor of the Bristol Turnpike Trust, that he began to gain a nationwide reputation. His methods were popular with the turnpike trusts because they were ideal for carrying out low-cost improvements to old roads, rather than building new ones. Although Macadam assisted dozens of separate trusts all over the country, he realised that improvements would have a greater effect if groups of trusts amalgamated to produce long, *continuous* sections of good road. He eventually persuaded Parliament to consolidate all the turnpikes in the London area under one **Metropolitan Turnpike Trust** (1825) to which he was appointed Surveyor-General. This was a great step forward and the nation's debt to him was recognised by a special parliamentary grant of £10,000.

The Coaching Age

Between 1790 and 1830 the network of turnpike roads spread all over the kingdom. In that time Parliament passed 2,450 Turnpike Acts, compared with 1,600 in the previous forty years. There were parallel improvements in road vehicles. Wagons and carts gradually replaced packhorses for the carriage of goods. In the towns, sedan-chairs gave way to private horse-drawn carriages and hired cabs, and there were great advances in stage-coach travel. **Coaches** in the mid eighteenth century were heavily built and without proper springs, which made them slow and uncomfortable. But by the turn of the century they had improved to such an extent that it was faster to send mail by coach than by postboy on horseback.

The growth of a regular **postal service** was one of the chief results of better transport in this period. There was no really national system before 1720, when **Ralph Allen** of Bath was granted a monopoly of all postal deliveries outside London. Although his postboys were easy prey for highwaymen, he managed to run a regular service roughly three times a week between all the main towns. By the 1780s, stage-coaches on improved roads could out-speed the horse post. As a result **John Palmer**, also from Bath, was given a Post Office contract to carry the mails between London and Bristol by coach, beginning in 1784. Palmer's coaches did the journey in sixteen hours and were such a success that within a few years fast mail-coaches served all the main towns. They carried passengers as well as mail, and each coach had an armed guard as a protection against highwaymen. Like the postboys before them, mail-coaches were exempted from turnpike tolls. The guard sounded his post-horn on approaching the toll-gates to avoid unnecessary delay.

Mail-coaches also delivered **newspapers**. Most large towns had their own daily papers by this time, and London had several. They were a fairly recent development, for, although periodicals appeared well before 1700, the first *daily* newspaper – *The Daily Courant* – began in 1702. It was printed on one side of a sheet of paper measuring 35 by 20 centimetres. During the course of the century, papers of several pages began to appear. More than half their news space was normally

London–Exeter mail-coach

BOLT-IN-TUN

ROYAL MAIL & COACH ESTABLISHMENT,
Sussex Tavern and Family Hotel,
FLEET STREET, LONDON.

Royal Mails.

PORTSMOUTH & ISLE of WIGHT, With a Branch to Chichester, Bognor, & Petworth. | HASTINGS & TUNBRIDGE WELLS, With a Branch to Rye and Hawkhurst.

Every Evening .... at Half-past Seven o'Clock.

Fast Coaches.

	Morning	Afternoon
ABERYSTWITH, Kington, Penybont, and Rhayader	7	½ past 5
ALRESFORD, Alton, and Farnham	½ past 8	....
BATH, Melksham, Devizes, Marlborough, and Hungerford	7	¼ to 7
BIRMINGHAM and Stratford-on-Avon,	7	....
BLACKWATER, Sandhurst (Royal Military College,) Egham, and Staines	....	3
BRISTOL, Clifton, Bath, Devizes, and Newbury	7	¼ to 7
BRIGHTON, Reigate, and Crawley	½ past 8 ½ past 10	....
CHELTENHAM, Witney, and Oxford	7 & ¼ to 8	¼ to 6
CHICHESTER, Midhurst, Hazlemere, Petworth, and Godalming	9	½ past 7
CHIPPING NORTON, Enstone, Woodstock	10	....
CHERTSEY, Shepperton, Halliford, Sunbury, and Hampton	....	½ past 3
CAERMARTHEN, Llandilo, Llandovery, Brecon, and Crickowell	7	½ past 5
DOVER, Deal, Canterbury, Sittingbourne, and Rochester	9	½ past 6
ESHER, Claremont, Ditton, and Kingston	8 & 9	½ past 3
EXETER, Collumpton, Wellington, Bridgewater, Taunton, and Wells	7	¼ to 7
FROME, Trowbridge, and Devizes	7	....
GLOUCESTER, Cheltenham, Northleach, Burford, Witney, and Oxford (*In direct communication with Coaches for all parts of South Wales.*)	7 & ¼ to 8	¼ to 6
GODALMING, Guildford, Ripley, Cobham, and Esher	8 & 9	½ past 3
HAMPTON COURT, Hampton, Twickenham, and Richmond	8 & ½ p. 10	½ past 3 ½ past 6

	Morning	Afternoon
HEREFORD, Ross, Gloucester, Cheltenham, and Oxford	¼ to 7	¼ to 6
HASTINGS, Battle, Robertsbridge, Flimwell, and Tunbridge	10	½ past 7
MARGATE and Ramsgate	9	½ past 6
MONMOUTH, Whitchurch, and Ross	7	½ past 5
OXFORD	7, 8 & 10	¼ to 6
PORTSMOUTH, Horndean, Petersfield, Liphook, and Godalming	½ past 11	½ past 7
READING, Wokingham, Bracknell, and Virginia Water	½ past 11	4
RYE, Northiam, Sandhurst, Hawkhurst, and Lamberhurst	11	½ past 7
SHREWSBURY, Bridgenorth, and Kidderminster	7	½ past 5
SOUTHAMPTON, Winchester, Alton, Farnham, and Guildford	½ past 8	....
St. LEONARDS and Hastings	10	½ past 7
SEVEN OAKS and Riverhead	10 & 11	½ past 2 ½ past 7
SWANSEA, Neath, Cowbridge, Cardiff, Newport, and Chepstow	7	½ past 5
TUNBRIDGE WELLS, Tunbridge, and Seven Oaks	10	½ past 2 ½ past 7
TROWBRIDGE and Devizes	7	¼ to 7
WEYBRIDGE, Oatlands, Walton, Moulsey, and Hampton Court	....	4
WINCHESTER and Farnham	½ past 8	....
WINDSOR, Eton, and Slough (Patronized by Her Majesty.)	½ past 9	½ past 2 4
WORCESTER and Tewkesbury	7	¼ to 6
WANTAGE, Wallingford, and Henley	8	....

ROBERT GRAY & CO. Proprietors.

Every information relative to the different STEAM PACKETS from
BRISTOL .... to Cork, Waterford, Swansea, Ilfracomb, Haverfordwest, and Tenby.
PORTSMOUTH .... to the Isle of Wight, Torquay, Plymouth, and Falmouth.
SOUTHAMPTON .... to the Isle of Wight, Guernsey, Jersey, St. Maloes, Havre de Grace, France, and Italy.

☞ NOTICE——No Parcel, or Passenger's Luggage, will be accounted for above the Value of Ten Pounds unless entered as such, and Insurance paid accordingly.

Timetable of mail-coach departures from London (1839)

devoted to parliamentary debates, and the remainder to articles, gossip, letters and columns of small advertisements. Since the great majority of the population could not read, 2,000 copies was considered a good daily sale for a leading London newspaper, even in the Coaching Age.

The mail-coaches were built for speed, with lighter, more streamlined bodies, steel springs and thinner wheels. These advances in design were taken up by private coach companies, which competed with each other to provide the fastest, most comfortable services. By the 1820s and 30s, a good stage-coach, changing horses frequently at coaching inns, could average up to 16 kilometres an hour on a long run. The 'Independent Tally-Ho' averaged 22 kilometres an hour from London to Birmingham. By the 1830s, when competition from railways began to be felt (see Chapter 13) improved roads, thorough-bred horses and better-designed coaches had brought about a remarkable reduction in travelling times since the mid eighteenth century.

Average travel times under favourable conditions

	1750s	*1830 (approx.)*
London–Newcastle	6 days	Just over 1 day
London–Edinburgh	10 days	2 days
London–Brighton	1 day	5½ hours

'Canal mania'

Even after road improvements it was still very costly to send freight by stage-wagon. Manufacturers continued to prefer water transport. For example, a Shropshire company, in 1775, sent pig iron 650 kilometres by sea and river to avoid the 100-kilometre journey overland. But navigable rivers were few, and many of these were too short or too shallow. By the second half of the eighteenth century growing industrial areas such as Lancashire and the West Midlands urgently needed more waterways. The answer was to follow the example of the Netherlands and France and cut artificial canals for carrying goods in bulk.

The beginning of the canal-building period in Britain is closely bound up with the lives of two men from very different social backgrounds. Francis Egerton, **Duke of Bridgewater** (1736–1803) was rich and educated. **James Brindley** (1716–72), his chief engineer, began life as a humble millwright and never learned to read and write properly. Their association began in 1759, when the Duke obtained an Act of Parliament allowing him to build a canal to Manchester from his estate at Worsley, 11 kilometres away. He had large deposits of coal on his land and wanted a better method of transporting it to Manchester than on the backs of packhorses. It was not the first 'deadwater navigation'. Liverpool was already receiving coal via the Sankey Brook Canal (1757) which linked the St Helens coalfield with the River Mersey at Warrington. But the **Bridgewater Canal** became the starting-point of a systematic network of waterways linking Britain's main industrial areas.

The construction of the Bridgewater Canal presented many problems. Brindley's method of tackling them was not to do complicated calculations but to retire to bed to think and stay there until he found a solution. In this way he hit upon the idea of carrying the canal over the River Irwell with an aqueduct, or bridge, at Barton. People came from all over Europe to stare at it in wonder. By 1764 the canal was carrying coal into the heart of Manchester. One horse pulled more on water than sixty packhorses could carry, with the result that the price of coal in Manchester was halved and the demand for it greatly increased. By 1762 Brindley was already working on a 56-kilometre extension of the canal, to meet the Mersey estuary at Runcorn. When it was completed (1776) the cost of carrying cotton and cotton goods between Liverpool and Manchester was reduced by five-sixths.

Meanwhile, in 1766, Brindley began his most ambitious scheme – the **Trent and Mersey Canal** – to provide a continuous waterway across England from coast to coast. It ran a distance of 150 kilometres, from the Bridgewater Canal, near Runcorn, via the salt and pottery districts of Cheshire and Staffordshire, to a point on the River Trent where it was navigable all the way to the Humber estuary. One of its main financiers was **Josiah Wedgwood**, the potter (see page 80). He had much to gain. Cornish clay, brought by sea to Chester or Liverpool, could be carried along the canal to his Etruria works, which were sited on its banks. The fragile finished goods could travel by barge to Liverpool or Hull instead of being jolted along the roads by packhorses.

Brindley called the Trent and Mersey Canal the **Grand Trunk**; for he made it the basis of a whole system of waterways linking England's greatest rivers. The Staffordshire and Worcestershire Canal joined the River Severn at Stourport, and a branch to Birmingham ran through the heart of the industrial Midlands. Brindley also surveyed another canal to link the Grand Trunk with the Thames at Oxford. But he did not live to see his schemes completed, dying as a result of overwork in 1772. His friends were not surprised. Five years earlier Wedgwood had written: 'I am afraid he will do too much, and leave us before his vast designs are executed.'

In the thirteen years they were together, Brindley and the Duke of Bridgewater built nearly 600 kilometres of canals. While the Duke provided the money, obtained the necessary Acts of Parliament and negotiated with the landowners, Brindley took charge of all the planning and construction. He even recruited and trained his own gangs

James Brindley's Barton aqueduct, on the Bridgewater Canal

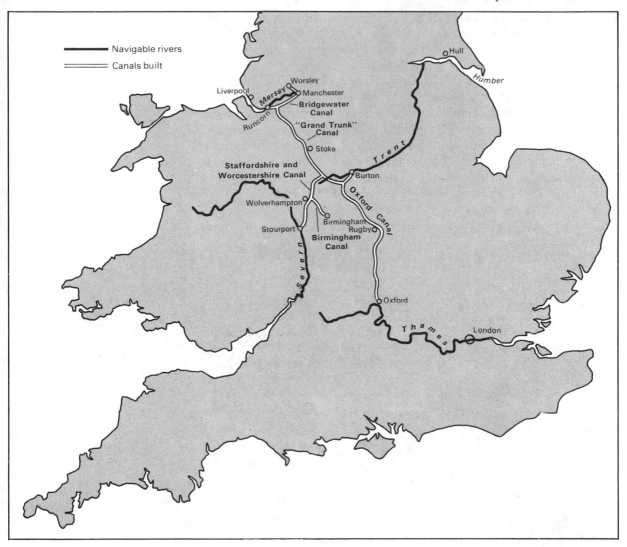

──	Navigable rivers
═══	Canals built

Liverpool • Worsley • Manchester — Bridgewater Canal — "Grand Trunk" Canal — Stoke — Burton

Staffordshire and Worcestershire Canal

Wolverhampton • Stourport • Birmingham — Birmingham Canal — Rugby

Oxford Canal — Oxford

Hull — Humber — Trent

Severn — Thames — London

Runcorn — Mersey

The 'Grand Trunk'
Canal System

of 'navigators' (called 'navvies') to do the digging – many of them Irish immigrants.

The Canal Age was in full swing by the time of Brindley's death. He had provided much of the framework for the great system of navigable waterways which served the main industrial areas by the early nineteenth century. South Lancashire and the West Midlands remained the chief areas of canal development, while Birmingham became the largest single centre – the 'canal metropolis'. With most canal companies making handsome profits and paying large dividends, there was no shortage of willing investors. However in the years 1791–6 this enthusiasm got out of hand. The urge for quick profits led to a *canal mania*, when scores of impossible schemes were eagerly supported, bringing ruin to those who put money into them.

When Brindley surveyed his canals he usually followed a winding course to avoid obstacles like hills and valleys. But later engineers, including **Thomas Telford**, tried to keep the line of the canal straight, by building high embankments over valleys and driving deep cuttings through hillsides. Every engineer aimed to keep the canal as level as possible, but, in crossing hilly country, **locks** had to be built. These were like stone-walled basins, with gates at each end. By means of sluices (inlet and outlet channels) in the gates, the water level could be changed within the lock to raise or lower barges, depending on the direction in which they were travelling. Long stairways of locks had to be built on the northern canals crossing the Pennines, where the hills were especially steep. The Rochdale Canal, for example, which was the first satisfactory water connection between Yorkshire and Lancashire (1804), had ninety-two locks in only 53 kilometres.

By 1830 Britain had over 6,500 kilometres of navigable waterways. So long as roads provided the only alternative, rivers and canals

A coal barge 'locking down' on the Staffordshire and Worcestershire Canal

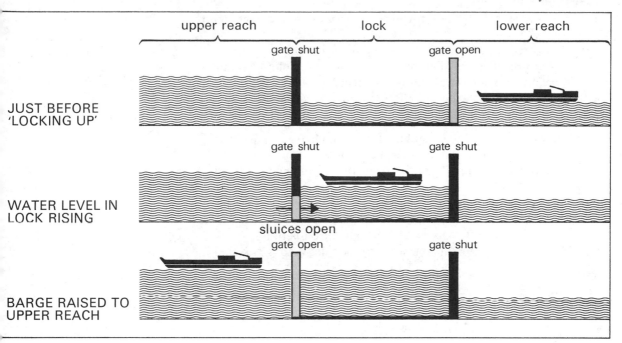

upper reach　　　　　lock　　　　　lower reach

gate shut　　　　　gate open

JUST BEFORE 'LOCKING UP'

gate shut　　　　　gate shut

WATER LEVEL IN LOCK RISING

sluices open

gate open　　　　　gate shut

BARGE RAISED TO UPPER REACH

The workings of a lock

enjoyed a clear superiority as carriers of freight. But the coming of railways (see Chapter 13) suddenly exposed their limitations. Although barges could carry anything from 30 to 100 tonnes, they were very slow – particularly in hilly country, where there were many delays in getting through locks. With the development of a railway network after 1830, the golden age of canals came to an abrupt end.

Timeline

1663	First Turnpike Act.
1702	*The Daily Courant* – the first daily newspaper.
1759–64	Bridgewater Canal (Worsley to Manchester).
1766–77	Trent and Mersey Canal ('Grand Trunk').
1772	Death of James Brindley.
1784	John Palmer's mail-coaches.
1791–6	'Canal mania'
1825	Metropolitan Turnpike Trust (Macadam Surveyor-General).
1826	Thomas Telford's Menai Straits Suspension Bridge.

Questions

1. 'I chiefly travelled upon turnpikes, of all which that from Salisbury to four miles the other side of Romsey ... is, without exception, the finest I ever saw. The trustees of that road highly deserve all the praise that can be given.' (Arthur Young, *A Six Weeks' Tour through the Southern Counties*, 1768)

   a) What was a turnpike? How did such roads get their name?

   b) Why was there a need for turnpike roads in the eighteenth century?
   c) What sorts of people were 'trustees' of such roads?
   d) Why were the roadbuilding methods of John Macadam especially popular with turnpike trustees?
   e) Why did long distance travellers not always get good value for the road tolls they paid?

2. Look at the picture of the London–Exeter mail coach (page 91).
   a) In what ways were mail coaches built for speed?
   b) What part did John Palmer play in the development of postal services?
   c) A guard on a mail coach carried a shotgun and a post-horn. What were these used for?
   d) What else did mail coaches deliver, apart from letters?
   e) Why do you think mail coaches were popular among travellers?

3. Outline the stages by which James Brindley provided a basic framework for the canal system of England and Wales. What part did the Duke of Bridgewater play in these developments?

4. 'Telford's is a happy life: everywhere making roads, building bridges, forming canals and creating harbours – works of sure, solid permanent utility.' (Robert Southey, the poet and a friend of Telford, writing in 1819)

   a) Name Telford's most famous road. Why was it badly needed?
   b) Where was part of this road carried by an equally famous suspension bridge?
   c) Name the great canal Telford built in Scotland.
   d) Why were Telford's roadbuilding methods more expensive than those of Macadam?
   e) How did Telford's approach to canal building differ from that of James Brindley?

5. Explain the following terms or descriptions:
   a) river 'cuts'
   b) turnpike 'fever'
   c) navvies
   d) the canal metropolis
   e) canal 'mania'

10

Storm Clouds over Europe
The French Wars, 1793–1815

William Pitt 'the Younger', 1759–1806

The American Revolution (1776–83) by which the Thirteen Colonies gained their independence (see page 26) also had important results for Britain and France. The failure of British forces discredited George III's ministers and assisted the rise to power of **William Pitt the Younger** – so called to distinguish him from his famous father. Pitt was only twenty-four when he became Britain's youngest Prime Minister (1783) but he proved to be one of the greatest. Remaining in power almost without a break until his death in 1806, he led Britain through one of the most difficult periods in her history.

In contrast, France, who had joined the colonists in the American War to settle old scores with Britain, paid a high price for victory. The French *National Debt* (money borrowed by the government on long-term loan) was no greater than Britain's, but, in the absence of wise and firm leadership, France failed to recover from the cost of the war. In the 1780s, while Pitt was putting Britain's finances on a firm footing, France went bankrupt.

The French Revolution

French governments had long been in financial difficulties, mainly because the wealthiest citizens – the nobles and the higher clergy – were like drones in a bee-hive. Unlike their British counterparts, most of them were exempted from paying taxes and did little to serve their country in return for the privileges they enjoyed. Very few even troubled to farm their land efficiently. At the other extreme, the peasants, who were generally worse off than the labouring classes in Britain, were severely taxed. Together with the middle-class merchants and manufacturers, they had to bear almost the entire cost of the eighteenth-century wars and of maintaining the extravagant royal court at the Palace of Versailles, near Paris. King **Louis XVI**'s advisers had pointed out the need for drastic reforms in taxation and royal expenditure. But Louis was too weak to risk the displeasure of the nobles by making them pay their share of taxes, and too stupid to realise the danger if he did not do so.

In May 1789 the French **States General** (similar to the early English Parliament) was called together, for the first time since 1614, to deal with the financial crisis and discuss possible reforms in government. Many members of the Third Estate (Commons) had been influenced by the views of the American rebels. The openly accused the aristocracy and monarchy of extravagance and misrule. Furthermore they demanded a full share in governing the country and justice and freedom

for all. When they were outvoted by the nobles and clergy, the commoners broke away to form their own **National Assembly**. Meanwhile the Paris 'mob', including thousands of starving peasants from the surrounding countryside, grew impatient. On 14 July they captured the **Bastille** (the state prison) and the Revolution began. In the next few years the Royal Government of France was swept away and thousands of nobles were executed.

The storming of the Bastille, 14 July 1789

At first, British public opinion strongly supported the ordinary citizens of France in their fight for 'liberty' and 'equality'. Leading MPs spoke in favour of the Revolution. For example Charles Fox called it 'the greatest event that has happened in the world'. All over Britain, working men formed societies to keep up regular correspondence with the French revolutionaries and to promote the views of reformers at home. The greatest influence on these **Corresponding Societies** was a political pamphleteer called **Thomas Paine** (1737–1809). He believed that the people as a whole had a right to choose their rulers. His pamphlet *Common Sense* (1776) had greatly influenced the American Declaration of Independence. Now his book, *The Rights of Man* (1791–2), applauded the French revolutionaries, attacked monarchy and aristocracy everywhere, and urged sweeping reform of the British system of government. Paine's influence was seen in numerous 'reform clubs' like the London Corresponding Society (1792) whose main aim was the extension of the vote to all adult males.

Meanwhile violence in France was increasing. By the winter of 1792–3, when Louis XVI and his Queen, Marie-Antoinette, were executed, Pitt's Government and large sections of the British public took a different view of the Revolution. There was now strong support for the views of **Edmund Burke** (1729–97), the only outstanding parliamentarian who had completely opposed the Revolution from the start. In his book, *Reflections on the Revolution in France* (1790), he claimed that revolution could never be justified, for it 'can only lead to bloodshed and disorder'. While events in France took the course forecasted by Burke, the British Government began to fear the spread of revolutionary ideas at home. Even demands for peaceful reform were regarded with suspicion; political societies were closed down and many of their leaders arrested. In 1794 Parliament went so far as to suspend the Habeas Corpus Act, making it possible for suspected persons to be imprisoned without a trial.

Britain goes to war

The main threat to the leaders of the Revolution came from outside France. Thousands of aristocrats had fled across the borders for safety, and these *émigrés* (emigrants) were urging the monarchs of Europe to help them put down the Revolution. In self-defence, the Revolutionary Government declared war on Austria and Prussia, two of the strongest military powers in Europe (April 1792).

Pitt did all he could to keep out of the war. He wanted the British to remain 'spectators of the strange scenes in France' so that he could continue his policy of financial reform without interruption. But events on the Continent soon left him no option. France's intention of carrying the Revolution outside her own frontiers was made clear in November 1792, when she offered 'assistance to all people who wish to recover their liberty'. Two months later, following the execution of Louis and his Queen, French troops occupied **Belgium**. Pitt could not stand by much longer. Had the French not declared war (1 February 1793) he would have done so himself.

Britain's more advanced industries should have given her a military advantage. But the **British army** was small and badly organised. Parliament would not allow a large army to be kept in peace-time, in case control of it got into the wrong hands, so whenever war broke out whole new regiments had to be raised. This was difficult, for conditions of service were so harsh that a man had to be desperate or stupid to enlist as a volunteer. Pay was low and almost always in arrears, and discipline was maintained by means of barbaric punishments. Consequently the ranks had to be filled mostly with men from the gaols and poorhouses – 'the scum of the earth', as the Duke of Wellington called them. In contrast, the officers came from wealthy, aristocratic families and lived in luxury, even during campaigns. Most of them had little or no knowledge of military matters and simply purchased their rank for social reasons.

A British force of about 50,000, together with some hired German troops, was sent to the Netherlands in 1793 under the Duke of York. It was soon clear that such an army stood little chance against France, which was, by this time, 'a nation in arms'. The population of

JOHN BULL Happy.

JOHN BULL going to the WARS.

JOHN BULL'S Property in danger.

J: G? des. et fecit.

JOHN BULL'S glorious Return.

France was nearly three times greater than that of Britain, and French forces were fighting for the cause of the Revolution. The British were soon forced to return home (1794) and, one by one, their allies were defeated or dropped out of the struggle. In 1793 France had faced a great coalition of practically all the major countries of Europe, including Britain, Austria, Prussia, the Netherlands and Spain. By 1797, 'the year of peril', Britain faced France alone.

Cartoon showing the perils of soldiering

Naval mutiny and Irish Rebellion

Britain's last line of defence was the English Channel, which throughout history has been her greatest ally in war-time. Provided the navy did not lose its command of the seas, Britain would be safe. Before the war Pitt had built and repaired many ships and improved the dockyards. His policy now paid off, as the navy blockaded French ports, kept trade routes open and won several major sea battles. But then it seemed disaster had struck when, in the 'year of peril', mutiny broke out in the fleet – at Spithead, near Portsmouth, and in the Nore anchorage, at the mouth of the Thames. While enemy ships prepared for invasion, Britain's navy was suddenly paralysed.

Less than 5 per cent of all British sailors in this period were volunteers. The navy was no more attractive than the army. More than half the average crew was obtained by **'press gangs'**. These were groups of sailors (usually volunteers) who swooped on coastal towns and villages, and even merchant vessels, to 'press' civilians into service. They were supposed to capture only seafaring men. But when the need for sailors was urgent, as it was during the French Wars, they were less choosy and sometimes searched many kilometres inland. In addition to captives of press gangs, large numbers of orphans were put in the navy when they reached fourteen or fifteen; and, after 1795, each county had to supply a yearly quota of men for the fleet. The size of the quota depended on the population; so Yorkshire supplied 300 while Rutland only had to find 30. Captains refused shore leave when ships were in home waters because they feared that most of their sailors would desert if allowed to set foot on land.

Refusal of shore leave was one of the grievances of the mutineers. But their chief complaint concerned the rates of pay, which had not been increased since 1652 even though the cost of living had doubled since then. Pay was often years in arrears, for it was withheld until the home port was reached. To make matters worse, the food rations frequently went bad, and the discipline was so severe that a hundred strokes of the 'cat o' nine tails' was a common punishment, even though the legal maximum was thirty-six.

When petitions to the Admiralty failed, carefully laid plans to mutiny were put into effect at **Spithead** on Easter Sunday 1797. The leaders wisely turned down vague promises of better pay and conditions, and refused to return to work until an Act of Parliament dealt

A press gang at work, capturing men to serve in the navy

with their complaints and an official pardon was given by the King. The mutiny at **the Nore**, which began in May, was less well organised and many of the men's demands were unreasonable. The Admiralty managed to put it down and hang thirty of the ringleaders.

In the following spring, Britain faced a new threat to her security in the shape of an **Irish Rebellion**. Trouble had long been brewing in Ireland, where the great majority of the people, because of their Catholic religion, were treated as second-class citizens. The Irish Parliament could only pass laws approved by the Parliament in London, and the entire population – Protestant and Catholic – felt the effect of severe trade restrictions, particularly on the export of wool and cattle.

The Irish took advantage of every British difficulty to press for fairer treatment. During the American Revolution, they had gained freer trade and wider powers for the Irish Parliament. Now, influenced by the French Revolution, a **Society of United Irishmen** was formed (1791) which sought French aid in expelling altogether English landlords and English influence from Ireland. Only bad weather prevented a French fleet from landing in Ireland in 1796 and again in 1797. However, when the long-awaited Rebellion came (1798) many leaders of the United Irishmen had already been arrested. Without French support, the rebels were heavily defeated at the Battle of **Vinegar Hill**.

Pitt realised he had been lucky. If the French had established a base in Ireland they might have altered the course of the war. In the interests of security Pitt proposed a full political union with Ireland, similar to the one with Scotland in 1707. After much argument, the **Act of Union** was passed in 1801. The separate Irish Parliament was abolished. Henceforward the two countries shared the same king, parliament and army; and all trade restrictions on Ireland came to an end. One hundred Irish MPs sat in the Commons and twenty-eight Irish peers and four bishops in the Lords. Unfortunately, a vital part of Pitt's plan – **Catholic emancipation** (freedom for Catholics to hold any public office) – was blocked by George III, who feared it as a threat to the Church of England. Pitt resigned, realising the Union was a fraud if Irish Catholics could only be represented by Protestant MPs. The Irish continued to press for Catholic emancipation until it was finally granted in the reign of George IV (1829).

The struggle against Napoleon

In 1790 Edmund Burke prophesied that in France 'bloodshed and disorder...will give place to a military tyrant'. Nine years later, **Napoleon Bonaparte** (1769–1821) overthrew the Republican Government and became dictator of France (November 1799). He was, without question, a military genius. Born in the island of Corsica, he began his career as an artillery officer in the Revolutionary army. By the time he was twenty-six he had risen to the rank of general, and four years later he controlled the destiny of France. Time and again in the next fifteen years he destroyed the mightiest armies on the

Pitt (left) and Napoleon as shown in a cartoon of 1805

Continent, only to see his ambition of becoming master of Europe checked by British sea power.

After crushing a second European coalition (1800–1) and reorganising the French government and legal system during a brief period of peace (1802–3), Napoleon prepared for his **Grand Design** – the invasion of Britain. Thousands of flat-bottomed boats and 150,000 of his finest troops were assembled at Boulogne, while the British built coastal defences. But the climax never came. The French fleet failed to gain control of the Channel and make it safe for the troop carriers. In disgust, Napoleon broke up his invasion camp (1805) and moved eastwards to smash yet another hostile coalition on the Continent.

Having helped to postpone the Grand Design, the British Mediterranean Fleet, commanded by **Lord Nelson**, now made it impossible. On 21 October 1805 Nelson destroyed the French and Spanish fleets at the Battle of **Trafalgar**, near Gibraltar. 'Our dear Admiral Nelson', as an ordinary seaman described him, was fatally wounded; but he died knowing that he had removed all danger from the French at sea. The last great battle between sailing ships was one of the most decisive in history.

The war now entered a new phase. Napoleon decided his best chance of defeating Britain was to destroy her foreign trade. In 1806 he issued the **Berlin Decree**, forbidding any country under his control

from trading with Britain or accepting any ship that had called at a British port. Napoleon hoped this *Continental System* of blockades would make the 'nation of shopkeepers' bankrupt, for over half Britain's trade was with Europe. The British reply was a series of **Orders in Council (1807)** claiming the right to seize neutral shipping bound for French-controlled ports. This policy caused much bitterness abroad, and even led to a brief war with the USA (1812–14), but it helped Britain to survive.

Clearly, if either side were to win, the deadlock between French land power and British sea power had to be broken. Britain's chance to end the deadlock came in the **Peninsular War**, beginning in 1808. While the Spanish were in revolt against French rule, a small British expeditionary force landed in Portugal, which was also refusing to co-operate with Napoleon. Under the command of the **Duke of Wellington** (1769–1852) the British built a series of fortifications, called the Torres Vedras Lines, near Lisbon (1809). Wellington now showed his tactical skill, wearing down the French army in Spain with short campaigns followed by orderly retreat behind his defences. By 1813 he was able to advance right across Spain and over the Pyrenees into France. On arriving at Toulouse (April 1814) he heard that the French had already surrendered.

Napoleon suffered his first land defeat when shortage of supplies forced him to give up an attack on Russia and retreat from **Moscow** (1812). The bitter winter and Russian flank attacks reduced his Grand Army of 600,000 to a quarter of its former size. Total defeat

Death of Lord Nelson on board the 'Victory' at the Battle of Trafalgar (October 1805)

The Duke of Wellington

for France was now almost certain, and the Allies finally entered Paris early in 1814. Napoleon was banished to the island of Elba. But in March 1815, while the peace conference was still sitting at Vienna, he escaped, landed on the French mainland and rallied support.

For a hundred days the outcome was again in the balance, until 18 June, when the Allied forces under Wellington and the Prussian General Blücher defeated Napoleon at **Waterloo** near Brussels. The battle was, in Wellington's words, 'the nearest run thing you ever saw in your life'. Napoleon was again banished, this time to St Helena, where he died in 1821. The Allies, influenced by Britain's Foreign Secretary, Viscount Castlereagh, treated the French leniently so that they would have no cause to reopen the war. France was restored to her old frontiers, and Britain kept only Malta, Ceylon (now Sri Lanka), the Cape of Good Hope and a few West Indian islands.

Life and work in wartime

During previous foreign wars, life at home had hardly been affected. Britain's empire in Canada and India had been secured by a few thousand soldiers and sailors. But the French Revolutionary and Napoleonic Wars were different. In the latter stages of the struggle, over 10 per cent of the male population of military age was in arms – a total of almost half a million men. The remainder of the population had to put up with invasion scares, food shortages, high prices, periodic unemployment and increased taxation.

For wealthy families in remote country mansions it was a time of increasing prosperity and comfort. But even the rich were firmly reminded of the war when Pitt introduced **income tax** in 1798. It ranged from twopence (1p) to two shillings (10p) in the pound, according to size of income. Since those earning less than £60 a year were exempted, it did not affect the labouring classes. Nevertheless higher taxes on food, manufactures and raw materials were a great burden on the poor, for these were paid at the same rate by all citizens, regardless of income.

In the countryside, the war years were marked by an acceleration in the progress of **enclosure** (see Chapter 5). In a normal year British farmers still produced just about enough to feed the rising population, but in years of poor harvests grain was usually imported from Europe. The war on the Continent made this increasingly difficult, especially during the Napoleonic blockade, so there were frequent shortages. In years of scarcity, the price of grain rose to double or almost treble its pre-war level and landlords and farmers made large profits. Therefore, where open fields were still in existence, there was a great rush to enclose them and concentrate on the large-scale production of corn. For the same reason, thousands of hectares of wasteland were enclosed and ploughed up for grain crops.

Parliamentary Enclosure Acts

1760–93 (33 years)	1,355 Acts
1793–1815 (22 years)	1,934 Acts

High prices benefited farmers and landlords, but only at the expense of the rest of the community, who had to pay more for bread. Serious distress appeared in the countryside quite early in the war, with thousands of **agricultural labourers** existing on starvation wages. In Berkshire the county magistrates met at Speen, near Newbury (1795), with the intention of fixing a minimum wage which all employers in the county would have to pay. Unfortunately, after strong objections from landowners, they decided on an alternative scheme which proved to be disastrous. Labourers who earned less than a certain basic minimum (calculated according to the size of their family and the price of bread) would have their wages made up out of the parish rates.

Ever since the first Poor Law (1598) in the reign of Elizabeth I, every parish had been obliged to collect rates in order to provide relief for its poor, handicapped and destitute people. The Poor Law authorities usually discouraged the 'able bodied' from applying for relief, in the hope that they would find regular work. But the **'Speenhamland'** or **'Allowance System'**, which was soon taken up all over southern England, paid relief to those who were not only 'able bodied' but *in regular work* as well. It was humiliating for fully employed labourers to receive part of their income in the form of parish charity. Farmers took advantage of the Allowance System to refuse deserved increases in wages, for they knew their workers could always fall back on parish relief. Needless to say, rates went up alarmingly, and in 1834 the whole system was swept away by Parliament (see pages 121–2).

The Allowance System did not spread to the industrial areas of the Midlands and North – mainly because wages in industry were normally higher. Even farmers in these areas had to pay better wages than their counterparts in the South, to prevent their labourers from moving to the towns. Nevertheless, **industrial workers** had hardships of their own as a result of the war. Napoleon's Continental System was designed to prevent British manufacturers from selling their goods in Europe. Although it was partly overcome by smuggling and by increased trade with the rest of the world (especially the Americas) many industries were seriously affected. When trade was lost there were periods of severe unemployment.

Workers in industries directly concerned with the war effort enjoyed the greatest regularity of employment. This was particularly true of the metal industries, where the demand for cannon, firearms and shot accelerated the introduction of steam power and the new techniques of puddling and rolling (see page 65). Similarly, the Yorkshire woollen industry, which specialised in making coarse cloth, was kept busy with government contracts for army uniforms. Elsewhere, the textile trades were not so fortunate. The cotton industry, for example, suffered from the difficulties and uncertainties of trading in wartime. All its raw material came from overseas and three-quarters of its output was exported. During the war with the USA (1812–14) supplies of raw cotton were often insufficient and thousands of workers suffered periodic unemployment.

A group of Luddites shooting Mr Horsfall, a factory master

The most desperate period for the poor was 1811–12, following a serious failure of the harvest in 1810. As the price of bread soared, the Napoleonic blockade resulted in ships laying idle and people being thrown out of work. There were serious outbreaks of machine-breaking and factory-burning in the textile districts, especially in Nottinghamshire, where a thousand stocking frames were smashed in this period alone. These machine-breakers were said to have been organised by one Ned Ludd – from whom they got the name **Luddites** – but it is doubtful if such a person existed. The Government, wrongly thinking that Luddite activities were part of an organised political conspiracy, put them down with great severity. Machine-breaking was made punishable by death, and roughly twenty persons were hanged as a result. But this was only a foretaste of even more severe distress and disorder when the wars ended.

Timeline

1783	Pitt 'the Younger' Prime Minister, aged twenty-four.
1789	French Revolution begins.
1793	Britain at war with France.
1795	'Speenhamland' or 'Allowance System'.
1797	Naval mutinies at Spithead and the Nore.
1798	Irish Rebellion – Battle of Vinegar Hill.
1799	Napoleon Bonaparte dictator of France.
1801	Act of Union with Ireland.
1805	Battle of Trafalgar.
1806	Napoleon's Berlin Decree – start of 'Continental System'.
1807	Orders in Council.
1808–14	Peninsular War.
1811–12	Machine-breaking – the 'Luddites'.
1812	Napoleon's Russian campaign.
1815	'Hundred Days'; Battle of Waterloo; Napoleon banished to St Helena.

Questions

The execution of Louis XVI (January 1793). This helped to change initial British reactions to the French Revolution (see Question 1)

1. 'Bliss was it in that dawn to be alive,
   But to be young was very heaven'
   (William Wordsworth, *Hope for Man*, 1792)

   a) To what extent did other people share the poet Wordsworth's view that the French Revolution was the dawn of a new age of liberty and equality?
   b) Which parliamentarian opposed the Revolution from the start? What were his reasons?
   c) What were the Corresponding Societies?
   d) Once the mass execution of French nobles began, how did the British Government react?
   e) What do you think was the point of suspending the Habeas Corpus Act in 1794?

2. 'They write from Marlborough that the Press was so hot last week at that Place that People were taken out of their Beds, and Strangers stopt upon the Roads.' (*Jackson's Oxford Journal*, 1756)

   a) What was 'the Press'?
   b) Why was it necessary to recruit for the navy by this method?
   c) Why would the navy have needed men in 1756 (see Chapter 3) and again in 1793?
   d) Marlborough is a long way from the coast. What does this suggest about the state of naval recruitment at that time?
   e) How did the army overcome similar recruitment problems?

3. Look at the cartoon of Pitt and Napoleon (page 105).
   a) Why can Napoleon be identified by his slice of the plumb-pudding?
   b) Pitt can also be identified by his 'slice'. Explain why.
   c) Which great sea battle took place in the year this cartoon was drawn? Why was its result important?
   d) Explain how Pitt's 'slice' helped Britain to defeat Napoleon's Continental System after 1806.
   e) Napoleon did not enjoy his 'slice' for long. What part did Britain play in his eventual defeat on land?

4. 'At a General Meeting of the Justices of this County...on Wednesday the 6th day of May, 1795, at the Pelican Inn in Speenhamland...for the purpose of rating Husbandry wages... Resolved unaminously,
   That the present state of the Poor does require further assistance.' (*The Reading Mercury*, 11 May 1795)

   a) In which county did this meeting take place?
   b) Why did the poor 'require further assistance' at this time?
   c) What is meant by 'rating Husbandry wages' (the original intention of the magistrates)?
   d) What did the magistrates do instead, and why did they change their minds?
   e) Why did the resulting 'Allowance System' prove disastrous?

5. Write a paragraph on each of the following:
   a) the naval mutinies of 1797
   b) the Act of Union with Ireland
   c) the Duke of Wellington
   d) 'Luddites'

11

The Darkest Hour and the Dawn
Social Distress and the Beginnings of Reform

The Allied victory at Waterloo (1815) ended the threat from Napoleon but brought no immediate end to the hardships of the war years. A severe depression in trade and industry caused widespread unemployment and distress in Britain. Mass meetings, protest marches and reform societies voiced the discontents of the poor, but the Government, still haunted by the ghost of the French Revolution, continued its policy of repression and opposition to reform. There is a saying that 'the darkest hour comes before the dawn'. This is true of the post-war years in Britain, for conditions got worse before they got better. It was only after 1820 that an improvement in trade led to relative calm, and Parliament gradually became less opposed to the demands of reformers.

'The post-war discontents'

After the collapse of Napoleon's blockade in 1813 European countries were again free to export corn to Britain. This should have brought down the price of bread, for the imported corn was cheaper than the home product. But landlords and farmers, many fearing bankruptcy, used their great influence in Parliament to protect themselves against foreign competition. A **Corn Law (1815)** prohibited the import of corn unless the home price rose to eighty shillings (£4) a quarter.* This gave home growers a virtual monopoly, for prices remained well below £4. As a result, the price of bread was kept artificially high after 1815, and the poor suffered great hardship.

The ending of government contracts for armaments, ships and clothing meant industries which had prospered during the French Wars now experienced **unemployment**. The rapid demobilisation of over a quarter of a million soldiers and sailors only increased the numbers out of work. To make matters worse for the labouring population, they now had to pay a greater share of **taxation**. The National Debt rose from £228 million in 1793 to £876 million in 1816. Yet the Government kept an earlier promise to abolish Pitt's income tax when the war ended. Consequently the only way of paying off the yearly interest on the debt was to increase taxes on ordinary goods. These were a great burden on the poor – unlike income tax, which did not apply to those with low incomes.

Expensive bread, high unemployment and rising taxation led to widespread discontent among the poorer classes. They began to put

*A measure of capacity, equal to 64 gallons or 291 litres.

William Cobbett, 1763–1835. As well as attacking the government in his weekly newspaper, the 'Political Register', he did much to publicise the desperate poverty of agricultural labourers in his book, 'Rural Rides' (1830), which was based on his observations while travelling through England in the 1820s. Cobbett eventually entered Parliament in 1832 as MP for Oldham

their faith in political reform, believing that if they could get a share in the government of the country their hardships would receive attention. Political clubs again flourished; so did newspapers representing the views of reformers. There were strong demands for reform of Parliament and the granting of the right to vote to all adult males. **William Cobbett**, a political journalist, was the chief inspiration behind the reform movement – through his weekly *Political Register*. It is said that when the coach carrying it arrived in the industrial towns, eager crowds tore open the parcels and read aloud in the streets.

However the Tory Government had other ideas. **Lord Liverpool**, Prime Minister 1812–27, had been in Paris at the start of the French Revolution and never forgot it. He and his Cabinet did not trust the masses and had no intention of giving them any political power. Like Pitt after 1793, Liverpool concentrated on keeping law and order, believing that weakness would lead to disaster. This fear of revolution was exaggerated, but the Government's anxiety when faced with any kind of mass movement is understandable. After all, there was no proper police force, and weapons and communications were not as efficient as they are today. Governments of this period were not only poorly equipped to deal with serious disorders, they were also *incapable of preventing their causes*. They could not have controlled variations in wages, prices and unemployment, even if they had been prepared to interfere with the rights of employers.

Discontent soon came to the surface. Before the end of 1815 there were riots against the Corn Law in several northern towns. In the following year, when unemployment was at its worst, reform meetings were held in many areas. After one such gathering, at **Spa Fields** in London, a mob marched through the streets, breaking into shops. As in 1794, the Government was so alarmed that it suspended the Habeas Corpus Act for a year – again allowing suspects to be imprisoned without a trial. Soldiers even broke up a peaceful 'hunger march' of unemployed workers from Manchester (1817). The **Blanketeers**, as they were called (they carried blankets for bedding), intended to walk to London and present petitions about their grievances to the Prince Regent. But soon after setting out they were dispersed and their leaders arrested.

The post-war reform movement reached a climax in the summer of 1819, with a great open-air demonstration in St Peter's Fields, Manchester. On Monday 16 August, roughly 80,000 people from all parts of south-east Lancashire assembled to hear several well-known speakers – notably **Henry Hunt**, who first came into prominence at the Spa Fields meeting. Although the crowd was in good order the magistrates lost their nerve and demanded the arrest of Hunt while he was on the platform. The soldiers sent to carry out the order were unaccustomed to such a large gathering. They panicked and began to cut their way through with swords. In the resulting stampede, eleven people were killed and hundreds injured. Public opinion was shocked, and the episode was called **Peterloo** – in mocking memory of the Battle of Waterloo. Nevertheless, the Government congratulated the magistrates, and strengthened the powers of law and order

with **Six Acts**, which severely restricted the right to hold public meetings and prevented the publication of newspapers and pamphlets likely to stir up unrest.

The 'Peterloo Massacre'. Soldiers cut their way through the crowd

Peel at the Home Office; Mrs Fry at Newgate

The Six Acts made it much more difficult for the labouring classes to express their grievances. So it was fortunate for them that they had less cause to protest in the years following Peterloo. A general improvement in trade from about 1820 brought fuller employment and therefore less hardship. By 1822 Lord Liverpool's Cabinet reflected these changing conditions. Several younger, more open-minded men were brought in, including **Robert Peel** (1788–1850), who became Home Secretary (the minister responsible for law and order). Peel

Elizabeth Fry – 'the Angel of the Prisons'

now made the first serious attempt to reform the prisons and make punishments less severe. Previously the efforts of humanitarians like John Howard (see page 35) had brought little action on these issues, but now reformers began to have a real influence on government policy. A good example can be seen in the persons of Robert Peel and **Elizabeth Fry** (1780–1845).

Even before her marriage at the age of twenty to Joseph Fry, a London banker, Elizabeth Gurney, daughter of a wealthy Norwich merchant, had opened a free school for poor children. She was a Quaker, and her strong religious beliefs made her eager to serve less fortunate people. Her interest in prison reform dates from 1813, when a visiting American Quaker told her about the wretched conditions in **Newgate**. There were no proper beds, only filthy straw, no doctors or medicine for the sick, and great overcrowding. Mrs Fry and her friends first took bundles of clothing for the children and clean straw for the women to lie on. Eventually she went into the prison yard to speak directly with the women. The gaolers tried to stop her, fearing she would be attacked, but, to their astonishment, the entry of the dignified figure of Mrs Fry, in the dress of a 'plain Quaker', made the prisoners stop in their tracks. After listening quietly to her words of comfort they begged her to come again.

A cell for condemned prisoners in Newgate Gaol, London

For thirty years Mrs Fry worked tirelessly to make prisons and convict ships more humane. 'Punishment', she said, 'is not for revenge, but to lessen crime and reform the criminal.' Her visits to Newgate became regular events and she arranged a rota of visitors, set up a prison school and began women's sewing classes. It was some time before she had any effect on government policies. Lord Sidmouth, Home Secretary 1812–22, resisted her suggestions, believing that nothing was gained by 'soft' methods. Peel, on the other hand, was influenced by her. While he was Home Secretary (1822–30) prisons began to be regularly inspected, gaolers were paid, instead of taking 'fees' from the inmates, and women prisoners were supervised only by women warders. Many other reforms suggested by Mrs Fry were not carried out until after her death. The abolition of transportation (1853) is one example. But in the meantime her influence resulted in women no longer being put in irons on the convict ships.

A London policeman, photographed in 1856

For Peel, prisons were only one aspect of the legal system that needed reforming. He considered the **Penal Code** (the range of punishments imposed on law-breakers) to be both savage and stupid. Over 200 separate offences carried the death penalty. Nearly all were crimes against property, including setting fire to a farmer's hay, horse and sheep stealing, forgery, and absurd crimes like cutting down a tree in Downing Street. Offenders were encouraged to commit murder to escape arrest – for, as the saying goes, 'you might as well be hanged for a sheep as a lamb'. Even when convinced of a prisoner's guilt, juries often refused to convict if they thought the penalty was too severe. This made a mockery of the law. Peel got Parliament to abolish the death penalty for about half the crimes to which it then applied. His successors continued this policy. After 1861 no-one was hanged in Britain for any crime other than murder or treason.

Peel was more concerned with preventing crime than punishing it. This led him to establish the first regular **police force**. The lack of any effective means of keeping order was one of the main reasons why governments were so easily alarmed by mass meetings or demonstrations. Large towns were particularly lawless, and the authorities often used troops to keep the peace – a much-hated practice, especially after Peterloo. In London, the 'runners' from Bow Street Magistrates' Court performed a useful service, but there were too few of them to deal with any serious disorder. Peel established a regular police force in London and the suburbs (1829). At first, there were 3,000 'Bobbies' or 'Peelers' (nicknamed after their founder), recruited and controlled by the Home Office. They wore top-hats and blue frock-coats and were armed only with wooden truncheons, but their presence soon forced many criminals to move out of the capital. Consequently other towns began to employ 'Peelers' until finally, in 1856, every county and borough was obliged to maintain a police force.

The great Reform Act

Peterloo and the Six Acts were a setback to the reform movement among the labouring classes. But nothing could stop the growing *middle* classes of factory-owners, merchants and professional people from demanding changes in the outdated system of parliamentary representation. They complained that corrupt elections and an unfair distribution of seats (both dealt with in Chapter 2) produced a House of Commons dominated by the landowning gentry. The Corn Law (1815) was a striking example of the way landowners could use their majority in Parliament to protect their own interests, while ignoring the protests of the bulk of the population. The middle classes in the towns rightly demanded a greater say in the running of the country – to be achieved by parliamentary reform.

Changes in the old system were debated in Parliament on several occasions in the eighteenth century, but nothing was done. Pitt introduced a Bill in 1785, aiming to abolish thirty-six 'rotten boroughs' and transfer their seats to the more populated areas. But MPs rejected even this mild proposal. Soon afterwards, the French Revolution (1789) turned Parliament even more strongly against the idea of reforming itself. Nevertheless, during and after the French Wars the repressive policy of the Government could not conceal the fact that the people as a whole were dissatisfied with their political system. Demands for reform varied considerably. While many of the working classes wanted nothing less than 'one man, one vote', the industrial and commercial middle classes urged that seats should be taken from the rotten boroughs and redistributed among the new industrial towns.

In November 1830 the main obstacle to parliamentary reform was removed. The Tory Party, which had consistently opposed any change in the constitution, lost its majority in the Commons for the first time in half a century. Soon afterwards (March 1831) a **Reform Bill** was introduced by Lord Grey's Whig Government. The Tories still had a majority in the Lords, and it was only after a long and bitter struggle that the Bill was finally passed in June 1832. Meanwhile 'political unions' of workers organised marches and demonstrations to protest at the delay, and there were reform riots in some towns. Nottingham Castle was burned, and so were several public buildings in Bristol, where a mob broke into the prisons.

The changes made by the Act did not justify all the fuss it caused. They can be briefly summarised under two headings:

1. *Distribution of seats*. Most of the rotten boroughs were abolished, leaving 143 seats for re-allocation. The counties and large towns got 65 each, and the remaining 13 went to Scotland and Ireland.
2. *Voting rights*. In the boroughs, owners or tenants of houses worth at least £10 rental a year could vote. In the counties, ownership of land worth £10 or more a year was the main qualification. The existing rights of freeholders were maintained.

To qualify for the vote on these terms, a man probably needed an annual income of at least £150. Since ordinary workmen seldom earned more than £50 a year, it is safe to say that the Act did nothing for the working classes, in spite of their enthusiastic demands. It was the factory *owners* rather than the factory *workers* who benefited. Only about 300,000 new voters were added to the existing electorate

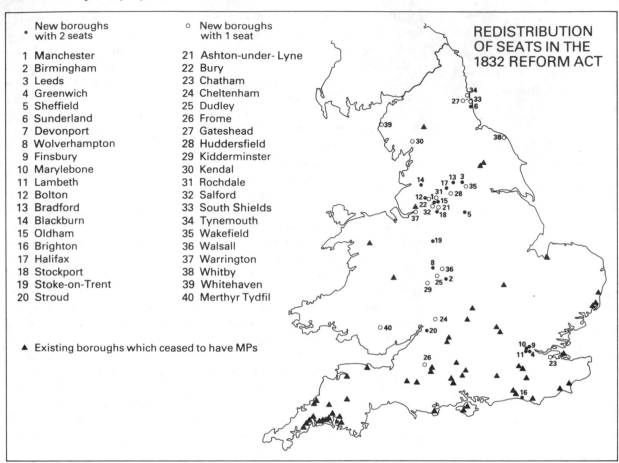

REDISTRIBUTION
OF SEATS IN THE
1832 REFORM ACT

• New boroughs with 2 seats
○ New boroughs with 1 seat

1 Manchester
2 Birmingham
3 Leeds
4 Greenwich
5 Sheffield
6 Sunderland
7 Devonport
8 Wolverhampton
9 Finsbury
10 Marylebone
11 Lambeth
12 Bolton
13 Bradford
14 Blackburn
15 Oldham
16 Brighton
17 Halifax
18 Stockport
19 Stoke-on-Trent
20 Stroud

21 Ashton-under-Lyne
22 Bury
23 Chatham
24 Cheltenham
25 Dudley
26 Frome
27 Gateshead
28 Huddersfield
29 Kidderminster
30 Kendal
31 Rochdale
32 Salford
33 South Shields
34 Tynemouth
35 Wakefield
36 Walsall
37 Warrington
38 Whitby
39 Whitehaven
40 Merthyr Tydfil

▲ Existing boroughs which ceased to have MPs

of under half a million. In other words, the landed gentry had merely shared a little of its political power with the new industrial and commercial middle classes.

The abolition of slavery

The membership of the 'reformed' House of Commons was much the same as before. Nevertheless, although there were very few new faces, somehow the *spirit* of Parliament was changed by the 1832 Act. The Whig Government, having gained a reputation for reform, now seemed to feel obliged to live up to it. Consequently a number of major reforms were passed in the next few years.

In 1833 the campaign to abolish slavery achieved its final triumph, after half a century of activity in and out of Parliament. (For details of the eighteenth-century slave trade, see Chapter 3.) The outstanding leader of the movement was **William Wilberforce** (1759–1833), a wealthy businessman from Hull, who first entered the Commons in 1780. After leading a carefree and reckless life, he experienced a religious conversion and, in 1787, he was won over to the growing anti-slavery movement by the arguments of the Rev. Thomas Clarkson.

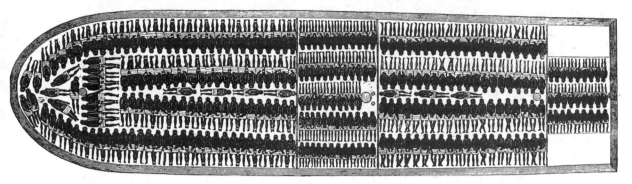

Plan showing the dreadful overcrowding on board a slaving ship. Part of the evidence brought before Parliament by Wilberforce and his friends

Anthony Ashley Cooper (1801–85), seventh Earl of Shaftesbury

As a boy of fourteen, Wilberforce had written a letter to a newspaper condemning the 'odious traffic in human flesh', and now he decided to devote his wealth and talents to fighting it. A **Society for the Abolition of the Slave Trade** was formed (1787) and received strong support from public figures such as John Wesley and Josiah Wedgwood.

The immediate aim of the Society – to end the *trade* in slaves – was finally achieved in 1807, when Parliament made it an offence for British subjects to take part in the capture and transport of slaves. The next step was to *set free* all the existing slaves in the British Empire – they numbered at least 800,000 as late as 1830. To this end the **Anti-Slavery Society** was founded in 1823, under the leadership of Wilberforce and Clarkson. They had little difficulty in winning over the general public, but met stiff resistance from merchants and plantation-owners in Parliament, who claimed they would be ruined and the valuable West Indian sugar trade destroyed if the slaves were freed. Ill-health compelled Wilberforce to retire from Parliament (1825) but he remained a great inspiration to the movement and lived just long enough to hear that the cause was won. By an **Act of 1833**, slavery was abolished throughout the British Empire. To compensate the planters, the Government paid them a total of £20 million – an average of about £37 per slave.

Lord Ashley and factory reform

Within months of the abolition of slavery, an important step was taken to improve the working conditions of factory children. It was well over fifty years since child labour was first introduced into textile mills (see page 58). Dragged from their beds in the early hours of the morning and set to work all day in foul, stuffy conditions, they often became so exhausted that they had to be beaten to be kept awake. Many slave children were better treated on the plantations. As a West Indian planter put it: 'I have always thought myself disgraced by being the owner of slaves, but ... never thought it possible to be so cruel as to require a child of nine years old to work twelve and a half hours a day.' Most factory-owners saw nothing wrong in this. When it was suggested that Parliament should pass laws to protect factory children they were quick to defend their 'rights', as employers, to run their businesses as they pleased.

A small group of enlightened factory-owners had long been in favour of parliamentary action to control hours and conditions of work, not just for children but for all workers in the mills. **Robert Owen** (see Chapter 12) showed in his New Lanark Mills that shorter hours and excellent conditions could still produce good profits. **John Fielden** owned one of Britain's largest textile businesses, at Todmorden in Yorkshire. His employees had a maximum working day of ten hours, yet handsome profits were made. **Robert Peel (Senior)** was another who tried to set a good example, but he soon realised this was not enough. It was he who got the first Factory Acts passed, in 1802 and 1819 – both attempts to protect children from excessive hours of labour. But these Acts had little effect because Justices of the Peace, often mill-owners themselves, failed to enforce them.

By 1830 textile factories employed a quarter of a million workers, most of them under the age of eighteen. At the same time a nation-wide reform movement was pressing for an effective Factory Act to limit the working day to ten hours. Leadership of the 'Ten Hours Movement' in Parliament soon fell upon **Lord Ashley** (Anthony Ashley Cooper, later Lord Shaftesbury). For Lord Ashley it was only the start of a long and distinguished career as a social reformer. He was concerned with many aspects of the welfare and education of working children – including apprentices in the coal-mines and 'climbing boys' (sweeps) who were sent up chimneys (until Parliament banned the practice in 1875). In later life, Shaftesbury was President of the Ragged Schools Union (see page 206).

It was some years before the Ten Hours Movement achieved its aim. However Parliament took an important step towards it with the **Factory Act of 1833.** Children under nine were barred from all textile factories, and the hours of older children were limited to a maximum of forty-eight a week for those under thirteen, and sixty-nine for 'young persons' of thirteen to eighteen. Four full-time inspectors were appointed to see that the regulations were carried out, and employers who broke the law could be fined. It was also laid down that every factory child should receive two hours' schooling a day. But this part of the Act was difficult to enforce and therefore often ignored. The reformers had hoped for more, and renewed their fight to get a ten-hour day for *all* textile workers. Nevertheless, the 1833 Act firmly established the *principle* of state intervention between employers and workers to control factory hours.

A chimney sweep's 'climbing boy'

Encouraged by Ashley and others, the Government appointed a Royal Commission on Children's Employment in 1840. Two years later it issued a report on underground workers in the mines. The public was horrified to learn that women and girls carried baskets of coal weighing up to 150 kilograms on their shoulders, or dragged loaded trucks, on all fours, along narrow underground passages. This work, said the Commission, 'makes them old women at forty'. Peel's Government took immediate action, despite the opposition of the coal-owners. A **Mines Act (1842)** prohibited the employment of women and girls underground, and a minimum age of ten was fixed for the employment of boys.

A child hauling coal underground

The Commission reported on other industries in the following year, and its findings led to another important **Factory Act (1844)**. This controlled women's hours for the first time, by including them under the same regulations as 'young persons' of thirteen to eighteen, whose hours were now reduced to twelve. The working day for children under thirteen was cut to six and a half hours, and all dangerous machinery had to be fenced.

Ashley's great aim, a **ten-hour day**, was achieved for women and young persons in the mills in 1847; although it was increased to ten and a half hours in 1850. Because the work could not be carried on by men alone, this had the effect of reducing *men's* hours as well. Ashley and his friends now worked to extend the principles of the Acts beyond textiles to other trades, and to workshops as well as factories. Hours were further reduced in 1874, to a maximum of fifty-six a week (ten hours Monday to Friday and six on Saturday). Until this time it had been usual to work a full six-day week. Meanwhile more factory inspectors were appointed, with greater powers, and safety regulations were tightened.

In opposing the Factory Acts many employers had claimed that they would be ruined, because their profit was made 'in the last hour of the day'. Yet within a few years they had to admit that the Factory Acts actually helped to increase output, because workers were more efficient when they were not exhausted by long hours.

The new Poor Law

The Poor Law was perhaps the most urgent of all the problems tackled by Lord Grey's Whig Government after 1832. The 'Speenhamland' or 'Allowance System' which was common in many farming areas of the South (see page 108) was highly unsatisfactory. The giving of Poor Relief to make up the wages of labourers with regular jobs encouraged farmers to pay less than a 'living wage'. It was also a

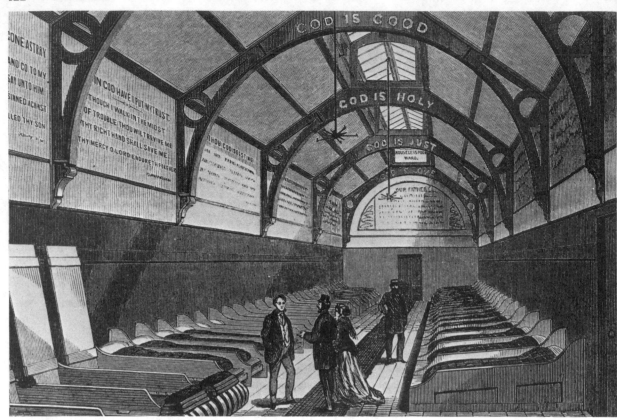

drain on the parish rates. In one parish in southern England the
annual cost of Poor Relief rose from £18 to £367 in the space of
thirty years.

Marylebone workhouse in London. A new ward for the homeless poor, 1867

A **Poor Law Amendment Act** was passed in 1834. It discouraged
the 'able bodied' poor from applying for relief by making it necessary
for them to enter a **workhouse** to get it. To deter idlers from trying to
get free board and lodging, life in a workhouse was deliberately made
less comfortable than that of the lowest-paid labourer. Workhouses
were intended to be nothing more than a *last resort for the totally destitute*. The inmates were set to work, in return for which they received the bare minimum of food and some kind of bed. Discipline
was strict – families were separated, visitors prohibited and smoking
and drinking not allowed.

Workhouses were paid for out of the parish rates, and the ratepayers elected local Boards of Guardians to run them. The Guardians
were ratepayers themselves, so they had a personal interest in keeping down the running costs of their workhouse. The food provided was
usually just enough to keep body and soul together. In a workhouse
near Leeds, inmates were fed in a trough like pigs, six at a time. By
the terms of the Act, the sick and aged on Poor Relief were allowed
to stay in their homes. In practice, it was cheaper for the Guardians
to herd everyone together under one roof. In some places the sick
were looked after by the insane in filthy workhouse infirmaries. Children mixed with hardened criminals and destitute mothers with

prostitutes, while those who had led respectable lives but were forced to enter the workhouse in old age lived with those whose poverty resulted from drunkenness and vice.

These places were so hated and feared by the poor that many preferred to face starvation rather than enter a workhouse. So the aim of the authorities was achieved, for they intended the workhouses to be a deterrent. They were delighted to see the numbers applying for Poor Relief dropping sharply after 1834.

It was in the industrial areas of the North that the new Poor Law met most opposition. It swept away the money relief on which workers had relied during periods of unemployment. During a severe industrial depression in the years 1837–42, Guardians often had no option but to pay money relief to the unemployed and overlook the workhouse altogether. In the agricultural districts of the South, however, the Act was largely successful. It forced farmers to pay their labourers better wages, otherwise they would have lost their services altogether. For all its faults, the new system was more efficient than the old. As time went by conditions were gradually improved. Workhouse schools were introduced to prepare children to earn their own living, and care of the sick was made more humane.

Timeline

1807	British slave trade abolished.
1813	Elizabeth Fry's first visit to Newgate.
1815	Corn Law.
1816	Spa Fields meeting.
1817	March of the 'Blanketeers'.
1819	'Peterloo' and the 'Six Acts'.
1829	Metropolitan Police established (Peel).
1832	Parliamentary Reform Act.
1833	Abolition of slavery and first effective Factory Act.
1834	Poor Law Amendment Act.
1842	Mines Act.
1850	Factory Act – ten-and-a-half-hour day.

Questions

1. 'There was a general cry of 'Stand Fast, they are riding upon us'. The cavalry were in confusion; they evidently could not with all the weight of man and horse penetrate that compact mass of human beings; and their swords were used to hew a way through the naked held-up hands and defenceless heads.'
   (Samuel Bamford, an eyewitness of the 'Peterloo Massacre', 1819)

   a) Where was this crowd assembled and for what purpose?
   b) Why was the cavalry trying to get through the crowd?
   c) Roughly how many people were present, and how many died?
   d) Why was the incident called 'Peterloo'?
   e) What was the reaction of the Government afterwards?

2. 'In my opinion, the Government ought, without the loss of a moment's time, to adopt measures to form either a police in London or military corps . . . or both.' (Duke of Wellington, 1820)

   a) Why do you think this view was widely expressed in Britain in the years after 1815?

   b) A 'military corps' to keep law and order would not have been acceptable to many people. Why?

   c) Name the Home Secretary who established a Metropolitan Police Force in 1829. What did he hope to achieve by it?

   d) What other legal reforms did he carry out in the 1820s?

   e) Why did towns outside London soon need their own police?

3. Which sections of the population a) were bitterly disappointed, and b) gained most, from the 1832 Parliamentary Reform Act? Give reasons for your answers, and refer to the terms of the Act.

4. Look at the picture above of children working in a coal-mine.

   a) Why do you think children were often employed underground?

   b) Why are the workers pictured here better off than some others employed to move coal to the surface?

   c) When did Parliament pass the first Act regulating the employment of women and children in mines? What were its terms?

   d) Similar attempts were made to regulate working conditions in factories. Summarise the main terms of the Acts of 1833, 1844 and 1850.

   e) Who led the factory reform movement in Parliament?

5. Write a paragraph on each of the following:
   a) causes of the 'Post-War Discontents'
   b) Elizabeth Fry
   c) the abolition of slavery
   d) the Poor Law Amendment Act, 1834

12

Combination, Chartism and Co-operation
Working-class Movements (I)

Workers were used to toiling long hours for low wages before the Industrial Revolution. Most of them accepted their fate as part of the natural order of things. But the beginnings of factory industry brought numbers of workers together in one place. They now began to feel a sense of unity and common purpose, for they were more aware of the weakness and inferiority of their position than their parents and grandparents had been. As the new 'working class' became established in the industrial towns, its members began to realise the power they could possess if they acted *together* instead of separately. So they organised themselves in various ways to press for improvements in their standard of living.

Early combinations and the law

Before the Industrial Revolution there were no trade unions in the modern sense. However during the eighteenth century **trade clubs** became established in many towns. These were groups of workers in a particular trade or occupation who usually met regularly at a local public house. Many pubs still bear their names today, like 'the Bricklayers' Arms'. Good company and strong ale were the first priority, but members also attended to more serious matters – such as accepting new apprentices, and putting aside a penny or twopence (less than 1p) a week to help those out of work. These taverns also became 'places of call', where employers could recruit extra workers. Occasionally, when their employers threatened to reduce rates of pay or refused increases when the cost of living rose, members banded together to defend their interests. As early as 1720 thousands of London tailors joined together in this way against their masters.

It was a short step from the activities of trade clubs to full-scale **trade unions**. These began when a number of clubs 'combined' to fight for a common aim. In the eighteenth century, trade unions usually arose to deal with a particular problem and then broke up when it was settled. Their most powerful weapon was a threatened stoppage of work, or **strike**. Workers realised that if they all asked for the same thing, and refused to go on with their jobs unless they got it, they would be in a good bargaining position with their employers. Faced with loss of business and possible ruin, employers were usually forced to reach some sort of agreement with the union. Strikes were quite common in the late eighteenth century. Among the most successful were those of the London tailors, who managed to push up their wages by a quarter as a result of strike action between

1775 and 1800. The naval mutinies of 1797 (see page 102) were really strikes against low pay and unsatisfactory working conditions.

Needless to say, employers strongly opposed the formation of trade unions. **The law** was on their side, for workers who planned joint action against their masters could be prosecuted for 'conspiracy in restraint of trade'. In addition, Parliament passed a number of Acts throughout the eighteenth century forbidding combinations in particular trades. After the outbreak of the French Wars (1793–1815) the ruling classes in Parliament suspected the intentions of *all* working-class organisations. Fearing the spread of revolutionary ideas from

France, they first outlawed political societies (see page 101). But trade unions did not escape for long. In an atmosphere of alarm and suspicion, it was feared that unions might provide a 'cover' for political activities, including plots to overthrow the government. In April 1799 the Commons received a petition from a group of master-millwrights complaining of 'a combination of . . . millwrights within the Metropolis and twenty-five miles [40 kilometres] round'. Parliament took the opportunity to pass a general law prohibiting *all* such combinations.

The **Combination Acts** of 1799 and 1800 forbade workers from meeting to plan joint action to raise wages or shorten working hours by bargaining with their employers or threatening them. The penalty was up to three months' imprisonment, with hard labour. Although a number of unions were driven out of existence, most continued their activities in secret. The Society of Ironfounders met at night in a remote country area and buried all books and records in the ground. Some workers combined quite openly, and there were even strikes, for example those organised by the Cotton Spinners' General Union in Lancashire and Cheshire (1810). There were few prosecutions under the Combination Acts, although nineteen printers on the staff of *The Times* were imprisoned in 1810 for what the judge called 'a most wicked conspiracy' to injure 'the very employers who gave you bread'.

Around 1820, a campaign was started to achieve the **repeal** (abolition) **of the Combination Acts**. It was led by **Francis Place**, a tailor, whose shop in London's Charing Cross Road was a meeting-place for reformers of all kinds. With the help of **Joseph Hume**, MP, a Parliamentary Committee of Inquiry was set up, and its report led Parliament to repeal the Combination Acts in 1824. Immediately there was an outbreak of strikes, as secret unions came into the open and pressed for wage increases. Employers blamed the 1824 Act and soon got Parliament to change it. By an Act of 1825, which no longer satisfied Place and Hume, workers could still form trade unions, *but* they were not allowed to 'molest' or 'obstruct' either employers or fellow workers. This meant, in practice, that it was difficult to strike without falling foul of the law, for courts could interpret the wording of the Act almost as they pleased. Nevertheless, after the Acts of 1824–5 at least the trade unionist was no longer an outlaw.

Robert Owen, the 'Grand National' and Tolpuddle

Most early trade unions were small, local organisations. It was not until after 1825 that large *national* unions began to combine workers in different parts of the country. An important figure in these developments was **John Doherty**, an Irishman and leader of the Lancashire cotton-spinners. In 1829 he formed a Grand General Union of Spinners, the first really national trade union. In the following year he went further and set up the **National Association for the Protection of Labour**, which aimed to unite *all* the trades in Britain. Such an ambitious scheme had little chance of success, but in the two years it

Robert Owen, 1771–1858

New Lanark cotton-mills

lasted it claimed over 100,000 members and had its own newspaper, *The Voice of the People*. More national unions followed – among builders, potters, textile workers and others. But overshadowing them all was the **Grand National Consolidated Trades Union** (GNCTU) established in October 1833. Within months it had over half a million members from every sort of trade.

The inspiration behind the GNCTU was **Robert Owen**, a remarkable Welshman from Newtown, Montgomeryshire. He rose from being a draper's apprentice to a great cotton manufacturer before he was thirty. In 1800 he became managing partner of the **New Lanark cotton-mills**, on the banks of the Clyde near Glasgow. He immediately made himself personally responsible for the welfare of the 2,000 workers – providing recreational facilities, replacing slums with decent houses and opening shops which sold essential goods at cost prices. He abolished child labour below the age of ten, giving these children free full-time schooling instead. No adults worked more than ten and a half hours a day; yet they were paid good wages which continued during sickness and temporary unemployment.

Other mill-owners were amazed to see that Owen made good profits, in spite of his lavish expenditure on workers' welfare. Owen explained that if factory hands were contented they would work harder and more efficiently. Nevertheless, few factory-masters followed his example and Owen soon took an active part in the Factory Reform movement (see page 120), realising that new laws were needed to give workers proper protection.

Owen was not satisfied with being just a 'model employer'. In his book, *New View of Society* (1814), he put forward ideas for changing the whole basis of people's lives. He wanted to replace the existing system of *competition* – 'between manufacturers for markets and between workers for jobs' – with *co-operation*, which he believed could bring peace and plenty for all. Owen suggested the setting up of **Villages of Co-operation**, where people could exchange their products with each other on equal terms and no-one would live on profits from another person's work. He proposed this as a remedy for the distress after 1815, but the ruling classes would have nothing to do with it. Formerly, they had admired him as a successful businessman, but now they distrusted him, realising that he was opposed to the whole idea of profit-making, on which their wealth and power depended.

After unsuccessful attempts to establish his own Co-operative Communities, in both the USA and Britain, Owen tried to put his ideas into practice in the trade union movement. The result was the 'Grand National' of 1833. It aimed to unite all trades, after which industry would be organised under National Companies according to the principle of co-operation. Employers were naturally alarmed by Owen's revolutionary scheme, and in self-defence set out to crush the GNCTU. Workers had to sign a statement, which became known as **The Document**, declaring that they were *not* members of the Grand National. All those who refused were sacked.

The six men of Dorset who were transported to Australia in 1834

Meanwhile an even more damaging attack on trade unions in general, and the GNCTU in particular, occurred in the Dorset village of **Tolpuddle**. In October 1833 some forty villagers formed a branch or 'lodge' of the Friendly Society of Agricultural Labourers, intending to join up with the Grand National. The authorities in the neighbourhood, most of them employers of the men, immediately set out to crush the lodge – with the agreement of the Home Secretary and a number of MPs. The villagers had taken the usual secret oath of loyalty to the Union, and this gave the magistrates their excuse. Six members of the lodge were arrested and charged with taking secret and unlawful oaths – under an Act of 1797, which had been passed to deal with the naval mutinies of that year. In March 1834, at nearby Dorchester, they were sentenced to be transported to Australia for seven years.

Members of the GNCTU, preparing for an all-out attack upon employers, now hesitated. They saw the Tolpuddle case as a threat to their right of combination, and feared that their political masters would stop at nothing to crush the Union. Within months the GNCTU fell apart in a series of bitter local disputes. In the end it proved too big and scattered to be manageable, at a time when most workers could neither read nor write and there was not yet rapid communication by letter, telegraph or rail.

The combined attack by employers and the Government in 1834 succeeded in crippling the trade union movement for the time being. But the workers had the last word. While the six men of Dorset endured the brutality of the convict settlements, a great movement of protest swept across England. There were countless petitions and public meetings, and a great procession of trade unionists in London's Copenhagen Fields. In 1836 the Government gave way and granted a free pardon and passage home to the 'Tolpuddle Martyrs'. Even then, it was a further three years before the last of the six returned.

The People's Charter

As the events of the 'black year' of 1834 showed, successful trade union action still depended upon the goodwill of Parliament. But Parliament was unlikely to be sympathetic towards working-class organisations so long as it was dominated by the upper and middle classes. Consequently the fight for parliamentary reform was soon renewed.

In 1836, a group of skilled tradesmen and small shopkeepers founded the **London Working Men's Association** (LWMA) which aimed to 'seek by every legal means to place all classes of society in possession of equal political and social rights'. The inspiration behind the LWMA was its Secretary, **William Lovett**, a cabinet-maker by trade. Under his influence, the LWMA drew up a **Charter** of political demands (1838) with the intention of presenting it to Parliament. It ran to many pages, but its core was in the following six points:

William Lovett (1800–77), Secretary of the London Working Men's Association

1. The vote for all adult males.
2. Election by secret ballot.
3. Equal electoral districts.
4. Abolition of the property qualification for MPs.
5. MPs to be paid a salary.
6. Annual Parliaments, with a general election every June.

Other societies of working men eagerly supported the Charter, and before long mass meetings and torchlight processions were held all over the country, particularly in industrial areas. Meanwhile at a great meeting in Birmingham (1838) the 'Chartist Movement' was officially launched, with the aim of getting Parliament to accept the six points.

Right from the start, the Movement lacked unity. Different sections had widely differing aims and tactics. In the Midlands, members of the Birmingham Political Union, led by **Thomas Attwood**, a banker and MP, wanted, among other things, a change in the monetary system – to be achieved by a reformed Parliament. Like the LWMA, the men from Birmingham believed in using 'moral force' (non-violent methods), through petitions, public meetings and the like. On the other hand, the largest group, from northern England and South Wales, represented the most depressed ranks of society, including unemployed industrial workers and the wretched handloom weavers. In their desperation, they were unlikely to stop short of violence and bloodshed. The 'physical force' Chartists, as they were called, wanted, above all, the repeal of the new Poor Law of 1834 (see page 121) which made it necessary for the unemployed to enter a workhouse in order to get Poor Relief.

The leader of the 'physical force' Chartists, **Feargus O'Connor** (1794–1855), was 'a hot-headed Irishman', capable of driving audiences into a frenzy with his violent attacks on the privileged classes. His Leeds newspaper, the *Northern Star*, soon achieved a circulation of 50,000 copies, giving him enormous influence over the Movement. Although London and Birmingham supported Lovett, the industrial workers of northern England and South Wales were under the spell of O'Connor, and they provided the most active support for Chartism. O'Connor was unreliable and had little self-control, but he had powers of leadership that Lovett lacked. By 1839 he had virtually taken over the Movement.

The **first National Petition**, containing 1,250,000 signatures, was presented to Parliament by Thomas Attwood in July 1839. Not surprisingly, the Commons rejected it by a large majority – 235 votes to 46. A general strike or 'Sacred Month' had been threatened if the Petition was refused, but this fell through because of poor organisation. However Chartists from the Welsh valleys, led by **John Frost**, an ex-mayor and magistrate, were not prepared to accept defeat so easily. On the night of 3–4 November, over 1,000 of them – mostly miners, armed with old muskets and clubs – gathered on the hills above **Newport**. Soon after dawn, they marched into the town in columns, but were surprised by a small military garrison which dispersed them with gunfire. Frost and two others were transported to Australia for life.

The most serious phase of Chartism was over, but the Movement was far from dead. In 1842 a **second National Petition**, more than 9 metres long, containing more than 3 million signatures, was rejected by a Commons vote of 287 to 49. Strikes and riots in the industrial areas followed, but the ringleaders were soon arrested and the authorities regained control. By now, Lovett and most of the 'moral force' Chartists had abandoned the Movement. 'Muskets are not what are wanted, but education and schooling of the working people', said Lovett. 'Violent words do not slay the enemies but the friends of our Movement.'

The Newport Rising, November 1839

O'Connor now began a scheme to establish co-operative communities of working people. The **Chartist Co-operative Land Society** (1845) quickly raised £80,000 in subscriptions and bought an estate in Hertfordshire. Members were allocated cottages and allotments of land, to enable them to be self-supporting. But success was short-lived. The Society was financially unsound and collapsed four years later.

Meanwhile, the return of distress and unemployment (1847–8) again resulted in the masses taking up the Chartist banner. A **third National Petition** was organised and, in April 1848, a demonstration was held on London's Kennington Common. The Queen was sent to the Isle of Wight for safety, and the aged Duke of Wellington, in charge of the defence of London, packed it with troops and special police. The huge Petition was carried in three cabs to Parliament, where many of the signatures were found to be forgeries – such as 'Queen Victoria' and 'Mr Punch'. The name of the Duke of Wellington appeared sixteen times. When the Commons threw out the petition, by 222 votes to 17, Chartism was as good as dead. Later attempts to revive the Movement failed, while O'Connor went out of his mind and died in an asylum (1855).

Chartism failed chiefly because its support came from the poorest and most powerless section of the population. Most of the more skilled and better-paid workers deserted the Movement when it fell under the control of the reckless O'Connor. The People's Charter

The great Chartist demonstration on Kennington Common, 10 April 1848. This is one of the earliest crowd photographs in existence

was little more than a banner, behind which flocked a vast assortment of discontented workers with different aims and tactics. It gained most of its support in periods of distress. The years of the three petitions were also years of severe unemployment and high corn prices. Increasing prosperity, in which the working classes shared to some extent, finally killed Chartism. Nevertheless it was the first nation-wide movement of working-class protest, and it drew the attention of the ruling classes to the sufferings of the poor.

Between 1858 and 1918 five of the six points of the Charter were partly or wholly accepted into the British parliamentary system.

Friendly Societies and Co-operatives

Today, we live in a so-called Welfare State. But in the nineteenth century there were no state schemes of social security for people who suffered hardship. Every family was expected to provide for itself entirely by its own efforts. It was not considered the duty of the government to interfere in these matters, with the exception of the Poor Law, which provided a 'last resort' for the destitute. This attitude was summed up by **Samuel Smiles**, an Edinburgh doctor, in his book *Self-Help* (1859). He said hard work was the *only* answer to poverty, for 'they who work in the truest spirit will invariably [always] be the most successful'. But this was just wishful thinking as far as unskilled workers were concerned. They rarely earned enough to make ends meet in a normal week, let alone when their income was suddenly reduced by sickness or unemployment.

However the better-paid, more highly skilled workers *could* help themselves. They could afford weekly subscriptions to a **Friendly Society**, in return for which they got cash benefits in time of need – usually an allowance during sickness, a pension in old age, and a sum of money at death to help with funeral expenses. Friendly Societies of various kinds had been a feature of working-class life since the late seventeenth century. They were mostly small, local organisations (like trade clubs) providing members with social activities and comradeship. Some, like the Oddfellows and Foresters (the two largest), were run on a national basis, with branches all over the country.

The Industrial Revolution, by bringing workers together in large numbers, led to a rapid rise in the membership of Friendly Societies, especially in Lancashire. They were the only working-class organisations not outlawed in the period of government repression during and after the French Wars. By the early nineteenth century there were over a million members of Friendly Societies in England and Wales alone, and the numbers were increasing every year.

Lower-paid workers were unable to join Friendly Societies because they could not afford the weekly subscriptions. But many of them supported **Co-operative Societies**, which began to be established in the 1820s under the influence of Robert Owen. Some Co-operatives were simply small grocery stores which tried to cut out shopkeepers' profits by buying goods in bulk and selling them to members at reduced prices. Others concentrated on spreading the gospel of Robert Owen,

WORKING-CLASS MOVEMENTS (Remember that each overlapped the others)

Trade Unions	Reform Movements, Societies and Parties	Friendly Societies and Co-operatives
'Industrial action' To get a better standard of living.	*'Political action'* To get a share in government.	*'Self-help'* Schemes of security and welfare.
AIMS Higher wages. Shorter hours. Better working conditions.	AIMS The right to vote. General reform of Parliament to make the vote effective.	AIMS Insurance against sickness, unemployment etc. Production and/or distribution of goods on non-profit making basis. Encouragement to save.
METHODS Negotiation with employers. Strikes.	METHODS Meetings and demonstrations. Newspapers and pamphlets. Petitions.	METHODS Collection of weekly subscriptions. Joint ownership of non-profit making shops, factories, etc.

or attempted co-operative production of goods. By 1832 there were altogether nearly 500 Co-operative Societies in Britain, but scarcely any were successful, mainly because they lacked sufficient funds to finance their schemes.

The real history of the Co-operative Movement began in 1844, when twenty-eight weavers each invested £1 towards setting up a grocery store in **Toad Lane, Rochdale**. Goods such as flour, oatmeal, sugar, butter and candles were sold at normal prices. Then, after running costs had been deducted, the 'dividend' (profit) was shared out among the customers in proportion to the amount of goods they had bought. Dividends could be left in the business to accumulate as shares on which interest was paid. This encouraged members to build up savings, and also provided a steady growth of funds which helped the store to expand. After a year the original membership had risen to seventy-four and profits of £22 were made. By 1875 it had no less than 8,415 members, with annual dividends totalling nearly £50,000.

The example of the 'Rochdale Pioneers' was soon followed throughout Lancashire and the North. As early as 1851 there were 130 similar societies, some of them in the industrial towns of Scotland. An important reason for their popularity was that they sold *pure* food. A co-operative store had no reason to swindle its members by watering down milk and butter or putting sand in the sugar, as many shopkeepers did in this period.

In 1863 a **Co-operative Wholesale Society** (CWS) was established in Manchester to buy from producers in large quantities (wholesale) and

Some of the 'Rochdale Pioneers', photographed in 1860

supply individual stores. At first, it confined its activities to the North, but within ten years it became a nationwide organisation. In 1875 the CWS began manufacturing its own products. Beginning with flour-mills and factories making biscuits, shoes, soap and clothing, it soon offered a wide range of goods.

Total Membership of the Co-operative Movement

1851	1881	1914
15,000	546,000	over 3 million

By the end of the century, some profits of co-operation were being used to provide adult education and other services for members.

Timeline

1799–1800	Combination Acts – trade unions illegal.
1824–5	Repeal of Combination Acts.
1833	Robert Owen's Grand National Consolidated Trades Union (GNCTU).
1834	The 'Tolpuddle Martyrs' and collapse of the GNCTU.
1838	The People's Charter.
1844	The 'Rochdale Pioneers'.
1848	Collapse of the Chartist Movement.
1863	Co-operative Wholesale Society (CWS).

Questions

1. '...every journeyman or workman, or other person, who shall...
   enter into any combination to obtain an advance of wages, or to
   lessen or alter the hours or duration of the time of working, or to
   decrease the quantity of work...and who shall be lawfully
   convicted of any of the said offences, shall...be confined in the
   common gaol...for any time not exceeding three calendar
   months.' (Combination Act, 1800)

   a) Why was this and a similar Act in 1799 passed?
   b) What effect did the Combination Acts have on the developing
      trade union movement?
   c) How and why was this Act repealed in 1824?
   d) Trade unions could still fall foul of the law after 1824. Explain
      how this happened in Tolpuddle, Dorset, in 1834.

2. 'We were present at many of the meetings of the Grand National
   Consolidated Trade Union, and have a distinct recollection of the
   excitement that prevailed in them – of the apparent determination
   to carry out its principles in opposition to every obstacle.' (A trade
   unionist, writing in 1841)

   a) What were the 'principles' underlying the GNCTU?
   b) What were the 'obstacles' to its success and why did they
      quickly lead to its collapse?
   c) Who was the inspiration behind the formation of the GNCTU?
   d) Why was he known as a 'model employer'?
   e) In what way did he aim to change the whole basis of society?

3. Look at the six points of the People's Charter listed on page 130.
   a) How would points 4 and 5 be to the advantage of the working
      classes?
   b) Which one of the six points has never been obtained? Why do you
      think this is so?
   c) Name *three* Chartist leaders. How did their aims differ?
   d) What happened on the three occasions when the Charter was
      presented to Parliament?
   e) What were the main reasons for the failure of Chartism?

4. In what ways were a) Friendly Societies and b) Co-operatives
   examples of 'self-help' among the working classes? Account for
   their success.

5. Write a paragraph on each of the following:
   a) eighteenth-century trade clubs b) John Doherty
   c) the Newport Rising, 1839   d) Samuel Smiles

13

The Railway Age
Transport and Communications (II)

*Poster advertising the Surrey
Iron Railway (1804)*

'Canals will last my lifetime, but what I fear is those damned tramways.' So said the Duke of Bridgewater, 'the father of inland navigation', shortly before his death. The **tramways** he referred to had been in use in mining areas for about 200 years. Their purpose was to ease the passage of horse-drawn wagons carrying coal from the pithead to the nearest navigable waterway. At first they were made of wood. Later, iron plates were fixed to the rails to reduce wear, until about 1790, when rails made entirely of iron came into general use. But such railways were still confined almost entirely to mines and quarries. Not until 1804 was the first *public* railway built – from Croydon in Surrey to the River Thames at Wandsworth.

It seemed unlikely that tramways would put either the canal companies or the turnpike road trusts out of business. Both were enjoying great prosperity, together carrying vast quantities of freight and thousands of passengers every year. The Duke's forecast was only proved correct by an entirely new development which even he did not foresee – the combination of iron rails *and* steam-powered locomotives.

Richard Trevithick and 'strong steam'

The application of Watt's engine to driving a wheel (1781) aroused interest in the possibility of steam-powered transport. Watt himself opposed the idea, saying that it was unsafe. When his foreman, William Murdock, built a working model of a high-pressure steam locomotive (1784) he discouraged him from proceeding any further. Watt preferred to keep the steam at atmospheric pressure, or very little above it, so that the creation of a vacuum was the most important part of the working process (see Chapter 8). His refusal to use high-pressure steam removed the risk of explosion, but it also made his engine unsuitable for any kind of wheeled transport.

Richard Trevithick (1771–1833), a young Cornish engineer, did not share Watt's fears. In 1802 he patented a **high-pressure steam-engine**, without all the clumsy mechanism of condenser and beam. The piston was driven directly by 'strong steam' (super-heated steam at higher than atmospheric pressure). Critics said the boiler would burst, but Trevithick safely let in steam at more than three times atmospheric pressure. Before long he was using pressures six or seven times greater than that of the surrounding atmosphere. His compact little engine not only required less fuel to do the work of pumping (his original aim) but was light enough to be carried on a cart. Trevithick immediately realised the possibility of making the engine drive the cart. After experiments with steam road-carriages in Cornwall and London, he hit on the idea of building a railway locomotive.

On a cold February morning in 1804 an historic journey was made along 16 kilometres of tramway in South Wales. Trevithick's locomotive drew five wagons, a coach and about seventy passengers from **Penydaren** Ironworks (near Merthyr Tydfil) to the Glamorganshire Canal. After frequent stoppages, mostly caused by the 5-tonne locomotive cracking the tramway, it completed the journey in four hours, to become the first steam-engine to run on rails and haul a train behind it.

Four years later Trevithick displayed his latest locomotive on a special circular track near Euston Square in London. He called it the *Catch-me-who-can* and gave shilling (5p) rides to the public at speeds of up to 20 kilometres per hour. But lack of money forced him to dismantle it a few weeks later. After more unsuccessful ventures, including an attempt to introduce his engine into the silver-mines of Peru, the forgotten Cornishman died in poverty, leaving others to benefit from his work.

George Stephenson and the *Rocket*

Although London businessmen failed to give Trevithick's invention the necessary financial support, it aroused great interest in the coal-mining areas of the North. Fodder for horses was in short supply during the Napoleonic Wars, so mine-owners were willing to consider any alternative means of moving coal. In 1805 Trevithick had built a locomotive for a colliery near Newcastle. It proved too heavy for the track and was never used, but it impressed many northern engineers. Before long they were building locomotives of their own. In 1812, *Prince Regent*, designed by **John Blenkinsop**, a colliery engineer, began to operate a regular steam railway on the outskirts of Leeds. A year later, in the North-East, **William Hedley** produced *Puffing Billy*, which could draw nine laden wagons at 7 or 8 kilometres per hour.

These developments greatly interested a young engine-wright at Killingworth Colliery in Northumberland. His name was **George Stephenson** (1781–1848). He is often credited with the invention of the locomotive, but, like James Watt, he was a great improver rather than a pioneer. The main features of an efficient steam piston-driven locomotive were already present in Trevithick's engines.

George Stephenson

From the age of fourteen, when he became an assistant colliery fireman, Stephenson devoted his life to engineering. He was skilfully repairing all kinds of machines, including steam-engines, before he learned properly how to read and write. His employer, Lord Ravensworth, had heard of Blenkinsop's and Hedley's locomotives, and when Stephenson suggested building one he provided the money. The result was *Blücher* (named after a Prussian general) which pulled eight laden wagons at 7 kilometres per hour on its first run in 1814. In the next seven years, Stephenson built sixteen locomotives and many kilometres of track, gaining a high reputation as an engineer.

Richard Trevithick's
'Catch-me-who-can' (1808)

The turning-point in his life came in 1821. Edward Pease, a wealthy landowner, appointed him engineer in charge of a new public railway to join the coal-mines of South Durham with the river-port of Stockton. Stephenson surveyed and constructed a route of 43 kilometres, running from Witton Park Colliery, via Darlington. He laid the rails 4 feet 8½ inches apart (just under 1.5 metres – the gauge still used today) after measuring the wheelbases of over 100 country carts and taking an average. Pease had assumed that all the traffic on the railway would be horse-drawn, but Stephenson convinced him of the advantages of steam. So at the ceremonial opening of the **Stockton–Darlington line** (September 1825) twelve loaded wagons, a coach and twenty-one passenger-cars were hauled by

1829.

GRAND COMPETITION

OF

LOCOMOTIVES

ON THE

LIVERPOOL & MANCHESTER RAILWAY.

STIPULATIONS & CONDITIONS

On which the Directors of the Liverpool and Manchester Railway offer a Premium of £500 for the most Improved Locomotive Engine.

I.

The said Engine must "effectually consume its own smoke," according to the provisions of the Railway Act, 7th Geo. IV.

II.

The Engine, if it weighs Six Tons, must be capable of drawing after it, day by day, on a well-constructed Railway, on a level plane, a Train of Carriages of the gross weight of Twenty Tons, including the Tender and Water Tank, at the rate of Ten Miles per Hour, with a pressure of steam in the boiler not exceeding Fifty Pounds on the square inch.

III.

There must be Two Safety Valves, one of which must be completely out of the reach or control of the Engine-man, and neither of which must be fastened down while the Engine is working.

IV.

The Engine and Boiler must be supported on Springs, and rest on Six Wheels; and the height from the ground to the top of the Chimney must not exceed Fifteen Feet.

V.

The weight of the Machine, with its complement of water in the Boiler, must, at most, not exceed Six Tons, and a Machine of less weight will be preferred if it draw after it a proportionate weight; and if the weight of the Engine, &c., do not exceed Five Tons, then the gross weight to be drawn need not exceed Fifteen Tons; and in that proportion for Machines of still smaller weight — provided that the Engine, &c., shall still be on six wheels, unless the weight (as above) be reduced to Four Tons and a Half, or under, in which case the Boiler, &c., may be placed on four wheels. And the Company shall be at liberty to put the Boiler, Fire Tube, Cylinders, &c., to the test of a pressure of water not exceeding 150 Pounds per square inch, without being answerable for any damage the Machine may receive in consequence.

VI.

There must be a Mercurial Gauge affixed to the Machine, with Index Rod, showing the Steam Pressure above 45 Pounds per square inch; and constructed to blow out a Pressure of 60 Pounds per inch.

VII.

The Engine to be delivered complete for trial, at the Liverpool end of the Railway, not later than the 1st of October next.

VIII.

The price of the Engine which may be accepted, not to exceed £550, delivered on the Railway; and any Engine not approved to be taken back by the Owner.

N.B.—The Railway Company will provide the Engine Tender with a supply of Water and Fuel, for the experiment. The distance within the Rails is four feet eight inches and a half.

THE LOCOMOTIVE STEAM ENGINES,

WHICH COMPETED FOR THE PRIZE OF £500 OFFERED BY THE DIRECTORS OF THE LIVERPOOL AND MANCHESTER RAILWAY COMPANY,

DRAWN TO A SCALE ¼ INCH TO A FOOT.

THE "ROCKET" OF MR. ROBT. STEPHENSON OF NEWCASTLE,

WHICH DRAWING A LOAD EQUIVALENT TO THREE TIMES ITS WEIGHT TRAVELLED AT THE RATE OF 12½ MILES AN HOUR, AND WITH A CARRIAGE & PASSENGERS AT THE RATE OF 24 MILES. COST PER MILE FOR FUEL ABOUT THREE HALFPENCE.

THE "NOVELTY" OF MESSRS. BRAITHWAITE & ERRICSSON OF LONDON,

WHICH DRAWING A LOAD EQUIVALENT TO THREE TIMES ITS WEIGHT TRAVELLED AT THE RATE OF 20¾ MILES AN HOUR, AND WITH A CARRIAGE & PASSENGERS AT THE RATE OF 32 MILES. COST PER MILE FOR FUEL ABOUT ONE HALFPENNY.

THE "SANSPAREIL" OF MR. HACKWORTH OF DARLINGTON,

WHICH DRAWING A LOAD EQUIVALENT TO THREE TIMES ITS WEIGHT TRAVELLED AT THE RATE OF 12¼ MILES AN HOUR, COST FOR FUEL PER MILE ABOUT TWO PENCE.

Stephenson's *Locomotion*, one of four engines specially built for the new railway. The triumphant journey to Stockton Quay was witnessed by thousands of cheering spectators.

The Stockton–Darlington railway aroused great interest among the merchants of **Liverpool** and **Manchester**. They had become dissatisfied with their canals, which were not only slow but likely to run short of water in the summer or freeze in the winter. In 1826 they got parliamentary permission to build a railway and appointed Stephenson Chief Engineer at the princely salary of £1,000 a year. But despite generous offers of compensation this pleased neither the canal-owners nor those who owned land between the two towns. They raised all kinds of objections to the proposed use of locomotives, saying these would pollute the countryside and terrify livestock. They claimed passengers would be blinded and deafened by the appalling speed of the trains and suffocate in the tunnels. When words failed to have an effect, they resorted to spoiling tactics. Surveyors were forced to work at night with lanterns to avoid pitched battles with farmers and their hired thugs.

The hostility of man was matched by that of nature. Stephenson, now working with his son **Robert** – an engineer as capable as himself – had enormous obstacles to overcome in laying the track. The greatest of these was Chat Moss, a huge spongy bog, which threatened to swallow up the track until a solid foundation of earth was sunk right to the bottom. In 1829, with the line nearing completion, the directors of the company offered a £500 prize for the best steam-engine to work it. The contest, held on part of the new track at **Rainhill**, was a triumph for the Stephensons. Their entry, the *Rocket*, was the undisputed winner, reaching a speed of 46 kilometres per hour. From now on there could be no doubt that people were going to travel faster than horses could carry them. When the two-way track was opened in 1830, worked by eight engines from the Stephensons' Newcastle factory, it was the first to be devoted entirely to steam locomotives. The real 'Railway Age' had begun.

The Railway Revolution

The Liverpool to Manchester line connected two great cities whose combined population totalled 350,000. With over 1,000 passengers a day and a large volume of freight, profits reached £80,000 in 1831 alone. Businessmen all over the country, seeing these rich rewards, rushed to promote railway companies by private Act of Parliament. Canal 'navvies' provided a ready-made labour force to carry out the work of railway construction. This tough new labouring breed, working almost entirely without machinery in all weathers, became the backbone of the Railway Age. Meanwhile canal-building came to an abrupt halt. Canal companies and turnpike trusts were ruined as the growing railway network claimed an increasing share of long-distance traffic. Short-haul road traffic in and around towns actually increased, but country roads and their coaching inns became almost deserted. If ever there was a 'revolution' in inland transport this was it.

Opposite: *The competitors at the Rainhill Trials (1829)*

There was no attempt to plan a proper railway system. Parliament allowed a general 'free for all', which resulted in a haphazard network with frequent duplication (more than one line to the same place). Nevertheless, progress was remarkably rapid. By 1843 London was linked with Dover, Brighton, Southampton, Bristol, Birmingham, Lancaster and York. In the next three years (1844–6) Parliament gave permission for a further 438 lines to be built. A *railway mania* had gripped the nation and the urge for quick and easy money led to great speculation in railway shares on the Stock Exchange. Small companies amalgamated or were swallowed up by larger ones, and a handful of financiers gained great power. The most famous of these was **George Hudson**, 'the Railway King', who bought control of most of the Midland and Northern companies. But his success was short-lived. When some of his schemes collapsed, he continued to pay dividends to shareholders with money he had raised to form new companies. By 1848 his double-dealing was exposed and he was ruined, along with thousands of investors.

The railway mania had constructive results too. By 1852, when most of the railways resulting from it were completed, almost all the *main* lines of the present day network had been laid.

Total railway track in Britain

1840	2,988 kilometres
1855	12,900 kilometres (approx.)
1870	25,031 kilometres

The scheduled time for fast trains between important business centres was already above 65 kilometres per hour in 1850. Passengers travelled in first-, second- or third-class **coaches**. The first-class compartments were like stage-coaches inside, usually with eight cushioned seats. But there was no lighting or heating in the early years and no lavatories before the 1870s. Second-class coaches provided shelter but little else, while the earliest third-class passengers travelled in open trucks with perhaps a few planks for seating. Third-class travel was rare before an **Act of 1844** compelled all future companies to provide it. At least one train a day in each direction had to stop at all stations and give third-class passengers a seated and covered ride at no more than a penny per mile (about ½p per 1.6 kilometres).

George and Robert Stephenson continued to play a leading part in railway development after 1830. They engineered the London to Birmingham line (1833–8) and made further progress in locomotive design. Other great engine-builders included **Sir Daniel Gooch** of the Great Western Railway (GWR). By the late 1840s, his expresses like *Great Western* could reach 100 kilometres per hour and get from London to Bristol in two and a half hours.

The London to Bristol line was a fine piece of engineering. It was built between 1835 and 1841 under the direction of **Isambard Kingdom Brunel** (1806–59), Chief Engineer of the GWR. With slight gradients and few bends, it is still the fastest major route in Britain. Brunel's skill was displayed to great effect in the course of driving the

Box tunnel – built by Isambard Brunel in the 1830s

line through the Cotswolds. A 3-kilometre tunnel was built at Box Hill – the longest and most difficult so far attempted. Brunel showed his complete mastery of the situation by setting the incline so that the rising sun shone through from end to end on his birthday (9 April)!

Brunel's colourful personality was in complete contrast to that of the careful and reserved Stephensons. He delighted in breaking with tradition. For example, he laid his rails 7 feet (2.1 metres) apart, to help trains hold the track more firmly on bends, especially at high speed. He hoped other companies would follow suit, but he was fighting a losing battle. By the mid 1840s, well over 80 per cent of Britain's railways had been built on Stephenson's 4 feet 8½ inches gauge. Parliament, seeking to establish a standard gauge for the whole country (1848), had little alternative but to forbid any extension of the broad gauge outside GWR territory. By 1892 the GWR had converted the last of its broad tracks to the standard gauge, and what might have been Brunel's greatest monument was gone for ever. Today the chief remains of his work are his fine bridges – notably the 300-metre **Royal Albert Bridge** across the river Tamar at Saltash. It was completed in 1859, just before his death.

By this time railways had begun to affect almost every aspect of national life. Country areas, previously isolated, were brought into

*Brunel's magnificent
Royal Albert Bridge*

direct contact with towns and cities. All branches of industry benefited – especially iron and steel, mechanical engineering, coal and agriculture. Railways themselves became a major industry, with valuable export markets in four continents. 'Railway towns', with big engine sheds and workshops, sprang up in places such as Swindon, Eastleigh and Crewe. The population of Crewe increased from a mere 203 in 1841 to nearly 18,000 thirty years later.

Meanwhile social habits were changing as a result of railways. Quick daily travel enabled many people to live away from their work. Consequently suburbs grew up on the outskirts of large towns. Railways also made it possible for increasing numbers to take annual holidays by the seaside, at expanding resorts such as Brighton and Blackpool. Only the middle classes could afford this luxury at first, but by the end of the century the 'holiday habit' was spreading among better-off working-class families.

Electric telegraph and Penny Post

To ensure safe and efficient operation of the railways, various methods of signalling were introduced. At first, signalmen stood by the track holding coloured flags – or lanterns after dark. They were soon replaced by mechanical 'arms' attached to posts and connected by rods to a shed (signal-box). But by far the most important development was that of *telegraphy* or distance communication.

The discovery that electric signals could be sent along wires dates back to the eighteenth century. In the earliest experiments with 'electric telegraph' a separate wire was used to represent each letter of the alphabet. But this method was very complicated, particularly if numbers were used as well. In 1837 two British scientists, **Charles Wheatstone** and **William Cooke**, invented a 'needle telegraph', with an

*Cooke and Wheatstone's
five-needle telegraph*

The famous 'penny black' (1840) – the world's first postage stamp

appropriate signalling code. Five magnetic needles were deflected by electricity to point to letters of the alphabet arranged on a board. The first telegraph wires were set up between Euston and Camden Town railway stations in London. Then Paddington was connected with Slough on the GWR. In 1845 the success of the new device was assured when a suspected murderer was arrested at Paddington following a telegraph message sent ahead of his train.

The electric telegraph was confined almost entirely to use on the railways before 1850, by which time the inventors had perfected a single-needle model. In 1851 a cable was laid across the Channel to establish contact between London and Paris. From then on telegraphy progressed rapidly. A transatlantic cable was laid in 1866. Three years later, Parliament granted a monopoly of all inland telegraph business to the Post Office, paying £11 million in compensation to the private companies. Meanwhile the needle device had been given up in favour of the system invented in America by **Samuel Morse**, which employed a code of dots and dashes.

Another great advance in communications during the Railway Age was the introduction of a nationwide **penny post**. Reform of the postal service was long overdue. Letters were charged according to weight and distance, and payment was made by the receiver – a complicated and expensive procedure. Parliament's decision to tax letters (1801) only made matters worse, and encouraged the public to find ways of sending mail privately. By the 1830s, when a single sheet from London to Edinburgh cost 1s 3½d (6½p – equivalent to several pounds at today's prices) a Parliamentary Committee discovered that three-quarters of the mail on some long-distance routes was not carried by the Post Office at all.

At this point, an ex-schoolmaster named **Rowland Hill** (1795–1879) published a plan for Post Office reform (1837) based on cheapness and simplicity. He calculated that the main cost of the postal service resulted from the need to tax each individual letter and collect the postage on delivery. Hill argued that if a prepaid standard rate of a penny (½p) were charged for every letter, regardless of distance, the volume of mail would so increase that the government's total revenue would rise. His plan was accepted and he was asked to supervise its introduction early in 1840. All letters up to half an ounce (14 grams) cost a penny, after which additional charges were made for extra weight. To enable payment to be made quickly and in advance, the world's first **postage stamps** were produced – the famous Victorian 'penny blacks'. They had to be cut out with scissors until 1854, when sheets began to be perforated. Meanwhile Hill's idea spread rapidly to other countries.

'Smokeboats'

Steamships were invented *before* railway locomotives – for it was possible to use a low-pressure 'condensing engine' on the water. But whereas railways quickly established superiority over other forms of land transport, steamships met stiff opposition from sailing vessels

and did not replace them on the main ocean routes until the second half of the nineteenth century.

William Symington's 'Charlotte Dundas'

Following experiments with steam-powered boats in France and North America, the first British steamer went noisily afloat on a Scottish loch in 1788. It was a double-hulled paddleboat, designed by **William Symington** (1763–1831), a Scottish millwright. His second effort, the *Charlotte Dundas* (1802), pulled two heavily-laden barges for 30 kilometres on her maiden voyage along the Forth–Clyde Canal. Symington was asked to build eight steam-tugs for the Bridgewater Canal, but the Duke of Bridgewater's death (1803) resulted in his contract being cancelled. This was the nearest Symington got to business success. Like Trevithick, he eventually died in poverty while others profited from his invention.

Robert Fulton, an American, had inspected the *Charlotte Dundas* during a visit to Britain. In 1807 he launched the *Clermont*, powered by a Boulton and Watt engine, which proved the merits of steam navigation in a series of voyages on the Hudson River. Within ten years 'smokeboats', as the Red Indians called them, were running regularly on the Mississippi. Meanwhile, paddle-steamers were becoming equally familiar on the River Clyde. Europe's first commercially successful steamship service was started in 1812 by **Henry Bell's** *Comet*, which he advertised 'to ply upon the River Clyde, from Glasgow; to sail by the power of wind and steam'. In addition to her three horse-power engine, *Comet* had a sail, to catch any favourable wind. Most steamships carried sails for another fifty years or more, to economise on fuel and as a safeguard in case of engine failure.

Regular cross-Channel steamers between Dover and Calais started in 1818. The next step was for steamships to meet the challenge of the oceans. This was no easy task, for their high coal consumption restricted their range. When the American steamship *Savannah* crossed the Atlantic to Liverpool (1819) her engine could only be used for eighty-five hours of the twenty-seven-day voyage. Nevertheless she was the first steam vessel to cross *any* ocean – a clear pointer to the future. In 1838 at least three British ships crossed the Atlantic using steam all the way. The first was *Sirius* from London, followed, only a day later, by the faster *Great Western* from Bristol, designed by **Isambard Kingdom Brunel**. He aimed to link it up with the London to Bristol railway (then under construction) to provide a combined land and sea route from London to New York. The age of long-distance steam navigation had begun. Two years later, the first regular line of ocean-going steamships was started by **Samuel Cunard**, a shipowner from Halifax, Nova Scotia.

All the early steamships were driven by paddle-wheels, but these were very exposed and hence easily damaged. The Admiralty in particular had misgivings about using ships which could be crippled by a single shot. The answer was to replace paddles with a propeller under the stern. The first successful 'screw-steamer,' the SS *Archimedes* (1838), was designed by an Englishman, **Francis Pettit-Smith**. Seven years later, Brunel's *Great Britain* made the first screw-propelled Atlantic crossing. More important still, she was the first ocean-going ship constructed entirely of *iron*. Previous steamers, like *Great Western*, had iron bands round the hull to give additional strength, but they were basically made of wood.

John Wilkinson, the great ironmaster, successfully launched an iron barge as early as 1787, but it was not until 1822 that an iron ship put to sea. This was the *Aaron Manby*, a steamer, which crossed the Channel after being built in sections in the Midlands and assembled on the banks of the Thames. Most shipbuilders still preferred to work with wood, but the growing shortage of timber gradually forced them to use iron – and so discover its great advantages. It was so much stronger than wood that iron plates of little more than 1 centimetre could be used in place of timbers 30 centimetres thick. Consequently an iron ship was lighter than a wooden one of the same size.

The added strength of iron made it possible to build much larger ships, a fact which did not escape the inventive mind of Brunel. The last years of his life were devoted to his most ambitious project, the **Great Eastern**. She was 215 metres long, with five funnels and six masts, a double hull and both screw-propeller and paddle-wheels (the

Isambard Kingdom Brunel, photographed in front of the 'Great Eastern'

The 'Great Eastern'. She burned nearly 300 tonnes of coal a day – much more than Brunel had calculated – and this made her unsuitable for the very long voyages for which she was intended

only ship to combine the two). Built at Millwall (East London) she was eventually floated on the Thames in January 1858, after defying all attempts at launching for three months previously. With accommodation for 4,000 passengers and a top speed of 14 knots (about 25 kilometres per hour) she was a triumph of engineering. The *Great Eastern* remained the world's biggest ship for over forty years – yet she was a commercial failure, like many of Brunel's daring schemes. She was intended for the Far Eastern trade, but the only profitable use to which her vast storage space could be put was laying telegraph cables in the Atlantic.

The challenge of the clipper

Steamships were faster and more punctual than sailing vessels. They did not have to wait for favourable winds, so their time of arrival could be advertised with reasonable accuracy. Nevertheless, the need to carry great loads of coal severely reduced their cargo space and often made them unprofitable on a long voyage. Right up to the 1870s, sail held its own on the longest trade routes – in the shape of the **clipper**, the swiftest and most graceful of all wind-driven ships. Originating in the USA in the 1840s, clippers were long and narrow, with sharp bows, almost straight sides and an enormous spread of sail. Their great cargo space and relatively small crew made possible a big reduction in long-distance freight charges. In favourable conditions they were capable of very high speeds. In 1854, the American *James Baines* crossed the Atlantic to Liverpool in twelve days – three days faster than the *Great Western* on her maiden voyage.

British shipbuilders went one better than their American rivals, making clippers with hulls of iron instead of timber. These were not

The 'Cutty Sark'. This famous British clipper of the mid nineteenth century can be seen in dry dock at Greenwich, London

only cheaper to construct but held even more cargo. Famous British clippers included the *Cutty Sark, Thermopylae* and *Sir Lancelot*, whose sails would have covered fifteen tennis courts. They were mostly employed in bringing tea from China and wool from Australia.

Even in the heyday of the clipper the scales were tipping in favour of steam. In 1854 **John Elder**, a Scotsman, invented a **compound engine**, with two cylinders. The steam exhaust from the first was used again, at reduced pressure, to drive the piston in the second, resulting in a reduction of nearly 60 per cent in fuel consumption. Steamships gained a further advantage when the **Suez Canal** was opened (1869). Their passage to the East was shortened by nearly 5,000 kilometres, while sailing ships continued to go round the Cape of Good Hope because of unfavourable winds in the Mediterranean and the expense of hiring canal tugs. Meanwhile **coaling stations** on the main sea routes, at places such as Gibraltar, Suez, Aden and Singapore, further assisted steamships by allowing them to give more space to cargo. By the last quarter of the nineteenth century the steamship was supreme.

Timeline

1802	Richard Trevithick's high-pressure steam-engine.
	William Symington's *Charlotte Dundas*.
1804	Trevithick's Penydaren locomotive.
1825	Stockton to Darlington railway.
1829	Stephenson's *Rocket* wins the Rainhill trials.
1830	Liverpool to Manchester railway.
1837	Wheatstone and Cooke's electric 'needle telegraph'.
1838	*Sirius* and *Great Western* cross Atlantic under steam.
1840	Rowland Hill's Penny Post.
1844–6	'Railway mania'.
1854	John Elder's compound steam-engine.
1858	Isambard Kingdom Brunel's *Great Eastern*.
1869	Suez Canal opened.

Questions

1. 'Wednesday, 8th October. An exciting day, for Braithwaite burst his bellows and Hackworth's boiler began to break and all the time the ROCKET was running up and down to everyone's cheering.' (Diary of John Kennedy, a director of the Liverpool and Manchester Railway)

   a) A week later the *Rocket* was declared the winner of the Rainhill Trials. What was the year and where was Rainhill?
   b) Who designed and built the *Rocket*? What speed did it achieve?
   c) What connection did the winning designers already have with the Liverpool and Manchester Railway?
   d) Name the other two locomotives referred to in the passage.
   e) The rails were laid 4 feet 8½ inches (just under 1.5 metres) apart. Why was this gauge chosen?

2. 'A murder has just been committed at Salthill and the suspected murderer was seen to take a first-class ticket for London by the train which left Slough at 7.42 p.m. He is in the garb of a Quaker with a brown coat on.' (Extract from a message received at Paddington Station, 1845)

    a) How was the message sent ahead of the train?

    b) Who invented the device and how did it work?

    c) How did Samuel Morse improve this method of communication?

    d) When was it possible to send similar ·messages to i) France and ii) the USA?

3. 'On the 15th September I lost my oldest and best friend ... By his death the greatest of England's engineers was lost ... The commercial world thought him extravagant; but although he was so, great things are not done by those who sit down and count the cost of every thought and act.' (Diary of Sir Daniel Gooch, Locomotive Superintendent of the Great Western Railway)

    a) The year was 1859. Who was Gooch referring to?

    b) What was his connection with the Great Western Railway?

    c) Give two examples of his 'extravagant' schemes which ended up as commercial failures. In each case, what went wrong?·

    d) How did he provide a faster journey from London to New York?

    e) What are the chief remains of his work? Give an example.

4.

TOTAL TONNAGE BUILT FOR UK SHIPOWNERS				
Figures are percentages rounded to whole numbers – which explains why totals do not necessarily add up to a hundred				
	Sail		*Steam*	
	Wood	Iron/Steel	Wood	Iron/Steel
1850–4	75	4	3	17
1855–9	71	7	1	19
1860–4	47	22	1	32
1865–9	35	32	1	33
1870–4	11	14	1	74

    a) When did the tonnage of iron ships built first exceed that of wood?

    b) What are the advantages of iron in shipbuilding?

    c) When did steam tonnage built first exceed that of sail?

    d) Why did it take so long for the supremacy of steam to be established on the longest sea routes?

    e) What effect do you think the opening of the Suez Canal had on these figures?

5. Write a paragraph on each of the following:

    a) 'tramways'   b) Richard Trevithick

    c) the penny post   d) William Symington

14

'Free Trade'
Foreign Trade, the Corn Laws and Agriculture

Governments got much of their income from taxes on overseas trade. Of these, the most important were **tariffs** (customs duties on imported goods). But tariffs often had an additional purpose. Like the Navigation Acts or 'Laws of Trade' (see page 24) they were one of the ways by which Parliament *controlled* the nation's trade. For example, the French and Italians could produce high quality silk goods at prices below those of British manufacturers. To protect the home industry from foreign competition, Parliament raised the price of imported silk by putting a tariff on it. Duties were also put on certain *exports* which Parliament considered 'undesirable', such as the sale of armaments or scarce raw materials to foreign rivals.

By the early nineteenth century, however, most of these trading restrictions were no longer needed. Britain was the world's greatest industrial nation, mass producing large quantities of cheap goods, and so had little to fear from open competition with other countries. In fact, many tariffs had become more of a hindrance than a help. They increased the cost of imported raw materials and so put up the prices of finished articles. Consequently, the period up to about 1860 saw a gradual withdrawal of trading restrictions, giving the British greater freedom to buy and sell where they pleased.

Adam Smith, 1725–90

Followers of Adam Smith

The real starting-point of the movement towards 'free trade' was a book published in 1776 by **Adam Smith**, a Professor at Glasgow University. It was called *An Inquiry into the Causes of the Wealth of Nations* and it criticised attempts to restrict foreign trade by tariffs, which made cheap goods from abroad artificially dearer. Smith considered it natural for each country to export goods it could produce most cheaply and import goods that were more cheaply produced elsewhere. As he put it: 'The tailor does not attempt to make his own shoes, but buys them of the shoemaker. The shoemaker does not attempt to make his own clothes, but employs a tailor.... What is prudence [common sense] in the conduct of every private family can scarce be folly in that of a great kingdom.'

The purpose of many tariffs was not to control trade but simply to raise revenue for the government. Duties on imported tobacco and tea, for instance, were straightforward taxes, because in neither case was there a home industry to 'protect' from foreign competition. Adam Smith did not regard these 'revenue duties' as a hindrance to free trade. On the contrary, he had them in mind when he suggested

that enough revenue for the government 'might be drawn from duties upon the importation of only a few sorts of goods of the most general use and consumption.'

Smugglers bringing their goods ashore

Pitt the Younger was one of the first to be influenced by *The Wealth of Nations*. In 1784, soon after becoming Prime Minister, he began to reduce some of the heaviest duties on imports. He did this in the hope of stopping the activities of smugglers, which Adam Smith had condemned. For example, Pitt cut the duty on imported tea from 119 per cent to 12½ per cent of its value, which made the profits of smuggling no longer worth the risk. He took up another of Adam Smith's suggestions in 1786, when he made a trade treaty with France. This lowered tariffs on imported French wines, spirits and silks in return for reduced French duties on British hardware and textile goods. But a change of policy was forced on Pitt by the outbreak of war with revolutionary France (1793), which brought the trade treaty to an end. The Government needed every penny it could get to pay for the war. Therefore duties were *increased* and a number of new trading restrictions introduced.

The move towards free trade was resumed by **William Huskisson**, President of the Board of Trade from 1823 to 1827. To help British manufacturers, he lowered tariffs on many imported raw materials, especially those used in textiles and the metal trades. Realising that British industry need no longer fear foreign competition, he reduced the maximum duty on imported manufactures from 50 to 30 per cent. He hoped this would set an example to other countries and perhaps encourage them to lower *their* tariffs against British goods. For similar reasons, Huskisson removed many of the restrictions in the old Navigation Acts, which had been strongly attacked by Adam Smith. British shipping, like British industry, no longer needed parliamentary protection. Huskisson also continued Pitt's policy of offering trade treaties to other countries, in order to achieve reduced tariffs on both sides.

Although Huskisson did a great deal in a short time, the main steps towards free trade were taken in the middle years of the century, by Robert Peel and William Gladstone. As Prime Minister (1841–6) **Peel** set out to encourage British industry and trade through a massive reduction of tariffs. By 1845 he had abolished all remaining export duties and nearly all tariffs on imported raw materials. The maximum duty on foreign manufactures was also reduced, to 10 per cent. Altogether, in the space of five years, Peel entirely abolished the duties on over 600 articles (more than half the existing total when he took office) and greatly reduced the remainder.

Partly as a result of Peel's policy, the volume of trade increased rapidly. The value of British exports rose from £47 million in 1842 to £57 million four years later. Although this brought increased revenue from the duties which remained, the Government still had to find another source of income to balance its tariff losses. Peel therefore reintroduced **income tax** (1842) at the rate of sevenpence (3p) in the

The chief steps to free trade

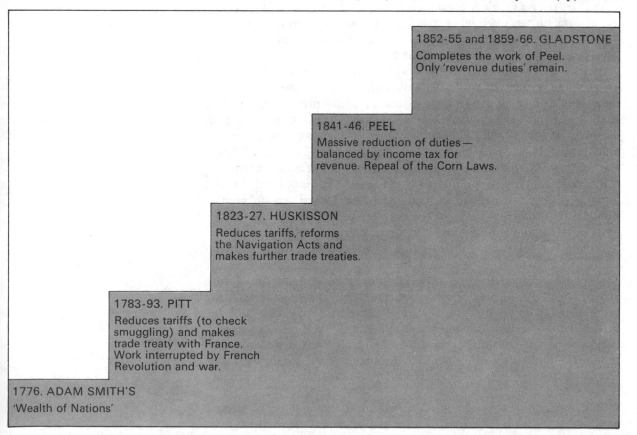

1852-55 and 1859-66. GLADSTONE
Completes the work of Peel.
Only 'revenue duties' remain.

1841-46. PEEL
Massive reduction of duties—
balanced by income tax for
revenue. Repeal of the Corn Laws.

1823-27. HUSKISSON
Reduces tariffs, reforms
the Navigation Acts and
makes further trade treaties.

1783-93. PITT
Reduces tariffs (to check
smuggling) and makes
trade treaty with France.
Work interrupted by French
Revolution and war.

1776. ADAM SMITH'S
'Wealth of Nations'

pound on incomes over £150 a year. It was intended to last for a trial period of three years, but has remained ever since. Nevertheless, income tax has advantages over other forms of taxation. It does not hinder trade, and, unlike most customs duties, it was at that time confined to the well-to-do classes.

The effects of Peel's free trade policy were felt not only by manufacturers and merchants but by the poor. The reduction of duties on everyday articles such as meat, sugar, tea and soap brought down the cost of living. Above all, busy export industries meant regular employment and often higher wages too.

Sir Robert Peel, 1788–1850

The repeal of the Corn Laws

British manufactured goods were normally cheaper than those of other countries. On the other hand home-grown food was often *dearer* than that produced overseas. Therefore landlords and farmers, unlike the rest of the community, *feared* the movement towards free trade. They claimed they would be ruined if cheap foreign food, especially corn, were allowed into the country free of duty. It was for this reason that the Corn Law of 1815 had been passed at the end of the French Wars (see page 112). It had the effect of preventing foreign corn from entering Britain and, as a result, artificially raised the price of bread. So it was a tax on the bulk of the population for the benefit of landlords and farmers alone. From the start, it was hotly opposed by manufacturers, town workers and, not least, agricultural labourers. No matter how prosperous farmers became, the wages they paid their labourers remained the lowest in the land.

In 1828 a new Corn Law replaced the prohibition on foreign corn by a 'sliding scale' of duties. These went down as the home price rose. But this change had little effect on bread prices. By the late 1830s, when a series of bad harvests coincided with a depression in industry, a small loaf weighing less than 1 kilogram could cost as much as a shilling (5p) – almost the entire daily wage of many labourers. In these circumstances there was a greatly increased demand for the repeal (abolition) of all laws restricting the import of foreign corn. To achieve this aim, an **Anti-Corn Law League** was formed in Manchester, early in 1839, by 'representatives from all the great sections of our manufacturing and commercial population'.

There now followed a bitter struggle between the rising industrial middle classes in the towns and the old landowning gentry in the countryside. Supporters of the League claimed that the future prosperity of Britain depended on the needs of manufacturers being given priority over the interests of landowners. They said that because Britain was the leading industrial nation, it was sensible to *concentrate* on manufacturing goods for export. If the Corn Laws were repealed, foreign countries would sell more food to Britain and, as a consequence, they would be able to afford to buy more British manufactures in return.

With financial backing from rich manufacturers, the League ran a nationwide publicity campaign. Cheap postage after 1840 enabled

millions of pamphlets and newspapers to be distributed, and full use was made of the new railways to send speakers on tours round the country. Almost everywhere, they received enthusiastic support. In the space of three months, early in the campaign, 150 meetings were held in London alone. Two of the League's main spokesmen, **Richard Cobden** (1804–65) and **John Bright** (1811–89), carried the campaign into Parliament after being elected to the Commons in 1841 and 1844 respectively. For them, repeal of the Corn Laws meant even more than an expansion of trade and cheaper bread. They considered free trade among nations the best means of securing international peace and friendship. Cobden and Bright were both fine speakers. Before long they gained the support of a large and powerful group of 'free traders' in the Whig Opposition Party.

As Prime Minister, Peel was in a very difficult position. Having set out to achieve free trade in manufactured goods, it seemed reasonable for him to do the same in the case of farm products. But the Conservative Party, which he headed, was dominated by landowners. They would regard any attempt by their leader to repeal the Corn Laws as downright treachery. Nevertheless Peel found the arguments of the League so convincing that they eventually converted him. On one occasion, early in 1845, while Cobden was speaking in the Commons, he screwed up his notes and whispered to one of his colleagues: 'You must answer this, I can't.'

The Irish potato famine: starving peasants at the gate of a workhouse

The Conservatives had been elected to maintain the Corn Laws. Therefore Peel's best plan was to wait until the next general election (1847 at the latest) before making his views public and trying to win over both his party and the voters to free trade in corn. But time ran out for him in the summer of 1845. Exceptionally heavy rain spoilt the English harvest and, worse still, blight destroyed three-quarters of the Irish potato crop. The plants withered and young potatoes turned black and rotten. The peasants of Ireland lived almost entirely on potatoes. Food had to be provided for them immediately, for they were already dying of starvation by the thousand. Faced with **famine in Ireland**, there was no alternative but to import large quantities of foreign corn. In such a situation it seemed senseless to stand by the Corn Laws, but it was realised that if they were suspended now they would probably not be brought back.

By October 1845 Peel had made up his mind. The Corn Laws must be repealed at once. His Cabinet was divided, so he resigned (December). However the Whigs failed to form a government and Peel returned to office. Although a majority of Conservatives opposed Repeal, they were outnumbered in the Commons, largely because almost all the Whigs supported Peel's decision. After a long struggle, Peel convinced most of his Cabinet and got the necessary approval of Parliament in June 1846. The Corn Laws were repealed at last – although a small duty on imports remained. One of the greatest political struggles of the century had ended in defeat for the landowners. Having lost their control of Parliament, they could never again force their will on the rest of the nation.

'Rotten potatoes have done it all', said the Duke of Wellington, 'they put Peel in his damned fright.' But this was not strictly true. Peel's views had already changed before the crisis came. In the end, it proved to be the ruin of his political career. On the very day that Repeal was accepted by Parliament, Peel was defeated in the Commons on a different issue, many Conservatives voting against him. He was forced to resign. But although many of his supporters felt he had betrayed them, the people as a whole admired Peel for his great services to the nation. When he died, four years later, after a riding accident, *The Times* described him as 'the greatest statesman of his time'. He put country before party when he realised that only he could command enough support on both sides of the House to repeal the Corn Laws. Above all, his great ministry of 1841–6 provided the basis for thirty years of unequalled prosperity, founded on a policy of free trade.

The Irish were not so fortunate. At least a million of them died during the Great Famine, which lasted until 1847. In the previous thirty years, the population of Ireland had increased from 6 to 8½ million. Yet because there had been no equivalent increase in food production, the country was unable to withstand the failure of its potato crop. The only immediate solution to the problem was mass emigration – to north-western England and particularly to the USA, where 2 million Irish settled in the next fifteen years. By 1871 the population of Ireland had fallen to 5½ million. Meanwhile, the rest of Britain continued to support a *rising* population by producing an ever-growing surplus of manufactures which could be sold to pay for food imports. The root cause of Ireland's difficulties was the backwardness of *both* her agriculture and her industry.

A task completed

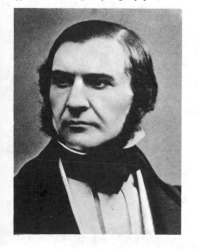

William Ewart Gladstone, 1809–98. After his financial reforms as Chancellor of the Exchequer in the 1850s and 60s, he became Liberal Prime Minister on four separate occasions between 1868 and 1894, when he retired from office at the age of eighty-four

Repeal of the Corn Laws removed the last major obstacle to free trade. Shortly after Peel's death his work was rounded off by one of his greatest admirers – **William Ewart Gladstone**. As Chancellor of the Exchequer (1852–5 and 1859–66) Gladstone's aim was to remove all tariffs except those needed to provide revenue for the government. Like Adam Smith, he came to the conclusion that sufficient revenue could be obtained from duties on a small range of articles in widespread use – for instance, wines and spirits, tobacco, tea, coffee and sugar. By 1860, when only forty-eight such articles continued to be taxed, Britain had become virtually a free trade country.

The move to free trade was achieved without harming Britain's industries because, at the time, there was little effective competition from overseas. Between 1842 and 1870 the annual value of British exports rose from £47 million to almost £200 million. Most of this trade (along with that of many other countries) was carried in British ships, even though the old Navigation Acts were finally abolished in 1849. These laws had long ceased to be necessary, for British merchant shipping dominated most of the world's major trade routes.

Although Britain remained a free trade country until the 1930s (see Chapter 22) few other nations followed suit. France, for example, was prepared to enter into a trade treaty with Britain (1860) but had no intention of allowing completely free trade. Countries such as the

USA and Germany, keen to build up their *own* industries, preferred to keep high tariffs in order to reduce competition from cheap British manufactures.

The rise and decline of British agriculture

In its *immediate* effects upon British farming, repeal of the Corn Laws justified neither the hopes of the free traders nor the fears of landowners. Supporters of the Anti-Corn Law League had argued that large quantities of cheap grain were being kept out of the country. This may have been so at the time of the first Corn Law (1815), but now it proved to be an exaggeration. Nowhere was there a great surplus of corn freely available to Britain – at least, not before the 1870s. For over twenty years after Repeal, wheat prices remained steady at about the same level as in the five years *before* 1846. Nevertheless, since bread was almost the only thing that did not rise in price during the 1850s and 60s, it is fair to say that repeal *did* keep down the cost of food – even if its results were less spectacular than the free traders had promised.

The campaign against the Corn Laws had coincided with a period of growing prosperity for British agriculture. Helped by quicker transport, more farming machinery and the steadily rising demand for food in the towns, many larger farms became, in the words of William Cobbett, 'factories for making corn and meat'. To the delight of the farmers, Repeal did not turn back the tide of prosperity. In fact, the threat of foreign competition led to greater efficiency, so that the period from around 1840 to 1875 is often referred to as the **'Golden Age' of British agriculture**. It was a time of great technical advance and steady profits for farmers. The rising standard of living among nearly all classes meant a greater demand not only for grain crops but also for meat and dairy produce. The output of meat, butter and cheese rose rapidly on enclosed dairy farms of the kind popularised by Robert Bakewell (see page 43).

Meanwhile arable farming was also improved. Underground drains made of tile pipes replaced the old methods of surface drainage, especially on heavy soils. Seed-drills at last came into general use, and steam power was more widely applied, for threshing, ploughing and reaping. There was also a greater application of science to agriculture. Here the chief British pioneer was **Sir John Lawes** (1814–1900). Following important German research into soil chemistry, he tried to discover which chemicals plants took from the soil and tested the nourishing effects of various kinds of manures. In 1843 he established an experimental farm on his family estate at **Rothamsted**, near Harpenden in Hertfordshire. It was like an open-air laboratory, made up of scores of separate plots. At the same time Lawes opened a factory in London to manufacture artificial fertilizers, including 'superphosphate of lime', which he patented. Use of fertilizers became normal farming practice during the 'Golden Age'.

However the threat to British agriculture that had been expected in 1846 was not avoided, it was merely delayed. The prosperous years

Rothamsted Experimental Station in Hertfordshire

came to an abrupt end in the mid 1870s. Five unusually bad summers in a row (1873–7) marked the turning-point, but there were more serious factors than the weather. Up to this time there had been little foreign competition; but countries such as the USA, Canada, Argentina, Australia and New Zealand now entered upon a period of great agricultural expansion. From the 1870s onwards they began to flood European markets with enormous quantities of cheap food.

The first of the 'new lands' to begin exporting on a large scale were the **prairies** of the American Mid-West – taking advantage of mechanisation, particularly combine harvesters, and cheaper long-distance transport. Between 1860 and 1880, the railway network of the USA trebled in size, as trans-continental lines opened up the Mid-West. Meanwhile improved steam navigation brought great reductions in shipping freight charges and made it possible to sell American corn across the Atlantic at well below European prices.

Cost of carrying corn from Chicago to Liverpool

1868	£3.25 a tonne
1882	£1.20 a tonne

By the 1880s, with the construction of the Canadian Pacific Railway, large quantities of Canadian wheat increased the competition from North America.

As foreign competition forced down British wheat prices, farmers pleaded for the reintroduction of a tariff on imports. This was the policy of other European countries, including France and Germany. But in Britain, where the landed gentry had lost much of their political influence, it was not seriously considered. Both major political parties had become firmly committed to free trade. After all, the more food foreign countries sold to Britain, the more they could afford to spend on British manufactures. The majority of voters were now town-dwellers (see pages 196–7). They were more interested in cheap food than the prosperity of farmers. Governments knew that if they protected British agriculture with tariffs they would suffer almost certain defeat at election time.

Falling profits and rents forced many farmers to convert arable land to pasture and take up livestock- and dairy-farming. The total area under wheat fell by nearly 400,000 hectares in the years 1875–85. But this was no answer to foreign competition. Before long, 'new lands' in the southern hemisphere, taking advantage of the invention of refrigeration, began massive exports of meat and dairy produce. The first cargoes of frozen meat (mostly mutton) from **Australia** and **New Zealand** arrived in London in the early 1880s. They were soon followed by chilled beef from **Argentina**, and butter, cheese, poultry and fruit from all parts of the British Empire. Foods that were not frozen were usually canned.

British livestock- and dairy-farming was saved from total collapse by the rising demand for milk and the willingness of some customers to pay more for *fresh* meat. Some specialised branches of agriculture actually expanded in these years – notably market-gardening, in areas near the main centres of population, including Cheshire, the Vale of Evesham and Greater London. In the end it was arable farming that suffered most from foreign competition. With unemployment rising and wages falling, labourers drifted off the land to find work in the towns or emigrate overseas. From 1870 to 1914 the number of workers on the land fell from 1¼ million to well below a million, even though the total population rose by about 40 per cent in the same period. The result was a decline in the traditional life of the countryside, made worse by the tendency for go-ahead young people to leave the villages in order to 'better themselves' in the towns.

Timeline

1776	Adam Smith's *An Inquiry into the Causes of the Wealth of Nations*.
1815	Corn Law.
1828	New Corn Law – 'sliding scale' of duties.
1839	Anti-Corn Law League founded.
1842	Peel's Income Tax.
1843	Rothamsted Experimental Station (Sir John Lawes).
1845–7	Irish Potato Famine.
1846	Repeal of the Corn Laws.
c. 1840–75	'Golden Age' of British agriculture.
c. 1875–1914	Agricultural Depression.

Questions

1. Explain clearly the meaning of each of the following:
   a) tariffs   i) as 'revenue duties'
                ii) for 'protection'
   b) free trade
   c) income tax
   d) trade treaties

2. 'At the next Parliamentary election, you will be entitled to choose between a bread-taxer (one who withholds corn from the people) and a candidate who will untax the poor man's loaf.' (Extract from a pamphlet issued by the Anti-Corn Law League)

   a) Anti-Corn Law League speakers always referred to the Corn Laws as the bread-tax. Why?
   b) How would the policy supported by the League 'untax the poor man's loaf'?
   c) Why did landlords and farmers want to keep the Corn Laws?
   d) How did events in Ireland affect the struggle over the Corn Laws?
   e) What effect did Repeal of the Corn Laws have on bread prices?

3. 'Agriculture . . . is a science which requires a first-rate education . . . the active brains of men and their advancing knowledge of mechanics have given to the scientific farmer . . . almost endless machines.' (William Howitt, *The Rural Life of England*, 1840)

   a) Outline the contribution of John Lawes to 'scientific farming'.
   b) Name some of the 'almost endless machines' that came into general use in this period.
   c) Why did British farming enjoy a 'Golden Age' after 1840?
   d) How did i) cheaper long-distance transport, and ii) the invention of refrigeration, help to end this 'Golden Age'?
   e) Why did Britain stick to her policy of free trade in the face of growing competition from foreign agriculture after 1875?

The Reverend Thomas Malthus (1766–1834). He argued that man's ability to increase population is greater than his ability to produce the necessary additional food supplies (see Question 4)

4. In 1798 a Cambridge University teacher, the Reverend Thomas Malthus, published a book entitled *An Essay on the Principle of Population*. In it he argued that if a country's population went on increasing without a check a point would be reached eventually when it would outstrip available food supplies. The laws of nature would then apply and famines would reduce the population.
   a) How far did events in Ireland in the nineteenth century provide an illustration of Malthus's theory? (For a graph of Ireland's population figures, see page 225).
   b) The population of mainland Britain went on increasing rapidly without any such disasters. How was this possible?

5. Write a paragraph on the contribution of each of the following to Britain's move towards free trade:
   a) William Pitt 'the Younger'   b) William Huskisson
   c) Robert Peel   d) William Ewart Gladstone

15
Prosperity and Progress
Industry in the 'Victorian Age'

Queen Victoria came to the throne in June 1837, at the age of eighteen. For the greater part of her sixty-four-year reign – the longest in British history – her people were the richest and most powerful on earth, with the greatest empire, the strongest navy and, above all, the most advanced industries. Of course, these things were not achieved by the Queen herself. She had little say in the government of the country which was, by now, firmly in the hands of Members of Parliament. Yet Victoria was the *symbol* of British greatness. We speak of this period as the 'Victorian Age', a time of peace, security and seemingly unlimited prosperity.

The Great Exhibition

In 1840, the year in which her image appeared on the world's first postage stamps, Victoria married **Prince Albert** of Saxe-Coburg-Gotha in Germany. At the outset, many people were reluctant to

Queen Victoria and Prince Albert, photographed in 1854

accept a foreigner as the first man of the kingdom, but Albert gradually won their trust and affection. His keen interest in science and the arts soon left its mark on his new country. Today he is best remembered as the chief inspiration behind the Great Exhibition of 1851.

The Society of Arts, of which Albert was President, put on several trade fairs in London in the 1840s. Their success led to the suggestion that a really spectacular trade show should be held – to display the latest industrial, scientific and artistic achievements from all over the world. A Royal Commission was appointed to plan it, under the leadership of Prince Albert. He firmly believed that such an exhibition would not only assist overseas trade (by displaying the fruits of Britain's advanced industries) but also help peace and understanding between nations. That the Victorians should want to display their achievements alongside the pick of those from abroad was an indication of their great confidence in the superiority of British skill and workmanship. It was the same attitude that had brought about free trade – the belief that Britain need fear no competition. Indeed some of the strongest support for the Great Exhibition came from 'free traders' such as Gladstone and Cobden.

Throughout 1850 and the early months of 1851, preparations went ahead for what was officially entitled **The Great Exhibition of the Works of Industry of All Nations**. A spacious site was chosen by Prince Albert on the south side of Hyde Park and a competition held to choose a design for the buildings. However none of the 245 entries proved acceptable. It was only at the last minute that **Joseph Paxton**, the Duke of Devonshire's head gardener, came to the rescue of the organisers with a revolutionary design in glass and iron. **The Crystal Palace**, as it was called, looked like a huge greenhouse, about 500 metres long and high enough to house several tall elm trees beneath its roof. Two thousand workmen laboured through the winter of 1850–1 to finish it on time.

There were 7,381 exhibitors from the British Isles and 6,556 from other countries. Needless to say, the machinery and manufacturing sections were dominated by Britain. Railway locomotives, boats, bridges, textiles and machine tools showed the progress of steam power and the supremacy of iron. Other manufactures included telescopes, cameras, barometers, an electric telegraph and surgical instruments. The Exhibition also showed the taste and fashion of the age: furniture that was well made but lacking in simplicity, hardware, china, glass, gold- and silverware which was excellent in craftsmanship but often over-ornamental in design.

'God bless my dear country which has shown itself so great today.' So wrote Queen Victoria in her diary on 1 May 1851, the day of the official opening of the Exhibition. In the next five and a half months, before it closed on 11 October, over 6 million visitors came to the Crystal Palace – an average daily attendance of more than 43,000. In the end a clear profit of £186,437 was made – a great fortune in those days. The money was well used. A large plot of land was purchased in South Kensington, where today the Victoria and

Albert Museum, the Science Museum, the Royal Colleges of Art and Music, the Royal Albert Hall and many other fine buildings stand – a monument to the success of the Exhibition and the foresight of Prince Albert. The Crystal Palace was re-erected at Sydenham in South London, where it was accidentally destroyed by fire in November 1936.

The Crystal Palace – home of the Great Exhibition of 1851

The new steel

The Great Exhibition marked the height of the Iron Age. The framework of the Crystal Palace was made of iron, as were many of the outstanding exhibits in it. But within a few years the domination of iron was ended by the discovery of cheap methods of mass producing steel.

Henry Bessemer (1813–98), the pioneer in the making of cheap steel, was a professional inventor. Among his earlier achievements were a perforated stamp which could not be re-used and a new method of making plate glass. During the Crimean War against Russia (1854–6) he was employed in trying to find a way of making better cannon. Cast iron, being brittle, was liable to shatter under the force of an explosion. Steel, which is hard yet not brittle, seemed the obvious answer, but methods of making it were too slow and expensive. There was still no satisfactory alternative to Benjamin Huntsman's century-old 'crucible casting process' (see page 70). After many difficult and costly experiments, however, Bessemer found a quick and simple method of converting large quantities of pig iron *directly* into steel (1856).

Molten pig iron, straight from the blast-furnace, was poured into a **converter** – a large vessel like a concrete-mixer, which could be tilted for filling and emptying. A blast of air was then blown through holes in the base of the converter. After only twenty minutes the impurities in the liquid iron had either been expelled in the form of burning gases or turned into slag. Finally, small quantities of carbon and manganese were added, to produce **mild steel**. 'While it is much harder and is not worn or indented so easily as soft iron,' wrote Bessemer, 'at the same time it is not so brittle or hard to work as ordinary cast steel.' Moreover, the liquid steel could be cast immediately into girders, rails or whatever shape was required, without having to be forged like bar iron.

After further experiments, Bessemer set up his own works in Sheffield (1859) and was soon producing steel at around £5 a tonne (compared with normal prices in the region of £50). Orders flooded in for steel rails and girders, tools, steel wire ropes and many other articles. In the early 1870s he was able to sell his works for twenty times its original value. By then he had also received over £1 million from other firms in patent rights.

Meanwhile an alternative method of making cheap mild steel had

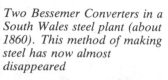

Two Bessemer Converters in a South Wales steel plant (about 1860). This method of making steel has now almost disappeared

been developed. A big disadvantage of the open-topped converter was that it wasted a lot of heat and some of the iron was carried away with the blast. To remedy this **William Siemens**, a German who settled in England, introduced the **open-hearth process** (1866) which owed much to the work of two Frenchmen, the brothers Pierre and Emile Martin. His converting vessel was a large, shallow bath or 'open hearth', which held up to 300 tonnes of pig iron and scrap metal. A mixture of coal-gas and air was burned over it to melt the iron and expel the impurities. The key to its success was the very high temperature of the hearth (about 1,650 °C). This was partly achieved by using the hot exhaust gases to pre-heat the incoming coal-gas and air.

The open-hearth process took longer than the Bessemer converter, but it allowed greater control over the quality of the steel. Its chief advantage was that its high temperature enabled large quantities of *scrap iron* to be converted directly into mild steel. In 1867 Siemens set up his own works at Landore, near Swansea. The business grew steadily in importance, and many other companies took up his process, until, by the end of the century, the quantity of steel produced by open-hearth methods exceeded that from the Bessemer converter.

At first both new processes had a serious drawback. They could only be used with iron containing very little phosphorus, because neither could get rid of it. Since many types of British iron ore were phosphoric, additional supplies had to be imported from Spain and Sweden. But this defect was overcome by **Sidney Gilchrist Thomas** (1850–85), clerk in a London magistrates' court, assisted by his cousin, Percy Gilchrist, who was a chemist. Working in a tiny laboratory in his backyard, Gilchrist Thomas had the idea of lining a Bessemer converter with limestone. This absorbed the phosphorus from the pig iron and deposited it in the slag as calcium phosphate (which proved a valuable fertilizer). The same principle could be applied to the open-hearth process.

Gilchrist Thomas announced his discovery in 1878, but little notice was taken of it. In the following year he gave a successful demonstration in Middlesbrough, using highly phosphoric ore from the nearby Cleveland iron ore field. He was at once internationally famous. Countries such as Germany and the USA had enormous fields of phosphoric ore which could now be exploited. They gained much more than Britain did from the new process. Unhappily, Gilchrist Thomas did not live to fully enjoy his success. His health was ruined by overwork and he died in 1885 at the age of thirty-four.

Mild steel was now so cheap and plentiful that it rapidly replaced iron in structural engineering. Railway companies were the first to buy it in large quantities, because steel rails could safely carry heavier locomotives. Bridges could be made stronger and therefore larger, like the great Forth Bridge (1886). Steel plates, lighter yet stronger than wrought iron ones, made possible the construction of larger ships. In building, steel girders were used for reinforcing concrete. The list does not stop there; cheap steel also led to immediate improvements in guns, boilers and all kinds of machinery.

The Forth railway bridge (1886), made of steel. It greatly improved communications between Edinburgh and the north of Scotland

'The Workshop of the World'

The Great Exhibition demonstrated to the world the long lead held by British manufacturers over all rivals. Yet it came only at the *beginning* of a period of even greater prosperity for the country's industries, in the third quarter of the nineteenth century. From 1850 to 1872, the annual value of Britain's exports increased by more than three and a half times, from £71 million to £256 million. It was with good reason that Britain became known as 'the Workshop of the World' in these years.

The most important development since the Industrial Revolution was the growth of **mechanical engineering** as a separate, highly-skilled industry. *Machine tools* (machines which are themselves tools) were replacing the old hand-tool methods of engineering, which depended upon the accuracy of the human eye. For the first time standardised parts could be made and large numbers of identical articles could be mass produced.

At the end of the eighteenth century, while Boulton and Watt were still dependent upon hand tools, two of the earliest 'master engineers', **Joseph Bramah** and **Henry Maudslay**, were laying the foundations for the mechanical engineering industry. Bramah (1748–1814) made machine tools for the manufacture of his 'unpickable locks', and his former pupil Maudslay (1771–1831) perfected a screw-cutting lathe in 1800. Screws had previously been made with a crude hand tool called a burr, which often broke the metal and rarely produced two screws that were alike. Maudslay's lathe could cut any number of screw-threads of fixed proportions. He also invented a machine which measured up to a thousandth of an inch (0.025 of a millimetre), making possible finer work on the lathe. These and many other machine tools were coming into common use at the beginning of the Victorian Age, resulting in far greater accuracy throughout British industry.

Around 1840, when Henry Bessemer was ordering machinery for one of his early inventions, he gave out the work, 'some in Manchester, some in Glasgow, some in Liverpool and some in London'. When he assembled the parts they fitted and worked. This would have been impossible at the beginning of the century. It was a clear illustration of the progress of mechanical engineering; progress which was reflected in many exhibits at the Crystal Palace (1851).

Two of the leading firms in the growth of precision engineering were those of James Nasmyth and Joseph Whitworth. Both were ex-pupils of Maudslay, and both established their workshops in Manchester in the 1830s. **James Nasmyth** we have already encountered as the inventor of the steam hammer (see page 69). He was also well known for his power-driven tools, including planing machines. **Joseph Whitworth** (1803–87) had no fewer than twenty-three exhibits in the Great Exhibition, which together earned him a worldwide reputation. They included lathes, accurate measuring devices and self-acting machines for planing, drilling, slotting and shaping. Whitworth is most famous for his **classification of screw-threads** (1843). After examining sample screws from many workshops, he proposed that the angle between the sides of the threads should be 55 degrees and the number of threads to the inch should be standardised for various diameters. By the 1860s, these 'Whitworth gauges' were in general use.

Whitworth's tools mostly originated in the Iron Age, but it was in the new Steel Age, following Bessemer's discovery, that they came into general use. By the 1870s, British engineers were capable of dealing with almost any problem industry could set them.

Meanwhile, the basic industries were still coal, iron and textiles – each of which roughly doubled its total production in the period 1850 to 1875. **Coal** continued to be the foundation of all industrial development, providing the fuel to drive the machines.

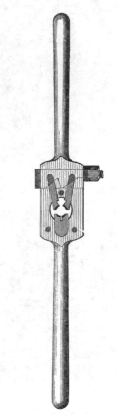

This apparatus, invented by Joseph Whitworth, was used to cut screw-threads to a standard gauge

British coal production

1846	45 million tonnes
1870	112 million tonnes
1891	188 million tonnes

Despite the enormous increase in output, coal-mining remained almost entirely a hand industry. The bulk of the work was done by pick and shovel, and pit ponies and manual labour were still generally used for moving the coal. As late as 1900, well under 5 per cent of British coal was cut by machinery. However more powerful steam-engines were introduced for draining mines and operating the winding gear, and pits were sunk to greater depths than ever before. When all the needs of industry had been satisfied, Britain still managed to

A coal-mine in South Staffordshire in the nineteenth century. Notice the pillars of uncut coal which support the ceiling

export thousands of tonnes of coal, to north-western Europe and the Mediterranean countries.

Unlike the coal industry, **textiles** were completely mechanised by the second half of the nineteenth century. Most technical developments consisted of improvements to existing machines rather than wholly new inventions. For example, the spinning-mule was now fully automatic. Cotton goods were still Britain's major export. Almost nine-tenths of the total output was sold overseas. In 1880 this amounted to a third of *all* exports. Britain was the world's clothing shop as well as its workshop. But as the output of finished goods increased so did imports of raw cotton. This dependence on foreign raw material proved a serious handicap in the early 1860s, when the American Civil War interrupted supplies and caused widespread unemployment in Lancashire. At one time, almost half the population of Preston was receiving Poor Relief.

The **heavy industries** – mainly iron, steel and hardware – were expanding even faster than textiles. For instance, pig iron output increased threefold in the period 1850–75. An increasing proportion of it was converted into steel after the introduction of the new processes of Bessemer, Siemens and Gilchrist Thomas.

British output of steel (approximate figures)

1850	40,000 tonnes
1870	240,000 tonnes
1880	1,250,000 tonnes

The West Midlands, especially South Staffordshire, was still the chief iron manufacturing area. However, in the year of the Great Exhibition (1851) the greatest English iron ore field was discovered, in the Cleveland district of North Yorkshire. As a result, Middlesbrough grew from a village to a town of 40,000 people within twenty years.

The chill wind of competition

In 1870 the total volume of British foreign trade was greater than that of France, Germany and Italy combined. But this unchallenged supremacy could not last long once countries such as the USA and Germany began to exploit their greater resources more fully. In the last quarter of the nineteenth century, British manufactured goods began to be seriously rivalled in the markets of the world for the first time since the Industrial Revolution.

'The superiority of the United States to England is ultimately as certain as the next eclipse.' So said *The Economist* newspaper in 1851. It was a warning that few people took seriously then, in the

This 'Punch' cartoon of 1896 highlights the growth of trading competition from Germany

CAUGHT NAPPING!

'THERE WAS AN OLD LADY AS I'VE HEARD TELL, | SHE WENT TO MARKET ON A MARKET DAY | BY CAME A PEDLAR—GERMAN—AND STOU
SHE WENT TO MARKET HER GOODS FOR TO SELL, | AND SHE FELL ASLEEP ON THE WORLD'S HIGHWAY. | AND HE CUT HER PETTICOATS ALL ROUN

triumphant year of the Great Exhibition, but it proved correct. After the American Civil War (1861–5) the **United States** entered upon a period of remarkably rapid industrial growth. While railways opened up the interior and linked the expanding manufacturing towns in the eastern states, vast numbers of settlers from Europe swelled the labour force. Similarly, the new **German Empire**, established in 1871 out of many smaller states, increased its industrial production at an astonishing rate. While Britain maintained a policy of free trade (see Chapter 14), the USA, Germany and other European rivals protected their own developing industries from foreign competition by means of high tariffs.

A reliable guide to a country's industrial capacity in this period was its production figures for coal and steel and the size of its population. Both Germany and the USA exceeded the British output of steel by the 1890s. At about the same time the USA overtook Britain in coal production too – Germany somewhat later. There was little that Britain could do about it, since both her main rivals had far greater supplies of coal and iron ore. In addition, their populations were larger and growing at a faster rate:

Growth of population (in millions)

	United Kingdom	Germany	United States
1871	32	41	38
1911	45	66	93

Britain's loss of industrial supremacy should not be exaggerated. The basic industries were still expanding and the overall standard of living was rising. Despite tariffs, large quantities of British goods continued to sell in the USA and Europe, and there was a massive increase in sales to the colonies and dominions. Britain still dominated the world's trade routes long after her industrial production had been surpassed. In 1885 no less than a third of all sea-going ships were registered in Britain. Moreover the country's shipyards had no serious rival. In the early years of the twentieth century the British were building almost two-thirds of the world's shipping tonnage.

Electric power

For a hundred years there was no real alternative to the steam piston-engine in providing power to drive machines. However, by the 1880s electric power stations began to appear. At about the same time the internal combustion engine was introduced from Germany, providing a relatively cheap power unit for the use of craftsmen in small workshops. (The internal combustion engine is dealt with in Chapter 21, since its greatest impact was on transport.)

These new forms of power, together with new materials such as rubber, petroleum, aluminium and celluloid, gradually changed the whole basis of industry. Indeed, the period from about 1880 to the 1930s is often referred to as the 'Second Industrial Revolution'. However, great as these changes were, they were not 'revolutionary' like those of the late eighteenth and early nineteenth centuries, which led to a new kind of society. The industrial advances of the last hundred years have resulted in the *fuller* development of a way of life already well established.

Scientists of many nations contributed to the understanding and use of electricity. However it was an Englishman, **Michael Faraday**, who first found a mechanical method of producing a continuous flow of electric current. In 1831 he showed that an electric current was produced when a coil was rotated between the poles of a horseshoe magnet. His principle of *electro-magnetic induction* was the starting-point for both the dynamo and the electric motor. A dynamo turns 'mechanical power' (needed to rotate the coil) into electric current. An electric motor (based on the same principle in reverse) converts the current back into mechanical energy, which can be used to drive a machine.

Many problems had to be overcome before the first dynamos were manufactured and sold (1867). There was a further timelag before electric power stations were built. The earliest ones (in the 1880s) began by providing current for **electric lighting** – another new invention, made by **Joseph Swan** in England (1878) and **Thomas Edison** in America (1879). They later joined forces to produce 'Ediswan' bulbs. Meanwhile electricity gradually replaced gas in the lighting of streets, public buildings and, finally, private houses.

Michael Faraday, 1791–1867

Ordinary steam piston-engines drove the dynamos in the first power stations. But they could not achieve a sufficiently high speed of rotation to be really efficient generators of electricity. The need for a faster-running steam-engine led to the invention of the **steam turbine** in 1884 by **Charles Parsons** (1854–1931), an engineer from Newcastle. It worked on the same principle as a windmill. A continuous blast of high-pressure steam was forced along a tube containing a *rotor*, made up of vanes (blades) mounted on a central shaft. This turned at great speed. By replacing the back and forward motion of a piston with the *spinning* motion of the turbine, Parsons made it possible to drive a dynamo much faster.

Electric-powered factories were cleaner and simpler. No shafts or belts were needed for driving the machines, which could be switched on or off individually. Yet British manufacturers were much slower in changing to electric power than most of their foreign rivals. By the outbreak of the First World War (1914) only a few areas, including Tyneside and Manchester, had sufficiently large generating stations to supply power as cheaply as in Germany or the USA. The newer industries made most use of electricity. Since the current was carried by means of wires, new factories could be built in areas where there was no local coal supply. It was not even necessary for the power station itself to be on a coalfield if **hydro-electric power** (h.e.p.) was generated. This was done by using falling water instead of steam-engines to drive the dynamos. After 1900, hydro-electric power stations began to appear in areas such as the Scottish Highlands, where coal was difficult to obtain yet there was no shortage of fast-flowing streams.

As the demand for electricity increased, in both industry and the home, Parliament decided to create a **National Grid** or network

Sir Charles Parsons's steam turbine, with part of the casing removed to show the 'rotor'

(1926) to carry the current all over Britain. In the towns, cables were buried below the streets, while tall steel pylons carried wires across the countryside, to avoid unnecessary interference with agriculture. The output from the power stations now went into a common pool. Consequently an area with a specially heavy demand could draw immediately on electricity produced elsewhere. The National Grid led to the development of industry in south-east England, around London, and other regions away from the congested coalfields (see page 268). This in turn brought a general drift of population from North to South in the twentieth century.

Timeline

1800	Henry Maudslay's screw-cutting lathe.
1831	Faraday demonstrates electro-magnetic induction.
1837–1901	Reign of Queen Victoria.
1843	Joseph Whitworth's standard system of screw-threads.
1851	The Great Exhibition.
1856	Henry Bessemer's Converter.
1866	William Siemens's Open-Hearth Process.
1878	The Gilchrist Thomas Process.
1878–9	Electric light bulb (Joseph Swan and Thomas Edison).
1884	Sir Charles Parsons's steam turbine.
1926	The National Grid.

Questions

1. '. . . a living picture of the point of development at which mankind has arrived, and a new starting-point from which all nations will be able to direct their future exertions.' (Prince Albert on the Great Exhibition)

'God bless my dear country which has shown itself so great today.' (Queen Victoria, on the opening day of the Great Exhibition)

a) How far do Queen Victoria and her husband appear to have had differing views of the significance of the Exhibition?
b) What part did Prince Albert play in the 1851 Exhibition?
c) How did the Duke of Devonshire's head gardener come to the rescue of the organisers?
d) Why were 'free traders' strong supporters of the Exhibition?
e) How was the profit made from the Exhibition used?

2. '. . . as the result of thirty minutes' blowing, wholly unaccompanied by skilled labour or the employment of fuel . . . we had as much metal as could be produced by two puddlers and their two assistants, working arduously for hours with an expenditure of much fuel.' (Sir Henry Bessemer, in his *Autobiography*)

a) What was the 'blowing' to which Bessemer referred?
b) What work did 'puddlers' do and what kind of metal did they produce?
c) Why did Bessemer's invention bring down the price of steel?
d) Bessemer's invention only worked properly with non-phosphoric pig iron. Who overcame this drawback, when and how?
e) What alternative method of producing mild steel was introduced ten years after Bessemer's invention? What were its advantages?

3. Look at the cartoon on page 170.
a) In what ways was Germany's industrial capacity greater than that of Britain?
b) What other nationality might the pedlar have been?
c) Which discovery, demonstrated in Middlesbrough in 1879, helped Germany and other trading rivals more than Britain?
d) Name *one* industry in which Britain was still unrivalled at this time.

4. Outline the contribution of Michael Faraday, Joseph Swan and Charles Parsons to the understanding and uses of electricity. How did electric power a) change factories and b) affect the geographical location of industry in Britain?

5. Write a paragraph on each of the following:
a) Henry Maudslay
b) Joseph Whitworth
c) the Lancashire 'cotton famine' (1860s)
d) a 'Second Industrial Revolution'

16

The Fight Against Disease
Public Health and Medical Science

In Britain in recent years the death of a child or of an adult in the prime of life has become sufficiently rare to be considered a tragic misfortune. This could not be said of any earlier period in the country's history. It is estimated that in the early eighteenth century almost half the children born died before reaching the age of five. On average, a family of eight would have had a death in the house once every five years. More than a hundred years later, despite advances in medicine, people still lived in the shadow of the graveyard. In some industrial towns in the early Victorian Age the death-rate was actually higher than it had been anywhere a century before.

Most of the major improvements in the health of the nation belong to the last hundred years or so. In that time, infectious diseases such as typhoid and typhus, tuberculosis, cholera and diphtheria – which together claimed hundreds of thousands of victims every year – have been almost eliminated as a cause of death. The hazards of childbirth and infancy have also been largely conquered, so that many parents now regard the motor car as the greatest threat to the safety of their children. Broadly speaking, progress has been made in two directions – the practice of medicine and the organisation of public health facilities.

The world of Edward Jenner

In the eighteenth century most medical practice was a combination of guesswork and superstition. *Physicians* (qualified doctors with university training) numbered only a few hundred in the whole kingdom. They practised almost entirely among the wealthy classes, who alone could afford their fees. The poor person's doctor was usually the *apothecary* (pharmacist) who dressed wounds, set broken bones and performed many other medical duties in addition to his main work of

Interior of a ward in Guy's Hospital for incurables, London

providing drugs. Routine operations were carried out by the *barber-surgeon*, who pulled teeth and let blood (a popular remedy in those days) as well as cutting hair, shaving chins and trimming wigs. Hospitals were few in number and mostly lacking in sanitation. Nevertheless, more than 150 hospitals and dispensaries were founded between 1700 and 1825, largely through private charity, to provide the poor with free medical attention. Many had their own medical schools, which helped to raise both the quality and quantity of trained doctors and surgeons.

At this time many poor people suffered from *malnutrition* (not enough of the right kind of food). Knowledge of vitamins and the part they play in a healthy diet belongs to the twentieth century, but many earlier discoveries were made simply by careful observation. In the eighteenth century two of the commonest 'deficiency' diseases were *rickets* and *scurvy*. Rickets is found in young children. Because of a shortage of what we now call 'vitamin D' their bones fail to harden, with the result that they suffer deformities of the spine or limbs. Farming improvements made sources of vitamin D – milk, butter, eggs and cheese – more plentiful, and so helped to reduce the danger of rickets. Nevertheless it was still very common in the nineteenth century.

Meanwhile, scurvy – a horrible disease in which blood escapes from the veins and causes swellings all over the body – was almost eliminated by 1800. It results from a lack of 'vitamin C', found in fresh fruit and vegetables, which explains why it was common among seamen on long voyages. In the mid eighteenth century it was suggested that the seaman's restricted diet of salted meat and biscuits might be the vital clue to the cause of scurvy, and Captain James Cook provided clear proof of this on his long voyage of 1772–5. He took every opportunity to land and collect fresh fruit and vegetables, and consequently lost only one of his crew of 118. In 1791 the Admiralty began to issue lemon or lime juice to all warships.

However by far the most important medical advance of the eighteenth century was achieved by **Edward Jenner** (1749–1823), the son of a Gloucestershire vicar. It was he who introduced the first satisfactory method of preventing **smallpox** – a highly infectious and often deadly disease which leaves hundreds of pits or 'pock marks' on the skin. In the eighteenth century it was at least as common as chicken-pox is today. Roughly one person in ten died of it, more than half of them in childhood, and many of the survivors were disfigured and made lame, deaf or blind. Eastern countries had long practised *inoculation* – an injection of a mild form of the disease in the hope of making the patient immune to further infection. This was introduced into Britain in the early eighteenth century, with some success, although a small proportion of patients died from it. But inoculation also helped the disease to spread, for the patient could pass on smallpox in its full strength.

As a youth, Jenner overheard a milkmaid saying she would not get smallpox because she had suffered from **cowpox**, a mild disease common among dairy-maids. This was believed by many country folk, but

Portrait medals of Edward Jenner, in honour of his discovery of vaccination

doctors dismissed the idea when they found cases of smallpox among those who had previously caught cowpox. Nevertheless, after finishing his studies in London and becoming a doctor in his home county, Jenner decided to investigate the effects of cowpox. He found that those who had suffered from it *rarely* got smallpox and, even if they did, they only had a *mild* attack. After many years of careful observation, he put his theory to the test. His most celebrated experiment, although it was only one of many, occurred in 1796, when he transferred matter from a cowpox sore on a dairy-maid's hand to the arm of an eight-year-old boy, James Phipps. Six weeks later, when young James was injected with discharge from a smallpox sore, there was a negative reaction.

In 1798 Jenner finally published details of his experiments, together with his conclusion that a *vaccine** of cowpox provided immunity against smallpox. Within two years Jenner's writings had been translated into several languages and circulated round the world. But although the practice of **vaccination** was soon established, Jenner had to fight much ignorance and jealousy among other physicians. One even suggested that the human body would gradually take on the features of a cow if vaccination became general practice. Nevertheless, Jenner's great service to mankind was widely recognised. Parliament granted him a total of £30,000 for his work. Soon after his death inoculation became illegal (1840) after which free vaccination was made available to all who could not afford it. By about 1880 smallpox had been almost wiped out in Britain and Jenner's methods were being used to prevent other diseases.

Cholera and Edwin Chadwick

In 1831 an epidemic of **cholera** broke out in Britain for the first time. Spreading from Asia, it began in the port of Sunderland and killed many thousands of people all over the country. Cholera is swift and deadly in its effect. Violent pains in the stomach are usually followed by diarrhoea, sickness and death. People were panic-stricken, especially as doctors could find no answer to the disease. However, one thing was clear. It struck hardest in poor, overcrowded and insanitary areas, particularly the working-class slums of the towns. It was in these districts that other epidemic diseases such as typhoid and typhus claimed most victims. Yet despite the obvious connection between dirt and disease little had been done to provide pure water supplies and effective sewerage and drainage facilities, which experience showed were the best safeguards against infection.

This neglect resulted partly from lack of scientific knowledge and ignorance of town planning. But a more important reason was simply that public health was no-one's special responsibility. Local authorities had little power, and Parliament was reluctant to interfere with the freedom of property-owners. However the sensational nature of cholera at last began to scare governments into action. Following a

*The word comes from the Latin *vacca*, a cow.

further outbreak in 1837, detailed investigations were made into public health facilities and living conditions. The most revealing of these studies was a nationwide survey compiled by **Edwin Chadwick**, Secretary of the Poor Law Commission.

Chadwick's *Report on the Sanitary Condition of the Labouring Population (1842)* revealed a grim state of affairs – hundreds of thousands of families living in waterlogged cellars; extreme overcrowding in damp, unventilated houses; unpaved streets full of refuse, and an almost total lack of proper drainage and sewage disposal. Fresh running water – the first essential for hygienic living – was found only in the houses of the wealthy. The poor had to fetch it from pumps, and a regular flow could not be relied on. In many towns the water was only turned on for a few minutes a day. Under these conditions, it is not surprising that Chadwick found 'the minor comforts of cleanliness . . . foregone, to avoid the greater discomforts of having to fetch the water'. In London, the Thames was used for both drinking-water *and* sewage disposal. So great was the stench from the river that the windows of the House of Commons had to be closed during debates.

'Disease', said Chadwick, 'is always found in connection with damp and filth, and close and overcrowded dwellings.' Consequently the *death-rate* (the number of people dying in a year per 1,000 population) was higher among the working classes than the well-to-do, and higher in the town than in the country. Chadwick's Report gave a striking illustration of these differences:

Average age at death (1840)

	labourers	gentry
Rutland (an agricultural area)	38	52
Manchester (an industrial town)	17	38

Such variations in life expectancy had existed for centuries – although in a less exaggerated form. But they were especially alarming in this period because the extent of Britain's disease-ridden slums was increasing year by year. Indeed, the overall death-rate rose slightly in the thirty years following Chadwick's survey (see graph opposite).

In these circumstances it is perhaps surprising that the total **UK population** doubled during the reign of Queen Victoria (1837–1901). The reason was the consistently high *birth-rate* (the number of births a year per 1,000 people). Births greatly outnumbered deaths throughout the nineteenth century, so the population continued to grow rapidly. Nearly all the increase was concentrated in the towns. When Victoria came to the throne about half her people were town-dwellers, but the proportion had increased to three-quarters by the time of her death.

Public health, housing and local government reform

No matter how great the advances in medical knowledge, there could be no real improvement in the nation's health until attention was paid

Sir Edwin Chadwick, 1800–90. He produced figures to show that the yearly death-rate from typhus fever alone was double the number of casualties suffered by the allied armies at the Battle of Waterloo (1815)

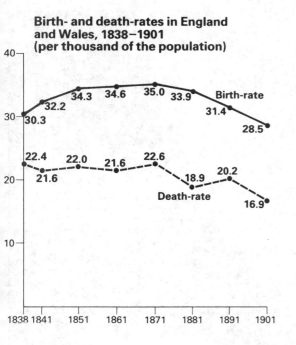

Birth- and death-rates in England and Wales, 1838–1901 (per thousand of the population)

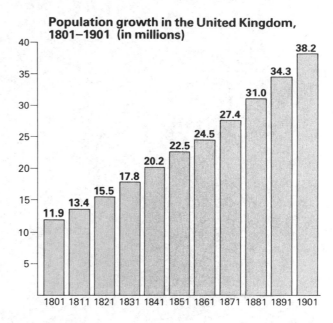

Population growth in the United Kingdom, 1801–1901 (in millions)

to the *environment* (surroundings) in which people lived. An important reason for the lack of public health facilities was the absence of effective **local government**. There were about 250 'chartered boroughs' in England and Wales, but most had been granted their status long before the Industrial Revolution and very few were in the expanding manufacturing areas. It was not until 1835 that a **Municipal Corporations Act** provided for the creation of town councils, elected every three years by all male ratepayers. At this time places such as Manchester, Birmingham and Sheffield still depended on JPs (Justices of the Peace) for any kind of local government.

As the newer towns established elected corporations under the 1835 Act, some began to construct proper sewerage and water systems and to pave and cleanse the streets. But in most towns progress was hindered by the powerful opposition of property-owners. They feared that sanitary regulations would involve them in heavy expenses, and objected to the necessary increases in the rates. Chadwick and his fellow reformers wanted *Parliament* to take responsibility for improving public health. But this was easier said than done. The idea that the state should intervene to safeguard the welfare of its citizens was not generally accepted until the twentieth century. Nevertheless Chadwick argued that parliamentary action was in the national interest. 'The annual loss of life from filth', he said, 'is greater than the loss from death or wounds in any wars in which the country has been engaged in modern times.'

Chadwick and cholera eventually prompted the government to take some action. The first **Public Health Act (1848)** set up a Board of Health in London, with Chadwick and Lord Ashley among its members. It had the power to create *local* boards of health around the country, to control necessary services such as cleansing, paving

Benjamin Disraeli, Earl of Beaconsfield (1804–81). His talents as a writer and parliamentary debater helped him to overcome the prejudice against Jews and the disadvantage of never having attended a university. Disraeli became leader of the Conservative Party in 1868, and his reforming Ministry of 1874–80 took positive steps to improve living and working conditions for the mass of the population

Opposite: *Street scene in a Newcastle slum (1882)*

and draining the streets. But nothing was compulsory. A district need not have a health board unless its death-rate was exceptionally high. When the national Board of Health was disbanded, six years later, only a sixth of the population was served by local boards. In many other areas there had been strong opposition to parliamentary interference – an attitude summed up by *The Times*, which called the 1848 Act 'a reckless invasion of property and liberty'.

However the Act created opportunities for local action, and where this was taken epidemic disease was reduced. In London, **John Simon**, a young surgeon, was made the first Medical Officer of Health (1848). He set out to provide a pure, filtered water supply and an efficient sewerage system, and began medical inspection of the houses of the poorest people. Meanwhile Chadwick took a hand himself, experimenting with glazed earthenware pipes for making sewers. He found them a great improvement on the brick-lined tunnels then in use. Pipes prevented blockages, and they were soon regarded as essential for sanitary engineering.

Not until the Conservative ministry of 1874–80, led by **Benjamin Disraeli**, did the state make itself responsible for really large-scale improvements. 'Health is the first essential' was Disraeli's motto, and his Home Secretary, Richard Cross, got a very important **Public Health Act (1875)** through Parliament. It set up a nationwide system of sanitary authorities, with responsibility for sewerage, drainage, street cleansing and water supply. Minimum standards of sanitation were to be observed in building new houses, and medical officers of health and sanitary inspectors were to be appointed in every locality.

By the end of the century British towns were much healthier, although still far below present day standards. The average expectation of life increased by ten years in the period 1850–1900, by which time the public health problem had become largely a **housing problem**. Overcrowding was the root of the trouble. The enormous increase in population meant that the demand for houses was far greater than the supply. Whenever things are scarce they become more expensive and people with the lowest incomes have to go without. Housing is no exception. Even the cheapest houses were let at rents which lower-paid workers could not afford. Millions of families rented single rooms or were forced to *share* a room with others. In the mid nineteenth century, it was common to find four or five families living in one room.

Not until 1868 was any attempt made to give town councils power to deal with housing. Even then very little was achieved, for the authorities were, as always, reluctant to interfere with private property. However in 1875 Disraeli's Government passed an **Artisans' Dwellings Act** which permitted councils to take over and clear whole slum districts. Although it was not compulsory, prompt action was taken in some areas. Nearly 30,000 people were rehoused in London in the next thirty years. In Birmingham, under its reforming mayor, **Joseph Chamberlain** (1836–1914), over 16 hectares of slum land were cleared to make way for new houses and a shopping centre (Corporation Street). Between 1873 and 1876 Birmingham was, in Chamberlain's words, 'parked, paved, assized, marketed, gas and watered and *im-proved*'.

Unfortunately many councils that were willing to pull down slums were not prepared to provide low-cost houses to replace them. Private builders redeveloped the cleared sites and let their houses to higher-paid workers – the rents the former slum-dwellers could afford were insufficient to meet even the costs of building. Local authorities were not urged to build houses themselves until 1890. Even then, little was done until after the First World War (1914–18), when the Treasury began to give grants for council housing schemes (see page 284). It was easy to remove slums but quite another matter to replace them with better homes at rents within the reach of the lowest-paid.

In step with these developments it was necessary to reshape the system of local government. No reform could be effective without proper local authorities to carry out the day-to-day administration. Borough councils had been established in many industrial towns since the 1835 Act, and Birmingham under Joseph Chamberlain showed how effective the best of them could be. But progress was much slower in the countryside. As late as the 1880s most people in villages and small towns had no say in the running of their locality. A Local Government Act (1888) remedied this by setting up elected **County Councils**. At the same time, some sixty large towns were made separate County Boroughs, with the same powers as the county councils. London became a separate county. A further Act of 1894 established nearly 7,000 Parish Councils and also a system of Urban and Rural District Councils, all based on direct election by the inhabitants.

The foundations of modern surgery

In the early nineteenth century surgical operations were performed without proper anaesthetics. Drugs were used – including Indian hemp and opium, rum and other kinds of 'hard liquor' – but they failed to produce complete unconsciousness. In 1800 Humphrey Davy found he could make himself unconscious by inhaling *laughing gas* (nitrous oxide vapour). Some twenty years later, his pupil, Michael Faraday, showed that *ether* produced a similar effect. But neither of these was suitable for long operations. The effects of laughing gas quickly wore off, so its use was restricted almost entirely to dentistry. Ether lasted longer, but made the patient feel very sick. In 1847 **James Simpson** (1811–70), Professor of Midwifery at Edinburgh University, demonstrated anaesthesia with **chloroform**. He invited two students to his home and together they inhaled the sweet-smelling vapour. A few minutes later, Mrs Simpson heard a crash and came running in to find all three unconscious on the floor. But they suffered no ill-effects and were delighted with the results.

Chloroform remained the chief anaesthetic until well into the twentieth century. No longer hindered by the cries and struggles of the patient, surgeons could perform long and delicate operations. But in the meantime a greater problem had to be overcome – the danger of *infection* of the operation wound. When **Joseph Lister** (1827–1912)

Joseph Lister

*Artist's impression of James
Simpson and his friends
experimenting with chloroform*

was appointed Surgeon to Glasgow Royal Infirmary (1861) internal
operations were hardly ever attempted because of the risk of infection.
Even after amputations, or in cases of compound fracture, about a
third of the patients died from *sepsis* (poisoning) of the wound. The
cause was not understood, so the importance of cleanliness was not
realised. Surgeons wore their old clothes, spattered with blood, and
rarely washed their hands or their instruments. Lister, who found the
stench of the surgical wards revolting, insisted on cleanliness at operations and ventilation of the wards. This brought some improvement, although sepsis remained an everyday occurrence.

Then, one day in 1865, Lister read accounts of the work of **Louis
Pasteur**, a great French scientist. Pasteur's recent researches showed
that it was tiny living organisms (microbes) that caused wine to
ferment. Lister wondered whether a similar explanation could be
applied to the infection of wounds. If sepsis resulted from different
kinds of living organisms (bacteria) present in the air then it only
remained to find a way of killing the bacteria. As events showed,
Lister's assumption was correct. He had, in fact, anticipated part of
Pasteur's later **Germ Theory of Disease** – the most important medical
discovery of all time.

When Lister heard that a thick black fluid called **carbolic acid** was
being used in Carlisle for purifying sewage, he decided to experiment
with it. A dilute solution of up to 5 per cent carbolic acid was used to
clean the wound and to disinfect the hands and instruments of the
surgeon and his helpers. In addition, a fine spray of the solution was
blown over the patient during the operation. The immediate effect of
Lister's *antiseptic* method was a great reduction in the death-rate
from sepsis. Internal operations previously considered too dangerous
could now be done safely.

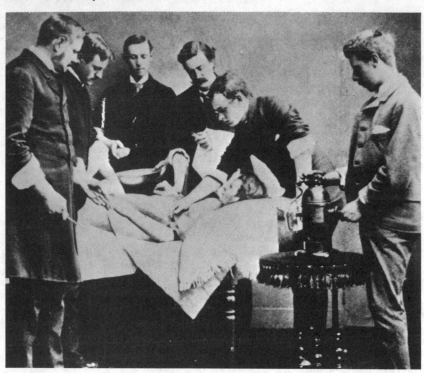

*Lister's carbolic spray in use
during an operation in
Edinburgh (1870)*

Further researches showed that the germs existing in the air were of
little importance and that sepsis was normally caused by *direct* infection from the surgeon's hands or instruments, towels, sponges and the
like. So Lister's spray (a great hindrance to the surgeon) was
eventually discarded in favour of the *aseptic* method, based on the
principle that simple cleanliness was sufficient. The healing of the
wound was left to nature, and everything brought into contact with it
carefully sterilised. Today the risk of death through infection of an
operation wound is practically non-existent.

'The Lady with the Lamp'

Simpson made operations painless; Lister made them safe. But this
revolution in surgery could only be really effective if hospitals were
clean and nurses efficient. In both these respects conditions in the
first half of the nineteenth century were unsatisfactory. Hospitals in
the towns frequently became so overcrowded that they were breeding
grounds for disease. Some patients who did not have fatal diseases
when they were admitted acquired them in the normal course of treatment. It was often safer to stay at home. As late as 1869 James Simpson found that two-thirds of the operations carried out in the hospitals
of London, Edinburgh and Glasgow proved fatal, compared with only
one in nine performed in private houses. But positive remedies were
already on the way, in the shape of antiseptic surgery and the long
overdue development of a trained nursing profession.

In 1854 Britain, supported by France, went to war in the Near
East, with the aim of protecting Turkey against Russian aggression.

The Crimean battleground

The Allies landed in the **Crimea**, a peninsula on the northern shores of the Black Sea, and began to attack the Russian naval base at Sebastopol. Before long cholera and dysentery swept through the British ranks. The emergency British hospital, established in a Turkish barracks at **Scutari**, was quickly overwhelmed. The filth and overcrowding were almost indescribable. Men from the battlefield in blood-soaked bandages shared the floor with rats; the lavatories were blocked and stinking, and there was a serious shortage of basic stores such as bandages, soap, blankets and even beds.

At this point **Florence Nightingale** (1820–1910) entered the scene. She was the daughter of a rich family, brought up to a life of luxury and idleness; but, to the astonishment of her friends and relations, she chose to go to Germany in 1851 to train as a nurse. By the autumn of 1854 she was in the Crimea, leading a party of thirty-eight nurses. She immediately set about the mammoth task of cleaning up the wards, corridors and lavatories of the hospital at Scutari. Next the kitchens and laundry were reorganised and a proper nursing service introduced. After six months of efficient administration and almost superhuman effort, the number of deaths per 1,000 patients had been reduced from 420 to 22. Her remarkable achievement won her the love and devotion of thousands of sick and dying soldiers. They called her 'the lady with the lamp', because of her daily practice of touring the wards last thing at night to make sure all her instructions had been carried out.

The war ended in 1856, with the prohibition of Russian fortifications in the Black Sea. Florence Nightingale was a national heroine. But her life's work had only just begun, despite the ruin of her health in the Crimea, which made her an invalid at forty. After assisting in a thorough reform of army medical services, she turned to her greatest

Florence Nightingale in the military hospital at Scutari during the Crimean War

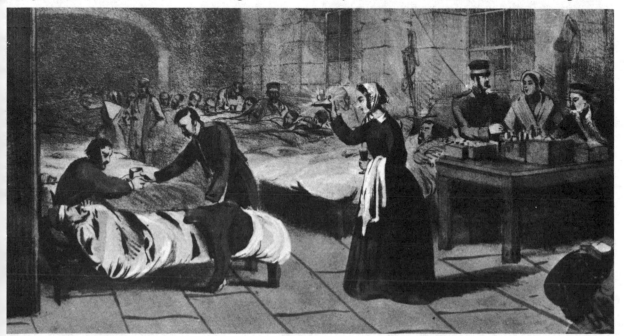

ambition, the establishment of nursing as a trained profession for women. It had previously been regarded as an unskilled job, fit for the lowest class of domestic worker. In 1860 Miss Nightingale founded a **nurses' training school** at St Thomas's Hospital in London. It set the pattern of training for the future and inspired similar establishments in most of the country's major hospitals. Entrants had to be of good character and have some educational background. After a course ranging from two to four years, a certificate was awarded on the result of a final examination. By 1900 there were 64,000 trained nurses in Britain, bringing much higher standards of hygiene and discipline to hospital wards. Parliament began the first State Register of qualified nurses in 1919.

The march of medical science

In the last hundred years or so the advance of medical knowledge has been greatly assisted by international co-operation. While British doctors have made important contributions to tropical medicine (notably **Ronald Ross**, who, in 1898, traced the cause of malaria to a species of mosquito) millions of British lives have been saved by new forms of treatment discovered abroad. For example, in *bacteriology* (identifying the particular germs responsible for each disease) and the accompanying search for prevention and treatment, very few major discoveries have been British. Foremost in this field was a German doctor, **Robert Koch**, who identified the microbes that cause tuberculosis and cholera (1882–3). At about the same time typhoid and diphtheria were similarly traced.

It was another German, **Wilhelm Röntgen**, who discovered *X-rays* (1895). Hidden parts of the body could now be observed easily, with the result that all kinds of surgery were improved (especially the setting of broken bones), and the treatment of tuberculosis and other diseases was greatly advanced. Röntgen's work, together with experiments on uranium carried out in France, inspired a further great achievement. In 1898, at the Sorbonne University of Paris, **Marie Curie** and her husband Pierre discovered *radium*. It could be made to act *selectively* on the body, destroying diseased cells without harming healthy ones. Radium was soon applied to the treatment of cancers and other deadly growths beyond the reach of surgeons.

The chief medical achievements of the twentieth century have been discoveries of new drugs. The outstanding example is *penicillin*, found accidentally by **Alexander Fleming**, a Scotsman, working at St Mary's Hospital, Paddington. One day in 1928 Fleming noticed that on a dish where he was growing bacteria a mould had formed which killed all the cultures of bacteria around it. The mould turned out to be penicillium, from which he developed the famous drug, or 'antibiotic', which revolutionised the treatment of pneumonia, meningitis and septic conditions. More than ten years of further research was necessary before penicillin could be processed by chemical firms and given by injection (1939–40). Soon afterwards Fleming received the Nobel Prize, as did two other doctors who worked with him.

Sir Alexander Fleming (1881–1955) being presented with the Albert Medal – one of many honours he received for the discovery of penicillin

An example of modern medical technology. This machine carries out the function of the patient's kidneys artificially

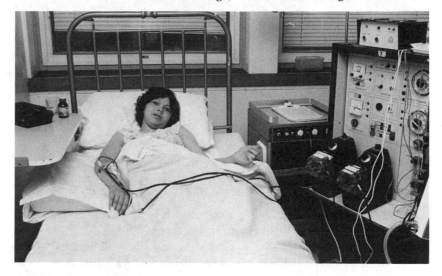

Since the Second World War many more antibiotics have been developed to attack infections. Other types of drugs produced by the growing pharmaceutical industry include powerful pain-killers, 'tranquilisers' and fertility drugs which make reproduction possible for women who previously could not have children. There have also been rapid advances in recent years in medical technology, such as the kidney machine which performs the function of the kidneys artificially. Moreover surgical skills have been extended to include the transplanting of human organs from the dead to the living. The first heart transplant operation was carried out in South Africa in 1968 by **Christian Barnard**; and kidney and lung transplants are now also performed in many countries. However such surgery is still in its infancy: it is very expensive for only a short-term result and has so far been used on relatively few patients.

Medical science has now almost eliminated major 'killer diseases' of the past such as tuberculosis and pneumonia. Yet these advances have been partly counterbalanced by increases in deaths from heart disease and **cancer**. The search for ways of curing cancer in its various forms remains the greatest challenge facing modern medical research.

Timeline

1798	Edward Jenner's smallpox vaccine.
1842	Edwin Chadwick's *Report on the Sanitary Condition of the Labouring Population*.
1847	James Simpson's chloroform anaesthetic.
1848	First Public Health Act.
1854–6	Florence Nightingale in the Crimea.
1865	Joseph Lister's antiseptic surgery.
1875	Public Health Act (Disraeli). Artisans' Dwellings Act.
1878	Louis Pasteur's *Germ Theory of Disease* published.

1895   Wilhelm Röntgen's X-rays.
1898   Marie Curie discovers radium.
1928   Alexander Fleming's discovery of penicillin.

Questions

1. 'Shepherd's Buildings consist of two rows of . . . what are styled back and front houses – that is, the houses placed back to back . . . The cellars are let off as separate dwellings . . . between the two rows is . . . the common gutter, into which all sorts of refuse is thrown . . . In many of these dwellings there are four persons in each bed.' (Report from a Poor Law Medical Officer in Stockport)

   a) The above was quoted in a famous Report which appeared in 1842. What was it called and who compiled it?
   b) Why would 'back to back' houses be especially unhealthy?
   c) What evidence is there of severe overcrowding in these houses?
   d) Why was Parliament slow to take action on public health?
   e) What was achieved by the Public Health Acts of 1848 and 1875?

Joseph Lister's carbolic spray (see Question 2)

2. Explain how the work of James Simpson and Joseph Lister helped to make operations   a) painless and   b) safe from infection.

3. 'It is with feelings of surprise and anger that the public will learn that no sufficient preparations have been made for the proper care of the wounded. Not only are there not sufficient surgeons . . . not only are there no dressers and nurses . . . but what will be said when it is known that there is not even linen to make bandages for the wounded?' (*The Times*, 9 October 1854)

   a) Where and why was Britain fighting a war at this time?
   b) Why do you think proper arrangements for the wounded had not been made?
   c) What would have been the job of a 'dresser'?
   d) Explain in detail what Florence Nightingale did to remedy this situation.
   e) What part did she later play in the development of a trained nursing profession?

4. Explain how each of the following contributed to medical progress:
   a) the large number of sailors who got scurvy on long voyages
   b) the small number of dairy-maids who got smallpox
   c) epidemics of cholera from 1831
   d) the discovery that living organisms cause wine to ferment
   e) a mould which accidentally killed cultures of bacteria

5. Write a paragraph on each of the following:
   a) nineteenth-century population changes
   b) the Municipal Corporations Act, 1835
   c) the Artisans' Dwellings Act, 1875
   d) reform of local government, 1888, 1894

17

Trade Unions Take Root
Working-class Movements (II)

Many trade unions had failed in the 1830s largely because they attempted to do too much too quickly (see Chapter 12). Influenced by Robert Owen's schemes for workers' control of industry, they set out to displace their masters. But the employers, backed by Parliament and the law courts, were much too powerful to be defeated by uneducated and often disorganised trade unionists. By the middle of the century, a new generation of working men had learned from the mistakes of the past. They aimed to establish trade unions that were well organised, financially sound and capable of improving members' conditions of work *gradually* by more peaceful means.

The 'new model unions'

In January 1851 a new kind of trade union was born. Well over a hundred local trade societies of millwrights, machinists, engineers and toolmakers came together to form the **Amalgamated Society of Engineers (ASE)**. The members of this union were well-paid, highly-skilled technicians – men on whom the future prosperity of Britain depended. They could afford the high weekly subscription of a shilling (5p) at a time when most working men still earned less than £1 a week. Many of the benefits they received in return were similar to those of a Friendly Society (see page 133). For example, the rules of the Union stated that one of its tasks was 'to promote the welfare of its members; to assist them when out of work or in distressed circumstances, to support them in case of sickness, accident or superannuation [old age] and loss of tools by fire, to provide for their burial and the burial of their wives'. Within nine months the ASE had 11,000 members and a permanent headquarters, with a full-time, paid Secretary.

The ASE became the 'model' for several national **craft unions** formed in the 1850s and 60s, among boilermakers, carpenters and joiners, bricklayers, plasterers and others. Each craft union deliberately set out to restrict the number of new entrants into its trade. In this way it could increase the 'scarcity value' of the skilled worker and make it easier for him to obtain good wages, without the need for strikes. Indeed, head-on collisions with employers were avoided as far as possible. But if they were considered really necessary these unions had ample funds for strike pay. The ASE, for instance, astonished everyone in 1859 when it presented the London Builders with £3,000 in three weeks, and so helped them to defeat their employers in a dispute.

The strength of their financial position enabled the 'model unions' to become firmly established. So did their willingness to accept the existing organisation of industry and to work *with* their employers rather than against them. Because the emphasis was on negotiation (discussion) rather than strike action as a means of settling disputes, each union had to have strong central control over its 'lodges' or local branches. So *executive committees*, normally based in London, tried to handle local grievances on behalf of the men. Employers came to respect the patient and responsible attitude of experienced union secretaries such as **Robert Applegarth** of the Carpenters and Joiners and **William Allen** of the ASE.

The new type of trade unionism was not favoured by all workers. The lower-paid could not afford to establish such elaborate

Robert Applegarth, Secretary of the Amalgamated Society of Carpenters and Joiners

societies and remained largely unorganised. Even among the skilled trades, members of some smaller unions had no wish to submit to such control and discipline. Unionists in the Sheffield cutlery trades even resorted to violent and murderous attacks upon *blacklegs* (fellow workers who refused to join them). Middle-class opinion was shocked in 1866 when a tin of gunpowder was exploded in the house of a non-unionist. These **Sheffield Outrages** undid some of the work of the craft societies in gaining a more respectable reputation for trade unions. However a Royal Commission of Inquiry (1867) decided that the incidents in Sheffield were exceptional and that most unions were peaceful and constructive.

By the 1860s, union representatives from many parts of Britain began to meet together from time to time to discuss matters of common interest, such as the regulation of working hours, technical education and conditions of apprenticeship. In 1868, at one such gathering in Manchester, it was proposed that regular meetings should be held every year in future. The **Trades Union Congress (TUC)** was born. At Birmingham in the following year there were forty-eight delegates, representing the interests of nearly a quarter of a million unionists. Within a few years well over a million members were represented and the TUC rapidly became an important unifying force in the trade union movement.

The struggle for legal protection

One of the chief concerns of the TUC was the question of legal rights. Trade union activities had always been hampered by a lack of legal protection. Long before they were outlawed in the Combination Acts (1799–1800) unions had run the risk of prosecution under the law of conspiracy. Even after the Combination Acts were repealed (1824–5) they frequently fell foul of the law, as in the case of the 'Tolpuddle Martyrs' of 1834 (see page 129). Trade unions were, in fact, fighting two powerful opponents at once – their employers and the state.

Influenced by the Royal Commission of 1867, Gladstone's Liberal Government passed two important new laws in 1871. The first, the **Trade Union Act**, enabled unions to register themselves in the same way as Friendly Societies. There was no longer any difference between collecting money for benefit purposes and collecting it to support strike action. Consequently trade unions could in future claim legal assistance in recovering stolen funds. This Act was favourable to them, but a **Criminal Law Amendment Act** which followed it seriously restricted union activities. With the Sheffield Outrages in mind, the Government repeated the old warnings against 'molesting' or 'obstructing' fellow workers, and then went on to outlaw even peaceful forms of *picketing* (attempting to prevent non-unionists from working during a strike). This was a big handicap because in those days union members were nearly always a minority in any group of workers. To carry out a successful strike picketing was almost essential.

A number of working men had recently been granted the right to

PROPOSED CONGRESS OF TRADES COUNCILS

AND OTHER

Federations of Trades Societies.

MANCHESTER, FEBRUARY 21st, 1868.

FELLOW-UNIONISTS,

The Manchester and Salford Trades Council having recently taken into their serious consideration the present aspect of Trades Unions, and the profound ignorance which prevails in the public mind with reference to their operations and principles, together with the probability of an attempt being made by the Legislature, during the present session of Parliament, to introduce a measure detrimental to the interests of such Societies, beg most respectfully to suggest the propriety of holding in Manchester, as the main centre of industry in the provinces, a Congress of the Representatives of Trades Councils and other similar Federations of Trades Societies. By confining the Congress to such bodies it is conceived that a deal of expense will be saved, as Trades will thus be-represented collectively: whilst there will be a better opportunity afforded of selecting the most intelligent and efficient exponents of our principles.

It is proposed that the Congress shall assume the character of the annual meetings of the British Association for the Advancement of Science and the Social Science Association, in the transactions of which Societies the artizan class are almost entirely excluded; and that papers, previously carefully prepared, shall be laid before the Congress on the various subjects which at the present time affect Trades Societies, each paper to be followed by discussion upon the points advanced, with a view of the merits and demerits of each question being thoroughly ventilated through the medium of the public press. It is further suggested that the subjects treated upon shall include the following :—

1.—Trades Unions an absolute necessity.
2.—Trades Unions and Political Economy.
3.—The Effect of Trades Unions on Foreign Competition.
4.—Regulation of the Hours of Labour.
5.—Limitation of Apprentices.
6.—Technical Education.
7.—Arbitration and Courts of Conciliation.
8.—Co-operation.
9.—The present Inequality of the Law in regard to Conspiracy, Intimidation, Picketing, Coercion, &c.
10.—Factory Acts Extension Bill, 1867: the necessity of Compulsory Inspection, and its application to all places where Women and Children are employed.
11.—The present Royal Commission on Trades Unions: how far worthy of the confidence of the Trades Union interest.
12.—The necessity of an Annual Congress of Trade Representatives from the various centres of industry.

All Trades Councils and other Federations of Trades are respectfully solicited to intimate their adhesion to this project on or before the 6th of April next, together with a notification of the subject of the paper that each body will undertake to prepare; after which date all information as to place of meeting, &c., will be supplied.

It is also proposed that the Congress be held on the 4th of May next, and that all liabilities in connection therewith shall not extend beyond its sittings.

Communications to be addressed to MR. W. H. WOOD, Typographical Institute, 29, Water Street, Manchester.

By order of the Manchester and Salford Trades Council,

S. C. NICHOLSON, PRESIDENT.
W. H. WOOD, SECRETARY.

vote – in the Reform Act of 1867 (see the last section of this chapter). Angry with Gladstone's Government, many trade unionists voted against the Liberals in the 1874 election and helped to return a Conservative Government under Disraeli. The Conservatives repaid the unions by passing the **Conspiracy and Protection of Property Act (1875)**. It permitted picketing during a strike, so long as no violence was used, and made the law of conspiracy no longer applicable to industrial disputes. Union members now had the same rights as any other citizens, even when acting together. In future they could only be prosecuted under the ordinary criminal law of the land.

'The dockers' tanner' and the rise of 'unskilled unions'

The 'new model unions' covered only a small section of the working classes – probably not above 10 per cent, even in the 1870s. Meanwhile the great mass of unskilled and semi-skilled labourers remained largely unorganised. There were some exceptions, such as the Miners' National Union and the Agricultural Labourers' Union (1872) started by Joseph Arch, a Warwickshire labourer. But it was not until the late 1880s that large numbers of poorer workers began to organise themselves. Their opportunity came with an improvement in overseas trade, which resulted in almost full employment for a time. The 'bargaining position' of unions is strengthened in such conditions because employers can rarely break strikes by bringing in new workers.

The turning-point was marked by a number of successful strikes among unskilled and semi-skilled workers in the years 1888–9. London was the main centre of the revival. It was there that the match girls of Bryant and May's organised a stoppage in 1888. They gained great public sympathy and financial assistance when it became known that they earned about a penny (½ p) an hour for the dangerous work of dipping matches in phosphorus. Within three weeks they gained considerably better pay and conditions. In the following year 20,000 **London gas-workers** struck, to achieve a reduction in their twelve-hour day. Led by **Will Thorne**, a young Birmingham-born Irishman who could barely read and write, they quickly forced the South Metropolitan Gas Company to cut the working day to eight hours. Immediately after this triumph, a strike began among the London dockers which captured the attention of the whole nation.

Most dockers were casual labourers who were taken on, as required, to unload cargoes and carry goods in and out of warehouses. During slack periods, when few ships were in port, thousands of men were idle, waiting at the dock gates or standing about the streets of the East End. A small Society of Tea Warehousemen had recently been formed. It was a remarkable achievement of discipline and organisation when its Secretary, **Ben Tillett**, brought 10,000 poverty-stricken dockers out on strike in the hot summer of 1889. They demanded at least four hours' continuous work at a time, with a minimum rate of sixpence (2½p) an hour – the '**dockers' tanner**' – and eightpence (3½p) for overtime. While the Port of London was closed and the Thames crowded with shipping, the strikers paraded through

Annie Besant, a London journalist and member of the Fabian Society (see page 197), took up the cause of the Bryant and May's match girls. She organised them into a union, gave publicity to their grievances and helped them to obtain better pay and working conditions

Ben Tillett (1860–1943), the dockers' leader

the City carrying fish-heads and rotten vegetables on sticks, to show what they had to live on.

At first the dock directors refused all the demands of the strikers, believing it was just a matter of time before their funds ran out and they were forced to surrender. But just as the dockers were on the verge of defeat they were saved by a flood of public sympathy and support. Subscriptions to their strike fund began to pour in from all over Britain and even from abroad. Every other union made a donation, so did the Salvation Army. Some football clubs sent their gate money. Above all, Australian sympathisers contributed a staggering £30,000. After five weeks, with the tide of public opinion running strongly against them, the employers realised they were beaten and granted all the dockers' main demands. The triumphant union was now established on a permanent basis, with Tillett as its full-time Secretary. Only three months after the end of the dispute it claimed a total of 30,000 members.

The dockers had won a victory not only for themselves but for *all* lower-paid workers. Their strike immediately inspired the formation of several powerful national unions among unskilled and semi-skilled workers. For instance, a **General Railway Workers' Union** was formed (1889) to cater for those who could not afford to join the existing 'craft' union – the Amalgamated Society of Railway Servants. At the same time the **Miners' Federation of Great Britain** was created, to represent most miners in England, Scotland and Wales. This great union was at the centre of some of the bitterest struggles of the next forty years. All these developments in the trade union movement were reflected in rising membership figures:

Total membership of trade unions (approximate figures)

1888	750,000
1900	2 million
1914	4 million

These new unions differed from the older 'model unions' in several ways. They were usually organised on an 'industrial' rather than a 'craft' basis – in other words, they set out to enrol *all* workers in a particular industry, no matter what their jobs were. They rarely collected money for benefit schemes, preferring to keep subscriptions to a minimum. Above all, they were less prepared to co-operate with employers. They wanted higher wages and better working conditions right away and would not listen to excuses.

There were many strikes in the years ahead. Great successes mingled with bitter defeats. Yet the worst setback of all occurred not on the 'industrial battlefront' but in the law courts. In 1901, following a strike by members of the Amalgamated Society of Railway Servants, the **Taff Vale Railway Company** in South Wales sued the union for damages. It was granted £23,000 in compensation; a decision which was confirmed by the House of Lords when the Union appealed against the judgment. This new ruling virtually eliminated the unions' major weapon, for every strike automatically causes employers to lose money. Eventually, in 1906, a newly elected Liberal Government passed a **Trade Disputes Act** which protected unions against similar claims for damages in the future.

Rising prices in the early years of the twentieth century led to frequent strikes for higher wages, reaching a climax in the period 1910–14. A railway stoppage in 1911 paralysed most of the country. It also led to an amalgamation of railwaymen's unions. Three of the four existing societies joined together in 1913 to form the **NUR** (National Union of Railwaymen). In 1912 the Miners' Federation organised the largest single strike that had ever taken place in Britain up to that time. Over a million miners came out in support of a claim for a minimum wage of five shillings (25p) a day for men and two shillings (10p) for boys. After six weeks Parliament intervened and set up a Minimum Wage Board which settled the dispute to the satisfaction of the strikers.

The railway strike had brought many other industries to a standstill. Likewise the coal stoppage forced factories to close and railways to restrict services. With this in mind, representatives of the 'big three' – the Miners' Federation, the NUR and the National Transport Workers' Federation (formed in 1910 out of various dockers' and transport workers' unions) – met in April 1914 to discuss ways of cooperating in future strike action. The outcome was the **Triple Industrial Alliance**, representing almost 1½ million trade unionists. It was intended that each section of the alliance should be prepared to strike 'in sympathy' with the other members. The outbreak of the First World War (August 1914) meant the scheme had to be shelved, for an 'industrial truce' was agreed between unions and employers, in the national interest. But it was clear that this powerful alliance could provide the basis for a future general strike (see page 277). As the President of the Miners' Federation said: 'it may well be found advisable later on to extend the scope of the alliance in the general interests of labour as a whole'.

Parliamentary reform and the origins of the Labour Party

The right to vote in parliamentary elections was still based on wealth and ownership of property after the 1832 Reform Act (see page 117). It was the continuing lack of working-class political rights that inspired the Chartist Movement (see page 130). But Chartism failed to achieve its aims and collapsed in 1848. By about 1860, when five out of six adult males were still without the vote, a new campaign for working-class *franchise* (voting rights) began. A **National Reform League** was established, with the support of trade union leaders, a few ex-Chartists and many middle-class Liberals. Meetings were held all over the country, reaching a climax in 1866 with a great demonstration in London's Hyde Park.

The new model unions had increased the influence of skilled tradesmen and made them seem more 'respectable' in the eyes of the middle classes. A growing number of MPs now believed that such men should be given the vote. The resulting second **Parliamentary Reform Act (1867)** was strongly influenced by MPs who supported the National Reform League. Consequently it extended the franchise far more

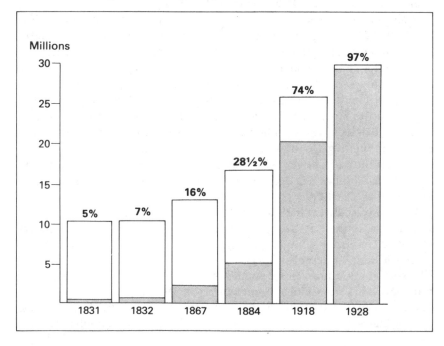

Percentage of the adult population entitled to vote, 1831–1928. (For later parliamentary reforms see pages 238, 275)

widely than the Conservative Government had originally intended. Voting rights in the boroughs were granted to all male householders and to lodgers paying at least £10 a year for unfurnished accommodation. In the counties, owners of property worth £5 a year (instead of £10 as in the 1832 Act) were given the vote, together with occupiers of property with a rental value of £12 a year. In addition, forty-five seats were taken from small boroughs and re-distributed to counties or boroughs with expanding populations.

Altogether the 1867 Act created nearly 1 million new voters – mostly better-off workers in the towns – and almost doubled the size of the electorate. Five years later, open voting was replaced by **secret ballot (1872)**. It was now unnecessary for a man to declare his political views in public. This stopped property owners from putting pressure on their tenants at election time, and it finally ended the buying and selling of votes – for no-one could now tell which way a man had voted. However it was still possible for rich candidates to spend vast sums on their election campaigns – until the **Corrupt Practices Act (1883)** fixed strict limits on a candidate's election expenses.

The number of working-class voters remained relatively small, until a third **Reform Act (1884)** gave the franchise to all male householders in the counties. This put agricultural labourers on the same footing as town workers. As a result the UK electorate increased substantially, from about 3 million to over 5½ million. In the following year the **Redistribution Act (1885)** abolished separate county and borough seats. The country was now divided into *constituencies* (voting areas), each with roughly the same number of voters returning one MP.

After 1884 almost half the electorate was working class, but many such voters were dissatisfied with having only Conservatives and Liberals to chose from. They felt it was time they had a political party of their own. The first really working-class MPs (two miners) had been elected in 1874. They sat with the Liberals in Parliament but were often known as 'Labour' or **'Lib-Lab'** members. Their numbers slowly increased until there were eleven 'Lib-Labs' in 1885. But there was little prospect of the Liberal Party carrying out the kind of far-reaching social reforms that many working people wanted. The creation of a separate workers' political party was just a matter of time.

In 1892 **Keir Hardie**, a Scottish miner, was elected for West Ham and created a sensation by sitting among top-hatted MPs dressed in cloth cap and working clothes. He soon took the lead in forming an **Independent Labour Party (ILP)** in 1893. Its policies were based on *socialism* – the belief that the state rather than private individuals should control the main sources of the country's wealth, including key industries and the banking system, for the benefit of the whole community. Small socialist societies already existed, notably the **Fabians (1884)** which included several well-known writers such as George Bernard Shaw and H.G. Wells. But the Fabian Society consisted mainly of middle-class reformers. It had no direct working-class support, unlike the ILP, which had many followers in the industrial North. Nevertheless, in the 1895 election all twenty-eight ILP candidates were defeated, including Hardie himself.

George Bernard Shaw (1856–1950), one of Britain's foremost playwrights, helped to establish the Fabian Society in the 1880s. He made speeches and wrote many articles and pamphlets in support of socialist principles

James Keir Hardie (1856–1915), addressing a meeting in London's Trafalgar Square in 1913

There seemed little chance of success without *official* support from the trade unions, the only workers' organisations really large enough to launch a new political party. Growing support for socialism among younger trade unionists finally led to the formation of a **Labour Representation Committee (LRC)** in 1900, backed by the Trades Union Congress. A fund was started to pay the expenses of Labour candidates and salaries to those who were successful (MPs were not yet paid). The election of 1900 came too soon for the LRC to get to work. Only two of its candidates were elected, including Keir Hardie.

James Ramsay MacDonald (1866–1937), Secretary of the Labour Representation Committee. He later became Britain's first Labour Prime Minister

In the next few years, however, under its busy Secretary, **James Ramsay MacDonald**, a Scottish journalist, the LRC built up a nationwide following. The Taff Vale decision of 1901 (see page 195) had finally convinced trade unionists of the need for an independent party to defend their interests in Parliament.

In the general election of 1906, no fewer than twenty-nine LRC candidates were successful – plus twenty-four miners and 'Lib-Labs'. The Labour Party, as it was now called, was at last capable of having some influence, although it had far fewer seats than the Liberals and Conservatives. Its main task was to gain wider support beyond the areas of mining and heavy industry, where most Labour voters were concentrated. This was difficult, because many people who sympathised with Labour policies were frightened away by the revolutionary ideas of a few extremists who preached 'class war' against the rich.

Money subscribed by trade unionists made these early successes possible. But not all union members voted Labour. **W.V. Osborne**, an official in the Amalgamated Society of Railway Servants, was a Liberal, and he took his union to court for allocating part of members' subscriptions to Labour Party funds. He won his case, and the House of Lords confirmed the decision in 1909. This was a great setback for Labour, since the 'political levy' from the unions was its main source of income. However in 1911 the old Chartist demand for **payment of MPs** was granted, at the rate of £400 a year (allowing for tax, this was worth more than the present day salary). Working men could at last support themselves as MPs. Nevertheless the Labour Party continued to demand a reversal of the Osborne Judgment. It finally succeeded when a **Trade Union Act (1913)** allowed union funds to be used for any lawful purpose, provided a majority of members showed approval in a ballot. Individuals could 'contract out' (be exempted) from the political levy if they wished.

Timeline

1851	Amalgamated Society of Engineers.
1854–66	'Sheffield Outrages'.
1867	Second Parliamentary Reform Act.
1868	Trades Union Congress.
1871	Trade Union Act (Gladstone).
	Criminal Law Amendment Act.
1875	Conspiracy and Protection of Property Act (Disraeli).
1884	Third Parliamentary Reform Act.
1889	The 'dockers' tanner'.
1900	Labour Representation Committee, became Labour Party, 1906.
1901	Taff Vale Case.
1906	Trade Disputes Act (reversing Taff Vale decision).
1909	Osborne Judgment.
1911	Payment of MPs.
1913	Trade Union Act (reversing Osborne Judgment).
1914	'Triple Industrial Alliance'.

Questions

1. Read carefully the Trades Council broadsheet on page 192.
   a) What are thought to be the likely benefits of holding an annual congress of trade union representatives?
   b) A Royal Commission is mentioned. What events in Sheffield did it investigate before making its recommendations?
   c) How far were the writers of this document correct in thinking that Parliament would soon 'introduce a measure detrimental to the interests' of trade unions?
   d) Why were unions concerned with 'Limitation of Apprentices'?
   e) Where did the congress take place in the following year, and how many trade unionists were represented?

2. '80,000 of the poorest men in London, the men who can less than any others afford to be out of work, are doing nothing, and, in spite of the help which they are receiving from outside, the sight is . . . pitiable . . . The net result of the present state of affairs is that the trade of the greatest port in the world is paralysed.' (*The Times*, 30 August 1889)

   a) What strike is being described here? Who was its leader?
   b) What help were the strikers 'receiving from outside'?
   c) How many more men were involved in the strike on 30 August than at its start, a fortnight earlier?
   d) What were the strikers demanding? Were their demands met?
   e) Why is this strike an important landmark in union history?

3. How was Parliament reformed and made more representative of the people between 1867 and 1885?

4. 'The money difficulty, which is the great bar to parliamentary representation of the working class, does not exist for bodies which can raise a thousand pounds by a levy of from a penny to sixpence per member . . . On the whole, then, we may take it that the representation of the working classes at the General Election will depend on the great national trade unions.'
   (Fabian Society article of 1893)

   a) What was the 'money difficulty' referred to here?
   b) How could the trade unions help to overcome the problem?
   c) When did the trade unions take the course of action recommended here, and what effect did it have?
   d) What happened in 1911 to reduce the 'money difficulty'?
   e) How did the 'Osborne Judgment' affect the political activities of trade unions? Why was its effect temporary?

5. Write a paragraph on each of the following:
   a) the Amalgamated Society of Engineers
   b) the Conspiracy and Protection of Property Act, 1875
   c) the Taff Vale Case
   d) James Keir Hardie

18
Schools for Everyone
The Beginnings of a National System of Education

Nowadays we are all required by law to devote roughly a seventh of our lives to full-time education. But the growth of 'state schools', financed out of rates and taxes, has only taken place in the last hundred years or so. Before then schooling was a private matter, left for parents to decide.

In the days before compulsory school attendance, there were great differences in education north and south of the Border. Most villages in Scotland had their own schools, maintained by local rates, as early as 1700. These took children from the poorest families as well as those of the *lairds* (landowners). 'You find very few [Scottish] gentry either ignorant or unlearned', said Daniel Defoe, writing in the early eighteenth century. 'Nay, you cannot ordinarily find a *servant* in Scotland but he can read or write.' In England and Wales (our chief concern in this chapter) the situation was different. Full-time education was a privilege, enjoyed by only a minority of the population. The well-to-do could afford the necessary school fees, but many working-class children were deprived of education because their parents were unable to pay for it. Even when free elementary schools were provided by private charity, many parents felt it was more important to keep their children at work to make up the family income.

The education of the well-to-do

In the eighteenth century, sons of the 'landed gentry' received private tuition in basic skills, including reading and writing, and were then sent as boarders to expensive **public schools** such as Eton, Winchester, Harrow and Rugby. Life in many of these schools was harsh and sometimes even violent. The boys fought and bullied each other, and the teachers usually maintained discipline by means of savage floggings. Since most public schools had insufficient staff, the senior boys virtually ruled the younger ones, using them as 'fags' (servants). The public school curriculum consisted almost entirely of Latin and Greek (together known as 'Classics') and teaching methods were dull and mechanical. Few pupils acquired any real knowledge and fewer still showed a genuine interest.

Much the same was true of the Universities of **Oxford** and **Cambridge**, where the sons of the upper classes normally finished their education. Most of the staff and students neglected their studies, preferring hunting, gambling and drinking. University teaching, like most schoolmastering, was in the hands of clergymen, many of whom had no qualifications in the subjects they taught. In the 1760s,

In this scene from Oxford University in the eighteenth century, the artist, William Hogarth, portrays the heavy drinking in which staff indulged, to the neglect of their studies

it was said that the Professor of Chemistry at Cambridge had never read a book on the subject! Examinations for degrees were a formality, presenting no difficulty to the most idle and stupid.

The daughters of the upper classes rarely went to school. They were thought to be less in need of 'mental cultivation' than their brothers. But they were expected to have certain 'accomplishments', which would help them to enter fashionable social circles and find desirable husbands. Therefore most well-to-do parents engaged **governesses** to teach their daughters reading and writing, music, painting and dancing, and a little 'general knowledge' such as the dates of kings and queens. Mothers often assisted governesses, particularly in the teaching of sewing, cookery and the management of household accounts.

Victorian 'young ladies' learning geography with the help of their tutor

Sons of the lesser gentry usually attended a **grammar school** in the nearest town. Many of these schools had been *endowed* (provided with a regular income by their founders) in the sixteenth century, and were intended for able boys of any social class. But, as prices rose, fixed endowments became insufficient for the upkeep of free schools. A good schoolmaster earned about £10 a year in the sixteenth century, but by the early nineteenth century, some headmasters were paid up to 100 times as much. Therefore fees were charged. This was how the public boarding-schools first developed. They grew out of a few local grammar schools which managed to attract paying pupils from a wide area. Meanwhile most of the remaining grammar schools declined rapidly. As the number of free places diminished and fees increased, smallholders and tradesmen no longer sent their sons. In any case, the curriculum, based on Classics, was particularly unsuitable for such pupils.

In general, the best schools of the eighteenth and early nineteenth centuries were the **Dissenters' academies**, run by Nonconformists (especially Quakers) who were excluded from most other schools because of their religion. These gave a general education which was more suited to the world of business, where many of the pupils were highly successful. Book-keeping, science and natural history were normally taught, as well as English and Classics.

Dr Thomas Arnold, 1795–1842

By the early nineteenth century rapidly growing numbers of wealthy manufacturers and merchants were sending their sons to public boarding-schools in order to get them accepted in the highest ranks of society. At about this time the public schools began to reform themselves, under the inspiration of a few exceptional headmasters. **Samuel Butler**, Head of Shrewsbury 1798–1836, set an example by introducing mathematics and history into the curriculum. **Thomas Arnold**, the famous Headmaster of **Rugby** from 1828 to 1842, added modern history, mathematics, geography and French. Dr Arnold wanted, above all, to make his pupils 'Christian gentlemen'. The chapel became the centre of school life, and he chose only outstanding boys in the sixth form to be prefects, for he expected the highest standards of conduct from them. 'What we must look for', he said, 'is first, religious and moral principles; secondly, gentlemanly conduct, thirdly, intellectual ability.'

Pupils at Rugby School

Rugby became the model for other public schools, both old and new. Altogether, fifty-four were founded during the nineteenth century, to meet the growing demand for a 'gentleman's education'. Some taught a wide variety of subjects, including science and handicrafts, and team games became increasingly popular. In the 1860s it was estimated that a typical pupil at Harrow School might devote fifteen hours a week to cricket. A number of new ideas were put into practice by **Edward Thring**, Head of Uppingham, 1853–87. He introduced a gymnasium and a swimming-bath, music rooms and workshops for carpentry. But despite such improvements most public schools failed to provide satisfactory courses in technical and scientific subjects. Although many of the pupils were sons of manufacturers, they mostly became politicians, civil servants, teachers and clergymen, and rarely took up the kind of work on which the country depended for its livelihood.

Meanwhile many of the old grammar schools were reformed along similar lines (particularly after 1869, when Parliament made extra charitable funds available to them), and the education of girls at last began to receive attention. In 1850 **Frances Buss** founded the North London Collegiate School, and, eight years later, **Dorothea Beale** became Principal of Cheltenham Ladies' College. Both set out to prepare young women for a serious career, and several new girls' public schools soon followed their example. In the past, girls' schools had concentrated on accomplishments such as music and dancing. But the

work of Miss Beale and Miss Buss, like that of Florence Nightingale (see page 185), made people realise that daughters of wealthy families could play a fuller part in national life if they had a broader education.

University College, London, founded in 1828

Finally, there were important developments in university education. The monopoly of Oxford and Cambridge ended in 1828, when **University College, London**, was founded. It was open to men of all religious views, unlike the older universities where Nonconformists could not take degrees before the 1850s and were barred from joining the teaching staff until 1871. The first women's colleges at Oxford and Cambridge were established in the 1870s, by which time many new subjects were being introduced, including sciences and modern languages. Meanwhile, **civic universities** began to appear in the major towns. Durham (1832) was the first, but by 1914 Manchester, Liverpool, Birmingham, Leeds, Sheffield and Bristol had followed suit, and the University of Wales was founded in 1893. They all took students of either sex and any religion, most of them day scholars who lived in the area. The civic universities were soon well known for their degrees in engineering, science and medicine. They gave higher education to many young people who would not otherwise have had the chance. Oxford and Cambridge continued to be dominated by ex-public school students from rich families until well into the twentieth century.

Voluntary schools for the poor

Despite the work of parish charity schools and the newer Sunday schools (see page 34) most children from poor families in England received no education of any kind at the beginning of the nineteenth century. Many charity schools had, in any case, run short of money and fallen into decay by this time – throwing a greater burden on the Sunday schools and various new foundations run by church societies.

Sunday schools were particularly important in manufacturing towns, where they provided almost the only education for the working classes during the first fifty years of the Industrial Revolution. **Robert Raikes**, who founded the first Sunday school, in Gloucester (1783), did so *not* for the benefit of the poor but to prevent the hooliganism which broke out in the streets when a nearby factory was closed. Although elementary instruction in reading and writing was normally given, Raikes and his imitators aimed above all to teach the children 'a sense of subordination and of due respect to their superiors', as well as some knowledge of the Bible.

The desire to give the poor free instruction in the Christian religion led **Andrew Bell**, an ex-army chaplain, and **Joseph Lancaster**, a Quaker, to set up rival elementary schools in London (1798). Both were short of money and teachers, so they operated a **monitorial system**. By this method (which Bell and Lancaster each claimed to have invented) one master could supervise the teaching of hundreds of children. He simply gave each lesson to a group of older pupils – the 'monitors' – and these, in turn, passed it on to the juniors. 'Give me twenty-four pupils today', said Bell, 'and I will give you twenty-four

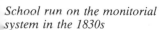
School run on the monitorial system in the 1830s

teachers tomorrow.' Two **church societies** were founded to run schools on the same pattern. Bell established the Church of England National Society for the Education of the Poor (1811) and Lancaster's Nonconformist supporters organised the British and Foreign Schools Society (1814). But the 'teaching' in these voluntary schools was almost worthless. Pupils were drilled to reply to set questions in chorus. On one occasion an inspector rearranged the questions, only to receive the replies in the original order.

Although the church societies provided many schools (the National Society alone founded 3,000 in twenty years) they only catered for a small fraction of England's children. In many areas the only education available to the working classes was that provided in small private **dame schools** – so called because they were usually run by women. In the absence of government regulations, there was nothing to stop people from opening schools in their own homes and charging a few coppers a week, even though they might be totally ignorant. Many 'dames' were little more than child-minders. They often attended to a shop or did washing and sewing while the children were in their care. 'If I can keep them quiet', said one, 'it's as much as I can do and all I'm paid for.'

Such was the sorry state of education for the poor at the beginning of the Victorian Age. The first sign of parliamentary interest came in 1833, when £20,000 was granted to the church societies for school-building. But considering that more was spent that year on the royal stables, education remained very low on the list of priorities. In 1839 the grant was slightly increased and a special Education Committee set up. Its secretary, **James Kay-Shuttleworth**, was not satisfied with the monitorial system, so he made great efforts to increase the supply of teachers. He started a Teachers' Training College at Battersea (1840) which soon led to the development of voluntary colleges in other areas. Meanwhile, to get over the immediate shortage, he encouraged a 'pupil teacher' system. Starting about the age of thirteen, **pupil teachers,** who were like apprentices, helped the teachers during the day and studied in their spare time. After five years they took exams to become assistant teachers or qualify for entry to a training college. Meanwhile, to help raise standards, Kay-Shuttleworth appointed more inspectors (there were only two in 1839).

By the middle of the century, the annual parliamentary grant for education had risen to £500,000. But there was still nothing like a proper state system of education. Voluntary societies continued to depend largely on private subscriptions. Several new societies had been founded, including the **Ragged Schools Union.** By about 1850, when it had established roughly 100 schools for poor children (many of them orphans), it received welcome support from **Lord Ashley,** the factory reformer. He became President, and set about building new schools and improving old ones. Lack of money was always a problem, especially as food and clothing had to be provided for many pupils before they were in a fit state to learn anything. Ashley contributed every penny he could lay hands on. He even resorted to begging money from MPs as they entered Parliament.

A 'ragged school'

'Payment by results'

By the mid nineteenth century, probably the great majority of children had *some* schooling, if only for a short period. However a Royal Commission on elementary education (1858–61) found that less than half of the 3½ million children in England and Wales went *regularly* to school, and of these only a tenth learned reading, writing and arithmetic successfully. In an attempt to raise standards, the Commission suggested a system of **payment by results**. In other words, the amount of taxpayers' money granted to each school would depend on 'the attainment of a certain degree of knowledge by the children ... during the year preceding the payment'. **Robert Lowe**, the

Vice-President of the Department of Education, liked the idea. It promised something definite in return for money spent. 'If it is not cheap, it shall be efficient', he said, 'and if it is not efficient, it shall be cheap.'

'Payment by results' was started almost immediately (1862). Her Majesty's Inspectors visited grant-aided schools once a year to test pupils in the '3 Rs' (reading, 'riting and 'rithmetic) and up to twelve shillings (60p) per child was paid on the result of the examination. Teachers, whose salaries normally depended on the size of the grant, sometimes resorted to underhand methods – such as signalling the answers to pupils from behind the Inspector's back. The new system helped to even out standards from one district to another, and it spurred many teachers to make a greater effort. But in other ways it was a backward step. It encouraged 'parrot learning' of facts, regardless of whether they were understood. Bright children were neglected while the teacher concentrated on bringing the slower ones up to the required standard; and many schools taught nothing else but the elementary work necessary for the exam.

Robert Lowe. As Vice-President of the Department of Education, he helped to introduce 'payment by results' in the 1860s

This method of paying grants to schools continued until 1897. But long before then it was realised that voluntary schools *alone* could not satisfy the urgent need for more elementary education. The state would have to take direct responsibility. In industry, there was an increasing demand for people who could read and write. Great strides were being made to meet this demand in countries such as Germany and the USA, Britain's main trading rivals. To some observers it seemed certain that British industrial supremacy would be lost if many of the nation's children remained uneducated. Moreover among the middle and upper classes it was now widely believed that crime, unrest and drunkenness were the result of ignorance, and that uneducated workers might be a danger to the peace and security of the country.

Reformers wanted elementary schools to be provided in *all* areas out of local rates. But Parliament was reluctant to make such a scheme compulsory because of the great difficulties involved. Many of the well-to-do were opposed to paying extra rates for the education of their social inferiors. Moreover, the Churches had been squabbling among themselves for thirty years about how the available money should be spent. Ratepayers who belonged to the Church of England objected to paying for the upkeep of schools which did not teach their religion. Nonconformists took a similar view when they were asked to give aid to Church of England schools. Feelings were so strong on both sides that many churchgoers preferred children to have no education at all rather than attend schools run by their rivals.

The event which finally forced the Government to take decisive action was the 1867 Parliamentary Reform Act (see page 196). It gave the vote to working-class householders in the boroughs, but they could hardly be expected to understand political affairs and use their vote wisely if they were unable to read or write. Most MPs agreed with Robert Lowe when, referring to the new voters, he said: 'We must educate our future masters.'

'Board school brats'

The outcome was the **Education Act of 1870**, introduced by W.E. Forster on behalf of Gladstone's Liberal Ministry. 'Our object', he said, 'is to complete the present voluntary system; to fill up the gaps.' Therefore the existing church schools, which now numbered 20,000, carried on as before, assisted by larger government grants. In all other areas, where proper schools were not provided, Parliament ordered that local **School Boards** were to be elected by the rate-payers. The Boards would provide elementary schools for the five to ten age group, paid for partly out of local rates and partly by direct government grants. Parents were charged a small weekly fee, unless they were very poor, in which case they were excused. Attendance was not yet compulsory, since it would take time for enough schools to be built. But individual Boards were given the right to make schooling compulsory in their own districts.

To get over the religious problem, the Forster Act stated that Christian teaching should be restricted to reading and explaining the Bible. In other words, there was to be no attempt to teach religion according to the views of any one church or denomination. Parents were given the right to withdraw their children from Scripture lessons if they wished. These arrangements did not satisfy a number of religious leaders, but it was clearly better to force them to accept a compromise than to allow their disagreements to hold up reform any longer.

An infants' school in London at the beginning of the twentieth century

By modern standards, board schools were drab and poorly equipped. Classes of eighty or ninety were common. All the different age groups often had to be taught together in one large hall. There were not enough trained teachers, so school managers had to recruit many unqualified assistants and pupil teachers. The children themselves were mostly dirty and ragged, with skin diseases and running noses. More fortunate middle-class children, from expensive private schools, called them 'board school brats'. Before the 'brats' could be educated they had to be civilised, and often fed and clothed as well. In 1889 over 50,000 pupils in London alone were reported to be 'attending in want of food'. The curriculum still consisted of little more than the bare essentials of reading, writing, arithmetic and Scripture. Elementary education in this period was designed to teach the poor to 'know their duty and keep their place', *not* to help them rise above their station.

Nevertheless it was from these beginnings that Britain's 'state system' of education developed. This alone makes the 1870 Act the most important milestone in the country's educational history. By 1880 there were enough schools for attendance to be made compulsory up to the age of ten. (The leaving age was raised to twelve in 1899 and fourteen in 1918.) **Compulsory attendance** brought to light hordes of children who were starving, suffering from infectious diseases, and without shoes or proper clothes. Many school boards had to arrange for cheap meals, free medical attention and the distribution of charity clothing for the most ragged ones. Fees were low, yet many families had great difficulty in paying even a penny or twopence (less than 1p) a week. Consequently elementary education was made free to all in 1891.

One immediate result of the spread of elementary education was the rise of the 'popular press'. Its chief creator was Alfred Harmsworth, later **Lord Northcliffe** (1865–1922). He realised that most of the new reading public found existing **newspapers**, with their stress on parliamentary news, too dull and difficult. After a successful start with a weekly paper called *Answers* (1888) he founded the *Daily Mail* in 1896. Its eye-catching headlines and photographs and its 'chatty' style quickly attracted a mass readership. Within three years, its daily circulation was over half a million, twice that of any other newspaper. The *Daily Mail* set the standard for the 'popular' newspapers of the twentieth century, including the *Daily Mirror* and the *Daily Express*.

The 1902 Act and the 'educational ladder'

Full-time education *beyond* the elementary stage was still only available to those who could afford the fees of private, grammar or public schools. The rest mostly had to make do with Mechanics' and Working Men's Institutes, which provided evening lectures, reading-rooms and lending libraries in return for a small subscription. By the 1890s, some local Boards provided 'higher grade schools', and County Councils began to run evening classes – mainly in technical and commercial subjects. But these opportunities were only available in a few areas.

The beginnings of the 'popular press': a copy of the 'Daily Mail' from 1896. The spread of elementary education had created a new reading public

Playground drill in a London girls' school (1908)

Most children from board schools had little chance of continuing their education, even if they were gifted.

No industrial country could afford such wastage of ability. In the 1890s a Royal Commission was set up 'to consider what are the best methods of establishing a well-organised system of secondary education in England'. Some of its proposals became law in the **1902 Education Act**, which made secondary schools for the first time a concern of the state. The 2,568 School Boards were abolished and their duties handed over to County and County Borough Councils. The Boards had achieved a great deal, providing nearly 2½ million school places, but they were too small to be really efficient. The newly created **Local Education Authorities** (328 in all) were large enough to build and maintain elementary *and* secondary schools.

It was intended that all secondary schools, both old and new, should charge fees. But in 1907 an important change was made. Secondary schools receiving public grants were instructed to make a quarter of their places available free of charge to the cleverest children from the elementary schools. These **free places**, later called scholarships, at last made it possible for a child from a poor family to get a full secondary education, continuing beyond the normal leaving age. In the early years, up to the First World War (1914–18), places were scarce, and less than one child in twenty from the elementary schools won a 'scholarship'. Nevertheless it was an important departure from the traditional view that education should teach children to 'know their station in life'. An 'educational ladder' had been built which could be climbed by able and hardworking children from any social background.

Meanwhile rapid strides were made in organising social services for

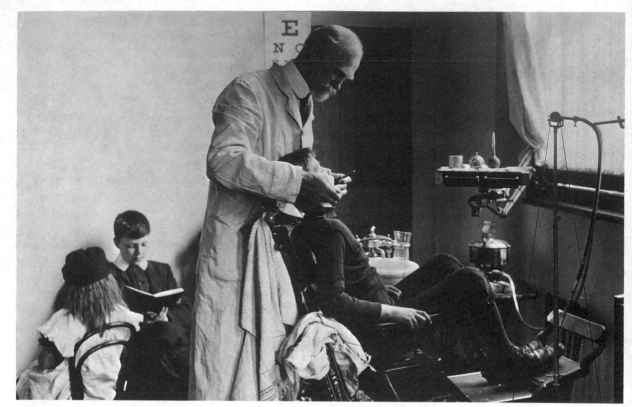

Schoolchildren receiving dental attention (1911)

schoolchildren. Parliament in 1906 encouraged the provision of school meals, and in the following year medical examinations were made compulsory in elementary schools (see page 240). Medical attention was extended to secondary schools in the **Education Act of 1918**. The same Act (largely the work of **H.A.L. Fisher**, President of the Board of Education) fixed the school leaving age at fourteen and restricted the employment of schoolchildren to little more than a paper round. Fisher also encouraged part-time education up to the age of sixteen, but lack of money almost ruled this out from the start (see page 298). The next big educational advance – free secondary schooling for *every* child, regardless of ability – had to wait until the second quarter of the twentieth century.

Timeline

1783	Robert Raikes founds the first Sunday school.
1798	Introduction of the 'monitorial system'.
1828	University College, London founded.
1828–42	Thomas Arnold Headmaster of Rugby.
1833	First parliamentary grant for education (£20,000).
1862	'Payment by results' introduced.
1870	Elementary Education Act (W. E. Forster).
1880	Elementary education made compulsory.
1891	Elementary education made free.
1902	Education Act.

1907 'Free places' in grant-aided secondary schools.
1918 Education Act (H.A.L. Fisher).

Questions

1. Look at the picture of a monitorial school (page 205).
   a) Name the two men who each claimed to have invented this type of school, and the Church Societies they inspired.
   b) Describe the teaching method being used. Was it effective?
   c) What was the attraction of this kind of school from the point of view of the organisers?
   d) Describe briefly *two* other types of school attended by children of poor parents in the early nineteenth century.

2. In what ways were the public schools unsatisfactory in the eighteenth century? How did they reform themselves in the nineteenth century and why did they enjoy rising popularity?

3. Give definitions of each of the following:
   a) Classics   b) governess
   c) endowed grammar school d) dissenters' academy
   e) civic university   f) pupil teacher

4. 'Now that we have given them political power we must not wait any longer to give them education...with the hope of doing great good, by removing that ignorance which we are all aware is pregnant with crime and misery...and danger to the community.' (W.E. Forster, House of Commons, February 1870)

   a) To what extent had those in need of elementary education been given 'political power' before 1870?
   b) What other reason does Forster give for making more education available?
   c) Why was there a dispute about religious teaching in schools financed by ratepayers? How did the 1870 Act tackle the problem?
   d) What were the duties of the School Boards set up by the Act?
   e) When was schooling made i) compulsory and ii) free to all?

5. Write a paragraph on each of the following:
   a) 'payment by results'
   b) Education Act of 1902
   c) free places in secondary schools
   d) the 'Fisher Act' of 1918

The British Overseas
The Empire (1783–1914) and the Irish Problem

After the loss of the Thirteen Colonies in America in 1783 (see page 26) the British had second thoughts about the value of overseas settlements. If colonists were likely to revolt against the mother country as soon as they were strong enough to stand on their own feet, then it was felt that all the trouble and expense of establishing colonies would not be worthwhile. For some years after the American Revolution the British tried to increase their trading connections while *avoiding*, as far as possible, the responsibility of founding settlements.

However interest in *imperialism* (the founding of colonies) gradually revived in the early nineteenth century. It was encouraged by Britain's control of the seas, the discoveries of explorers such as Captain Cook and, above all, by the desire of growing numbers to emigrate and start a new life elsewhere. The tide of **emigration** began to flow strongly in the 1830s and early 1840s (a time of hardship among the poor). It became a flood after gold discoveries in California (1849) and Australia (1851). Altogether in the period 1815–1914, about 19 million Britons, many of them Irish, left for foreign lands. After 1865 the yearly total of emigrants never fell below 100,000, and the British built 'an empire on which the sun never sets' – stretching into every corner of the world.

The growth of the Dominions

In the eighteenth century Britain obtained, almost by accident, vast, underpopulated territories – Canada, Australia and New Zealand – which were suited to European settlement. However their future prospects were not realised at the time. **Canada**, gained at the Treaty of Paris (1763), was thought by many people to be less valuable than the small West Indian sugar islands of Martinique and Guadeloupe, which were returned to France. Pitt's Canada Act (1791) divided the inhabited area into two provinces: Upper Canada (**Ontario**) where British settlers lived, and Lower Canada (**Quebec**) which was populated by the earlier French colonists. Each was granted an elected assembly to control local affairs, but in most other ways the two provinces were very different. French Quebec consisted mainly of isolated farmers and fur traders, scattered along the banks of the St Lawrence river. Ontario had busy, thriving towns, inhabited largely by 'Empire Loyalists' who had left the Thirteen Colonies after they became independent.

The two races did not get on well together. French-speaking Canadians feared that the British wanted to impose their own customs

Original provinces of the Dominion of Canada established 1867 by the British North America Act

Dominion of Canada 1912

Canadian Pacific Railway 1885

The Dominion of Canada

Driving the last spike in the Canadian Pacific Railway, 7 November 1885

upon them, while British settlers complained that their trade was hampered by the French along the St Lawrence. In 1837 there were riots in both provinces. They were easily put down, but the British Government sent Lord Durham to investigate the causes of unrest. On his return he wrote a report which became the basis of all future relations between Britain and her 'white colonies'. The **Durham Report (1839)** suggested, first, that the separate provinces should be reunited, and, second, that Canadians should be given responsibility for managing their own affairs. Then they would have no cause to rebel against the British connection, as the Thirteen Colonies had done. The first proposal was accepted almost immediately. The second eventually became law in the **British North America Act (1867)**. Quebec, Ontario and the coastal provinces of New Brunswick and Nova Scotia were formed into a self-governing colony, or *dominion*, with a central government at Ottawa.

Dominion status gave Canadians control of their country yet maintained close and co-operative relations with Britain. It coincided with a period of expansion into the vast territories of the interior. Beyond the Rocky Mountains, parts of the western coastal region of British Columbia had already been populated by a 'gold rush', beginning in 1857. British Columbia agreed to join the Dominion (1871) provided a railway was built to link it with the east. The result was the great **Canadian Pacific Railway**, which ran for nearly 5,000 kilometres through lonely prairies and rugged mountains. Its completion (1885) united Canada more securely than any Act of Parliament could do.

Settlers followed the engineers, and soon the prairies of Manitoba (which joined the Dominion in 1870), Alberta and Saskatchewan (1905) were transformed into vast wheatlands. The total wheat crop increased by twenty times in the period 1870–1914, while the population doubled – from under 4 to 7½ million.

The first British landings in **Australia** were made in 1788, when 700 convicts were transported there. But a further forty years went by before the new continent was officially declared a British territory. Meanwhile it continued to be a dumping ground for convicts, who outnumbered free settlers until the 1830s. The long voyage and the presence of thousands of criminals discouraged emigration from Britain – even though the crossing of the Blue Mountains (1817) opened up fine grazing land suitable for sheep-farming. The colony of Victoria was founded in the same year, as an alternative to the original convict settlements in New South Wales and Van Diemen's Land (Tasmania).

The next stage in the development of Australia resulted from the efforts of **Edward Gibbon Wakefield** (1796–1862). He wanted the new colonies to become 'real British nations', not just places of refuge for the poor and unfortunate. He therefore worked out a method of *systematic colonisation*. This involved selling the land to wealthy settlers and using the money to pay for the passages of new immigrants who would farm the land for wages. In this way a colony would contain people of all social classes – a true cross-section of Britain – and be capable of governing itself. Wakefield established a company which successfully applied his principles to the settlement of South Australia (founded in 1836). Land was sold to 16,000 settlers and the proceeds used to bring labourers out from Britain. It soon became a prosperous wheat-growing area..

However, not until the **discovery of gold** in New South Wales and Victoria (1851) did free settlers come in large numbers. The population rose from about 400,000 in 1850 to over a million ten years later. Meanwhile, by 1855, most of the colonies had been granted 'responsible government', with their own parliaments. Queensland obtained the same rights in 1859 and Western Australia in 1890. All the states depended largely on sheep- and cattle-farming. At first livestock were bred mainly for hides and fat. Much meat was wasted because the small population could consume only a fraction of it. But the introduction of refrigeration in the 1880s led to mounting exports of beef and mutton carcasses to Britain and Europe. In 1914 Australia had about a sixth of the world's sheep. They far outnumbered the small human population of 5 million.

Australia's isolated settlements went their own separate ways at first. But by the 1890s they began to seek closer unity, because of the colonial ambitions of other countries. Germany controlled nearby Papua. The French were in Tahiti. Japan was growing powerful and eager to expand overseas. A single Australian government was needed to organise the defence of the continent. Therefore by the **Commonwealth of Australia Act (1900)** Parliament joined the separate states in a self-governing dominion. Soon afterwards a 'white

The Dominion of Australia

The harbour at Melbourne, Victoria (1883)

Australia' policy was declared. It was feared that if immigrants from the overpopulated countries of South-East Asia were admitted, they would quickly outnumber white Australians and swamp their Western way of life.

The settlement of **New Zealand** followed a similar pattern. In 1839 Gibbon Wakefield formed the New Zealand Company, which followed his principle of selling land and using the money to bring out more emigrants from Britain. It was a successful start, although there were many disputes with the native Maoris over land ownership. In the 1870s a central government was established at Wellington, and New Zealand became the third self-governing dominion in 1907. Her prosperity depended on export of chilled lamb and mutton, and by 1914, when the population was less than 1 million, she had begun to rival Denmark as a dairy-farming nation. Meanwhile rapid social progress was made. All men were given the vote in 1889, and all women in 1893. New Zealand had old age pensions, state-aided hospitals, labour exchanges and many other social services well before they were introduced into Britain.

The British in India

English merchants founded the East India Company (1600) in order to trade with the East *not* to conquer India. But in the eighteenth century the Company was forced to wage war and take control of certain territories to secure its trading stations against attack, especially from the French (see Chapter 3). As a result the British Government became directly involved in Indian affairs. **Pitt's India Act (1784)** set up a Board of Control in London which supervised many of the Company's activities. It was hoped that further conquests would be unnecessary, but dangers from native rulers and continued French interference led to more wars and more British gains. By 1819 the conquest of India was almost complete and Britain was responsible for law and order throughout the subcontinent.

The British soon began to influence the Indian way of life. For example, they tried to stamp out cruel customs such as *suttee* (the burning alive of a widow on her husband's funeral pyre). During **Lord Dalhousie's** term as Governor-General (1848–56) a cheap postal service and the electric telegraph were introduced, and 6,500 kilometres of good roads and the first railways were built. Dalhousie also began a system of elementary education in village schools. But the pace of reform was too fast. The British took it for granted that Indians wanted to be Westernised, and ignored many Eastern customs and religious practices. Consequently there was mounting opposition to 'British interference', especially among landowners, who objected to Dalhousie's policy of deposing native rulers who were weak or incompetent. Even the setting up of village schools was suspected of being the start of a drive to convert Indians to Christianity.

In the midst of the unrest brought about by Dalhousie's reforms, a serious revolt, known as the **Indian Mutiny**, broke out among the 'sepoys' (native troops) in the Bengal army of the East India Company. Discipline had been bad for some time when, in May 1857, sepoys from three regiments murdered British officers and their

Sikh officers in the Indian army (1858)

families in order to release from gaol 85 of their comrades who had disobeyed orders. Fortunately for the British, the rising that followed did not spread over the whole country. Only about a quarter of the sepoys in the Bengal army took part. Nevertheless the British were outnumbered and in great danger. The mutineers quickly occupied Delhi, the capital, but then they hesitated, allowing the Company's troops time to organise and counter-attack. Within a few months the British were back in control, but order was not fully restored for two years.

Neither side emerged from the Mutiny with credit. Indians massacred British families after they had surrendered, and the British, in turn, took merciless revenge before peace was officially declared. The resulting hatred and distrust between the races was never quite forgotten. But at least the British learned not to push their Westernising policy too far in the future. There were no more conquests of Indian territory after 1858, when the East India Company was abolished and its army transferred to the Crown. As an extra precaution, the proportion of British troops in each regiment was raised to at least a third.

India now settled into a period of calm, during which new irrigation schemes and railways improved the cultivation and distribution of crops. But, with a population of more than 200 million, terrible famines were still unavoidable if the rains failed – as they did in 1877, when at least 5 million people died of starvation. By the end of the century, Indians had been granted a small share in government. This was increased in 1909, but educated Indians were not satisfied. They were still members of a conquered race, treated by the British as second-class citizens. As late as 1914, only about 5 per cent of senior posts in the civil service were filled by Indians, and all important government decisions were made by the British.

South Africa – the Boer War

The first British foothold in South Africa was the **Cape of Good Hope**, taken from the Dutch during the Napoleonic Wars and purchased for £14 million in 1815. It was a valuable naval base on the sea route to India and the Far East, particularly before the opening of the Suez Canal (1869).

From the start, British settlers found the black Africans easier to handle than the Dutch farmers (**Boers**) who had established the colony. Boers were tough, religious folk who disliked all government and hated paying taxes to the British. They used Africans as slaves, but in 1833 slavery was abolished throughout the British Empire. Disgusted with the 'soft' attitude of the British, and eager to have greater freedom and more land, the Boers clambered into their ox-wagons and started the **Great Trek** inland. From 1835 onwards Boers left Cape Colony in their thousands, to set up new homes in Natal and in the territories later known as Orange Free State and Transvaal.

The trekkers wanted complete independence. But when fighting broke out with the African tribes of the interior, British troops

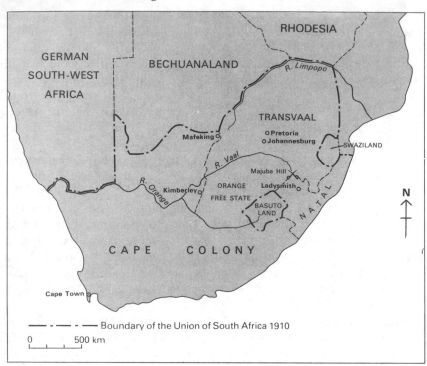

GERMAN
SOUTH-WEST
AFRICA

RHODESIA

BECHUANALAND

R. Limpopo

TRANSVAAL

Mafeking○   ○Pretoria
○Johannesburg

SWAZILAND

R. Vaal

Majuba Hill

R. Orange

Kimberley○   ORANGE   Ladysmith○
FREE STATE
BASUTO
LAND

NATAL

CAPE   COLONY

N

Cape Town○

— · — · — Boundary of the Union of South Africa 1910

0   500 km

South Africa in the early twentieth century

arrived to help restore order. This happened in **Natal**, which Britain took over in 1843 (causing the Boers to move out again). **Transvaal** and **Orange Free State** were granted self-government in the 1850s. Britain occupied Transvaal for a brief period after 1877, to defend it against the warlike Zulus on its frontiers. But after the Zulu danger had been removed, the Boers demanded that their independence should be restored. While Gladstone's Government hesitated, the Boers routed a small British force at **Majuba Hill** (**1881**). Britain now gave in to their demands, rather than fight a difficult and costly war.

Lasting peace between the two Boer republics and the two British territories of Cape Colony and Natal seemed unlikely. Any chance of it was ruined when rich seams of **gold** were discovered in Transvaal (1886). The Boers were farmers and took no part in exploiting the gold for themselves. But thousands of settlers, mostly British, poured into the republic and created a thriving town – Johannesburg – around the diggings. The Boers strongly disliked these **Uitlanders** (outsiders) who were upsetting their simple, independent way of life. **Paul Kruger**, the President of Transvaal, was a bitter opponent of Britain. Although he did not want to expel the foreigners, for they were making his country rich, he refused to give them the vote and made them pay heavy taxes.

Kruger's policy, though unfair, was understandable. 'Those who do not like my laws can leave my country', he said. This attitude infuriated **Cecil Rhodes**, the Prime Minister of Cape Colony. After making a fortune in diamonds and gold, Rhodes had set out to use his wealth to make the British masters of Africa. His greatest ambition was to

Paul Kruger (1825–1904), President of the Transvaal

Cecil Rhodes (1853–1902), Prime Minister of Cape Colony

establish a wide belt of British territory running the length of the continent, from the Cape to Cairo. He therefore encouraged British settlement in the area north of Transvaal (later Rhodesia). This, together with British control of Bechuanaland, prevented the Boers from extending their territories. A clash between Rhodes and Kruger was unavoidable, for the Boer republics stood in the way of Rhodes's ambitions.

Rhodes planned to crush Transvaal by encouraging a Uitlander rebellion in Johannesburg and supporting it with his own British South Africa Company police. But the scheme collapsed disastrously. The Uitlanders failed to revolt, and Dr L.S. Jameson, in command of the British force, grew tired of waiting. In December 1895 he crossed the Transvaal border with only 470 men, and was easily overpowered. The **Jameson Raid** discredited Rhodes, who was forced to resign, and blackened Britain's reputation in the eyes of the world. The German Emperor, William II, even sent a telegram to congratulate Kruger. This encouraged the Boers in the mistaken belief that they could expect German support in any decisive contest with Britain. Transvaal's expenditure on armaments – most of them German – rose 400 per cent in the next two years, and an alliance was made with Orange Free State (1897). Britain sent troop reinforcements to Natal, but Kruger demanded their withdrawal from his frontiers. When the British refused (October 1899) the **Boer War** began.

The Boers took the offensive immediately, besieging the British in **Ladysmith** (Natal) **Kimberley** (Cape Colony) and **Mafeking** (Bechuanaland). However, early in 1900 reinforcements arrived and a series of British successes followed, under the leadership of Lord Roberts. The three garrisons were relieved, and by 5 June Roberts was in **Pretoria**, the Transvaal capital. But although the last of the Boer armies was defeated in August, Kruger refused to surrender. For another eighteen months Boer riflemen raided and ambushed the British, forcing **Lord Kitchener**, now in command, to conquer every inch of the countryside. Farms were destroyed and Boer families crowded into **concentration camps**, where insanitary conditions caused 20,000 deaths in fourteen months. There were storms of protest from all over the world. Foreigners accused Britain of bullying the Boers in order to steal their gold. Even at home, the Leader of the Liberal Party denounced Kitchener's 'methods of barbarism'.

The war was finally ended by the **Peace of Vereeniging (May 1902)**. The two Boer republics lost their independence and Britain paid £3 million towards restocking the devastated farms. It had taken 450,000 British troops nearly three years to defeat 50,000 Boers – at the cost of 22,000 lives and £220 million of British taxpayers' money. Never again were the British people so enthusiastic about their empire. In 1906–7 the newly elected Liberal Government tried to wipe out some of the bitterness by restoring the independence of Transvaal and Orange Free State. Soon afterwards the four independent South African states came together in a self-governing dominion, the **Union of South Africa (1910)**. Louis Botha, one of the Boer generals, was its first prime minister.

'The scramble for Africa'

At the beginning of the nineteenth century, British possessions in Africa were confined to forts and slave-trading stations along the west coast. The interior of the continent was still largely unknown to Europeans. However as the century progressed explorers revealed the courses of the great rivers and mapped the lakes, forests and mountains. None stirred the public imagination more than **David Livingstone** (1813–73), a self-educated Scotsman who started work in a cotton-mill at the age of ten. After taking a degree in medicine when he was twenty-seven, Livingstone spent the rest of his life journeying in 'darkest Africa'. Risking death from disease and hostile tribes, he became the first white man to discover the Victoria Falls, Lake Nyasa, the upper waters of the Congo and many other great landmarks.

To the ordinary person, African exploration was an exciting adventure. But to businessmen and politicians it uncovered great new sources of wealth and power. By this time European factories were mass producing goods in such large quantities that manufacturers were constantly searching for new regions of the world where they

The British army relieves the siege of Ladysmith (1900) during the Boer War

Africa 1875

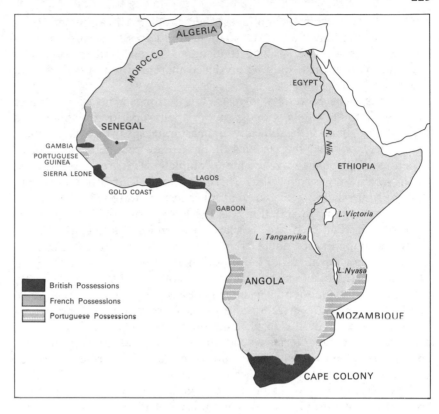

British Possessions
French Possessions
Portuguese Possessions

Africa 1914

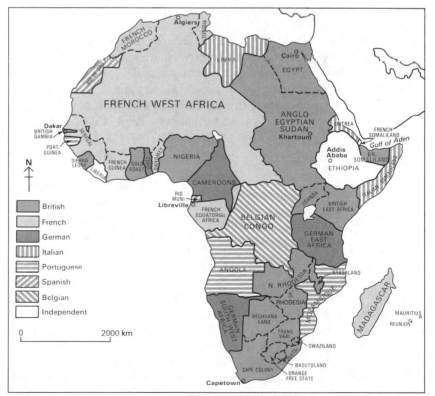

British
French
German
Italian
Portuguese
Spanish
Belgian
Independent

could sell their products and invest their profits. Africa seemed likely to provide not only markets for manufactured goods but also valuable supplies of raw materials and foodstuffs. Cotton, timber, vegetable oils and mineral ores could be produced there and fed into European industries.

Africans were powerless to resist this European 'invasion'. White men, with their warships and cannon, their superior discipline and organisation, had little difficulty in mastering spear-throwing tribesmen. They rejected the customs of those they conquered and introduced a European way of life, complete with roads, railways, factories and mines, as well as Christian churches. It is not surprising that the 'imperialists' were hated as much as they were feared.

The real **Age of Imperialism** was the last quarter of the nineteenth century. The Far East had its share of attention, particularly China, where Britain, France and Germany were rivals in establishing trading posts and naval stations. But the main objective was Africa. In 1875 only a tenth of the continent was governed by Europeans. By 1900 more than nine-tenths had been colonised (see map on page 223), Britain led the way in redrawing the map of Africa, taking over a large proportion of the fertile and productive regions. But France, Portugal, Belgium, Germany and Italy all claimed a share. In 1885 they even signed a treaty in Berlin which laid down rules by which the 'scramble' was to be conducted.

Apart from the colonies in the South and West, which continued to expand in this period, the other main area of British activity in Africa was in the north-east, **Egypt** and the **Sudan**. In Egypt, the influence of France had been strong ever since French engineers built the Suez Canal (1869). Moreover, half the shares in the Canal Company were French-owned. But British interest in this region grew rapidly after 1875, when Disraeli's Government purchased almost all the remaining Canal shares from the bankrupt Egyptian ruler, Khedive Ismail. Following a rebellion, Britain occupied Egypt (1882) and began to reform its administration and finances. **Lord Cromer** became 'adviser' to the Egyptian Government (1883–1907) and organised the building of dams, reservoirs and canals, to make better use of the precious Nile waters.

Egypt's dependency, the Sudan, was in the hands of a religious fanatic, the Mahdi. The isolated Egyptian garrisons were evacuated, but not before Britain's **General Charles Gordon** had been killed at Khartoum (January 1885) after refusing to retreat. Eleven years later Lord Salisbury's Government sent Lord Kitchener, in command of the Egyptian army, to reconquer the Sudan and gain control of the Upper Nile. Kitchener defeated the Sudanese, but when he arrived at **Fashoda** (July 1898) he found a French flag flying. It was the work of Captain Marchand of the French army, who, together with 7 officers and 120 native troops, had travelled nearly 5,000 kilometres from the Atlantic coast with orders to secure the Upper Sudan for France. Kitchener and Marchand wisely referred the matter to their governments. While British and French newspapers flung insults at each other, Salisbury openly prepared for war. Realising he was serious,

Following rumours that Livingstone was dead, the 'New York Herald' sent another explorer, H.M. Stanley, to find him. The famous meeting of Stanley and Livingstone (shown here in an artist's impression) took place at Ujiji on the shores of Lake Tanganyika in 1871

the French reluctantly gave way and ordered Marchand to leave. A joint British and Egyptian government then ruled the Sudan.

Ireland and Home Rule

Ireland never really recovered from the Great Famine of the 1840s (see page 156). The resulting mass emigration, mostly to the USA, almost halved the population in the next fifty years. Emigrants left with bitter feelings towards Britain. They believed Parliament could have *prevented* famine conditions from arising if it had taken more interest in Irish affairs. In 1858, in New York, discontented Irish-Americans founded the **Fenian Society**, which aimed to achieve an Irish republic totally independent of the United Kingdom. Fenians believed in using force. They soon began a series of bombings and violent demonstrations in England, which acted as a sharp reminder of Irish grievances.

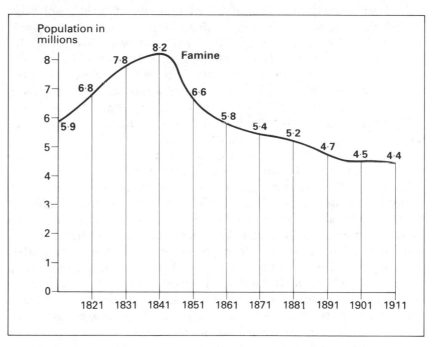

The population of Ireland – before and after the Great Famine

'My mission is to pacify Ireland', said **William Ewart Gladstone**, who first became Prime Minister in 1868. During the next twenty-five years he led the country on four separate occasions, and tried desperately to find a lasting solution to the Irish problem. First, he dealt with religious grievances. Only one Irishman in ten belonged to the Anglican Church, so Gladstone **'disestablished' the Anglican Church of Ireland (1869)**, taking away its property (worth £15 million) and giving half to charity and education. This pleased the Catholic majority. The other major grievance concerned land, much of which was owned by Englishmen. Every year, hundreds of families were evicted from their smallholdings because their landlords found new tenants capable of farming the land more effectively and paying more rent.

Gladstone's **Land Act (1870)** made landlords pay outgoing tenants compensation for improvements they had made. His second **Land Act (1881)** went much further, stating that tenants could not be evicted so long as they paid their rent, and allowing them to sell their leases without consulting the landlord. Moreover, Land Courts were set up, to fix fair rents in cases where landlord and tenant disagreed.

Rents now dropped by about a quarter. But the Irish Party in the Commons was not satisfied. It demanded nothing less than **Home Rule** by a separate Irish parliament. Meanwhile there was great unrest in Ireland, with frequent outbreaks of violence against landlords. By 1886 Gladstone gave up hope of 'pacifying Ireland' through a policy of reform and introduced a Home Rule Bill. However his sudden conversion aroused opposition among his own Liberal supporters. Ninety-three of them joined the Conservatives to defeat the Bill. Gladstone tried once more, in 1893, but his Bill was overwhelmingly rejected by the House of Lords, having narrowly passed the Commons.

The large Conservative majority in the House of Lords, which included many owners of land in Ireland, seemed a permanent stumbling block to Irish Home Rule. But the situation was changed by the Parliament Act of 1911 (see page 240). The Lords could now only *delay* Commons' Bills; they could not reject them completely. In 1912 the Liberal Government introduced a **third Home Rule Bill**. It passed the Commons only to be rejected, as expected, by the Lords. However, by the terms of the Parliament Act, it would become law after two years, despite the opposition of the peers. Ireland would have its own parliament in Dublin, although it would still send MPs to Westminster, which retained control over defence and foreign affairs.

But Home Rule was strongly opposed by Protestants in the northern counties (together called **Ulster**). They preferred to remain part of the United Kingdom rather than be governed by an Irish parliament in which Catholics would outnumber them. Ulster was the country's main industrial region. Its more prosperous inhabitants anticipated that they would have to pay the largest share of taxation, to support the agricultural South. Determined to resist the wishes of the Catholics, Ulstermen began to arm themselves. In March 1914 Northern Irish officers serving in the British army at the **Curragh** base, near Dublin, resigned rather than march into Ulster to enforce Home Rule. Ireland seemed on the point of civil war when the outbreak of the First World War (August 1914) caused Home Rule to be postponed for the duration of the war.

Equally serious opposition to the Bill came from a secret organisation called **Sinn Féin** (Ourselves Alone). Like the earlier Fenians, Sinn Féiners wanted *complete* separation from Britain. Yet the terms of the 1912 Bill offered Ireland *less* self-government than a dominion like Canada. On Easter Monday 1916 Patrick Pearse, a poet and teacher, led a rising in Dublin. About 2,000 Irish Volunteers, an armed force with the same aim as Sinn Féin, occupied key points in the city, including the General Post Office, and opened fire on British soldiers. The **Easter Rising** had no chance of success; but its leaders seemed prepared to give up their lives as an example to their

The Easter Rising, 1916: British soldiers among the ruins of the General Post Office, Dublin

countrymen. For six days, the streets and squares of Dublin became a battlefield. When the rebels were finally captured Dubliners cursed them for causing the ruin of their city.

However the British made a terrible mistake when they tried and executed Pearse and fourteen others. This turned them into heroes, and the Sinn Féin cause, which had almost collapsed, received an unexpected flood of support. In the 1918 election, Sinn Féiners won 73 seats out of 105. Led by their President, **Eamon de Valera**, they refused to sit at Westminster and in 1919 set up their own *Dáil* (parliament) in Dublin, which quickly commanded the support of the southern Irish. Meanwhile the Irish Volunteers, now called the **IRA** (Irish Republican Army), waged war on British soldiers and police. The British Government replied by raising a special force of ex-soldiers, nicknamed the **'Black and Tans'** because they wore the black hat of the Irish police with their khaki uniforms. A deadly struggle followed. Bloodstained bodies in the streets and wrecked or burning buildings became familiar sights.

By 1921 both sides were weary of fighting and ready to discuss peace. **David Lloyd George**, Britain's Prime Minister, made a truce with Sinn Féin leaders. He then offered southern Ireland independence on the same basis as the dominions, provided the six counties of Ulster (**Northern Ireland**) were free to remain part of the United Kingdom. De Valera rejected the British terms. Dominion status was not full independence, he argued, and Britain would be able to use her position as head of the Commonwealth to interfere in Irish affairs. He urged the Irish peace negotiators not to agree to any treaty which left the Irish subjects of the British Crown.

The Irish negotiators shared de Valera's dislike of the British proposals. But they knew that a renewal of the war would be unpopular at home, and that the IRA was in a weakened state. Reluctantly they signed a treaty, on 6 December 1921, which accepted the *partition* (division) of Ireland and stated that the new southern Irish parliament would take an oath of loyalty to the Crown. So the **Irish Free State** was created in 1922.

Ireland, showing the line of partition (1921)

Northern Ireland

Irish Free State

De Valera and his more extreme Sinn Féin supporters rejected the peace treaty. Their aim was a fully independent republic of all Ireland, free from all traces of British influence. A civil war followed (1922–3) in which the anti-treaty forces were heavily outnumbered and defeated. But de Valera did not give up. In 1926 he split away from Sinn Féin and formed a new party called **Fianna Fáil** (Gaelic for 'Warriors of Ireland'), which gradually gained support for the anti-British cause. In 1932 Fianna Fáil gained a majority in the Dáil and de Valera set about removing the Free State's remaining links with Britain. The oath of loyalty to the Crown was abolished, the King's representative, the Governor-General, was stripped of his powers, and the Free State began issuing separate passports to its citizens. Finally, in 1937, the Irish Free State was renamed **Eire** and a new constitution made it a republic in all but name (see page 316).

Eamon de Valera (1882–1975), pictured in 1921 – the year of Irish partition

Timeline

1788	First landings in Australia.
1815	Cape of Good Hope purchased.
1835	Beginning of the 'Great Trek'.
1839	Durham Report.
1857	Indian Mutiny.
1867	British North America Act (Dominion of Canada).
1882	British occupation of Egypt.
1898	Fashoda incident.
1899–1902	Boer War.
1900	Commonwealth of Australia Act (Dominion of Australia).
1907	Dominion of New Zealand.
1910	Union of South Africa.
1916	'Easter Rising' in Dublin.
1922	Irish Free State (renamed Eire, 1937).

Questions

1. 'Hundreds of poor people, men, women and children, of all ages from the drivelling idiot of 90 to the babe just born, huddled together, without light, without air, wallowing in filth . . . sick in body, dispirited in heart . . .

   The causes which produced the immense emigration of the past year still exist . . . and we shall have a repetition of the same scenes of misery, if prompt measures be not taken.'

   (Letter to an Emigration Commissioner from Stephen de Vere, who sailed with emigrants to Canada (1847) to observe their condition)

   a) Many emigrants at this time were Irish. What had happened in Ireland which forced many people to leave the country?

   b) Why would many emigrants have been 'sick in body, dispirited in heart'?

   c) What happened in California and Australia in the next few years to further swell the numbers of emigrants from Britain?

d) How did Edward Gibbon Wakefield encourage emigration to Australia and New Zealand?

e) Long voyages gradually got easier in later years. Why?

2. 'I am not ready to hand over my country to strangers.' (President Kruger of the Transvaal)

a) Who were the 'strangers'? What did the Boers call them?
b) Why had they gone to the Transvaal?
c) Who tried to encourage them to revolt so that he could gain control of the Transvaal?
d) Why did this scheme fail, and with what result?
e) How and why did the Boer War of 1899–1902 affect
   i) Britain's reputation abroad, and   ii) the attitude of the British people towards their empire?

3. What were the main grievances of the Irish after the Great Famine? How did Gladstone try a) to 'pacify Ireland', and b) to achieve Irish Home Rule? Why did both policies fail?

4. 'You are letting loose a river of blood, and, make no mistake about it, between two races who, after three hundred years of hatred and of strife, we had nearly succeeded in bringing together.' (John Dillon, Deputy Leader of the Irish Party in the House of Commons, May 1916)

a) What had recently happened in Dublin (starting on Easter Monday, 24 April)?
b) How did the British react to it?
c) Why did Dillon think the British reaction was 'letting loose a river of blood'?
d) What did Dillon mean when he said that Parliament had 'nearly succeeded in bringing together' the 'two races'?
e) After the end of the First World War (1918), what happened to force the 'two races' apart?

5. Write a paragraph on each of the following:
   a) the Durham Report, 1839
   b) the Indian Mutiny
   c) the 'Great Trek'
   d) the Fashoda Incident

'The Two Nations'

Social Life, Attitudes, Reforms – from the Victorian Age to the First World War

As a young man, **Benjamin Disraeli** wrote several novels. In one, called *Sybil* (1845), he described the rich and poor as *Two Nations* 'who are as ignorant of each other's habits, thoughts and feelings as if they were dwellers in different zones, or inhabitants of different planets; who are formed by different breeding; are fed by a different food, are ordered by different manners, and are not governed by the same laws.'

Although social divisions of this kind had long existed in the countryside, some interests and activities, such as farming and hunting, were shared to some extent by rich and poor. In the industrial towns this was not so. The rich, secure in their own neighbourhoods or suburbs, had no contact with the 'lower orders' and were often completely ignorant of living conditions in the slum areas. Many did their best to forget that the poor even existed. If Disraeli had been writing fifty or sixty years later, he would have found the situation little changed.

However there were more than two 'nations' in the nineteenth century. The Industrial Revolution and the growth of towns not only widened the gulf between rich and poor, it also increased the number of *middle* classes in between. Moreover, it raised the standard of living of the skilled worker far above that of the unskilled labourer and slum-dweller.

Townsmen and villagers

By the mid nineteenth century, the growth of manufacturing industry made Britain the first country in the world to have a majority of people living in towns. Meanwhile town and country were increasingly separated from each other. Villages became more purely agricultural as, one by one, craftsmen disappeared from the countryside. By about 1900 only the blacksmith remained in some villages.

Looking at the nation as a whole, those commonly referred to as 'the poor' still made up the largest social group. They were mostly unskilled workers without a regular trade: factory hands, dockers, 'navvies', farm labourers and the like. Much of what was written and said about the extent of **poverty** was guesswork, until, in 1889, **Charles Booth**, a Liverpool shipowner, published the first of seventeen volumes on *The Life and Labour of the People of London* (completed in 1903). He and a team of helpers carried out extensive social surveys, on the basis of which Booth calculated that about a third of London's families lived in poverty, on about £1 a week or less. Many critics said London was exceptional. But in 1899 **Seebohm Rowntree**,

Slum dwellers in London (1889)

a member of the famous cocoa- and chocolate-making family, conducted a house-to-house survey in York, with similar results. He discovered almost 28 per cent of the total population in poverty (which he defined in much the same way as Booth).

If these findings were true of Britain as a whole, roughly 10 million people in England and Wales alone were so poor that, in Rowntree's words, they were 'forced to go without some of the necessities of a civilised life'. Those below the 'poverty line' were unable to afford anything better than a damp, dark slum. Their diet may have contained enough bulk to fight off the feeling of hunger, but it almost certainly lacked sufficient nourishment for good health. Many families could not afford butchers' meat, only a little fat bacon. Extras such as clothing were often paid for by going short of food. As one woman in York said: 'If there's anything extra to buy, such as a pair of boots for one of the children, me and the children goes without dinner'.

Such conditions were not confined to the towns. **Agricultural labourers** were no better off. Although their wages rose gradually in the second half of the nineteenth century, they were still the lowest

Farm labourers in the late nineteenth century

paid of all workers. They mostly lived in cottages of mud, plaster and thatch, with one room up and one down. Few had more than two bedrooms, even though families of ten, twelve or more children were common. Such dwellings were often damp and draughty as well as overcrowded. More spacious brick-built cottages were normally found only on the larger estates. Cowmen and shepherds got higher wages than ordinary labourers, but less than they could have obtained in a factory or workshop. As the century progressed, emigration overseas and a steady drift to the towns led to depopulation of the countryside. Despite reports of the hardships of factory life, many villagers regarded the railway line to town as the route to better things. Wages were higher, and that counted for a lot.

Charles Booth estimated that 10 shillings (50p) a week marked the difference between poverty and 'solid working-class comfort'. **Artisans** (skilled tradesmen) normally earned about 25 to 30 shillings (£1.25 to £1.50) a week. They included mechanics, ironfounders, masons, carpenters and those in newer occupations such as railways and the police force. Their clothes were 'respectable' and their houses solidly built. 'In this class', said Booth, 'no-one goes short of food. Meat and vegetables are demanded every day'. Entry into the skilled trades was restricted by the craft unions (see page 189). Sometimes the most important qualification was to have a relative already in the trade. At the top of the scale, foremen and a few highly-skilled artisans earned up to 70 shillings (£3.50) a week. They lived very comfortably indeed, often owning their own houses and investing money in post office savings banks. There was a world of difference, both in attitudes and living standards, between the highly skilled and the labourers. So it is more accurate to speak not of the 'working class' but of the 'working class*es*'.

Throughout this period, hours of work were gradually reduced. The Saturday half-holiday was general by 1900, and Parliament introduced four Bank Holidays in 1871. As the **leisure time** of the working classes increased, their interests and activities became more civilised. Barbaric spectacles like bull- and bear-baiting (made illegal in 1835) were replaced first by prize-fighting and later by horse-racing and organised games such as soccer. The first professional football club, Notts County, dates from 1862. Working men's clubs grew in number, and music-halls became very popular by the end of the century. However public houses were still the main 'social centres' for the working classes. They housed the headquarters of Friendly Societies and clubs of various kinds – and also tempted the irresponsible to drink away a large proportion of their wages on a Saturday night.

Most people's living standards rose in this period, but the greatest gains were made by the **middle classes**, particularly factory owners, managers and other businessmen. Many could afford large mansions on the outskirts of towns, staffed with butlers, cooks, housemaids and gardeners, as well as public school fees for their sons. Alongside the growing industrial and commercial middle classes were members of the 'professions' – engineers, doctors, lawyers, accountants and higher civil servants. They too were increasing rapidly in numbers and in wealth. Victorians liked to believe that, with hard work, any man of

A middle-class family in the 1890s

good character could be successful, whatever his origins. But since the owners of most firms kept the best jobs for their relations, it was difficult for a young man without money or family connections to make his way in business. His best chance might be to gain a professional qualification, which would open the door to a secure and well-paid position.

The eventual aim of the successful businessman was usually to buy a country estate and become accepted as a 'gentleman'. Even at the turn of the century, when most people's incomes depended upon factories, mines and foreign trade, the **landed gentry** retained their social prestige. Country-house life, with its hunting and shooting parties and its lavish entertaining, was the envy of the town-bred middle classes. The term 'landed gentry' covered a wide range – from owners of quite small estates up to great aristocratic families, whose vast properties often included mines, quarries and parts of towns. Among the gentry, it was normal for the eldest son to inherit the family estate. His younger brothers, if any, entered occupations such as the army and the Church, where advancement still depended to some extent on family influence.

The gentry owned the land; **farmers** worked it. Some holdings were small enough for a tenant farmer and his family to manage on their own. But the trend was towards larger farms, on which labourers were hired. On the larger estates a farmer and his family could often live in some comfort; but they would rarely mix with the gentry – except in activities like the hunt, which involved the whole neighbourhood. Social barriers between the gentleman and the farmer were based on education rather than wealth. The gentry went to public schools, while farmers usually considered 'book learning' a waste of time.

Faith and doubt – religion and the influence of Darwin

The Victorian Age was a time of strong religious beliefs and strict moral attitudes. Most people went to church or chapel at least once on a Sunday. In the most 'respectable' households there were daily family prayers, while on Sundays games and entertainments were forbidden, including card-playing, dancing and theatre-going.

The middle classes were the most religious of all. Many of their number attended **Nonconformist chapels** – Congregationalist, Baptist or Wesleyan Methodist. The last, which had the biggest membership of the three, was also strongly supported by the better-off working classes. Members were called upon to be sober, hardworking and self-sacrificing. Their seriousness and strict moral conduct greatly influenced the Evangelical Movement, which set out to raise standards in the Church of England (see page 33). **Evangelicals** deplored the slackness of the eighteenth-century Church. They encouraged regular Bible reading and believed it was the duty of Christians to preach and work among the poor. Great social reformers such as Wilberforce and Shaftesbury came from their ranks (see Chapter 11).

The 'Evangelical revival' began to slacken by the mid nineteenth century. But its influence remained strong in the work of **Dr Thomas**

Barnardo (1845–1905) and **William Booth** (1829–1912). While he was a medical student in London, Barnardo founded the **East End Mission** for destitute children (1867). He gave up his intended career to devote his life to the welfare of London's homeless children. In the next thirty-five years, 60,000 orphans were given a new start in life through Dr Barnardo's Homes. William Booth, an ex-Methodist minister, founded the **Salvation Army** in 1878. Like Dr Barnardo, he considered social work to be part of the Christian mission. So Salvation Army relief and training centres were set up to help the poor and unfortunate. Popular methods of 'conversion' were used, including street bands and coloured uniforms, and the whole movement was organised on military lines, with Booth as 'the General'.

Meanwhile, the strict religious attitude of the middle classes in the towns influenced both the landed gentry and Anglican clergy. Parsons were normally much more conscientious and hardworking than their predecessors in the eighteenth century. Attempts were made to extend the influence of the Church of England in the working class districts of towns. New parishes were created and 'slum parsons' took on the difficult task of bringing the faith to the poor. But organised Christianity continued to have little effect upon the lower classes. Apart from the Methodists and growing numbers of Irish Catholics, the masses looked upon church going as something for the well-to-do, not for the ordinary person. They saw little reason to devote their day of rest and recreation to religion.

In the early Victorian Age, Christians accepted the exact word of the Bible, believing that its writers had been directly inspired by God. The account of the Creation in the Book of Genesis was taken to be historical fact. But scientists were beginning to cast doubts upon such beliefs. In 1830 **Charles Lyell**'s *Principles of Geology* set out to show that the earth had developed through millions of years of *evolution* (gradual change). If Lyell was right, the universe could not have been created in six days. An even more serious challenge to traditional views was the application of the principle of evolution to plant and animal life – notably by **Charles Darwin**. After nearly thirty years of detailed observation and research, he published his world-famous *Origin of Species* in 1859.

Darwin claimed that all species of living creatures had developed over millions of years from one original form of life, which may have been a simple cell. Gradual changes in each species had resulted from the struggle for existence. In other words, the weaker types died out while the stronger ones, which adapted to their surroundings, survived and passed on their superior characteristics. It was a 'survival of the fittest', or, as Darwin put it, *'evolution through natural selection'*.

His conclusion that man had not been separately created but had 'evolved' by pure chance directly challenged long-established religious beliefs. Darwin himself made no attempt to attack Christianity, but many other scientists claimed that his theory made belief in God not only unnecessary but impossible. If Darwin was correct, they said, man could hardly have been made in God's image. At first, most churchmen refused to accept evolutionary theory. The idea of 'man

Charles Darwin, 1809–82. At the age of twenty-two he was appointed naturalist to HMS 'Beagle', a ship which spent five years surveying the South American coast and parts of the Pacific. The plants, rocks and animals he studied on the voyage set him off on the line of thought which he developed in 'The Origin of Species'

descended from a monkey' horrified them. But Darwin's evidence was strong and the basic principles of his theory were soon widely accepted. Eventually most religious thinkers came to the conclusion that their beliefs had not been challenged after all. Genesis, they said, was written in such a way as to be understandable to ancient peoples. It answered the question *'who* made the world?' without attempting a scientific explanation of *how* it was done.

Nevertheless the 'great debate' between scientists and Christians destroyed much of the basic certainty of Victorian religion. By the end of the century the Church's hold upon the people had begun to slacken, and the growth of scientific doubt was partly responsible. Fewer people attended services, and Sunday observance became less strict. Other activities occupied people's leisure time, including outdoor sports, cycle rides and railway excursions. However the change was slow up to the First World War (1914–18). The decline of Christianity in Britain has largely occurred in the last sixty or seventy years.

The position of women

At the start of the Victorian Age men and women were even more clearly divided into 'two nations' than the rich and poor. The duties, rights and responsibilities of each were quite different. In well-to-do families, '**ladies**' were not expected to work. If they did, it was widely assumed that their menfolk could not afford to support them. Therefore, from the country mansions of the nobility and gentry down to the town-houses of the middle classes, women were encouraged to remain idle and to leave household chores to domestic servants. They were cut off from life and its interests. Such ladies were not even encouraged to take exercise, apart from riding and dancing.

Working-class women, on the other hand, had neither comfort nor leisure. Married women had the double burden of raising children and going to work to make up the family income. In the towns, large numbers were employed in factories, laundries or in trades such as dressmaking. In the countryside women worked in the fields, especially at harvest-time. However the largest single form of female employment was **domestic service**, which girls normally entered between the ages of ten and fifteen. Numbers of household servants rose steadily throughout this period – from about 700,000 in 1840 to a peak of almost 1½ million just before 1914. Life 'in service' could be hard and monotonous, especially in less wealthy families, but at least it provided women and girls with good food and accommodation and allowed them to see how the 'other half' lived.

Demands for the *emancipation* (setting free) of women from masculine control were rare before the development of **girls' education** in the second half of the nineteenth century. The rise of public schools and university colleges for 'young ladies' and the start of state elementary schools (see Chapter 18) led to important social changes. Women from wealthy families became increasingly dissatisfied with idleness. Having no money of their own, they were even less independent than factory women. Following the example of Florence

A group of domestic servants in the 1880s

Nightingale (see page 185) they demanded that the professions should be opened to women so that they could play a useful part in society. A start was made when the London School of Medicine for Women opened in 1874. Twenty-five years later there were over 300 lady doctors.

Lower down the social scale, a whole new range of **female occupations** came into being after the introduction of the telephone and the typewriter, from the 1880s onwards. Women and girls who wanted something other than factory work or domestic service now became telephone operators or typists. The idea of employing women in offices had previously been unheard of, yet by 1901 7 per cent of all business and commercial clerks were women. The rapid expansion of elementary schools after 1870 provided another career for women in teaching. Meanwhile thousands more became shop assistants. Now that women were more active, their styles of clothing changed. Cumbersome Victorian dresses, with long, trailing skirts and thick petticoats, were gradually replaced by simpler and healthier fashions.

As women became more independent, they demanded equal legal and political rights. One of their greatest grievances concerned ownership of property. When a woman married, all her money and possessions – and even her children – automatically belonged to the husband. In 1870 Parliament at last took action, allowing married women to keep their own earnings. But not until 1882 were they granted the right to own property and dispose of it as they wished. These **Married Women's Property Acts** gave women a new legal status, but they were still not entitled to vote in parliamentary elections. Women could vote for County and County Borough Councils after 1888, and they were allowed to become councillors in 1907, but they played no

part in central government. Even Queen Victoria opposed the granting of full political rights to her own sex, believing that politics did
not concern women. Many of her subjects thought otherwise, including **Emmeline Pankhurst** (1858–1928). In 1903 she founded the
Women's Social and Political Union (WSPU), which set out to organise public demonstrations in favour of women's *suffrage* (voting
rights). Members were soon known as **suffragettes**.

A Liberal victory in the 1906 election raised the hopes of suffragettes, for many Liberal MPs were on their side. But the Cabinet
was divided on the issue and no positive action was taken. The
WSPU replied by heckling speakers at political meetings, organising
petitions and even chaining themselves to railings outside the houses
of Cabinet ministers. By 1912 a campaign of violence and vandalism
was organised, largely by Emmeline's daughter, **Christabel Pankhurst**. Members of the WSPU smashed shop-windows, burned houses
and public buildings, cut telephone wires, tore up golf greens and
slashed pictures in the National Gallery. **Emily Davison**, a suffragette,
threw herself under the King's horse at the Derby (1913) and was
fatally injured. It was difficult to punish crimes committed by suffragettes because when they were imprisoned they went on hunger
strike. Prison authorities either had to release them or feed them by
force and risk a public outcry. To help enforce the law, Parliament
passed the so-called **'Cat and Mouse Act'** (1913) which enabled prison
governors to release hunger strikers and then rearrest them when
they had regained weight.

The use of violent methods did more harm than good to the suffragettes' cause. Their opponents could claim that women had shown
themselves to be irresponsible. However during the First World War
(1914–18) large numbers of women were employed in essential industries, including armaments factories. This valuable work had more
effect than the entire campaign of the WSPU. Immediately after the
war (1918) the vote was granted to women over thirty who were
householders or wives of householders (and also to all men over
twenty-one). Another **Parliamentary Reform Act, 1928,** put women
on the same footing as men, when they were all given the suffrage at
twenty-one.

Another, less obvious, aspect of female emancipation was the reduction in the size of families resulting largely from new methods of
birth control. After all, nothing restricts a woman's freedom more
than continual childbearing. Family planning, in the modern sense,
began among the well-to-do in the nineteenth century. But it was
some time before the poor, whose need was the greatest, came to
understand and practise it. In the 1890s, working-class women spent,
on average, fifteen years either pregnant or with a child under one
year old. By the 1950s, the equivalent figure was only *four* years.
This represented a rapid fall in the birth-rate (largely balanced by a
lower death-rate). It also meant far greater freedom for married
women, especially those wishing to follow a career. Nevertheless the
responsibilities of motherhood still put women at a disadvantage in
their fight for equality (see page 358).

*Emmeline Pankhurst being
arrested during a suffragette
demonstration (1914)*

Women war workers in an engineering shop

The foundations of the Welfare State, 1906–1911

The average family was a lot better off at the end of Victoria's reign (1901) than it had been at the beginning (1837). Working conditions and hours had improved, while wages had risen. There had been great progress in medicine, public sanitary services were well established, and a start had been made on the problem of slum clearance. Every child received elementary education, and recreational facilities such as public parks and libraries had been provided.

Victorian reformers had achieved a great deal, but they also left major problems unsolved. In particular, they did little to combat the root causes of **poverty**. Progress in this direction had been hindered by the belief that it was no business of the state to interfere in such matters. People were simply urged to be thrifty and hardworking and to 'save for a rainy day'. But lower-paid workers could not afford to live decently, even under favourable circumstances. Moreover, among quite highly-paid workers, sickness, old age, unemployment or some other misfortune might at any time force a family below the 'poverty line'.

The wealthy classes generally took the view that poverty would die out of its own accord as the country got richer. But by the turn of the century an increasing number of MPs in the Liberal Party thought otherwise. They were determined to attack poverty and other social evils by introducing new social services. Their chance came following the election of 1906, when, with strong working-class support, they gained a massive majority in the House of Commons. 'The cause of

Liberalism is the cause of the left-out millions', said **Winston Churchill**, then a young man of thirty-one. He became President of the Board of Trade in 1908 and played an important part in the reforms of this period.

The welfare of children was the first priority of the **Liberal Governments of 1906–14**. Several local authorities had recently opened clean milk depots and appointed health visitors to advise parents on infant care. After 1906, with Government help, **infant welfare clinics** were set up in many areas. Following the introduction of compulsory education (1880) charity organisations in many towns provided meals for children who were too hungry to learn. The Liberals now set out to extend **school meals** to all areas. By an Act of 1906, local authorities could either use existing voluntary schemes or, where these were lacking, provide their own. Meals were only given to children who were 'unable by reason of lack of food to take full advantage of the education provided for them'. Nevertheless it was an important step forward. By 1914 over 150,000 children had school meals; on Saturdays and during holidays as well as in term time. But undernourishment was only part of a general health problem among deprived children. In 1907 the Government compelled local authorities to have pupils in elementary schools medically examined.

The first truly nationwide social service was **Old Age Pensions**, introduced in 1908. Pensions were paid to citizens over the age of seventy, provided their incomes were not over 12 shillings (60p) a week. The amount varied between 1 and 5 shillings (between 5 and 25p) weekly, depending on the pensioner's income. Old people were delighted to have this regular money coming in. They were now less dependent on the goodwill of relations or the grudging help of the Poor Law. 'We are lifting the shadow of the workhouse from the homes of the poor', said **David Lloyd George**, the Chancellor of the Exchequer and the leading social reformer in the Cabinet.

To pay for social welfare schemes (among other things) Lloyd George estimated that an additional £16 million would have to be raised in the Budget of 1909. He aimed to 'make the rich pay'. In addition to higher taxes on drink and tobacco, and a new motor car licence, Lloyd George increased income tax. It was scaled, so that those with annual incomes above £3,000 paid 1s 2d (6p) in the pound, while those with lower incomes paid 9d (4p). A further 'supertax' of 6d (2½p) in the pound was imposed on those earning over £5,000 a year. Lloyd George also increased death duties on the estates of the rich and placed heavy taxes on profits gained from the ownership and sale of property.

'The People's Budget', as Lloyd George called it, met powerful opposition from the well-to-do. The Conservatives, many of them landowners who objected violently to property taxes, used their majority in the House of Lords to reject the Budget. The Government now decided it was time for a showdown with the Upper House, which had obstructed some of its other Bills. The Budget was forced through (1910) and, after a long struggle, the **Parliament Act (1911)** drastically cut the powers of the Lords. They were no longer

David Lloyd George (1863–1945) pictured in 1910

One of the earliest labour exchanges (1910)

allowed to prevent the passage of 'Money Bills', and they could not hold up other Bills for more than two years (reduced to one year in 1949). The social reformers had won an important victory, for one of the results of the struggles of 1909–11 was a steady growth of state spending on the welfare of the needy.

The Liberals now carried out their most important reform, by means of the **National Insurance Act (1911)**. Some workers already insured themselves through Friendly Societies, but the lower-paid could not afford the necessary subscriptions. Besides, whether they could afford it or not, many preferred to 'take a chance'. The Government therefore introduced compulsory insurance for those who needed it most, keeping contributions down to a minimum. There were two parts to the 1911 Act, providing separate insurance schemes for sickness and unemployment.

Unemployment insurance began on a small scale, applying only to a few trades, such as building, shipbuilding and ironfounding, where work was known to be irregular. It was intended to include other trades in the future. Workers over sixteen, their employers and the state each contributed 2½*d* (1p) a week – so spreading the cost over the whole community. In return, 7*s* (35p) a week was payable during unemployment for a maximum of fifteen weeks in any one year. Benefits were paid at **Labour Exchanges**. These were based on a German idea (like several other Liberal reforms). Their main purpose was to provide unemployed workers with information about job vacancies. The first eighty-three Labour Exchanges opened in 1910.

The other half of the 1911 Act introduced 'insurance against loss of health and for prevention and cure of sickness'. All wage-earners between sixteen and seventy had to join the scheme if they earned less than £3 a week. Their weekly contribution was 4*d* (just over 1½p), to which their employers and the state added a further 5*d* (2p) between them. Payments were recorded by means of stamps stuck on individual cards. In return, free medical attention, with medicine, was given. It did not include hospital or specialist services, however, just 'simple doctoring'. When work was lost through sickness, 10s (50p) a week was paid, from the fourth day of the illness. This lasted for a maximum of twenty-six weeks, after which 'disablement benefit' (half the full amount) could be claimed. An additional 30s (£1.50) 'maternity benefit' was paid on the birth of each child.

Churchill described the 1911 Act as 'the most decisive step yet taken upon the path of social organisation.... The cruel waste of disease and unemployment, breaking down men and women, breaking up homes and families, will for the first time be encountered by the whole strength of the nation'. Together with Old Age Pensions, National Insurance struck for the first time at some of the deepest roots of poverty. Instead of merely providing workhouses for the destitute, the Liberals tried to *prevent* destitution with specialised services to meet individual needs. It was on these foundations that the modern Welfare State was later built.

Poster advertising National Health Insurance. The 'doctor' is Lloyd George

Timeline

1859	Charles Darwin's *Origin of Species*.
1867	Dr Thomas Barnardo's 'East End Mission' founded.
1870–82	Married Women's Property Acts.
1878	Salvation Army founded by William Booth.
1903	Women's Social and Political Union founded.
1906	The Liberals come to power.
1908	Old Age Pensions.
1909	'The People's Budget'.
1910	Labour Exchanges introduced.
1911	National Insurance Act.
	Parliament Act.
1918	Representation of the People Act: votes for most women over thirty and men over twenty-one.
1928	Representation of the People Act: votes for women over twenty-one.

Questions

1. 'One knows there is a great deal of poverty in the East End of London but I wonder whether there is in provincial cities. Why not investigate York?' (B. Seebohm Rowntree, *Poverty: A Study of Town Life*, 1901)

   a) Who had recently provided a wealth of information on poverty in London?

   b) How did Rowntree's findings compare with those in London?

   c) Describe briefly what life was like for those below Rowntree's 'poverty line'.

   d) Were farm labourers better or worse off than town workers?

2. Look at the picture of domestic servants (page 237).
   a) A dozen servants was not unusual among middle-class families at this time. How does this reflect changes in the last 100 years in i) wages for manual work ii) opportunities for female employment iii) taxation of the well-to-do iv) the lives of middle-class women?
   b) Whose children do we see in the picture? Why do you think they were included?
   c) What jobs would have been done by (i) the women (ii) the men?

3. 'A Suffragette tried to stop the race by jumping in front of the horses at Tattenham Corner...She is suffering from severe concussion of the brain and other injuries.' (*Daily Mail*, 5 June 1913)
   a) What organisation did 'Suffragettes' belong to? What were they trying to achieve?
   b) Who is referred to here? What happened to her afterwards?
   c) Name the race and the owner of the horse that hit her.
   d) Give some examples of other ways in which 'Suffragettes' were trying to gain publicity for their cause at this time.
   e) Did these methods succeed? Give reasons for your answer.

4. 'We adopted the German plan of raising contributions from employers and employees by stamps attached to cards; but we should almost certainly have been forced to think of that ourselves.' (William Beveridge, on the 1911 National Insurance scheme)
   a) For what purpose were the 'contributions' to be used?
   b) What other contributions were made, apart from those of 'employers and employees'?
   c) Name another German idea which inspired a Liberal reform.
   d) The 1911 National Insurance scheme was limited to which groups in the population?
   e) How did William Beveridge influence the further development of Britain's social services? (See Chapter 24)

5. Write a paragraph on each of the following:
   a) the Salvation Army
   b) Charles Darwin
   c) Old Age Pensions
   d) 'The People's Budget' and the Parliament Act (1909–11)

The Shrinking World
Transport and Communications (III)

Just as the origin of railway locomotives and powered ships depended upon the steam-engine, so the birth of motor cars and aeroplanes resulted from the *internal combustion engine*. It was not a British invention. France and Germany pioneered the new form of power and, along with the USA, they were the first countries to make effective use of it. Similarly, the British played a minor part in the development of both the telephone and wireless telegraphy, which together revolutionised communications. All these advances, which have done so much to shape the modern world, were made before 1914, although their full effects were felt later.

The internal combustion engine

Like the steam-engine, the internal combustion engine turns heat into energy – in the form of the up and down movement of a piston in a cylinder. But the heat that makes a steam-engine work is produced by a boiler *outside* the cylinder. It is therefore an *external* combustion engine. To produce a smaller and lighter engine, suitable for road vehicles and aircraft, it was necessary to do away with the boiler-unit altogether and arrange for the combustion (burning) of the fuel to take place *inside* the cylinder.

The steam-engine was first developed for industrial use. Likewise, the internal combustion engine resulted largely from the search for a cheaper and more compact power unit to serve craftsmen in small workshops. These considerations led **Etienne Lenoir**, a French engineer, to produce a **gas engine** in 1859 – the forerunner of later developments. A mixture of coal-gas and air was sucked into a cylinder, where it was ignited by an electric spark. The force of 'expansion' following ignition pushed a piston, which, in turn, rotated a wheel. In Lenoir's engine, ignition took place at each stroke, on either side of the piston. This was wasteful. It was left to a German engineer, **Nikolaus Otto**, to produce a *four-stroke compression engine* (1876), the main principles of which are found in most modern cars. Although four movements of the piston are necessary to complete each cycle – suction, compression, combustion and exhaust – the real work is done on the third stroke (see diagram opposite).

Otto's gas engine had several important advantages over steam. It was smaller, its fuel consumption was less and it needed no preliminary heating-up. Above all, it developed more power in relation to its weight. But it could only be used satisfactorily as a stationary engine for driving machinery, because it depended upon a ready supply of

The workings of a four-stroke internal combustion engine

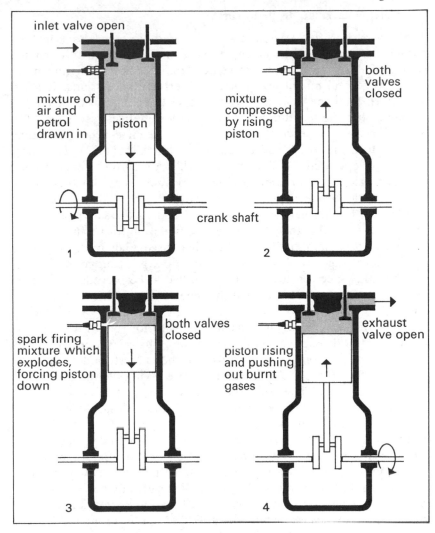

coal-gas. Before it could be used to move a vehicle, a different fuel had to be found which was as portable as the engine itself. The answer was **petrol** (refined petroleum) which had been drilled in the USA since 1859. At first, petrol or 'gasolene' was thrown away as waste in the production of paraffin. But in 1883, **Gottlieb Daimler**, formerly technical manager at Otto's works, found that petrol was more than just a replacement for coal-gas – it was superior to it, giving a much greater punch to the piston.

In 1885, Daimler fitted his petrol engine to a wooden cycle, and so invented the motor bike. In the same year, **Karl Benz**, another German, built a motor tricycle which ran at 13 kilometres per hour. Daimler made the first petrol-driven, four-wheeled car in 1887. It was a genuine 'horseless carriage' – a coach, with the shafts removed and an engine added. Meanwhile the British had not yet entered the Motor Age, although they shared in other developments in road transport which prepared the way for the coming of the motor car.

From steam carriages to 'baby cars'

The earliest horseless carriages were powered by steam. Back in 1769 **Nicholas Cugnot**, a Frenchman, drove a **steam carriage** through the streets of Paris. But he was prevented from developing his invention when his second model overturned and terrified pedestrians. **Richard Trevithick** built the first steam cars to travel on English roads (1801–3) before turning his attention to railway locomotives (see page 137). Several passenger services later employed steam coaches, including London to Bath (1827) and Paddington to the City (1883). The latter route was operated by Walter Hancock's *Enterprise*, which carried fourteen passengers at about 16 kilometres per hour. But these vehicles were far too heavy for the roads that carried them. Turnpike companies, fearing damage to their roads, charged steam coach operators such high tolls that they were mostly put out of business. Then, in 1865, Parliament passed the so-called **'Red Flag Act'**. It limited horseless carriages to 4 miles per hour (6½ k.p.h.) on country roads and half this speed in towns. They also had to be preceded by a man carrying a red flag. This effectively ended the brief life of the steam carriage.

The first really successful mechanical device for road travel was the **bicycle**. After becoming popular in France, bicycles were manufactured in Britain from 1869 onwards. On the earliest models the pedals were connected to the front-wheel axle. When it was found that greater speeds could be achieved with an enlarged front wheel, the famous 'penny-farthing' resulted. However the widespread popularity of cycling dates from the introduction of the modern 'safety bicycle' in the 1880s. Its wheels were almost equal in size and it had a rear-wheel chain-drive. In 1888 **John Boyd Dunlop** from Belfast produced a **pneumatic tyre**, with a separate, air-filled innertube. Bicycles were now both safe and comfortable, and cycling suddenly became a craze. Men and women from every walk of life began to explore the countryside, especially at weekends. Several discoveries prompted by the

An early 'safety bicycle' (1890)

A Rolls-Royce 'Silver Ghost'. It was produced for eighteen years (1906–24) – one of the longest production runs in the history of motor manufacture

bicycle helped the later development of motoring, including steel spokes, roller bearings and, above all, the pneumatic tyre – the chief British contribution to the motor car.

The Motor Age really began in Britain in 1896, when Parliament repealed the Red Flag Act and raised the speed limit to 14 miles per hour (22½ k.p.h.). This was celebrated by an 'emancipation run' from London to Brighton – still commemorated in the annual Vintage Car Rally. In the same year **F.W. Lanchester** built the first British four-wheeled car, after which the manufacture of motor cars quickly became a thriving industry. The famous Rolls-Royce Company was formed in 1906 by **Henry Royce**, a Manchester engineer, and **Charles Rolls**, one of the first racing motorists and airmen. Their first successful effort, the 40–50 horse-power 'Silver Ghost', was a magnificent piece of engineering. It gained a worldwide reputation for smooth, quiet running and reliability, and remained unequalled as a luxury car for the very rich.

In 1903, with the number of cars on British roads already approaching 20,000, Parliament compelled every motorist to obtain a licence costing 5 shillings (25p) from the local county council. In the same Act, the speed limit was raised to 20 miles per hour (32 k.p.h.). Most cars could comfortably go faster by this time. So carefree motorists on country roads frequently found themselves caught in police 'speed traps' and fined. No doubt they could afford it, for a motor car was then a very expensive 'toy', beyond the reach of all but the wealthier middle and upper classes.

The earliest models were open-topped, so travellers needed weather-proof clothing. Fur coats, gloves and goggles were commonly worn; so were capes, as a protection against the clouds of dust stirred up by the wheels. Except for the larger towns, where streets were normally paved with stone blocks, the roads were unsuitable for the new traffic. The iron-bound wheels of horse-drawn vehicles had helped to bind the loose stone surfaces, but soft rubber tyres sank

A 'B-type' London bus

into the cracks between the stones, loosening them and sucking out dust. The answer was to spray tar over the stones, or, better still, put down 'tarmacadam' (stones which are tarred *before* they are laid and rolled). Until such improvements were carried out, it was difficult to get through a day's motoring without at least one puncture.

Not all the early motor vehicles were built for pleasure. As early as 1905 the London General Omnibus Company, the largest owner of horse-drawn buses in Britain, decided to change to **motor buses**. After trying many different designs, they introduced the famous 'B-type' in 1910 – a double-decker, seating thirty-four passengers. No fewer than 4,000 were built before they were withdrawn from service in 1925–6. Other towns were slow to follow suit, mainly because many had recently introduced electric trams. They were reluctant to change again after all the expense of laying tracks and installing overhead wires. Not until the 1920s and 30s were motor buses in general use. Even then trams lingered on in some areas until the 1950s, or were partly replaced by trackless trolley-buses. These still took electric current from overhead wires but were easier to manoeuvre.

By the 1930s increasing numbers of buses and lorries had Diesel 'heavy oil' engines, invented by a German, **Rudolph Diesel**, in 1892. Combustion was produced not by a spark but by compressing the air in the cylinder so tightly that it became hot enough to ignite the heavy oil fuel the moment it was sprayed in. The Diesel was the most powerful internal combustion engine and the cheapest to run. But it needed cylinder walls of great strength, which made it too heavy to be fitted in motor cars. The earliest models were very large and were used to power ships and factory machines.

Meanwhile, private motoring gradually became more than just a sport for the rich. Cars were brought within the reach of a larger section of the population as a result of **mass-production methods**, pioneered by an American, **Henry Ford** of Detroit. Using assembly lines to bring the cars and the necessary tools to each worker in turn, Ford produced a strong, reliable 'family car' at a remarkably low price. Worldwide sales of his 'Model T' (1909) reached 15 million in eighteen years. As output increased, production costs per car grew less and Ford was able to reduce his price further. In 1915, when a twelve horse-power workshop-built car cost more than £350, a twenty horse-power Ford could be bought for £115. Ford's first British factory was opened in Manchester (1911).

Taxes on petrol and car licences were introduced in 1910, and a Central Road Board used most of the revenue for tarring main roads. A new Ministry of Transport took over in 1919 and made roadbuilding grants to local authorities, out of motor taxation. At this stage the amount of car tax paid depended on engine size, so designers set out to get more power from smaller engines by making them work faster. The result was the popular '**baby cars**' of the 1920s and 30s. When the Austin Seven appeared (1922) it was the smallest four-seater car ever made. It cost £165. In the same price range was the Morris Minor. Its maker, William Morris, later **Lord Nuffield**, was the first Englishman to take up Henry Ford's mass-production methods. Having started in business as a cycle-repairer at the age of sixteen, he eventually became the richest man in Britain.

William Morris's motor body shop at Oxford (1913)

By the 1930s, when a small Ford, Morris or Austin could be bought for little over £100, payable in instalments, cars were within the reach of the lower middle classes. In 1939 there were nearly 2 million private cars licensed – one to every twenty-five persons.

Total number of motor vehicles (all kinds) in Britain

1914	1920	1930	1939
400,000	650,000	2,300,000	3,000,000

The speed limit was abolished in 1930, but, following a rapid increase in accidents, a 30 miles per hour (48 k.p.h.) limit was introduced in 'built-up areas' (1934).

Motor vehicles had far-reaching effects on life and work. Two deserve special mention. First, they brought together the town and the countryside, reducing the isolation of remote villages. Second, they freed industry from dependence upon rail and water transport. New industries developed alongside the main roads leading out of towns.

The conquest of the air

Before the invention of the internal combustion engine, the only successful human flights were in **balloons** filled with hot air or a gas like hydrogen which is 'lighter than air'. But balloons cannot be properly controlled in flight. They are at the mercy of the wind and air-currents. Not until man had invented a powered, 'heavier-than-air' machine could he claim to have conquered the skies. Steam-engines were often tried in the nineteenth century, but they were much too heavy in relation to the power they produced. It was the lighter, more compact petrol engine that held the key to success.

Wilbur and Orville Wright were bicycle-makers from Dayton in the State of Ohio, USA. In 1903, after carefully studying the problems of flight, they fitted a wooden glider with a twelve horse-power petrol engine and two propellers driven by bicycle chains. Then, on a cold morning in December at Kitty Hawk, North Carolina, they became the first men to fly a 'heavier-than-air' machine. The longest 'hop' made that day lasted only 59 seconds, but it was enough to open a new chapter in the history of transport.

The British were slow to respond to the new invention. Five years went by before the first powered flight was made in England. In 1909, when the *Daily Mail* offered £1,000 for the first pilot to fly the Channel, it was won by a Frenchman, **Louis Blériot**. It took him 35½ minutes, from Calais to Dover Castle. Over 120,000 people saw Blériot's wood and sailcloth machine on exhibition in London. However when the First World War broke out, five years later, the vast majority of the population had not yet seen an aeroplane. The military possibilities of aircraft were quickly realised, so the war led to a rapid development of aviation. For the first time planes were mass produced from standard parts. They were mainly used for reconnaissance, although fighters and bombers had been developed by 1918, when the **Royal Air Force (RAF)** was formed.

Kitty Hawk, 1903: the first flight in a 'heavier-than-air' machine. Orville Wright is at the controls

The extent of the progress made during the war was shown in 1919, when two RAF officers, **John Alcock** and **Arthur Whitten-Brown**, made the first flight across the Atlantic. They covered the 3,040 kilometres from Newfoundland to Ireland at an average speed of 190 kilometres per hour, battling all the way against fog, ice and storms. At one point Brown had to climb on the wings to hack away ice with a knife. In August of the same year, the world's first daily air service began, carrying goods and passengers between London and Paris. By 1923 Croydon Airport, in Surrey, was handling up to thirty cross-Channel flights a day. A high standard of safety and reliability was achieved, although the journey was slow and bumpy and the passenger compartment noisy and cramped.

Services to other continental cities were soon introduced, but they failed to pay their way despite high fares and freight charges. Foreign airlines were given financial assistance by their governments, in the form of subsidies or grants. In 1924 the British Government did the same. A single company was formed – **Imperial Airways** – which took over all existing routes and began many new ones. By 1939 regular flights were being made to Australia (via India and Malaya), South Africa (via Egypt), Canada and many other British territories overseas. Air-mail was carried at ordinary rates of postage – often in flying-boats, since smaller territories lacked airport facilities. A transatlantic air-mail service began in 1939. Shortly afterwards, in April 1940, the Government merged Imperial Airways with a rival company, British Airways, which had held a monopoly of routes to Berlin and Scandinavia since 1935. The result was the state-aided **British Overseas Airways Corporation (BOAC).**

All these developments were on a very small scale in comparison with the progress of civil aviation since 1945 (see page 340). The number of passengers carried was relatively small and the luxurious conditions of present day air travel were unheard of. The most comfortable

The 'Graf Zeppelin' flying over Wembley Stadium during the 1930 Cup Final

(and costly) way to fly in this period was by **airship**, containing giant gas-filled balloons and powered by internal combustion engines. Airships were first built in Germany by **Count Zeppelin**. They carried out air raids in the First World War, but their great size made them more suitable for passenger services. All the comforts of an ocean liner, including separate cabins, lounges and dining-rooms, were provided on 'ships' like the German *Graf Zeppelin*, which flew round the world in twenty days (1928). But airships were liable to catch fire and explode, and a series of disasters soon put an end to their use. After 1930, when the great *R.101* burst into flames over France, no more were built in Britain.

More railways and ships

Almost all the main **railway network** was laid by the 1850s (see Chapter 13). Although thousands of kilometres of track were later added (using mass-produced steel rails from the 1870s onwards) most of the new routes were branch lines. By the end of the nineteenth century a few long-distance expresses had achieved *average* speeds of more than 100 kilometres per hour. Moveover, following the introduction of restaurant and sleeping-cars (1870s) and corridor carriages (1890s), the highest standards of comfort were not far removed from those of the late twentieth century.

Most railway companies had little interest in suburban services, regarding them as something of an interference with the free passage of long-distance expresses and coal trains. So travellers *within* London and other large towns mostly relied on horse-drawn buses and cabs. In 1863, however, the first **underground railway** was opened – the

London Metropolitan – running 6 kilometres, from Paddington to Farringdon Street in the City. The Metro, like several others after it, was a 'shallow underground', just below the surface. The first deep 'tube', the City and South London Railway (1890), was 12 metres down. It was also electrified; an improvement on previous undergrounds, in which passengers endured the choking smoke of steam-engines. 'Tubes' quickly gained great popularity. Within twenty years, they reached Hampstead, Shepherd's Bush, Finsbury Park and Clapham. Only two other cities provided an alternative to surface transport – Liverpool, with an overhead electric railway on viaducts (1893–6) and Glasgow, with tube trains worked by cable haulage (1896).

The ordinary railway companies, 123 of them, were amalgamated into four large systems in 1921 – the LMS (London Midland Scottish), LNER (London North Eastern Railway), GWR (Great Western Railway), and SR (Southern Railway). It was now easier to finance large projects, like the electrification of suburban services south of London (which began in 1898). Nevertheless railways suffered a decline after the First World War, largely because of growing **competition from road transport**. While cars and cheap motor coaches took away passenger traffic, lorries had the advantage of being able to deliver goods door-to-door. They rivalled railways on all but the longest hauls and in handling all but the heaviest freight. For every ten railway passengers in 1920, only six were carried in 1938. Freight traffic fell by 17 per cent in the same period. Railways tried to hit back with more return-ticket reductions and faster services, for example the LNER *Silver Jubilee Express* (1935) which ran from London to Newcastle in four hours. But most railways had ceased to pay their way, an important factor in their later nationalisation (see page 325).

The LNER 'Silver Jubilee Express'. A locomotive of the same type, 'Mallard', reached 202 kilometres per hour in 1938 – then the record speed for a railway engine

In 1882 the British Register of **Shipping** contained more steam ships than sailing vessels for the first time. This trend was accelerated when the steam-engine reached its final stage of development in the **turbine** of 1884 (see page 172). The steam turbine was first used to drive generators in electric power stations, but its inventor, **Sir Charles Parsons**, soon realised that its spinning motion made it ideal for driving the screw-propellers of ships. The superiority of the new engine was demonstrated beyond doubt in 1897, when Parsons went uninvited to the Naval Review at Spithead. His turbine-driven yacht, aptly named *Turbinia*, reached 34½ knots (over 60 kilometres per hour) which was then a world record. The whole fleet had suddenly become obsolete. From 1905 onwards all warships were fitted with turbines, and in 1907 the newly-built Cunarders *Mauretania* and *Lusitania* became the first big ocean liners to be powered by turbine engines.

The 'Queen Mary' under construction on Clydeside

Another important advance was the introduction of **oil fuel** instead of coal. Oil could be used for firing the boilers of steam piston-engines and turbines as well as for driving Diesel engines, which were first used for shipping in 1912. Oil was cleaner, easier to load and store, and produced more steam than the equivalent weight of coal. The Admiralty began using oil before 1914, but it was not in general use until the 1920s and 30s. These years also saw the building on Clydeside of the two great Cunard liners, *Queen Mary* (82,000 tonnes) and *Queen Elizabeth* (86,000 tonnes). The former went into service on the Atlantic route in 1936, but the latter was still under construction when war broke out (1939). Her maiden voyage, to New York, was made in secret the following year.

The telephone, wireless and the BBC

Rapid communication over long distances began with the electric telegraph (see page 144). By the 1870s, when telegraph cables were carrying Morse Code messages across continents and below oceans, a second great advance was made – the transmission of speech by **telephone**. This was first achieved in 1875 by **Alexander Graham Bell**, an American teacher born in Edinburgh. It was a highly complicated apparatus, in which vibrations made in the air by the speaker caused variations of electric current (supplied from a battery) in an electromagnetic coil. These were transmitted along the connecting wire, at the end of which the same process happened in reverse. The electric vibrations created sound waves on the same frequency as those of the speaker.

Unlike the telegraph, the telephone required no special training and could be used by anyone. Consequently it had a much greater effect upon both business and social life. The first British telephone exchange opened in 1879 in London. At the start, private companies operated under government licence, but by 1912 the Post Office had taken control of the country's telephone services. There were already 700,000 receivers. The first automatic exchange was built in the same year. Nevertheless progress was slow in comparison with the USA. In

A London telephone exchange in 1883

1920, when 12 per cent of Americans had a telephone, only 2 per cent of the British had one. By 1939 there were 3,235,000 receivers in the United Kingdom, roughly one to every fourteen persons.

Even before the invention of the telephone, scientists had begun to investigate ways of transmitting sound *without* wires. In 1864 **James Clerk Maxwell**, a British physicist, proved the existence of electromagnetic 'waves', and showed that they obeyed the same natural laws as light. Just over thirty years later, the first public demonstrations of wireless communication were made by **Guglielmo Marconi** (1874–1919), an Italian who came to England in 1896. After successful transmissions in London, on Salisbury Plain and across the Bristol Channel, he established communication with the French coast (1899). However the experiment that aroused most interest occurred in December 1901. At St John's, Newfoundland, Marconi picked up the 'dot, dot, dot' of the Morse letter 'S' from a transmitting station in Cornwall, nearly 3,200 kilometres across the Atlantic.

The value of wireless for communication with shipping was quickly realised, and Marconi's own company established a chain of coastal stations for this purpose. In 1912, when the giant British liner *Titanic* sank in the Atlantic after hitting an iceberg, its wireless distress signal brought other vessels to the scene to pick up survivors. In the First World War, wireless was used by the armies and navies of both sides, and air-to-ground communication was achieved with aircraft. Meanwhile progress was being made in the wireless transmission of speech. Keen radio amateurs began to build their own wireless transmitters and receivers and make private 'broadcasts'.

In response to the growing demand for a service of radio entertainment, the **BBC** (British Broadcasting Company) was established by radio manufacturers in 1922. Within a few years, millions were 'listening in' to music, plays, talks and news on homemade crystal sets with earphones. Later, large horn-shaped loudspeakers replaced headphones. The powerful position of the BBC was demonstrated in 1926, when its news bulletins kept the nation informed of the latest developments during the General Strike (see page 278). In the same year, the BBC became the British Broadcasting *Corporation*, a public body financed from licence fees paid by listeners. By 1939 very few homes were without a radio set.

Broadcasting Shakespeare from the BBC's Marconi House in 1923. The actor speaking is Harry Tate, a well-known comedian

Number of radio licences in Britain

1923	80,000
1927	2,300,000
1939	8,900,000

In 1922, the year in which wireless was established as a means of public entertainment, a Scotsman named **John Logie Baird** began to tackle the problem of transmitting *pictures* by electro-magnetic waves. Just as newspaper illustrations consist of large numbers of dots, almost disappearing in some places and forming dark patches in others, so **television** pictures have to be broken down into dots and built up again on the screen. After two years of experiments, using odds and ends such as a tea-chest, biscuit-tin and secondhand radio parts, Baird succeeded in transmitting the flickering outline of a Maltese Cross over a distance of a few metres. In the following year (1925) he first televised a human being. However others improved on Baird's invention, and when the BBC began a regular television service (1936) it chose an alternative system developed by Electrical and Musical Industries. The first television studios were at Alexandra Palace in North London. By 1939 there were about 80,000 television sets in use – all in the London area, within range of the Alexandra Palace transmitter. Services were suspended during the Second World War and resumed in 1946 (see page 366).

Just before the war broke out **Sir Robert Watson-Watt** and a team

John Logie Baird (1888–1946) and the apparatus with which he first televised a human being

of British scientists developed **radar** (radio detection and ranging). It enabled objects within a certain distance (roughly 50 kilometres at ground level) to be located by the echoes or rebounds from radio waves. Radar was put to immediate use in detecting approaching enemy aircraft during the Battle of Britain (1940). It soon proved to be of great value in all kinds of sea and air navigation, for darkness or fog make no difference to its ability to detect moving objects and measure their distances and speeds.

Timeline

1863	London Metropolitan underground railway.
1865	'Red Flag Act'.
1875	Alexander Graham Bell invents the telephone.
1876	Nikolaus Otto's four-stroke compression engine.
1887	First petrol-driven four-wheeled car (Gottlieb Daimler).
1888	John Boyd Dunlop's pneumatic tyre.
1892	Rudolph Diesel's 'heavy oil engine'.
1896	'Red Flag Act' repealed. Guglielmo Marconi's first wireless demonstrations in England.
1897	Sir Charles Parsons's *Turbinia* at the Spithead Naval Review.
1903	First powered flight (Wright brothers).
1921	Amalgamation of railway companies.
1922	BBC established.
1924	Imperial Airways formed. First television picture transmitted (John Logie Baird).
1936	BBC Television Service begins (London area).

Questions

1. 'In the year 1894 I . . . went to Messrs. Benz and Co., and ordered a two-seater 3 h.p. car which cost me about £80. They explained to me that, although motor cars were being used on the Continent, I should not be allowed on account of the English law to run it in England until a special Motor Car Act was passed.' (Henry Hewetson, the first man to run a car in England)

   a) One of the two main German pioneers of the motor car is referred to here. Name the other.
   b) What invention, also by a German, made the car possible?
   c) What was 'the English law' which initially prevented Mr Hewetson from running his car in England?
   d) In 1896 the 'special Motor Car Act' was passed. What new maximum speed did it allow?
   e) Give *two* examples of the hazards of motoring in the early years.

2. Look at the picture of William Morris's motor body shop (page 249).
   a) What evidence is there of the need for basic craftwork to be done on some of the fittings?

b) Why were cars made like this beyond the reach of the working classes?

c) Morris later took up the production methods of which American manufacturer?

d) How did this help to reduce the price of his cars?

e) Why was the Morris *Minor* a big seller in the 1920s and 30s?

3. Explain why powered flight came later than powered land transport. Outline the main developments in *British* aviation before the Second World War. Why did air travel have little direct effect upon ordinary people's lives in this period?

4. 'I still have amongst my junk a little home-made crystal set, which worked lovely with the iron bedstead for aerial and the gas stove for earth, and which told me and my wife (each with one earphone to the ear) what was really happening.' (An Old Age Pensioner recalling his experience of the General Strike, 1926)

a) Name the Italian pioneer of wireless communication.

b) To what uses was it put *before* public broadcasting?

c) How can we tell that the writer trusted the BBC? Why are people more inclined to believe the BBC than newspapers?

d) What change was made in the organisation of the BBC in the year of the General Strike?

e) What new form of broadcasting began in 1936? Why was it at first restricted to the London area?

5. Write a paragraph on each of the following:
a) steam carriages
b) bicycles
c) developments in shipping, 1880s–1930s
d) the telephone

22

War and Depression

The First World War and its Effect on Industry, Agriculture and Foreign Trade, 1914–1939

Britain was not involved in any major war for a century following the Battle of Waterloo (1815). Peace was interrupted only by distant campaigns such as the Crimean War against Russia (1854–6) and the Boer War of 1899–1902 in South Africa. By the late nineteenth century the British were concentrating their energies upon empire-building, mainly in Africa, and had ceased to have much influence on European affairs. Britain was said to be in *'splendid isolation'*. However, events in Europe led to a change of policy in the early years of the twentieth century.

The end of isolation

King Edward VII. His warm reception during an official visit to Paris in May 1903 helped pave the way for the Anglo-French 'Entente' in the following year

In 1871 a new and powerful **German Empire** was created out of a number of individual states. The military strength of the new nation had already been demonstrated when the armed opposition of Austria (1866) and France (1870) was overcome by crushing German victories. Having unified the German states, Otto von Bismarck (Chancellor of Germany 1871–90) tried to re-establish peace in Europe. He regained the friendship of Austria and signed an alliance in 1879. This became the **Triple Alliance** (1882) with the addition of Italy. But France and Russia were suspicious and fearful of their new neighbour. In 1893 they formed a **Dual Alliance** for mutual help and protection. So Europe was divided into two 'armed camps'.

A growing number of British politicians expressed concern at their country's isolation from the continental alliances. They urged the Government to 'come down off the fence' on one side or the other. If and when this happened, it seemed likely that Germany would be the natural ally of Britain. William II, the German Kaiser (Emperor), was a nephew of King Edward VII (1901–10), and the two peoples had a long history of goodwill and co-operation. But friendly approaches to Germany – made secretly by Joseph Chamberlain, the Colonial Secretary, between 1898 and 1901 – came to nothing. The two countries were beginning to drift apart. The Kaiser's decision to build a powerful navy alarmed the British, for it seemed to be intended for use against them. When they replied by strengthening their own fleet, a 'naval race' developed which soured Anglo-German relations.

Meanwhile, Britain and France, the 'traditional enemies', drew closer together. In 1904 they signed the **Entente Cordiale** (Friendly Understanding) recognising each other's areas of influence in North

Triple Alliance
Dual Alliance

N

GREAT
BRITAIN
NORWAY
SWEDEN
NORTH SEA
DENMARK
Baltic Sea
St. Petersburg

RUSSIA

London
NETHER-
LANDS
BELGIUM
GERMANY
oBerlin

ATLANTIC OCEAN

oParis

FRANCE
SWITZ.
oVienna
AUSTRIA-HUNGARY

PORTUGAL

oMadrid
SPAIN

ITALY
Adriatic Sea
oRome

oBelgrade
SERBIA
ALBANIA

ROMANIA
BULGARIA
oSofia

BLACK SEA

Constantinople

TURKEY

GREECE

MEDITERRANEAN SEA

0   600 km

Triple Alliance and Dual Alliance – the two 'armed camps' of Europe

Africa. Three years later Britain made a similar agreement with Russia, France's ally, which settled their colonial differences in Asia. The **Triple Entente** to which Britain now belonged was *not* an alliance. In other words, Britain was not legally bound to aid either France or Russia against an enemy. But it was now very likely that Britain would favour the Dual Alliance rather than the 'Central Powers' (as Germany and her allies were called) in the event of a European war. This likelihood increased when British and French naval chiefs began to hold secret talks.

Britain's policy of *semi*-commitment to the Dual Alliance had serious disadvantages. If war broke out, France and Russia would expect assistance; yet, because there was no definite alliance, Britain could not hope to influence their actions when they looked like getting into trouble. The danger of this position became clear in the summer of 1914. Britain was a helpless spectator while a quarrel between Austria and Russia developed into a world war.

The First World War, 1914–1918

On 28 June 1914 **Archduke Franz Ferdinand**, the heir to the Austrian throne, was shot dead by a Serbian student. The Austrians had long been looking for an excuse to crush neighbouring Serbia (part of present day Yugoslavia) and expand into south-eastern Europe. Now was their chance. By the end of July the two countries were at war. The speed of events now quickened. Russia mobilised forces in Serbia's defence, determined to resist any extension of Austrian territory. Germany immediately supported her ally and declared war on Russia (1 August) and France (3 August). It was the start of the greatest bloodbath the world had seen, costing 10 million lives in just over four years.

The Schlieffen Plan for a quick German 'knock-out blow' against France

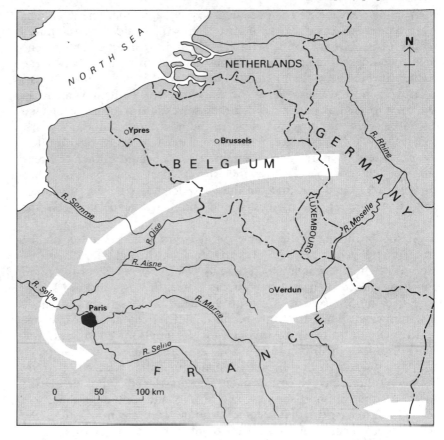

Faced by enemies on two fronts, the Germans put into operation the **Schlieffen Plan**, prepared by a former Chief-of-Staff in 1905. Their main attacking force was concentrated for a quick thrust against the French, hoping to knock them out of the fighting before Russia could fully mobilise on the Eastern Front. The German right wing aimed to sweep through Belgium and across the northern frontiers of France, the weakest point in the enemy's defences. Paris could then be attacked from the rear and the French army would be encircled.

Sir Edward Grey, Britain's Foreign Secretary, feared that if France were crushed the Germans would be able to dominate Europe. In his view, it was Britain's duty to fight simply to preserve the *balance of power* on the Continent. Several members of the Cabinet disagreed at first. But the German invasion of Belgium enabled Grey to get the full support of his colleagues and the nation for British entry into the war (4 August). Britain and the other great powers had signed a treaty in 1839 promising to defend Belgian independence. The German Chancellor now referred to it as a 'scrap of paper'. In any case, Britain could not stand by and see Belgium overrun, for it might provide a springboard for an invasion across the Channel.

The Belgians resisted bravely, slowing down the German advance. By the time Brussels, the Belgian capital, fell (20 August) the first British troops had arrived to assist France. Nevertheless the Schlieffen

Plan came very near to succeeding. By 5 September the Germans were within striking distance of Paris. The Allies, aided by reinforcements rushed to the front in taxis, rallied just in time. During the next seven days, the invaders were pushed back from the River Marne to the River Aisne. After this vital **Battle of the Marne**, the greatest crisis was over and the character of the war changed. Swift movements in the open ceased as both sides dug themselves into **trenches**, protected by barbed-wire and machine-guns. In the next three and a half years, the trench lines, extending from the Channel to the Swiss frontier, never varied by more than 30 kilometres. Repeated efforts to break through led to some of the bloodiest and most futile battles in history. Artillery and machine-gun fire gave defenders a clear advantage against troops advancing across the 'no-man's land' between the trenches.

At the beginning of the war cheering crowds had gathered in the streets, and young men had eagerly enlisted 'to fight for King and Country'. But the public mood quickly changed from cheerful optimism to grim acceptance of the horrors of trench warfare. **Lord Kitchener** became Minister of War (until his death at sea, 1916). He made a nationwide appeal for army recruits, and a million men came forward by the end of 1914. *Conscription* (compulsory enlistment) was not introduced in Britain until 1916 – so successful was the campaign for volunteers. Meanwhile the civilian population concentrated on supplying the armed forces. Women workers played a vital part in the factories, the transport services, and on the land. Although there was no fighting on British soil, people at home were given a taste of the war. Towns on the east coast were bombarded by the German navy, and occasional raids by aeroplanes and Zeppelins (airships, or powered balloons) claimed 1,400 victims.

To the great disappointment of Britain and France, the Russians failed to break through on the Eastern Front. They were heavily defeated at **Tannenberg** in East Germany (August 1914) and never fully

Volunteers for Lord Kitchener's Army (1914)

The Gallipoli Campaign, 1915

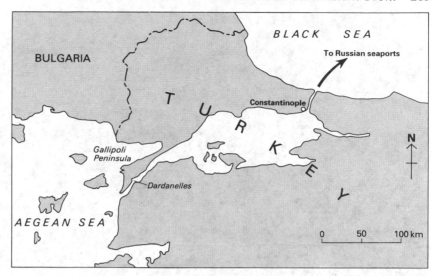

recovered. Russia was desperately short of military supplies, but it was difficult for Britain and France to make contact with their ally, especially after Turkey joined the Central Powers (October 1914). In the spring of 1915 the Allies began an offensive against Turkey, attempting to force a passage through the Dardanelles and attack Constantinople (see map above). A naval bombardment was tried first, but this gave the Turks warning and time to prepare their defences. When troops landed on the **Gallipoli** peninsula they suffered heavy losses and the campaign was abandoned after a few months. So 1915 was a disappointing year for the Allies, even though the Western Front held firm and they were joined by the Italians (who refused to support the Central Powers because they were the aggressors). But Italy had little effect on the outcome of the war, being hard pressed to hold her own against Austria.

Meanwhile the deadlock in the West continued. Both sides sacrificed hundreds of thousands of lives in hopeless attacks on enemy entrenchments. In 1915 Germany tried poisonous gas, but it was countered by the use of gas-masks. In the following year, German forces gathered for an all-out attack at **Verdun.** The French suffered appalling casualties, but held on by the skin of their teeth. To relieve pressure on them, the British staged a mass offensive on the **Somme.** Their losses were immense – 20,000 were killed on the first day (1 July). After four months a few kilometres of shell-torn countryside had been gained at the expense of 420,000 British casualties. There was great disillusionment at home, and this contributed to a change of leadership. **Lloyd George**, who distinguished himself while Minister of Munitions (1915–16), replaced Herbert Asquith as Prime Minister in December 1916. He formed a small War Cabinet of five members.

Like the fighting on land, the **war at sea** was a slow wearing-down process. With the Royal Navy in control of the oceans, the German battle fleet rarely ventured out of the Baltic. The only time the fleets came within striking distance of each other was in May 1916, off

Jutland (Denmark). But the Germans avoided a full-scale battle and disappeared in the evening mist, having sunk fourteen British ships and lost eleven themselves. Both sides were reluctant to risk defeat, especially the British, who needed command of the seas in order to supply the army, feed the people and blockade German shipping.

The British naval blockade deprived the Germans of vital supplies, including food. They replied by attacking British merchant shipping with **U-boats** (submarines). Early in 1917 the German High Command decided its best chance of victory was to starve Britain into surrender by *unrestricted* submarine warfare. From 1 February *all* ships approaching Allied ports were liable to be torpedoed, even if they belonged to neutral countries. The Germans realised that the United States would now almost certainly join the war against them, but gambled on defeating the Allies before the USA could mobilise her troops. The plan almost succeeded. By April, when the United States declared war on Germany, over 1,000 ships had been torpedoed in three months, and Britain had only six weeks' supply of food left. There were long queues outside the shops, and the Government introduced rationing to ensure fair distribution. After April, however, shipping losses were greatly reduced. Merchant vessels began to sail in *convoys*, escorted by destroyers equipped with depth-charges.

American support was especially welcome to Britain and France because Russia withdrew from the war soon after the Communists came to power in the Revolution of November 1917. Everything now depended on the Western Front. Another British offensive failed in the summer and autumn of 1917. Only 8 kilometres of muddy wilderness and the village of **Passchendaele**, near Ypres, were gained at a cost of 300,000 casualties. Nevertheless, Germany, in the grip of the naval blockade, was now drastically short of food and raw materials.

German U-boats in Kiel harbour (1917). They were able to take a short cut from the Baltic into the North Sea by means of the Kiel Canal – cut across the lower part of Jutland just south of the border with Denmark

British machine-gunners manning shell-holes near Passchendaele (1917)

Austria and Turkey were also in trouble. In December 1917 the Turks lost Jerusalem to Britain's General Allenby, who was ably assisted by **T.E. Lawrence** ('Lawrence of Arabia') leading the tribes of the Arabian desert.

Germany's only hope was an all-out attack in the West before United States forces arrived in full strength. With troops transferred from the Russian frontier, the Germans began their great **Spring Offensives** in March 1918. They broke through the Allied defences in several places. At one time Paris was again in danger and a second Battle of the Marne was fought to save France's capital. But by June the Allies, strengthened with American troops and under the sole command of the French **Marshal Foch**, began to drive the Germans back. A series of attacks all along the line soon led to its collapse. British tanks played a decisive part for the first time since their introduction in 1916. The Germans were too exhausted to rally. The Kaiser fled to the Netherlands, and the long-awaited **armistice** came on 11 November at eleven o'clock. In London and all the Allied capitals, people rushed into the streets, dancing and cheering. There were plenty of tears also. Britain and the Empire alone had lost over a million men killed and more than twice as many wounded.

Nine weeks later representatives of thirty-two countries attended the Peace Conference in Paris. The Germans were deprived of some European territory and all their colonies; their army was reduced almost to nothing and their armaments manufacture strictly controlled. In addition, Germany was expected to pay large sums of money to the Allies as *reparations* (damages). **President Woodrow Wilson** of the USA asked the Conference to accept his *Fourteen Points*, containing a recipe for world peace. He had to give way on many of them, but his chief hope was realised – the creation of a **League of Nations**, to meet regularly and discuss world problems. However Wilson's political opponents at home kept the USA out of the League, so reducing its effectiveness from the start.

The depression; industries old and new

For a short time after the war, British exports soared and industry prospered. Everywhere there was a great demand for manufactured goods that had been scarce during wartime. By 1920 the army was demobilised, most of the 3 million munitions workers were re-employed in peacetime industries, and everyone talked of 'business as usual'. But then, suddenly, this brief period of prosperity came to an end. In the winter of 1920–1, when more normal trading conditions returned, British exports slumped and there was a consequent rise in **unemployment**. By June 1921, 2 million men were out of work – one in every seven of working age. There was no immediate panic, for everyone expected the situation to improve quickly, as it usually had done in trade 'slumps' of the past. But this time there was no quick recovery. British foreign trade was entering a period of serious decline, and, from 1921 to 1940, the numbers of unemployed never fell below a million.

The First World War was partly to blame. While British industry concentrated on supplying the armed forces, many former customers overseas were neglected. They either increased their own production of goods previously bought from Britain, or found other sources of supply; for example, South American countries turned to the USA. Naturally, when peace returned, these countries found they could manage with fewer British goods than they had bought before 1914.

Britain's share of world trade had been decreasing slowly for half a century, as other nations developed their own industries. But the war greatly *accelerated* this trend. Until Britain could find new customers, or recover lost markets with new products, there was not enough work to go round. The effects of the depression were not evenly spread over the whole country. The areas which suffered most –

Unemployment 1900–40

Percentage of working population unemployed

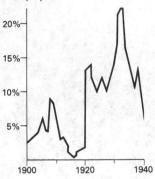

The rise and decline of three major industries

	Coal	Iron	Cotton textents
	Total output of coal in United Kingdom (million tonnes)	Output of pig iron in Great Britain (million tonnes)	Exports from United Kingdom of cotton piece-goods (million metres)
1873	131	7	3,186
1897	205	9	4,382
1913	292	10	6,469
1929	261	8	3,443
1938	231	7	1,324

All figures to nearest million

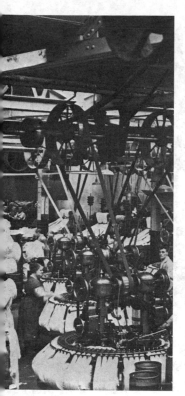

Part of a wool combing shed n West Yorkshire

north-east England, Lancashire, South Wales and Clydeside – were centres of the **old-established industries**: textiles (especially cotton), coal, iron and steel, heavy engineering and shipbuilding. Few of these industries regained the high level of output they had reached before 1914 and all failed to recapture fully their pre-war export trade.

The **cotton** industry was the hardest hit by the war, mainly because of its dependence on overseas customers. In 1914 there began a decline in the fortunes of the industry from which it never recovered. Like Britain during the Industrial Revolution, newly developing countries turned to cotton very early in their industrialisation. For instance, Japan and India gradually ceased to buy from Britain and became competitors instead. By 1935 the Japanese dominated Asian and Far-Eastern markets, and they were already exporting greater quantities of cotton goods than Britain. **Woollen textiles** fared much less badly. Woollen cloth had been in great demand for military uniforms during the war, and, in peacetime, a large proportion of Britain's output continued to be sold at home.

Coal-mining came under direct government control during the war, along with railways and munitions factories. When peace returned, the industry suffered a steady decline, in both its labour force and its production. The output of 292 million tonnes in 1913 has never since been equalled – despite much greater use of mechanical cutters and conveyors in later years. Only 8 per cent of UK production was machine-cut in 1913, compared with 61 per cent in 1939. Yet output per man rose much less rapidly than in Germany and Poland, Britain's main rivals in the export trade. British coal exports fell from 75 million tonnes in 1913 to 41 million tonnes in 1937. Meanwhile the growing use of electric power in industry reduced the demand for coal at home. It was still required to drive the generators in the power stations (see page 172) but it was used more economically than in the days of steam-powered factories. Furthermore, shipping was rapidly changing over from coal to oil fuel.

Iron, steel and engineering experienced varying fortunes. New iron ore fields were developed in North Lincolnshire and Northamptonshire, leading to the growth of iron and steel towns such as Scunthorpe and Corby. Nevertheless, an increasing proportion of Britain's iron ore had to be imported, while exports of pig iron to Europe dropped sharply. Steel and heavy engineering were hit by the depression, but revived in the late 1930s, stimulated by rearmament for war. Steel output in 1937 was more than a third above that of 1929. But **shipbuilding** suffered disastrously from the decline in international trade, which reduced the demand for new merchant vessels. In 1933 nearly two-thirds of Britain's shipbuilding workers were unemployed and many yards were being dismantled. However the industry recovered strongly in the late 1930s, largely because of the need to build up the Royal Navy. In 1939 Britain was still the world's leading shipbuilder.

A wide range of **newer industries** grew and prospered in the inter-war years (1918–39). There was a steady rise in the output of motor cars, aeroplanes, electrical equipment, chemicals, fertilizers, rubber

The De Havilland aircraft factory at Hatfield, Hertfordshire, in 1935. Along with Hawker Siddeley, it was one of Britain's leading aircraft manufacturers before the Second World War. From small beginnings in the 1920s, the aircraft industry became big business after about 1930

goods, medicines, cosmetics and packaged foods. Most of these were manufactured in the South Midlands and the South-East – for electric power encouraged the growth of factories away from the coalfields, in more pleasant surroundings. As George Orwell, the novelist, observed: 'The typical post-war factory is not a gaunt barrack or an awful chaos of blackness and belching chimneys; it is a glittering white structure of concrete, glass and steel, surrounded by green lawns and beds of tulips.'

In the early 1930s, when unemployment reached 30 to 40 per cent in many coal-mining, cotton or shipbuilding towns, only about 6 per cent of workers in the 'lucky South' were without jobs. In fact, despite the depression, a *majority* of the population enjoyed an improvement in living standards in the inter-war years. The main centres of **motor-car manufacture** – Coventry, Birmingham, Oxford, Bedford and Dagenham – were especially prosperous. The British motor industry was the first to copy American mass-production techniques and it became Europe's leading producer in this period. Between 1929 and 1937, when the old-established industries felt the worst effects of the trade slump, the output of motor vehicles more than doubled. By 1937 the yearly production of motor vehicles was half a million – three-quarters of them made by six companies: Morris, Austin, Standard, Rootes (whose trade names were Humber, Hillman, Commer and Sunbeam Talbot), and the US-owned Ford and Vauxhall.

Similarly, the **electrical industry** was little affected by the depression.

The production of dynamos, electric motors, light bulbs, radio sets, cookers and vacuum cleaners rose steadily. The manufacture of **chemicals** was one of the few expanding industries partly located in the 'depressed areas' – notably Merseyside and the North-East. In 1926 four large firms came together to form ICI (Imperial Chemical Industries Ltd), then the largest industrial concern in the British Empire. The chemical industry played an important part in the development of rayon, an artificial fibre made from cotton and cellulose (obtained from wood-pulp). The products of these newer industries were mainly sold in home markets. Britain failed to capture a sufficiently large share of world trade in goods such as cars, radio sets and rayon cloth to make up for the losses of the older industries.

State aid for agriculture

Farming, the oldest industry, enjoyed a brief period of prosperity during the First World War. U-boat attacks on merchant shipping, at a time when Britain imported about two-thirds of her food, made it essential to increase home production. The Government encouraged the ploughing-up of grassland in order to grow more cereals, and gained the co-operation of farmers by giving them guaranteed prices (1917). At the same time, agricultural labourers were granted a national minimum wage. With additional help from the Women's Land Army and prisoner-of-war labour, the wheat harvest was increased by 60 per cent, and there was a substantial rise in the production of potatoes, barley and oats – though partly at the expense of meat and milk.

But agriculture slumped again soon after the war. The average price of wheat halved in the years 1920–2. Farmers were no longer guaranteed against losses after 1921, so they were forced to return to the pre-war practice of converting arable land into pasture (see page 160). Livestock- and dairy-farming requires fewer workers than arable cultivation, so this trend increased the numbers of unemployed. Governments felt compelled to take fresh action, to help farmers and to restore the balance between the different branches of agriculture. **State subsidies** (money grants) were paid to growers of wheat (1932), barley and oats (1937), as well as to meat-producers (1934). After 1933 **import quotas** limited purchases of foreign food to fixed quantities. Meanwhile national **Marketing Boards** were established (1931–3) to control sales of milk, bacon, pork, hops and potatoes, at guaranteed prices. The influence of government policy was clearly seen in the case of sugar-beet. Sugar was entirely imported before 1914, yet, by the early 1930s, heavy state subsidies had created a home industry supplying a quarter of the country's sugar needs.

The combined efforts of successive governments and the farmers resulted in a slight recovery of agriculture in the 1930s. This was aided by greater use of **farm machinery**, especially for threshing and milking. Combine harvesters were used on some larger farms. Motor tractors, which were almost non-existent in Britain before 1914, numbered 50,000 in 1939. Nevertheless the drift from the land was

unchecked. A quarter of a million labourers left the countryside between 1918 and 1939. So the decline of village life continued and Britain remained dangerously dependent on foreign food supplies, as was shown in the Second World War (see page 326).

A new development in farming: large pneumatic tyres fitted to a plough tractor

The crisis of 1931 and the end of 'free trade'

In October 1929 there was a sudden fall in the value of shares on Wall Street (the New York Stock Exchange). Investments became almost worthless as thousands of share-holders panicked and tried to sell in a market where there were no buyers. The **'Wall Street Crash'** began a worldwide financial crisis and a further slump in international trade which seriously affected Britain and other industrial nations. British exports almost halved in value in the next two years (1929–31) while the total of unemployed reached nearly 3 million (roughly one worker in five).

Faced with the worst depression in history, the Prime Minister, **Ramsay MacDonald**, formed an all-party **National Government** in 1931. He split with Labour, his former party, in the process (see page 280). The National Government assisted manufacturers as well as farmers. For example, loans were given to certain industries to help finance worthwhile projects. One result was the completion of *Cunarder 534* (renamed *Queen Mary*) which lay half-built on Clydeside. Four of the most depressed regions – the North-East, South Wales, the Scottish Lowlands and West Cumberland (Cumbria) – became **Special Areas** (1934) and industries were encouraged to move to them.

Above all, the National Government decided to abandon 'free

trade' (see Chapter 14). Since the mid nineteenth century, foreign manufactured goods had entered Britain free of customs duties, even though other nations imposed duties (tariffs) to protect their own industries from outside competition. Back in 1903 **Joseph Chamberlain** had resigned from the Conservative Government to launch a nation-wide **Tariff Reform Campaign**. He proposed that Britain should give up free trade and impose tariffs which allowed for *imperial preference* (lower duties on Empire goods than on imports from other countries). His main aim was to strengthen the Empire, but he won support from many people who felt that Britain's rivals had an unfair advantage and that the Government should introduce tariffs equivalent to those placed on British goods abroad. However Chamberlain's scheme required substantial duties on *food* imports from countries outside the Empire. When his policy was put to the test of a general election (1906) the prospect of higher food prices caused most voters to reject it. Chamberlain retired from politics and the campaign against free trade was not seriously revived until the coming of the depression.

In 1915 wartime duties were placed on non-essential imports like cars, clocks and musical instruments. When peace returned they were not removed, even though this had been promised. Then, in 1921, Parliament imposed a few more duties to protect from foreign competition some small industries that had arisen during the war. This was 'the thin end of the wedge', but the decisive change came, in the depths of the depression, with the **Import Duties Act, 1932**. The National Government decided that while it was powerless to prevent the slump in overseas sales, it could at least preserve the *home* market for British producers. Therefore a 10 per cent customs duty was placed on a majority of imports – to make them less attractive to British buyers. The only goods exempted were most foodstuffs and

Cartoon showing Joseph Chamberlain searching for the remains of the Tariff Reform Campaign after the 1906 general election

some raw materials such as rubber, cotton and wool. Later in the same year, most duties were raised to 20 or even 33⅓ per cent. The Act did not apply to Empire products, so the way was clear for the immediate introduction of 'imperial preference' similar to that suggested by Joseph Chamberlain.

Despite the ending of free trade, recovery from the depression was painfully slow. Industrial production picked up in the late 1930s, as Britain rearmed to face the threat of Hitler. But it took the Second World War (1939–45) to bring mass unemployment to an end.

John Maynard Keynes – a voice in the wilderness

Government policies in the 1920s and 30s did little to lessen the effects of the depression. Low industrial output and high unemployment meant a reduced income from taxes on firms and people at work. So governments tried to reduce their spending in order to balance the annual budget. They cut back on social services, education, road-building and so forth to save money. This seemed common sense. After all, it was the way an ordinary household would manage its family budget. But such policies not only failed to cure mass unemployment, they actually *made it worse*. A different approach was suggested by a group of *economists* led by **John Maynard Keynes**, a Cambridge University teacher. Keynes's most important book, ***The General Theory of Employment, Interest and Money***, appeared in 1936. But well before this he had gained a reputation as a powerful critic of established economic thinking.

Keynes did not deny that an important cause of the depression was the decline of older industries such as cotton, coal and shipbuilding. Whatever happened, areas where these industries were concentrated could expect to suffer above average unemployment. The only answer to this so-called *structural* type of unemployment was a long and painful process of adjustment. Some of the jobless would have to move to areas of expanding industry, and new industries would have to be set up in the 'depressed areas'. But Keynes argued that there was a *more general cause* of unemployment which was not properly understood and which could be tackled by new government policies.

At the heart of Keynes's ideas is a very simple fact. Money spent by one person is earned by others, and then *re*spent on and on in a chain. For example, £100 spent by a family on clothes is shared out, as income, among those who produced and sold the goods. These people, in turn, spend their incomes – so the £100 is received, shared out and respent many times over. This works the same way in reverse. If, say, £100 is *not* spent the consequences become magnified as it is *not* earned, *not* respent and so on. This happened during the depression. Many people were out of work because there was *not enough spending altogether* by individuals, businesses and the government. Less spending led to less production, less earned in wages and salaries, even less spending, and so on in a downward spiral.

Keynes said that the government should take positive steps to boost spending – because *one man's spending is another man's work*.

John Maynard Keynes (1883–1946) had a brilliant academic and professional career at Eton, Cambridge University, in the civil service and the Treasury. He felt strongly about the misery of mass unemployment and argued for much more positive government policies to get the wheels of industry turning

Firms could be encouraged to invest in new equipment if, for example, money could be borrowed at a lower rate of interest. Above all, the government could increase its *own* spending – on social services, armaments and 'public works' such as roadbuilding. Government spending over and above its total income would be made up by borrowing. Keynes was not afraid of a budget *deficit* (where spending is greater than income). This was because the policies he put forward would result in more people at work, more wages earned and profits made. These extra wages and profits would be spent and so encourage further increases in production. The government would receive more in taxes on incomes and profits and could then repay the money it had borrowed.

'Keynesian economics' were to revolutionise government policies in the 1940s (see pages 302, 345). But until then ministers and their advisers were unwilling to put his theories to the test. The idea of deliberately running a large budget deficit so as to increase government spending was considered 'unsound', even reckless. Businessmen, too, expected the government to balance its budget. If Keynesian policies had been adopted in the 1930s, before the business world was ready to accept them, they might have backfired. Firms might have lost confidence in the government and, fearing a financial crisis, invested even less in new equipment. This could have outweighed the beneficial effects of extra government spending. As it turned out, Keynes remained a voice in the wilderness until after the outbreak of the Second World War, when he became an adviser to the Treasury. He then had a decisive influence on the whole shape of future government policy.

Timeline

1903–6	Joseph Chamberlain's Tariff Reform Campaign.
1904	'Entente Cordiale'.
1907	Anglo-Russian 'Entente'.
1914–18	First World War.
1920–1	Start of the depression.
1929	Wall Street 'Crash'.
1931–5	National Government (state aid for industry and agriculture).
1932	Import Duties Act.
1936	John Maynard Keynes's *General Theory of Employment, Interest and Money*.

Questions

1. 'The War . . . originated in a quarrel in which this country had no direct concern . . . We were bound by our obligations . . . to assert and maintain the threatened independence of a small and neutral State.' (Herbert Asquith, Prime Minister, August 1914)

   a) What was the 'quarrel' which led to the First World War?

b) Why were countries not directly concerned, including Britain, expected to assist those involved in the quarrel?

c) Name the 'small and neutral State' which was threatened.

d) What were Britain's 'obligations' to this State?

e) Why did Britain's Foreign Secretary think that Britain would have to fight in any case, regardless of her 'obligations'?

2. 'Although the first effects of the 1920 slump were felt by merchants in the form of cancelled orders . . . they were quickly transmitted to . . . spinning and weaving.

. . . attempts to undersell competitors tended more and more to take the form of supplying a yarn, a cloth or a finish a little cheaper or lower in quality than the competing article.

. . . the industry as a whole was working with a margin of profit which left it with no adequate balance to devote to re-equipment . . . Accordingly it stood still in its methods just at a time when new industries were growing up elsewhere.'
(Board of Trade Report on the Cotton Industry, 1946)

a) Why was there a 'slump' in 1920? How long did it last?

b) Why was the cotton industry hard hit by the trade slump?

c) Name *two* of Britain's rising competitors in cotton production.

d) How did attempts to compete with these countries further weaken the British cotton industry?

e) Why did Britain's woollen industry fare less badly than cotton in this period?

3. a) Take *two* examples (excluding cotton) of 'old established' industries which declined in the period 1919–39, and give reasons for their decline.

b) Give *two* examples of 'newer' industries which expanded in the same period, with reasons for their growth.

c) How did the varying fortunes of these industries affect the geographical distribution of industry in Britain?

4. Look at the cartoon on Tariff Reform (page 271).

a) Why did Joseph Chamberlain launch his Tariff Reform Campaign?

b) What was the main objection to his policy?

c) Why are the terms 'great storm' and 'snowed under' used in relation to Tariff Reform and the 1906 Election?

d) Did Tariff Reform 'disappear' completely, or did the 'snow' later melt? Give reasons for your answer.

5. Write a paragraph on each of the following:

a) trench warfare, 1914–18

b) the war at sea, 1914–18

c) government control of agriculture

d) J. M. Keynes's ideas on unemployment

23

The Troubled Years
Working-class Movements and Social Conditions, 1918–39

When peace returned in 1918, the British people looked to the future with high hopes. Lloyd George, the prime minister, talked of making Britain 'a fit country for heroes to live in', and promised an all-out attack on poverty and bad living conditions. Even before the peace treaty was signed, a **Parliamentary Reform Act (1918)** extended the right to vote to all men over twenty-one and most women over thirty. This more than doubled the size of the electorate. A general election was held almost immediately, and Lloyd George's wartime **Coalition Government** was returned to power with an enormous majority (December 1918). However, many of the easy promises made in the hour of victory could not be fulfilled in the difficult years which lay ahead.

Industrial unrest

The mass strike action on the eve of the First World War was halted by an 'industrial truce' between employers and trade unions which continued until 1918 (see page 196). There were still a few strikes – for example among shipbuilding workers on Clydeside and miners in South Wales – but in general the unions co-operated with employers and the Government. Because of this inactivity, they emerged from the war with greatly increased funds. Furthermore, the number of trade union members almost doubled between 1913 and 1919. The unions were stronger than ever before.

They soon had plenty to fight for. Steeply rising prices after the Armistice led to hundreds of claims for higher pay, and, where these were rejected, many bitter strikes. On average, more than 100,000 men were on strike every day throughout 1919. Some unions achieved their aims by peaceful means. The Government set up an **Industrial Court** where both sides in a dispute could state their case and obtain a settlement. Early in 1920 dockers gained a substantial wage increase in this way. Their arguments were skilfully put by **Ernest Bevin**, a remarkable union leader who left school at the age of eleven and rose from farm-labouring to become a Cabinet minister in the 1940s. Bevin played a leading part in the creation of the world's largest trade union in 1921. It was formed by the amalgamation of a number of separate unions into the **Transport and General Workers' Union**, which Bevin served as General Secretary. There were many other trade union amalgamations in the post-war years, each resulting in a more powerful organisation.

Although many wage increases during 1919–20 were wiped out by

Ernest Bevin (1881–1951), General Secretary of the Transport and General Workers' Union from 1921 to 1940

Dockers on strike after the First World War

the higher cost of living, the unions felt triumphant at having won a succession of victories over employers. But the coming of mass unemployment in 1921 (see page 266) caused a sudden reversal of fortunes. Employers now held the upper hand, for whenever there are more workers than jobs those who strike may be threatened with dismissal. The trade slump led employers to press for *lower* wages and *longer* hours. Unions were forced on the defensive. Instead of asking for more, they had to struggle to keep what they had got. This problem was greatest in the old-established industries, such as coal-mining, which were the hardest hit by the depression.

The miners' grievances and the General Strike, 1926

During the war, the coal industry was temporarily *nationalised* (taken under government control). Wages were increased and they no longer varied from one district to another. Miners were more contented than they had been under private employers, so when peace came their union, the **Miners' Federation of Great Britain**, demanded that nationalisation should continue. The Government, under pressure from the mine-owners, refused the demands of the union, even though a Royal Commission (1919) declared itself in favour of state control. The miners were angry, especially as the Government had promised to abide by the Royal Commission's decision 'in the spirit and in the letter'. The question of nationalisation remained a cause of discontent in the coal industry for almost thirty years.

By the time nationalisation came to an end (March 1921) the depression had begun. The export price of coal in the spring of 1921 was down to only a *fifth* of the summer 1920 price. Mine-owners gave

Employers' view of the Triple Industrial Alliance, as shown in a 'Punch' cartoon, April 1921

Stanley Baldwin (1867–1947) pictured in 1920

warning that when they resumed control of their pits they would make drastic wage cuts, and these would vary from region to region, because some mines were more profitable than others. The Miners' Federation refused to accept the new terms and gained the support of the railwaymen and transport workers, their partners in the **Triple Industrial Alliance** of 1914 (see page 195). A massive strike was arranged for 15 April, but when the day arrived the other unions withdrew their support. Trade unionists called it **'Black Friday'**, for the Triple Alliance had collapsed and the miners were left to fight alone. They eventually returned to work on 1 July, having gained very little improvement in the terms offered in March.

After a slight recovery, coal prices again fell sharply in 1925. Employers proposed immediate wage cuts and an increase of one hour in the working day. But the Miners' Federation protested that it was already 'stripped to the bone'. The Triple Alliance was revived and this time it held firm. The Prime Minister, **Stanley Baldwin**, saw that the only way of preventing a nationwide stoppage was for the

Government to intervene and make up miners' wages to their previous level. Therefore, on 31 July, miners were offered a state subsidy of £24 million to offset the owners' wage cuts. It would last for nine months. The unions called their success **'Red Friday'**, but in fact it settled nothing. Both sides realised there would be a showdown when the subsidy ended.

Neither the miners nor their employers were prepared to give way. The mine-owners continued to demand substantial wage cuts and longer working hours, and the miners replied with the slogan 'not a penny off the pay; not a minute on the day'. By the time the subsidy was withdrawn (1 May 1926) the Trades Union Congress had agreed to support the miners. Its members voted by an overwhelming majority for a **General Strike**, beginning on Tuesday, 4 May.

It was not necessary for all union members to strike. The country could be paralysed if workers came out in a few key industries. Therefore only railwaymen and transport workers, dockers, builders, iron, steel and chemical workers, printers, and gas and electricity workers supplying power for industry came out, in addition to the miners. Sanitary services continued and health and food services were not interfered with. There were altogether about 3 million men on strike (one in every five adult males). They formed the backbone of British industry.

It was the quietest Tuesday morning in living memory. Factories were deserted, there were no buses, trams or trains, and no newspapers. However, the 'great silence' was soon broken, for non-union business attempted to carry on as usual. In London crowds of people set out to walk from the suburbs to their offices in town. Bowler-hatted businessmén were seen on bicycles, while thousands of motor cars, crammed with hitch-hikers, caused enormous traffic jams on main roads leading to the City.

The Government had made careful plans for dealing with the strike. Troops were sent to work in the docks and power stations and to accompany food convoys in the towns. In London, Hyde Park became a vast milk depot. Most important of all, a voluntary **Organisation for the Maintenance of Supplies (OMS)** had for months been training ordinary citizens to drive buses and trains and to act as special constables. Within a week, nearly 3,000 trains were operating with amateur crews, and bus services were running in many areas. There were more crashes than usual, but few were serious.

Despite the printers' strike, Winston Churchill (the Chancellor of the Exchequer) and a band of willing helpers produced a government daily newspaper – *The British Gazette* – from 5 May. It accused the strikers of 'a direct challenge to ordered government', and 'a hold-up of the nation to ransom'. The TUC (Trades Union Congress) replied with a paper called *The British Worker*. This denied the Government's charges and emphasised that the strike was simply 'an industrial dispute, *not* an attack upon Parliamentary government'. Most of the regular daily papers, including *The Times* and the *Daily Mirror*, were reduced to single sheets. The BBC tried to make up for the newspaper shortage by putting out five news bulletins a day. Baldwin

A Strike Edition of 'The Times' compared in size with an ordinary alarm clock

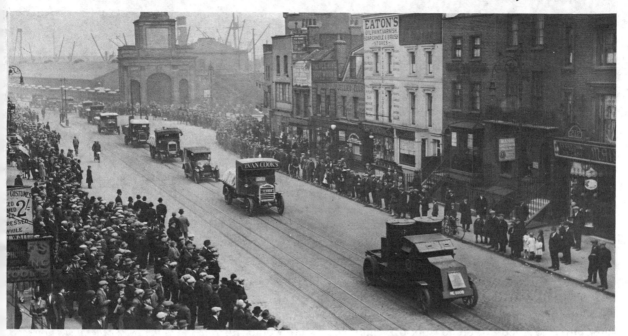

A food convoy leaves London Docks on the fifth day of the General Strike

made several broadcasts to the nation, but his Cabinet prevented both the TUC and the Leader of the Labour Party from speaking on the radio.

Some of the strikers occupied their time trying to wreck vehicles driven by members of the OMS. As a result, many buses had windows boarded up against stone-throwers and barbed-wire across the bonnet to protect the engine from sabotage. In Northumberland a gang of wreckers managed to derail the *Flying Scotsman* by removing a length of the railway track. But incidents of that kind were rare. Considering the serious nature of the dispute, most people were remarkably peaceful and good humoured. At Plymouth, for instance, a team of strikers played the local police at soccer. All over the country, entertainments and sports, including county cricket, helped to take people's minds off the crisis. Foreign observers were greatly impressed by the calmness of the British people. *The Philadelphia Record*, an American newspaper, pointed out on 11 May that after a week of the greatest industrial dispute in the nation's history 'not a single life has been lost, not a single shot fired'.

As the strike entered its second week, all seemed to be going well for the unions. But suddenly, on 12 May, the TUC called it off, after only nine days. They said they had been given 'assurances that a settlement of the mining problem can be secured'. But the Miners' Federation was dismayed to find that nothing *definite* had been promised by either the Government or the mine-owners. The TUC leaders seemed to be afraid of the great weapon they had created and unwilling to be branded as revolutionaries. So the miners were left to fight alone, until near-starvation forced them to return to work, on the owners' terms, *six months later*. Some mining districts never recovered. After standing idle for six months or more, many smaller pits were forced to close down, their workers swelling the already high numbers of unemployed. In the summer of 1927 a quarter of a million miners were out of work.

The Government pressed home its victory with a **Trade Disputes Act (1927)**, which made most kinds of general or 'sympathetic' strikes illegal. The Act was not necessary, however, because few trade unionists wanted a repeat of the events of 1926. The General Strike cost the unions involved about £4 million. In the next few years, while union funds recovered, strikes were fewer and generally short-lived. Under the leadership of **Walter Citrine**, General Secretary of the TUC 1926–46, the trade union movement set out to regain public confidence and build up a new kind of relationship with the government. By offering advice and assistance on a wide range of industrial issues, the unions exerted a growing influence on national policy.

Liberal decline and the mixed fortunes of Labour

After 1926 many working-class people took a greater interest in politics. They had learned from the General Strike that there was a limit to what they could achieve by withdrawing their labour. The best alternative seemed to be to support candidates who would further their aims in Parliament. So the defeat of the General Strike was followed by a rise in the fortunes of **Labour** – the only major political party which claimed to put the interests of the working classes uppermost (see pages 197–9).

The Labour Party had been growing in strength since 1918, when the right to vote was extended to all men and most women. In the 1923 election Labour, under **Ramsay MacDonald**, won 191 seats and formed the government for the first time (January 1924). But MacDonald depended on Liberal support in the House of Commons, because the Conservatives were the largest single party. His Government only lasted ten months; yet in that time it did much to convince doubters that Labour was 'respectable' and fit to govern. In the election of October 1924 the Liberals won only forty-two seats and ceased to be a major force in British politics. The **decline of the Liberals** was directly linked to the rise of Labour. Although the Liberals had a proud record of social reform, industrial workers increasingly switched their support to the party fathered by the trade unions to protect their interests. As the Liberal Party faded and Labour became the main opposition to the Conservatives, the customary *two-party system* was restored (see page 347).

In the first election after the General Strike (1929) Labour won 287 seats, more than any other party. However Liberal support was again required for an overall majority in the Commons. The second Labour Government had the misfortune to encounter the great financial crisis which followed the collapse of the American stock market in 1929 (see page 270). It broke up when MacDonald proposed cuts in government spending on social services, notably a reduction in unemployment benefit (1931). This was against the principles of a party which claimed to protect the 'underdog'. When MacDonald formed

J. Ramsay MacDonald pictured after his victory in the 1929 general election

an all-party **National Government** he was regarded as a traitor and the bulk of Labour MPs would have nothing more to do with him. The Party was divided and for a time its strength in Parliament dwindled.

The 'dole' and the 'means test'

For unemployed workers and their families, life was a grim struggle. Debts piled up, furniture, clothing and personal possessions were taken to the pawnbroker, men searched for coal in slag-heaps and railway sidings, and thousands of families went short of food. Things would have been even worse without weekly unemployment benefits and allowances paid by the state. The original unemployment scheme in the National Insurance Act of 1911 only covered about 3 million workers in a small range of industries (see page 241). However, by November 1920 everyone earning less than £5 a week was brought in, with the exception of farm labourers and domestic and civil servants. Cash benefits could be claimed for up to fifteen weeks in any year. In 1921 allowances for dependent wives and children were added.

The new insurance scheme was worked out just before the start of the depression. Almost as soon as it came into operation it was out of date. Calculations had been based on an unemployment rate of no more than 4 per cent of the working population; but in fact it hardly ever fell below 10 per cent for almost twenty years. Hundreds of thousands of workers used up their fifteen weeks of benefit without there being any sign of a job. 'Extended benefits' (nicknamed the '**dole**') were introduced. When they ran out the only alternative was Poor Relief. In 1929, however, the whole system of Poor Law Guardians and workhouses was abolished. Responsibility for the jobless who exhausted their insurance benefits eventually passed to a new **Unemployment Assistance Board (1934)**. It had offices all over Britain (relieving the overworked Labour Exchanges) and was financed out of national taxation.

Meanwhile the numbers out of work rose above 2 million in 1931, and remained at this high level for three or four years. As part of its 'economy drive', the National Government cut benefits for the insured by 10 per cent (1931) and introduced a **means test** for the long-term unemployed. This meant that the amount of cash each man received depended on his family's total income, including pensions and savings. Even if his son had a paper round he had to declare it and his 'dole' was adjusted accordingly. The means test saved the Government several million pounds a year, but at the cost of greater misery and discontent. It was hated by the unemployed, who resented officials enquiring into their family affairs. Worst of all, it caused bitterness between parents and children. If sons and daughters had regular jobs, father was 'knocked off the dole' and had to be supported by them. This could be very damaging to a man's self-respect.

Most of the time the unemployed suffered in silence. But occasionally public demonstrations and 'hunger marches' drew attention to the plight of the depressed areas. In 1936, for example, 200 men from Jarrow in County Durham marched over 450 kilometres to

London to present a petition to the Prime Minister. Because of the dismantling of the town's shipyard, almost three-quarters of its working population was idle. The **Jarrow Crusade** stirred the conscience of the nation. So did a BBC broadcast in 1934, when a group of men and women were invited to describe their experience of 'life on the dole':

'When there is a job going, anything up to twelve are sent for it', said an ex-metal turner who had served a seven-year apprenticeship. 'That means eleven of us are disappointed; and when this happens over and over again one gets real fed up.'

'My husband has worked about one year out of twelve and a half', said a mother of four children. 'His face was lovely when I married him, but now he's skin and bones.' Housekeeping was a nightmare. 'I can't manage more than one box of matches a week', she explained. 'Our kettle's got about six patches on it, made . . . from cocoa tins.'

Although the worst was over by about 1934, unemployment figures remained high for the rest of the 1930s. Families lucky enough to have a little savings could afford to move to one of the centres of the newer industries, where chances of a job were good. Hence there was a rapid growth of population in south-eastern England during this period. For the remainder who stayed in the depressed areas, often the only hope was to obtain a place in a government training centre,

The Jarrow marchers on their way to London – headed by their mouth organ band. Throughout the four weeks of marching the men took turns to carry a heavy oak chest containing a petition with 12,000 signatures to be presented to the Prime Minister, Stanley Baldwin

which prepared workers for new trades. Retraining was especially important for young men, many of whom had reached their mid-twenties without ever having a job. Older men, with little chance of finding work, were often given allotments of land where they could grow vegetables and fruit and rear poultry or rabbits for their families. This gave them some release from boredom and worry.

No 'homes for heroes'

Next to unemployment, **housing** was the greatest social problem of the inter-war years. Even under normal conditions house-building had lagged behind the growth of population, but during the First World War only 50,000 houses were completed in over four years – fewer than in a normal year before 1914. Consequently by 1918 there was an acute housing shortage. Moreover, many rows of dismal terraced houses in the towns or crumbling country cottages were unfit to be lived in. At the end of the war, Lloyd George declared that the slums would be swept away and replaced by 'homes fit for heroes'. But this promise, like many others made at the time, proved wildly optimistic.

The full effects of the housing shortage were felt by the poorest sections of the community. As is nearly always the case, those who could afford to pay more got what they wanted. George Orwell put it in a nutshell: '"Housing shortage" . . . means very little to anyone with an income of more than £10 a week.' Even before the war builders found it unprofitable to construct houses at rents lower-paid workers could afford (see page 181). Poorer families mostly had to make do with one or two rooms. After 1918 a rise in the cost of materials made this problem worse and brought greater overcrowding in the slum areas.

Pre-war governments had done little to increase the supply of houses. They were always reluctant to interfere with private property unless it was an urgent matter of public health. But after the wartime slowdown in building and Lloyd George's rash promise in 1918, government action seemed essential if poorer families were to have any hope of getting a decent home. Beginning with the **Housing Act (1919)** the Government offered subsidies to local councils to help them provide homes for families with low incomes. Private builders could also qualify for financial assistance if they built houses which could be let at low rents. In the same year local authorities were for the first time *obliged* (not just encouraged) to carry out surveys of their housing needs and take action to remedy shortages. Up to the early 1930s, when subsidies were ended in the National Government's economy drive, estates of **council houses** sprang up all over Britain. They were very plain and monotonous to look at; but with gardens, inside lavatories and bathrooms, they were far superior to most previous working-class houses.

Despite subsidies, councils still found it difficult to keep rents low enough. Most of their houses were let to higher-paid workers in fairly 'safe' jobs, while the poor and the unemployed had to be satisfied with what they had got. Only just over a quarter of all new houses in

the inter-war years were built by local authorities. The rest were
mainly sold to owner-occupiers with comfortable incomes. There was
a big increase in private house-building in this period – encouraged
by the growth of **building societies**. These lent up to 95 per cent of
the cost of a house, and charged rates of interest as low as 4½ per
cent in 1934. Indeed, by the 1930s there were *more than enough*
houses in the middle and upper price ranges. The shortage was entirely confined to cheap, rented accommodation for poorer families.

An early council estate in York

In 1930 a special subsidy was offered to local authorities for **slum
clearance**. The aim was not just to pull down slums but to rehouse
their inhabitants as well. So the payment was only made if occupants
of the demolished houses were given alternative accommodation at
rents they 'could reasonably be expected to pay'. In 1933 councils
were asked to prepare five-year programmes for the abolition of
slums. But despite great activity in many areas, much remained to be
done when the Second World War interrupted and put the clock back
by several years. In 1939 there were still half a million dwellings classed
as slums in England and Wales alone.

A fuller life

Although the depression cast a shadow of unemployment across many
parts of Britain, most people outside the depressed areas enjoyed
higher living standards and a fuller life than their parents and grandparents had done. Families were smaller, largely because of the
spread of birth control, yet wages were generally better. Working
hours had been reduced from about fifty-four to between forty-four
and forty-eight a week since the turn of the century. Most manual
workers had a week's paid holiday by 1939. On the whole the British

were healthier than they had ever been. Better food and improved sanitation helped to prevent disease, so that the annual death-rate nearly halved between 1900 and 1939. At the same time, social services like National Insurance, pensions, subsidised housing and education (including milk and meals for needy children) helped to reduce the amount of poverty and ignorance.

In the Victorian Age, most manual workers had little energy for anything besides drinking. But by the 1920s and 1930s they enjoyed a wide range of leisure activities and entertainments. Most towns had sports clubs and swimming-baths, as well as dance-halls, theatres and music-halls. **Cinema-going** became a national habit in these years. Its popularity was firmly established during and after the First World War, when American 'stars' like Charlie Chaplin, Mary Pickford and Rudolph Valentino became household names. At first films were silent and required captions to give necessary details of the action. A continuous musical background was provided, usually by a pianist. The introduction of the sound-track (1927) transformed the cinema. Natural acting and more complicated and realistic plots were made possible. By the late 1930s, about a quarter of the population went to the films twice a week or more.

For those who wanted to get out and about, there were cheap railway excursions, and many lower middle-class families could now afford motor cars, in which they set off for days in the countryside and holidays by the sea. The first of Billy Butlin's famous holiday camps was opened in 1937, at Skegness. Cycling was still popular, particularly among younger people. The YHA (Youth Hostels Association) was formed in 1930 to provide simple, inexpensive accommodation for cyclists and hikers.

The **radio** provided families with entertainment in their own homes (see page 255). So did public libraries, which reflected the progress of

A cinema in London's West End in the 1930s

education by lending a steadily increasing number of books each year. There was also a rapid rise in **newspaper** sales, particularly 'popular' dailies like the *Mirror, Mail, Express* and the trade union-sponsored *Daily Herald* (which ceased publication in 1964). They set out to appeal to the masses by including strip cartoons, competitions, racing and sports pages and plenty of news about royalty. Large headlines and photographs helped to give these papers an eye-catching appearance. All in all, the British were better informed and entertained than ever before.

Timeline

1919	Housing Act begins new policy of state subsidies.
1921	'Black Friday': failure of the Triple Industrial Alliance.
1924	First Labour Government.
1925	'Red Friday': nine month subsidy for the coal industry.
1926	General Strike, followed by great coal strike.
1927	Trade Disputes Act. First 'talkie' pictures.
1931–5	National Government (Ramsay MacDonald Prime Minister).
1931	Means test.
1934	Unemployment Assistance Board.
1936	'Jarrow Crusade'.

Questions

1. Look at the cartoon of the Triple Industrial Alliance (page 277).
    a) When was the Triple Alliance formed and with what aim?
    b) Why is the head marked 'MINES' the fiercest?

    c) The original caption to the cartoon said, 'The Problem Picture of 1921: How to Make the Tail Wag'. Explain why this was a 'problem'.

    d) The power of the Triple Alliance was tested in 1921 and 1925. What happened in each case?

    e) Why did the General Strike (the decisive 'test') fail?

2. 'The defeat of the miners ended a phase, and from then on the pendulum swung sharply to political action. It seemed to us that we must try to regain in Parliament what we had lost on the industrial battlefield.' (Aneurin Bevan, a member of the Labour Party, recalling the General Strike in his book, *In Place of Fear*, 1952)

    a) In what sense is Bevan talking about the end of a 'phase'?

    b) Why did the failure of the General Strike lead to a revival of 'political action' by the Labour Movement?

    c) How did this affect support for Labour in the next General Election?

    d) What effect did the rise of Labour have on the Liberal Party?

    e) How did the Labour Party suffer a setback in 1931?

3. 'During the last fifteen years, Jarrow has passed through a period of industrial depression unparalleled... Where formerly 8,000 persons, many of them skilled workmen, were employed, only a hundred are now employed on a temporary scheme.' (Ellen Wilkinson, MP for Jarrow, presenting a petition to the House of Commons, November 1936)

    a) How had this petition been carried from Jarrow to London?

    b) Where is Jarrow? What was the industry on which it depended?

    c) Why was this industry so badly depressed in the inter-war years?

    d) How did Britain's preparations to fight Nazi Germany help Jarrow and neighbouring towns?

4. '...the mere difficulty of getting hold of a house...means that people will put up with anything – any hole and corner slum, any misery of bugs and rotting floors and cracking walls.' (George Orwell, *Road to Wigan Pier*, 1936)

    a) Why did the First World War make the housing shortage worse?

    b) Did all sections of the population have difficulty in getting a house in this period? Give reasons for your answer.

    c) What action did the Government take after the First World War to increase the supply of cheaper homes?

    d) How far did this policy succeed in helping those most in need?

    e) What progress was made with slum clearance in the 1930s?

5. Write a paragraph on each of the following:
    a) Ernest Bevin (see also page 348)
    b) the Organisation for the Maintenance of Supplies
    c) the 'Means Test'
    d) the rise of the cinema

24

War and the Welfare State
The Second World War and the New Social Services

In November 1918, when the guns stopped firing and the nations of Europe counted their dead, most people felt they had witnessed 'the war to end all wars'. It was difficult to believe that statesmen and generals would ever again be capable of such madness and destruction. Yet only twenty-one years later Europe and most of the world was engulfed in another bloody struggle. No easy explanation can be offered, but undoubtedly part of the cause of the Second World War was the **Treaty of Versailles (1919)** which followed the first great conflict. The peace terms imposed on the Germans were unnecessarily harsh. They lost large slices of territory and were ordered to pay enormous *reparations* (damages) to the Allies. Although these were never paid in full, they hindered the defeated nation's recovery from the war. Germans felt humiliated and many became bitter and revengeful.

Adolf Hitler and German aggression

The disastrous slump in international trade after 1929 (see page 270) added the suffering and discontent of **mass unemployment** to the already strong grievances of the German people. By 1930, 6 million Germans were out of work, more than double the British total. Such conditions explain (but do not excuse) the sudden popularity of the National Socialist or **Nazi Party**, led by **Adolf Hitler** (1889–1945), a former house-painter and army corporal. Hitler declared that most of Germany's troubles stemmed from the peace treaty of 1919 and the activities of Jews and communists within the country. He promised social reforms, measures to cure unemployment, and a recovery of German national pride and prestige. The latter was to be achieved by overthrowing the terms of the Treaty of. Versailles and bringing all people of German nationality within the frontiers of a restored German Empire.

In 1932 the Nazis became the largest party in the Reichstag (Parliament). Within a year Hitler was Chancellor of Germany. He quickly set out to silence all opposition and make himself a dictator. Concentration camps were established for the torture and extermination of political opponents. The minds of the people, especially the youth, were filled with evil doctrines of German racial superiority. Jews, gipsies and other 'racially impure' elements in the population were cruelly persecuted. Meanwhile an industrial recovery, assisted by rearmament and public works like roadbuilding, greatly reduced unemployment.

Hitler speaking at a Nazi Youth rally in 1938

In March 1936 Hitler sent troops into the **Rhineland** area of Germany, which bordered France. It had been declared a demilitarised zone in the Treaty of Versailles, yet, as Hitler expected, Britain and France took no action against him. Their peoples were sick of war and anxious to avoid a repeat of the horrors of 1914–18. This suited Hitler's plans. Early in 1938 he occupied **Austria** and absorbed it into his new German Empire. **Czechoslovakia** was next on his list, for her population included 3 million Germans (see map on page 290). In September 1938, at a meeting in Munich, **Neville Chamberlain**, Britain's Prime Minister, got Hitler to agree to occupy only Sudetenland, the portion of Czechoslovakia containing people of German nationality. Hitler also promised he would attempt no more territorial gains.

The expansion of Nazi
Germany, 1933–39

Map legend:
- Germany 1933
- Rhineland remilitarised 1936
- Annexed 1938
- Annexed 1939

Chamberlain returned to London and announced to cheering crowds that he had achieved 'peace in our time'. Not everyone was so sure. Men like Winston Churchill and Duff Cooper (who resigned from the Government at this time) had long warned that there was no limit to Hitler's ambitions. It seemed they were right when, in March 1939, Hitler invaded the rest of Czechoslovakia and began to threaten **Poland**. Although Britain promised to help the Poles if they were attacked, only the Soviet Union was close enough to give them immediate support. But the Russians were unprepared for war. In August they signed a treaty of friendship with Germany, leaving Hitler free to attack Poland, which he did on 1 September. Britain and France could stand by no longer. With the deepest regret, they declared war on Germany (**3 September**). Crowds thronging the streets in London and Paris showed none of the enthusiasm which had marked the beginning of war in 1914.

The Second World War, 1939–1945

British cities prepared for immediate bombing and poisonous gas attacks. Children were evacuated into the countryside, gas-masks were issued, and all windows were blacked out at night to make it difficult for enemy bombers to find their targets. But the hurry was unnecessary. Throughout the winter of 1939–40 so little happened that the Americans called it **'the phoney war'**. Germany and the Soviet Union divided Poland between them (part of their August agreement) but, in the West, the rival armies stayed behind their fortifications. The British spent their time clearing the seas of German merchant shipping and establishing an army in France. Conscription had already been introduced in May 1939.

The phoney war ended suddenly in April 1940, when Germany

Neville Chamberlain's triumphant return from his meeting with Hitler at Munich (September 1938)

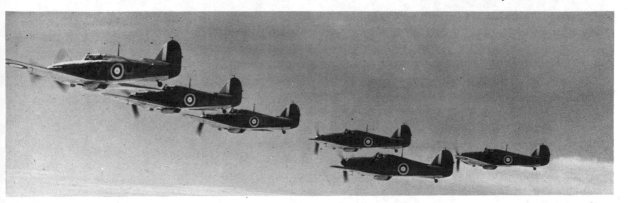

RAF fighters during the Battle of Britain

occupied Denmark and invaded **Norway**. A British naval squadron and a few Anglo-French troops were powerless to resist the German advance. Within a few weeks, Norway was in enemy hands. At home, Chamberlain was accused of being half-hearted in his conduct of the war. He resigned, and an all-party **Coalition Government** took over, led by **Winston Churchill**. He was the ideal man for the job. As Britain prepared to face the greatest challenge of modern times, the courage and confidence revealed in Churchill's leadership and in his stirring speeches proved a constant source of inspiration – not only to his own people but to the forces of freedom everywhere.

On the day Churchill became Prime Minister (10 May) Hitler launched his long-awaited offensive in the West. There was no repeat of the deadlock of 1914–18. With great superiority in tanks, the Germans swept all before them. As in 1914 they by-passed the main French defences and attacked from the north. The Netherlands and Belgium were soon overrun, and the British army was cut off and forced to retreat to the coast. From 24 May to 4 June, 320,000 British and French troops were evacuated from **Dunkirk** and nearby beaches. The Royal Navy was assisted by hundreds of small craft, including ferry boats, pleasure steamers, tugs and trawlers. Churchill called it 'a miracle of deliverance'; but all the tanks and artillery were lost.

The French army swiftly collapsed and surrendered on 25 June. A fortnight earlier the Italian dictator, **Benito Mussolini**, had brought his country in on the German side. The British Empire stood alone, while Hitler prepared a cross-Channel invasion. Some British politicians regarded the situation as hopeless, but not Churchill. 'We shall defend our island, whatever the cost may be', he said, 'we shall *never* surrender.' The beaches were covered with barbed-wire and landmines, and church bells were silent, reserved to sound the alert. However, before Hitler's invasion fleet could safely put out to sea, he had to gain superiority in the air. Hermann Goering, in command of the *Luftwaffe* (air force), assured his master that all he needed was 'five days of fine weather'.

Early in August the *Luftwaffe* began its task of destroying the RAF and the airfields of southern England. But for the first time it met highly efficient opposition, equipped with coastal radar stations and spearheaded by Spitfire fighters, which were slightly superior to the

German Messerschmitts. Although greatly outnumbered, British pilots inflicted such heavy losses on the enemy that by mid September the invasion plan was postponed indefinitely. The **Battle of Britain** was over. Hitler's plans had been upset by the skill and courage of a few hundred RAF fighter pilots, nearly all of them under twenty-five. 'Never', said Churchill, 'was so much owed by so many to so few.' The *Luftwaffe* switched to night raids on London and other major cities, hoping to cripple British war production. **The Blitz**, as it was called, lasted into the spring of 1941. Night after night, sirens warned families to take cover – in cellars, specially built air-raid shelters or, in London, the Underground Railway stations. Despite widespread destruction, British resistance was unshaken.

Meanwhile Italy's entry into the war threatened Britain's position in the Mediterranean. Tanks and troop reinforcements were sent to **Egypt**, to protect the Suez Canal and the vital oil supplies of the Middle East. At the end of 1940, when the Italians advanced from Libya into Egypt, British troops forced them back to Benghazi. But early in 1941 the German *Afrika Korps* arrived under General Rommel. The British were driven back into Egypt. Germany also rescued her ally in south-eastern Europe, conquering Greece, Yugoslavia and Crete (April–May 1941) after the failure of an Italian attack on Greece. However **Malta**, Britain's 'unsinkable aircraft carrier', managed to survive heavy air attacks from enemy bases in Sicily.

The Second World War in Europe and Africa

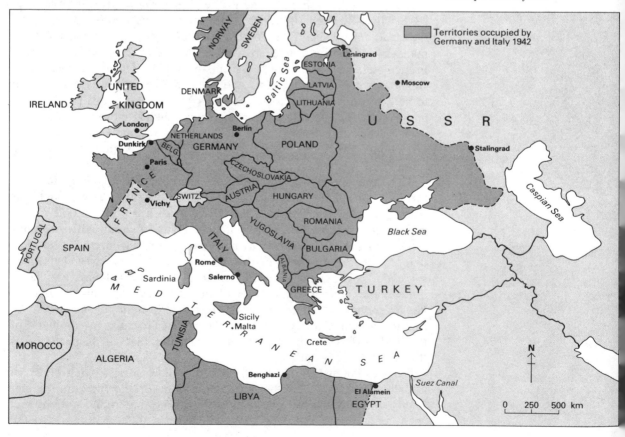

In June 1941 Hitler broke his treaty of friendship and attacked the **Soviet Union,** the only possible military rival left on the Continent. An enormous army, supported by the *Luftwaffe*, met little resistance as it advanced along a 2,400-kilometre front, stretching from the Baltic to the Black Sea. But as the Russians retreated they deliberately burnt towns, villages and farms. Short of food and deprived of buildings in which to quarter their troops, the German generals met a similar fate to that of Napoleon 130 years before. They were unprepared for a winter campaign, and their soldiers suffered terribly from the bitter weather and Russian counter-attacks. Instead of gaining a quick victory, Hitler sacrificed hundreds of thousands of troops and masses of equipment. In the following year advances made in good weather were again checked when winter set in.

The war became truly worldwide in December 1941, when Japanese aircraft made a surprise attack on the US Pacific Fleet at **Pearl Harbour** in the Hawaiian Islands. While European countries with possessions in the Far East were fully occupied, the Japanese aimed to acquire an empire in South-East Asia. They realised America would try to stop them, so they struck the first blow. Within six months, they conquered the whole of the Far East, including the British territories of Malaya and Burma, the Dutch East Indies and the Philippines. But in the end Pearl Harbour proved as decisive as Hitler's attack on the Soviet Union. Britain gained as an ally the

The Japanese attack on Pearl Harbour (December 1941)

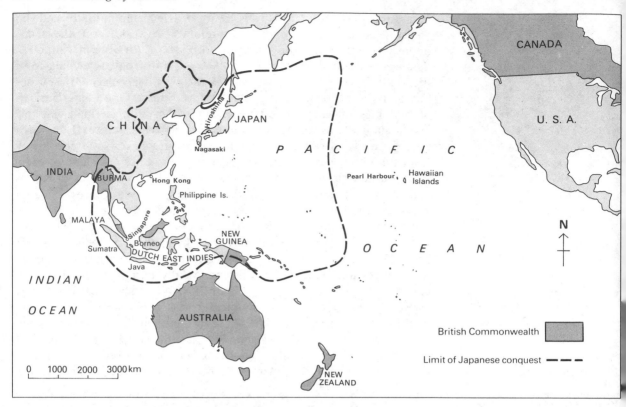

The Second World War in the Far East

most powerful nation on earth. Henceforward US forces not only set out to crush Japan but also led a counter-offensive in North Africa and Western Europe.

The turning of the tide in Africa came in October 1942, when the British Eighth Army, commanded by General Montgomery, defeated Rommel at **El Alamein**. The *Afrika Korps* retreated across Libya into Tunisia where it was trapped by Anglo-American forces under the US General Eisenhower. In May 1943 over 250,000 German and Italian soldiers were captured and Africa was cleared of the enemy. The Allies could now concentrate on freeing Europe.

In the summer of 1943 Anglo-American forces captured Sicily and invaded **Italy**. Mussolini was overthrown before they arrived and the new Italian Government gave up the struggle. But German troops quickly occupied the country and put up a stiff resistance. Elsewhere, things were going badly for Hitler. Allied bombers were reducing many German cities to ruins. The Russians had won a great victory at **Stalingrad** early in the year and were now on the attack. Even the menace of German submarines in the Atlantic was being mastered. During 1941–2, the British merchant fleet suffered terrible losses; but by 1943 U-boats were being hunted successfully with long-range aircraft using searchlights and radar.

Meanwhile the Allies made plans to recover a foothold in Western Europe. On 6 June 1944 Anglo-American forces, commanded by Eisenhower, landed on the beaches of **Normandy**. After three months

Allied troops landing on the Normandy beaches, 6 June 1944

of hard fighting, France and Belgium were recovered, making possible the destruction of many launching sites for Hitler's 'new weapons', the V1 flying-bomb and the V2 long-range rocket. By March 1945 Allied forces crossed the Rhine and struck into the heart of Germany. The Russians were closing in on the other flank. As they advanced through the suburbs of Berlin, on 30 April, Hitler shot himself. An armistice was signed on 8 May – **V.E.** (victory in Europe) **Day** – which was marked by scenes of rejoicing in Britain. Japan held out for another three months, until August, when the United States dropped the first **atomic bombs** on Hiroshima and Nagasaki. Over 100,000 people died, and countless thousands were scarred and disabled in the terrible blast of heat, fire and radiation. Japan surrendered almost immediately (14 August).

In the end, British and Commonwealth forces lost about 400,000 dead, less than half the total of 1914–18. A further 60,000 British civilians were killed in air-raids. On the other hand, the Russians, who withstood the full force of the German onslaught, lost no less than 6 million soldiers and almost as many civilians. Europeans had suffered terribly under Hitler, especially the Jews, 6 million of whom were exterminated in gas chambers. Yet the Western Allies tried to avoid repeating the mistakes of 1919. Some Nazi ringleaders were tried and executed, but the rest of the German people were encouraged to get their country back on its feet as soon as possible so that it could take its proper place in a peaceful world. However the attitude of the Russians proved a stumbling-block. They were unwilling to move out of East Germany, with the result that the country had to be divided into eastern and western occupied zones. The **Cold War** between the Western Allies and the Communist World had begun.

In October 1945 the **United Nations Organisation (UNO)** was created, with its headquarters in New York. It aimed to succeed where the earlier League of Nations had failed, by getting its members to settle their differences without the use of force.

The 'home front': warfare and welfare

Although there was no fighting on British soil, the menace of the *Luftwaffe* and shortages resulting from U-boat attacks on shipping affected everyone. The Government quickly saw that the safety and welfare of civilians was no less important than the need to supply the armed forces. **Food rationing** began in January 1940. It was at first restricted to sugar, butter and bacon, but then extended to the whole range of basic foods except bread. Everyone had a ration book containing coupons which were given up each time purchases were made. In this way the Ministry of Food, run with great efficiency by Lord Woolton, did its best to ensure a fair distribution and an adequate diet for all. Soap, clothing, footwear and petrol were also rationed, although in 1942 the petrol ration for inessential motoring was stopped.

Even before war was declared the **evacuation** began. Between 1 and 3 September 1939 well over a million people, mostly children, were transported into the countryside from areas close to probable air-raid targets. By 1941 the total number of evacuees had risen to about 3 million. The evacuated areas contained some of Britain's worst slums. From dockland London, Liverpool and Glasgow came thousands of undernourished children, some lacking outdoor shoes and wearing clothing so rotten it had to be cut off and burnt. Many were infested with vermin and suffering from skin disorders such as ringworm and impetigo. The more fortunate families who received them were appalled, and government officials readily appreciated the need to expand existing **social services**.

Apart from the needs revealed by the evacuation, help was urgently required by bombed-out families, wives of dead servicemen, old people cut off from their relations and young children whose mothers

The evacuation: children being sorted out after their arrival at Whaley Bridge in Derbyshire. Notice the identification labels round their necks

were working in essential industries. An **Assistance Board** was created (1940) out of the old Unemployment Assistance Board. It aided families in distress, provided home-helps for the sick and elderly, and distributed cash to those who needed it. For instance, supplementary (extra) pensions were paid to over a million old people and widows. The shortages, mishaps and dangers of war were shared by the whole population. So the Government set out to provide social services for all who had need of them, not just the poor. In the process, it took a vital step towards the idea of a *Welfare State*.

The health and nourishment of infants and young children was the first priority. During the Blitz, the Ministry of Health began a campaign to have children immunised against **diphtheria**, a killing disease which was likely to spread among families crowding in air-raid shelters. It was a wise decision. While wartime deaths from diphtheria rose alarmingly in most other European countries, in Britain they fell to a quarter of the pre-war figure by 1945. A **National Milk Scheme** was introduced in 1940. All children under five and expectant and nursing mothers were entitled to a pint (0.56 litres) a day for less than half the normal price of 4½d (2p). In the following year cod-liver oil and blackcurrant extracts (later replaced by orange juice from America) were provided for expectant mothers and young children. These *vitamin foods* were free at first, but a small charge was soon put on them. After the war the Welfare Foods Service continued, along with cheap milk for young children.

Until July 1940 **school meals** were provided mainly for under-nourished children. But then came a complete change of policy. With so many mothers working in wartime industries, the Government encouraged local education authorities to provide subsidised meals for as many children as possible. Similarly, from September 1941, **school milk** was provided for all children at a subsidised price, or free if necessary. There could be no going back on these advances when the war ended. School meals were provided for all who wanted them, at a reduced price or free in cases of need; and for many years milk was given free to every child (see page 359).

The Beveridge Report 1942

In the past, schemes of social security had been introduced from time to time without any overall plan. There were different rates of benefit for the sick and the unemployed, even though their needs were similar; more than one contribution card was necessary, and a number of government departments controlled separate funds for similar purposes. With this in mind, the Government appointed a Committee of Inquiry (1941) to investigate 'existing national schemes of social insurance' and to suggest improvements. Its Chairman, who had sole responsibility for the contents of the report, was a senior civil servant, Sir William (later **Lord**) **Beveridge**. He was ideally suited to the task, having a greater knowledge and experience of social insurance than any other man of his time.

In his Report (1942) Beveridge proposed that all the bits and

Sir William (later Lord) Beveridge, 'the father of the Welfare State', explains his Plan at a meeting in London's Caxton Hall (1943)

pieces of insurance and pensions should be replaced by *one* scheme, covering *all* citizens whatever their income. People of working age, together with their employers, would pay a weekly contribution, recorded by a stamp on a single card. In return, cash benefits would be paid on 'interruption of earnings' – sickness, unemployment, retirement or widowhood – for 'as long as the need continues'. All citizens would be equal members of the scheme, therefore no means test would be necessary. The actual rates of benefit would be based on a minimum standard of living 'below which no-one should be allowed to fall'. There would be special allowances to cover extra expenditure, including maternity and funeral grants. In addition to the insurance scheme, Beveridge urged the Government to pay weekly *family allowances* to parents for each dependent child. These were needed because parents' pay did not increase as their families grew in size.

The insurance scheme was not a complete system of social security. It dealt only with *want,* and, as Beveridge said, 'Want is only one of the five giants on the road of ... social progress.' The other 'giants' were *disease*, which would have to be attacked by a new health service 'for all citizens'; *ignorance*, which could be overcome with 'more and better schools'; *squalor*, which could be avoided with 'more and better houses', and *idleness* or unemployment. The latter could be kept in check only by much more positive government policies to stimulate business activity.

The Beveridge Report was the greatest single influence on the making of the Welfare State. The public received it like a new gospel. Long queues formed outside His Majesty's Stationery Office, where the Report was on sale, and a special pamphlet on it was printed for soldiers overseas. At first the Government refused to commit itself to the Beveridge plan. It was anxious not to raise false hopes, remembering the failure of the promises made after the First World War. But eventually, in 1944, a new **Ministry of National Insurance** was set up to prepare a scheme of social security along the lines proposed by Beveridge.

Secondary education for all

Plans to expand state education after the Fisher Act of 1918 (see page 212) were affected by cuts in government spending from 1921. Nevertheless many new schools were built in the 1920s and 30s, and the curriculum for older pupils was widened to include science, more handicrafts and physical training. About 10 per cent of eleven-year-olds gained 'free places' in grammar schools. There were also other types of school, mainly in large towns and cities, which provided an education beyond elementary standard. *Central schools*, pioneered by London County Council before the war, offered courses geared to careers in commerce and industry; and *junior technical schools* prepared boys for apprenticeships, especially in engineering. But there was still a great wastage of talent among children of poorer families. In the 1920s the full-time education of about 80 per cent of all children ended in the senior class of an 'all age' elementary school.

R.A. Butler – architect of the 1944 Education Act

In 1926 a special committee under Sir Henry Hadow recommended 'secondary education for all'. The **Hadow Report** criticised 'all age' schools, where pupils spent their entire school life until they left at fourteen. It proposed a separate infant and junior school, from which pupils would be transferred at eleven to either a grammar or a senior elementary school. The latter would have a broad curriculum modelled on that of the central schools. The Hadow Committee accepted the views of *psychologists* that intelligence could be measured by special tests, on the basis of which children could be selected for the type of secondary school best suited to their 'interests and abilities'. The Hadow recommendations were widely accepted by local authorities, and by 1939 about two-thirds of the resulting re-organisation was completed.

The urgent demand for skilled workers during the war revealed gaps in the education system, especially a need for more technical education. Consequently educational reform had high priority in the plans for post-war reconstruction. Under the guidance of **R.A. Butler**, President of the Board (soon to be the Ministry) of Education, the basis for the future was laid in the **Education Act of 1944**. (It applied only to England and Wales. The Scottish system continued to develop independently and required separate Acts of Parliament.) '*Free* secondary education for all' was the keynote of the 1944 Act. The Hadow re-organisation would be completed, with the important difference that fee-paying would be abolished in grammar schools – apart from 165 'direct grant' schools which could still charge fees for *half* their places. The Government wanted to lessen the influence of wealth on educational opportunity, although fee-paying schools were still allowed to flourish outside the state system.

The idea of 'elementary' education disappeared in the 1944 Act. In future there would be three successive stages – primary, secondary and further. The earliest leaving age was to be raised to fifteen (this was done in 1947) and to sixteen as soon as possible after that. Physically and mentally handicapped children were not left out. It became the duty of each local authority to provide suitable schools for all children according to 'age, ability and aptitude', and also milk, meals and dental services. A big expansion of higher education was also planned, together with more grants to enable students to study for degrees (see page 360). It was intended to provide three years of part-time further education for all early school leavers at *county colleges*. But shortage of money killed this plan. Instead, 'day release' classes at colleges of further education were expanded, to give young people technical or commercial training while they were in a regular job.

Many obstacles had to be overcome before the bright hopes of 1944 could be realised. Air-raids had destroyed or damaged 5,000 schools. This, together with a rise in the birth-rate during and after the war, caused great overcrowding of existing buildings. When the school leaving age was raised in 1947 there were not enough teachers for the extra classes. So the Government attracted people from all walks of life to register for 'emergency' teacher training courses.

An **'eleven plus' examination** was used to decide children's educational future. Those who reached a certain standard proceeded either to a grammar school, with an 'academic' curriculum, or, where provided, to a *technical high school*, with a bias towards applied science. The remainder, about 75 per cent, went to a *modern school*, where greater emphasis was placed on practical courses. All three types of secondary school were supposed to be of equal rank and importance, but this was just wishful thinking. Grammar schools were the aim of most parents and children because they provided the surest route to higher education and the most desirable jobs. Those who went to modern schools were considered 'failures'. This separation of eleven-year-olds into 'sheep' and 'goats' came under increasing attack in the 1950s, as support grew for *comprehensive* schools (see page 358).

One of the new post-war secondary schools – Smallberry Green Secondary Modern for Boys at Isleworth, Middlesex, opened in 1947

Social security and 'full' employment

Churchill's Coalition Government began the attack on the first of Beveridge's five giants – *ignorance* – with the wartime Education Act. The task of tackling the remaining giants fell, somewhat unexpectedly, to a Labour Government led by **Clement Attlee**. In the **1945 election,** Labour won 393 seats out of 640 and so gained an overall majority for the first time. It had been widely assumed that Churchill's war record would ensure victory for his party, the Conservatives. But many voters blamed them for the miseries of the depression, the 'dole' queues and the means test. To break with the past they turned to the Labour Party. Attlee's Government faced a mammoth task. Britain was deeply in debt, many towns had suffered appalling bomb damage, and food, clothing and fuel were in short supply and still strictly rationed. Yet the people demanded 'social security from the cradle to the grave' and would accept no excuses or delay.

Clement Attlee (1883–1967) was a member of the War Cabinet in Churchill's Coalition Government of 1940–45. After winning the 1945 election, he became the first Labour Prime Minister with an overall majority in the House of Commons

Family allowances had already become law in 1945, before the election, although the first payments were not made until 1946. Five shillings (25p) a week was paid for each dependent child *after the first*.

The money was given to all families, so no means test was needed. The chief proposals of the Beveridge Report formed the basis of the **National Insurance Act (1946)**. It made insurance compulsory for everyone of working age, except married women. In return for a single weekly contribution – 4*s* 11*d* (24½p) for employed persons when the scheme started in 1948 – there were sickness and unemployment benefits, retirement and widows' pensions, guardians' allowances, maternity benefits and a funeral grant. It was, in the words of James Griffiths, Minister of National Insurance, 'the best and cheapest insurance policy offered...to any people anywhere'. A separate, but linked, scheme was introduced by the **Industrial Injuries Act (1946)**. It dealt with compensation for those injured, disabled or killed at work.

To round off the attack on the 'giant *want*', the Government set up a new **National Assistance Board (1948)**. It catered for people who needed help even though they had not paid for it through the insurance scheme. These included the blind, deaf, crippled and mentally handicapped, the homeless, unmarried mothers and the wives and children of criminals. National Assistance also provided a 'safety net' for those whose needs were not fully met by National Insurance benefits. Beveridge had recommended that National Insurance should provide an acceptable 'minimum standard of living'. But the Government did not give this guarantee. National Insurance benefits were set lower than in the Beveridge plan. Consequently the 'safety net' was soon bulging, mainly with old people who could not live on their pensions. Instead of being just a prop to the system of social security, National Assistance increasingly became a basic part of the scheme (see page 361).

An employment exchange, opened in 1949. Compare these comfortable surroundings with the 1910 Labour Exchange pictured on page 241

Beveridge warned that his whole scheme could collapse if mass unemployment – the 'giant *idleness*' – returned after the war. His call for **'full' employment** reflected the ideas of **John Maynard Keynes** (see page 272) which now had a big influence on government ministers and led to a reversal of pre-war policies. In 1944 all parties in the Coalition Government pledged themselves to maintain 'a high and stable level of employment' when the war ended. If an industrial depression threatened, the government would *increase* its spending, on services and public works, to 'prime the pump' and get industry expanding again. It would also encourage new industries to move into depressed areas and help redundant workers retrain for new jobs.

'Full' employment does not mean that *everyone* willing and able to work has a job. There are always some people 'between jobs' or being retrained in new skills. In 1945 it was thought that 'full' employment would involve keeping the unemployment rate down to 3 per cent of the total labour force (the average figure in the inter-war period was 13 per cent). In fact, the average from 1945 to the early 1970s was only about 2 per cent. A steady expansion of world trade was a vital factor in keeping the wheels of industry turning, but the 'Keynesian' policies of successive governments also played an important part (see page 345).

Health and housing

The attack on the two remaining giants, *disease* and *squalor*, was led by **Aneurin Bevan** who, as Minister of Health, 1945–50, was responsible for both health and housing policy. The creation of a free health service for all was one of his great ambitions. Many people had become dissatisfied with the 1911 scheme of health insurance, which excluded the wives and children of insured workers from free medical treatment (see page 241). Doctors found themselves practising 'Robin Hood medicine' – overcharging the rich to cover the cost of treating the poor free. Partly because of such difficulties, there were not enough doctors practising in the poorer districts of towns. Most preferred to work in well-to-do areas where patients could afford to pay their bills. Britain's pre-war hospital services also left much to be desired. Alarming shortages of beds, nursing staff and medical equipment were discovered in 1938–9 when preparations were made for the reception of air-raid casualties.

Realising the urgent need for reform, the Coalition Government produced a plan for a free state medical service in 1944. Labour made some important changes in it before the **National Health Service Act** was passed in 1946. The whole range of medical treatment, including the services of dentists and opticians, became freely available to every citizen. To achieve a more even distribution of GPs (general practitioners) the Medical Practices Committee would draft new applicants to 'undoctored areas'. Hospital services were remodelled. All but the large teaching hospitals were taken over by Regional Hospital Boards under the Ministry of Health. Most county and county borough councils already provided ambulances, midwives, home

Aneurin Bevan, the minister responsible for introducing the National Health Service

Pressure on the new Health Service: out-patients waiting to see doctors at the London Hospital in Whitechapel (April 1949)

nurses and health visitors. Now it was compulsory for them to provide these services. Finally, *health centres* were to be set up, bringing together GPs, nurses and other medical staff to provide a range of services under one roof.

Many doctors bitterly opposed the Act, fearing that 'socialised medicine' would restrict their freedom and give them little say in organising the new services. Bevan made some minor changes and finally got most doctors to accept the National Health Service – just in time for it to start as planned (along with the new National Insurance scheme) on 5 July 1948. This was the so-called **Appointed Day** for the official beginning of the Welfare State. Immediately doctors' surgeries were invaded like bargain sales, and dentists and opticians were booked solid for months ahead. Within a year, 5 million pairs of spectacles were provided, 8½ million patients were treated by dentists and 187 million prescriptions were written by doctors! Critics said taxpayers' money was being squandered on people who only wanted to get something for nothing. But probably much of the early pressure on the health services resulted from previous neglect. Millions who needed spectacles did not have them, and millions more had allowed their teeth to decay rather than pay for dental treatment.

Although some private medical practice continued, well over 95 per cent of all doctors and patients joined the National Health Service. Its cost proved much greater than estimated, however, and shortages of staff and equipment continued. Health centres were intended to be the heart of the new service, but most local authorities were very slow to establish them. Consequently hospitals were overburdened with outpatients. Financial pressures soon led to **charges** being made on patients. From 1951, part of the cost of prescriptions, spectacles and dental treatment had to be paid. Bevan, then Minister of Labour, resigned from the Government. He protested that charges were against the principle of a *free* Health Service.

During the war, half a million houses in Britain were destroyed by enemy action. At the same time building almost ceased. The result was a desperate **housing shortage** – far worse than that of 1918. Army huts and aircraft factories were converted into temporary accommodation for the homeless, and estates of prefabricated homes (called 'pre-fabs') were built from factory-made sections bolted together on concrete bases. The Government severely restricted private building and directed men and materials towards providing more **council houses**. Subsidies (grants) were given to councils so that they could build at less than the normal cost and charge lower rents. Despite acute shortages of building materials and skilled tradesmen, Britain produced 1 million new homes in the five years after the war – more than any other European country. But much still needed to be done. In 1951 a third of all homes in England and Wales had no fixed bath, and more than 1 million households had no flush toilet.

A **New Towns Act (1946)** combined the need for more homes with the task of reducing overcrowding in the main centres of population. Aided by government subsidies, whole new communities were established to take the 'overspill' from London and other cities. Work on the first twelve began by 1950 (see map on page 363). Such developments allowed planners the freedom to put new ideas into practice, including traffic-free shopping centres and the separation of industrial zones from residential areas. A similar scheme (1952) led to the creation of *expanded towns* in places such as Aylesbury, Bletchley and Swindon. The Government aided the building of housing estates and

Part of Harlow New Town, in Essex – one of the original twelve new towns. Bevan insisted that all homes built with government subsidies, in new towns as well as on ordinary council estates, should be of good quality, with a natural life of about eighty years. They were expensive, but he refused to lower standards

factory accommodation to attract people from decaying inner city areas. Housing and land planning were closely linked. Under the **Town and Country Planning Act (1947)** all councils were required to submit a 'development plan' for government approval. Any scheme could be blocked if it looked like producing ugly or haphazard 'urban sprawl'.

The remarkable social progress of the period 1940–8 stands apart in British history. For the first time social services were planned and created as part of an overall scheme. The Second World War was a vital spur, coming as it did after a period of distress and hardship in many parts of Britain. It drew together the whole community in face of a common danger and kindled a desire to banish long-standing social evils. As Lord Beveridge said in his Report, 'War breeds national unity. It may be possible, through a sense of national unity . . . to bring about changes which . . . it might be difficult to make at other times.'

Timeline

1919	Treaty of Versailles.
1926	Hadow Report (proposes secondary education for all).
1933	Hitler comes to power in Germany.
1939–45	Second World War.
1940	Food rationing begins; National Milk Scheme; Assistance Board.
1942	Beveridge Report.
1944	Education Act (free secondary education for all).
1945	Family Allowances; first majority Labour Government.
1946	New Towns Act.
1947	Town and Country Planning Act.
1948	Appointed Day – 5 July – official beginning of the Welfare State: start of National Insurance, National Assistance and the National Health Service.
1951	Health Service charges imposed.

Questions

1. 'In the raid last night and early this morning bombs were dropped on one of London's most famous hospitals – the fifth hospital to be hit – a London theatre, a newspaper office, and a large block of offices . . . Again the Nazi murder bombers were sent against Buckingham Palace.

   The alert was sounded at 8.11 p.m., and it signalled a return to all-night attacks . . . Black-out zero hour tonight: 7.42 p.m.'
   (*Daily Express*, 16 September 1940)

   a) Why did the German bombers attack at night?
   b) The bombed hospital and other public buildings were not named. Can you think of a reason for this?
   c) What was the point of trying to bomb Buckingham Palace?

d) What was the 'alert'? What did it warn families to do?

e) The 'black-out' involved the use of heavy curtains, switching off street lights and 'masking' car lights to narrow the beam. What was the point of all this?

2. 'The Government believe that in the past the power of public expenditure, skilfully applied, to check the onset of a depression has been under-estimated.

. . . for the purpose of maintaining general employment it is desirable that public investment should actually expand when private investment is declining.' (Coalition Government 'White Paper' on *Employment Policy*, 1944)

a) What is meant by 'public investment'? Give some examples.

b) How was this policy different from that of pre-war governments?

c) Whose ideas did it reflect? (See Chapter 22)

d) How successful was this policy after the war? What were its drawbacks, if any? (See Chapter 27)

e) What factor outside Britain's control also helped to create jobs?

Winston Churchill broadcasting to the nation from 10 Downing Street during the Second World War (see Question 4)

3. What were the 'five giants on the road of . . . social progress' identified by Lord Beveridge? How was Aneurin Bevan involved in attacking two of them? What did his Ministry achieve, 1945–50?

4. 'We must make sure that the path to the highest functions throughout our society and empire is really open to the children of every family.' (Winston Churchill, in a BBC broadcast, 1943)

a) What Act was passed by the Coalition Government with the aim of increasing educational opportunity?

b) What changes did it make in secondary education?

c) How were pupils selected for different types of school?

d) Which of the Act's recommendations came to nothing? Why?

e) Why was there serious overcrowding in schools after the war and an acute shortage of teachers in 1947?

5. Write a paragraph on each of the following:
a) Winston Churchill
b) the evacuation, 1939–41
c) the National Insurance Act, 1946
d) the National Assistance Board

25

Sunset on the Empire
The Commonwealth, Ireland and the EEC

'We are the best race in the world, and the more of the world we inhabit the better.' So said the Englishman Cecil Rhodes, founder of Rhodesia, during the Age of Imperialism in the late nineteenth century (see Chapter 19). Similar views were expressed by French, Belgian and other European colonisers at this time. But in the twentieth century the right of one country to rule another was increasingly questioned. As more of the subject peoples in the colonies received education, they began to demand self-government. Strikes and demonstrations against foreigners grew more frequent in many colonies from the 1930s and 40s. At the same time European politicians showed a greater willingness to guide their colonies along the road to independence. From the end of the Second World War to the mid 1960s, almost the whole of Africa and southern Asia, along with many smaller regions, became self-governing. This wave of **decolonisation** began in the British Empire, which was by far the largest.

The Dominions go their own ways

The Dominions – Canada, Australia, New Zealand and South Africa – were populated largely by British and other European settlers. The first three in particular had close ties with Britain. Nevertheless, after the First World War, in which the Dominions lost nearly 200,000 men fighting on Britain's side, they were determined to go their own ways. In 1926 Britain recognised them as fully independent countries. This was later put into law by the **Statute of Westminster (1931)**, which declared the dominion territories to be equal partners with Britain in a free 'Commonwealth of Nations'. They were no longer bound by any laws passed by the UK Parliament, unless they agreed to them. However, legal freedom did not prevent these countries coming to Britain's assistance again in the Second World War.

  Canada was Britain's main ally between the fall of France (June 1940) and the entry of the USA into the war (December 1941). She produced vital war materials in factories safe from Hitler's bombers, and her armies fought in Europe and North Africa. Canada's development after the war was heavily dependent upon her giant neighbour, the USA, rather than Britain. For example the great **St Lawrence Seaway**, which enables ocean-going ships to reach ports on the Great Lakes, was a joint US–Canadian venture (1954–9). Over half Canada's manufacturing industry is American-owned and, in 1980, 70 per cent of her foreign trade was with the USA. By then trade with Japan was twice that with Britain, her third trading partner in order

of importance. Canada's population, boosted by immigration from Europe, rose from 7 million in 1911 to 23½ million in 1980. Yet she could comfortably support two or three times that number – and thereby exploit more fully her large mineral resources.

The Cornwall Dam, Ontario – part of the St Lawrence Seaway project

Until the Second World War, **Australia** and **New Zealand** traded mostly with Britain and, unlike Canada, had no close relationship with any other country. But as their political ties with Britain loosened, they found trading partners nearer home, in South-East Asia and the Pacific. Britain bought two-thirds of all New Zealand's exports in 1950, yet only half in 1966 and a mere eighth in 1978. Trade with Australia declined similarly. By 1978 Britain was only Australia's fifth largest customer, behind the USA, Japan, New Zealand and China. Apart from her large output of wool and meat, Australia has rich resources of coal, iron ore, copper, oil and uranium. Her industries are developing rapidly, even though her population (14½ million in 1980) is still relatively small. In New Zealand efforts to increase mining and manufacturing have been less successful. Her 3¼ million people still depend mainly on exports of meat and dairy produce.

Contacts with the wider world led Australians to give up their 'whites only' immigration policy (see page 216). Large numbers of

European refugees settled in Australia after the war, and in 1972 it became official policy to allow Asian immigration. When Britain entered the European Economic Community (EEC) in 1973 (see page 319) some of the last empire links were broken. The words 'British subject' no longer appeared on Australian passports, and a song called 'Advance Australia Fair' replaced the British National Anthem. Nevertheless when the Queen visited Australia in 1977 she was warmly received. The bonds of friendship were still strong between peoples with many family ties, a shared language and a similar culture.

India – independence and partition

Apart from the 'white Commonwealth', the earliest demands for freedom from British rule came in India – by far the most populated part of the Empire. After the First World War the cause of Indian independence came under the influence of **Mohandas Karamchand Gandhi** (1869–1948). Although he had studied at London University and practised as a barrister in South Africa, he lived with the simplicity of a peasant and refused to adopt Western ways. His sincerity and saintly qualities greatly impressed the many Indian people who called him *Mahatma* (Holy One). Gandhi hated violence. He wanted to achieve independence through 'non-violent non-co-operation', involving strikes, protest meetings and a refusal to buy British goods.

To give Indians less cause for complaint, the British granted them a greater share in governing themselves and promised independence some time in the future. By 1935 **provincial councils**, dealing with such matters as health, education and agriculture, were entirely under Indian control. But nothing short of 'immediate self-government' would satisfy the **Congress Party**, led by Gandhi. Real power was still in the hands of the British Viceroy, and the UK Parliament could overrule the decision of any Indian assembly.

During the Second World War, Gandhi refused to co-operate with the Allies, despite the Japanese conquest of neighbouring Burma. He ran a 'Quit India' campaign against the British, which infuriated Churchill and made him even more determined to resist Indian demands. But Clement Attlee's post-war Labour Government took a different view. In 1947 it decided to make India self-governing. This was easier said than done, for there were deep religious divisions within the country. The Muslims, outnumbered three to one by Hindus, were afraid that when British rule ended they would be unfairly treated. For some years their leader, **Mohammed Ali Jinnah**, had been demanding independence not only of Britain but of the Hindus as well. He wanted a separate state, to be called **Pakistan**. The Hindus were strongly against the idea, but serious riots convinced the British Government that immediate *partition* (separation) might be the only way to prevent civil war between Hindus and Muslims.

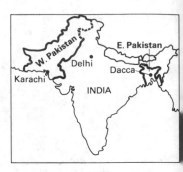

The partition of India. East Pakistan became Bangladesh in 1971, when it broke away from West Pakistan after a bitter civil war

So when the British withdrew (15 August 1947) *two* independent states – India and Pakistan – came into being. Pakistan was itself divided into two parts, the larger in the west, containing the capital, Karachi, and the smaller in the east. Massive population movements were required to get the two religious groups mainly within their own countries, although even then the new borders did not divide Hindus and Muslims neatly. In the confusion there were savage riots and massacres and more than 500,000 people were killed or died of starvation. Nevertheless the quick acceptance of the need for independence by the Attlee Government and its Viceroy in India, **Lord Louis Mountbatten**, probably helped to prevent greater bloodshed in the long run. Britain's prompt action also earned the goodwill of most Indians. Despite all their hostility towards colonial rule before 1947, Indians did not become anti-British afterwards – as they would probably have done if Britain had continued to resist their demands for freedom.*

'Wind of change' in Africa

The story of African independence really began after 1945, when there were only four self-governing states in the whole continent. Two world wars had seriously weakened the colonial nations of Europe. Moreover, in each colony there was by this time a group of educated black Africans who, as students or soldiers abroad, had become familiar with Western ideas of political freedom. Encouraged by events in India, they demanded self-rule and declared that if Europeans believed in freely elected governments for themselves they could hardly object when others wanted the same.

British politicians said they were willing to give up colonial rule just as soon as black Africans were ready to govern themselves. But African leaders saw a catch in this. They claimed that so long as they were denied experience in government this condition would not be

---

* Later developments in India and Pakistan lie outside the mainstream of British history and are not covered in this book. The same applies to most countries dealt with in the next section, once they became wholly independent of Britain.

Kwame Nkrumah, first President of Ghana (1957–66). He soon forgot the principle of free choice he had preached at the British in the years before independence and took on the powers of a dictator. After nine years of mounting corruption and overspending, he was deposed in an army revolt

satisfied. In some colonies in the 1930s Britain had created regional councils which included Africans. But real power remained in white hands. It was the agitation of black nationalist leaders, who organised or exploited strikes and other disturbances in the post-war years, which made Britain speed up moves towards independence.

Apart from Egypt, which gained full self-government in 1936, the first African states to become independent of Britain were in the old slave-trading areas of West Africa. Here, owing to the exceptionally hot climate, there were few white settlers to oppose majority rule. The Gold Coast was the first to gain self-government, as **Ghana**, in 1957. **Nigeria**, the largest and most populated British colony in Africa, became a federation of three separate regions in 1954 and achieved independence six years later. **Sierra Leone** got her freedom in 1961. Finally, when tiny **Gambia** became self-governing (1965) Britain's empire in West Africa was at an end. These changes were not trouble free. Ghana's new leader, **Kwame Nkrumah**, became a dictator and squandered vast sums of money on his presidential palace and other trappings of power. In Nigeria, the tribal regions never fully accepted the British idea of unity under a federal government. There was a military take-over in 1966 and a civil war in the following year.

In East Africa, moves towards independence were often complicated by the presence of quite large minorities of white settlers who clung to their privileged position under colonial rule. Self-government was achieved in Tanganyika (1961) and **Uganda** (1962) without great disturbance. The former became **Tanzania** when it was united with the island of Zanzibar (1964). However in **Kenya** there were fierce racial clashes. About 40,000 whites controlled the local Assembly and farmed the most fertile land, known as the 'White Highlands'. From the Kikuyu tribe, led by **Jomo Kenyatta**, there sprang a secret terrorist organisation, 'Mau Mau', which, from 1952, carried out murderous attacks on settlers. Britain flew in troops and imprisoned Kenyatta, although his part in terrorist activities was not proved. After order had been restored (1956) blacks were given a greater share in government. Kenyatta was eventually released and became Prime Minister (later President) of an independent Kenya (1963).

Further south, Northern and Southern Rhodesia and Nyasaland were linked in a **Central African Federation (1953)**. It was the hope of some British politicians that the powerful whites in **Southern Rhodesia** would help Britain keep control over the rich copper mines of the North. The Federation's second prime minister, Sir Roy Welensky, said he expected European control to extend into the future as far as he could see. Black Africans had other ideas. Those living in Northern Rhodesia and Nyasaland bitterly opposed the union with Southern Rhodesia. Here 200,000 whites ran the government and owned two-thirds of the land, while 4 million blacks were herded into 'reserve areas'. Increasingly violent protest by the black majority made Britain decide to break up the Federation in 1963. Northern Rhodesia and Nyasaland were given self-government, as **Zambia** and **Malawi** (1964).

Southern Rhodesia's white rulers, who, since 1923, had been partly

self-governing, now demanded complete independence. But Britain first wanted a promise that the black population would receive proper voting rights within a reasonable period. Such 'unimpeded progress towards majority rule' was unacceptable to the governing Rhodesian Front party. Its leader, from 1964, the Prime Minister **Ian Smith**, said he could not foresee black rule 'in a thousand years'. When talks with Britain reached deadlock, his Cabinet made a *unilateral* (one-sided) declaration of independence – **UDI** (November 1965). Britain's reply was to ban all trade with the rebel régime, until Smith agreed to her terms. The United Nations encouraged other countries to do the same. But such trade *sanctions,* as they are called, failed. Rhodesia found trading partners, and goods were carried through friendly South Africa and Portuguese Mozambique.

Until 1974 Ian Smith defied Britain and the world. But then a revolution far away in Portugal changed the situation. Portugal's new rulers promptly freed their African colonies, including Mozambique. Under black rule, Mozambique's long border with Rhodesia became a refuge and training ground for the **Patriotic Front** – an alliance of nationalist groups determined to overthrow Smith by force. A full-scale guerrilla war engulfed Rhodesia.

Rhodesian Prime Minister, Ian Smith, signs the declaration of independence in Salisbury, Rhodesia (11 November 1965)

Robert Mugabe, first Prime Minister of independent Zimbabwe. In the 1980 election his party won 57 seats out of a possible 80 (the remaining 20 were reserved for whites and all were won by Smith's Rhodesian Front)

As road ambushes and attacks on white farms multiplied, Smith reluctantly accepted the principle of rule by the black majority, now numbering 6½ million (1976). At first he brought about a government favourable to the whites, under the black **Bishop Abel Muzorewa**, who was elected in 1979. But the Patriotic Front denounced the election as a fraud, saying that Muzorewa was a 'puppet' of the whites who had not been opposed by any of the true leaders of the blacks. The guerrilla war continued and Britain also kept up trade sanctions. Smith and Muzorewa were forced to accept a new constitution drawn up at an all party conference in London. Fresh elections in 1980 resulted in a clear victory for the wing of the Patriotic Front led by **Robert Mugabe**. He became Prime Minister of a now independent **Zimbabwe** – the ancient name for the country.

Like their Rhodesian neighbours, the whites in **South Africa** resisted what Britain's Prime Minister, Harold Macmillan, had called 'the wind of change...blowing across this continent'. Most of South Africa's white minority (numbering 4½ million) are Afrikaners, descendants of the Boers who founded Cape Colony in the seventeenth century. To them Africa is home and they are determined to stay. Moreover they regard the black African as inferior and unfit for public responsibility or social mixing. Accordingly, the Afrikaner-dominated Nationalist Party, which gained power in 1948, introduced **apartheid**, or separation of the races. Blacks were forced to live in special suburbs and reserves, mixed marriages were forbidden, separate schools provided, and the races were kept apart on buses, beaches and in public buildings.

To enforce the laws of apartheid, South Africa developed the apparatus of a police state. The prisons filled, floggings and executions became common, the mail ceased to be private and spies and informers flourished. In 1960, at **Sharpeville**, a large crowd demonstrated against the Pass Laws, which required adult blacks always to carry their special identity documents. The police opened fire and killed over sixty blacks. Bitter protests from fellow members led South Africa to leave the Commonwealth (1961). Nevertheless she tried to defend her policies, describing apartheid as a system of 'separate development', not just a way of keeping the whites on top. Eventually apartheid is supposed to lead to a number of self-governing states, called **Bantustans**, within South Africa. Several have been set up, but they are really just black reservations because most men have to go off to work in the industrial areas, leaving their families behind.

In South Africa the whites still have the best land, and control industry and commerce. But they cannot do without the blacks. Their wealth depends on the cheap labour of 20 million blacks, Asians and 'Coloureds' (people of mixed blood) who mostly live in crowded townships away from the white residential areas. Recently the Government has relaxed some petty rules against blacks and improved black education in line with new technology in industry. But the Afrikaners will never willingly give the blacks equal voting rights. They know that if they do their privileged way of life will disappear.

When Prince Charles watched the Union Jack being hauled down

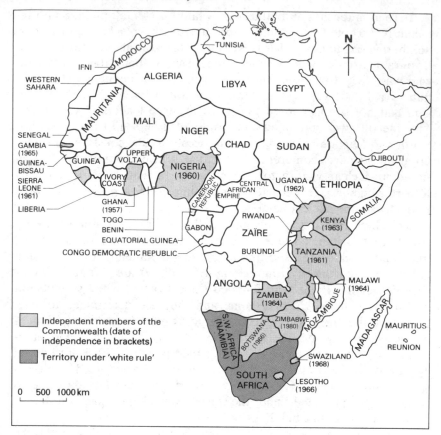

Africa 1982

in Zimbabwe (17 April 1980) the British Empire in Africa officially ended. However Britain's *effective* rule in Africa had ceased when **Botswana** (formerly Bechuanaland), **Lesotho** (formerly Basutoland) and **Swaziland** became independent (1966–8). Most of the new African states depended heavily on foreign aid. Some relied on sales of just one or two main crops or raw materials for their income, and were therefore badly affected by fluctuations in the demand for their products overseas. Meanwhile, European-style political systems often proved unworkable. Africans generally prefer a system based on a single party, usually representing the tribal organisation. Africa's political future is likely to be rooted in its own traditions rather than those of the former colonial countries.

A multi-racial Commonwealth

Almost the whole British Empire had been dissolved by the mid 1960s. In the **West Indies**, a federation of British islands was formed in 1958, but because of rivalries between the members it only lasted four years. Jamaica and Trinidad and Tobago became independent in 1962, followed by Barbados and Guyana (formerly British Guiana) in 1966. On the other side of the world, Malaya, Singapore, Sabah (formerly North Borneo) and Sarawak were formed into the self-governing **Federation of Malaysia** (1963). Singapore broke away two years later. In the Mediterranean, **Cyprus** (1960). and **Malta** (1964) became independent of Britain, the former after years of civil war between Greek and Turkish Cypriots. By 1981 the only British dependencies left were Hong Kong, on lease from China until 1997, Gibraltar and a scattering of tiny islands all over the world. Most were only protected or subsidised, not ruled directly, by Britain.

Colonial self-government carried with it the right to cut all ties with Britain. This was the immediate choice of some, notably Burma (1948), Sudan (1956) and Somalia (1960, formerly Somaliland). But the great majority of newly independent countries preferred to maintain contact by joining the **Commonwealth** – which now became a multi-racial association. Through regular contacts between heads of state, diplomats and officials, the 'New' Commonwealth promised to become a force in world affairs. Some British politicians who had lamented the end of the Empire hoped that this expanding 'community of equals', with shared traditions and interests, would partly compensate Britain for what she had lost. Britain continued to give preference to Commonwealth goods, and a definition of 'British Nationality', laid down in 1948, allowed Commonwealth citizens the right to enter the UK freely.

By the 1960s, however, it was clear that members of the

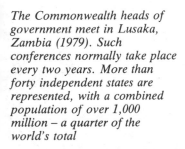

The Commonwealth heads of government meet in Lusaka, Zambia (1979). Such conferences normally take place every two years. More than forty independent states are represented, with a combined population of over 1,000 million – a quarter of the world's total

Commonwealth did not necessarily have common interests. A number of ex-colonies used the Commonwealth as a platform from which to air their grievances, especially against Britain. There was no unity of purpose. Some members quarrelled and broke off diplomatic relations with each other. South Africa, a founder member, left altogether in 1961. In the same year the British Government made its first attempt to join the European Economic Community. Closer ties with Europe seemed likely to be of greater benefit to Britain than her Commonwealth membership. Britain could not stake too much of her future in what was becoming little more than a debating club for people of different cultures.

Divided Ireland

Britain's colonial troubles really began in Ireland (see page 225). By the Treaty of 1921, Ireland was partitioned roughly in line with her religious divisions, as happened later in India. The six northern counties, together known as **Northern Ireland**, remained part of the United Kingdom, while the other twenty-six counties became self-governing as the Irish Free State (now the **Republic of Ireland**). The Irish Republic broke her remaining links with Britain during the inter-war years. She stayed neutral during the Second World War and, in 1949, left the Commonwealth.

Meanwhile all was not well in Northern Ireland. Ever since partition the Catholic leaders of the Irish Republic had hoped that North and South would one day be reunited, and the **IRA** (Irish Republican Army) often resorted to violence in pursuit of this aim. But the Protestants in Northern Ireland, who made up two-thirds of its population, were determined to stay in the United Kingdom. They did not want to live in a united Ireland where Catholics would outnumber them and control the government. This left the Catholics of Northern Ireland, the remaining third of its population, in an unhappy position. Most of them had never wanted to be separated from the South in the first place.

From the start, the Catholics in Northern Ireland felt themselves to be second-class citizens. The ruling **Ulster Unionist Party** (so-called because it upheld union with Britain) was led by wealthy Protestant businessmen who favoured those of their own faith. No Catholic ever became a Unionist MP. Indeed, very few even joined the Party. The political system itself was biased against Catholics. Only householders could vote in local elections, which penalised the poorer, Catholic section of the community. And council voting boundaries were frequently drawn in such a way as to keep the Protestants in power. Once elected, Protestant politicians often discriminated against the Catholic community in the allocation of council houses and the provision of health facilities and transport.

Discrimination did not end there. Northern Ireland was policed by two mainly Protestant forces: the **Royal Ulster Constabulary** (**RUC**) and the part-time **'B' Specials**, often accused of unfairness by Catholics. In the civil service Catholics were under-represented, and

Ireland – scene of 'the troubles' since 1968

they seldom got top jobs in any walk of life. During the depression of the inter-war years Catholics were hardest hit by severe unemployment in the shipbuilding and linen industries. After the Second World War, however, new industries such as aircraft building and artificial fibres created more jobs in the North. The British Welfare State was also extended to Northern Ireland, and helped to raise its living standards well above those in the Irish Republic. Consequently when the IRA, based in the Republic, began a series of attacks across the border in 1956, blowing up customs posts and power installations, they found less enthusiasm among the Catholics of the North for a reunited Ireland. IRA suspects were *interned* (imprisoned without trial) on both sides of the border and by 1962 their campaign had fizzled out.

By the early 1960s many Catholics in Northern Ireland were willing to abandon dreams of ending partition if they could achieve genuine equality with the Protestant community. But the Unionist-dominated parliament at Stormont Castle was slow to respond. **Terence O'Neill**, Northern Ireland's prime minister 1963–9, sympathised with Catholic demands. But his plans for reform were opposed by 'hard line' members of the Party. These included the **Reverend Ian Paisley**, founder of the Free Presbyterian Church, who accused O'Neill of betraying the Protestant cause when he tried to win Catholic support and improve relations with the Irish Republic.

In 1967 Catholics and sympathisers formed a **Civil Rights Movement** in Northern Ireland. They aimed to demonstrate peacefully, but extremists on both sides soon made this impossible. On 5 October 1968 a Civil Rights march in Londonderry roused the

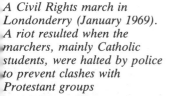

A Civil Rights march in Londonderry (January 1969). A riot resulted when the marchers, mainly Catholic students, were halted by police to prevent clashes with Protestant groups

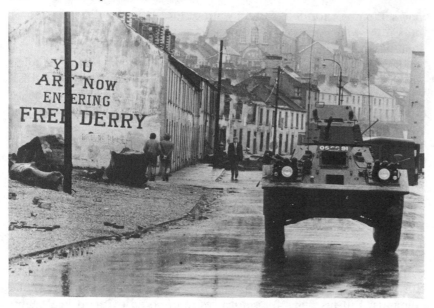

For a time the Catholic Bogside district of Londonderry (shown here) and Andersonstown in Belfast were run by the IRA, who built barricades manned by gunmen.
In August 1972 such 'no go areas' were cleared by the British army in 'Operation Motorman'

anger of influential Unionists who got the RUC to stop it. The resulting riot opened a new and bloody chapter in Irish history. Catholics and Protestants took to fighting in the streets in many parts of Northern Ireland. After savage riots in Londonderry and Belfast in August 1969, the British Government abolished the 'B' Specials and sent troops to Northern Ireland to restore order. The IRA, meanwhile, saw its chance. Its moderate 'Official' wing wanted to continue with peaceful protest, but members of the militant 'Provisional' wing saw themselves as armed protectors of the Catholic community. These so-called 'Provos' were soon involved in a shooting and bombing war with armed Protestant groups and the British army.

The Stormont Government re-introduced **internment of IRA suspects** (August 1971). The IRA responded by bombing shops, factories, hotels and public houses – killing many innocent people. An already tense situation worsened on 30 January 1972 when British soldiers opened fire during a Civil Rights march in Londonderry, killing thirteen people. The shock of 'Bloody Sunday', as the IRA called it, led the UK Government to dissolve the Stormont parliament (March 1972) and rule Northern Ireland directly from London. An attempt was made to set up a more broadly-based Assembly in Northern Ireland, elected on the basis of 'power-sharing' between Catholics and Protestants. But many Protestants objected that the Catholics had more seats than their numbers justified. They organised a **general strike** (May 1974) which paralysed Northern Ireland and led to the collapse of the Assembly within a fortnight. Britain was forced to re-impose **direct rule** on 29 May.

As the bombings and shootings continued, the majority of people in the North yearned for an end to violence. This was demonstrated when Betty Williams and Mairead Corrigan formed a **Peace People** organisation (1976) and attracted large crowds to peace rallies. By then direct rule was beginning to lessen fear and resentment in

Mairead Corrigan (below) and Betty Williams (right) who founded the Peace Movement in Northern Ireland

Northern Ireland. Measures like the **Fair Employment Act (1976)**, which banned job discrimination in Northern Ireland on religious or political grounds, dealt with long standing grievances. But although support for both the IRA and Protestant semi-military groups declined, the killing continued. The army's death toll reached 300 in August 1979 – the tenth anniversary of its arrival in Northern Ireland. In the same month the Queen's uncle, Lord Louis Mountbatten, was killed by an IRA bomb aboard his boat off the Irish coast. Fresh efforts were made to increase co-operation between the governments of Britain and the Republic to curb IRA activities. But a final solution to the 'troubles' still seemed a long way off.

Overtures to Europe

As Commonwealth ties loosened, it seemed that Britain's future prosperity and influence in the world might depend upon a closer relationship with Western Europe, particularly the **European Economic Community (EEC)**. The EEC, popularly known as the Common Market, was founded in 1957 when France, West Germany, Italy, the Netherlands, Belgium and Luxembourg signed the Treaty of Rome. 'The Six' agreed to form a free trading area by gradually removing all *tariffs* (customs duties) on trade among themselves, although they kept a common *external tariff* on trade with countries outside the Community. The Six also agreed to adopt common policies in agriculture, transport and welfare, and to prepare for eventual political unity. It was felt that only a truly united Western Europe could deal on equal terms with the USA and USSR.

At the outset Britain had not been prepared to commit herself so completely to Europe, and had therefore not applied to join the EEC. Half her foreign trade was with Commonwealth countries in the late 1950s, and EEC tariffs would have penalised her Commonwealth imports – especially from Australia and New Zealand. Nevertheless the British Government realised that European sales were becoming increasingly important for the more advanced industries. So Britain joined six other countries – Austria, Sweden, Switzerland, Norway, Denmark and Portugal – in a more loosely organised customs union, the **European Free Trade Association (EFTA)**, in 1960. Its members planned to abolish tariffs between themselves, but only in manufactured goods, and each chose its own external tariff.

EFTA was not a real alternative to the Common Market. Its members traded more with EEC countries than they did among themselves. Consequently in 1961 Harold Macmillan's Conservative Government changed direction and applied to join the EEC. Talks went on until January 1963, when the French President, **Charles de Gaulle**, called a halt. He said it would be impossible for Britain to be loyal to the Six, not only because of her Commonwealth commitments but also her close ties with the USA. Britain had just agreed to buy nuclear weapons from the USA. De Gaulle would have preferred her to join her European neighbours in making their own.

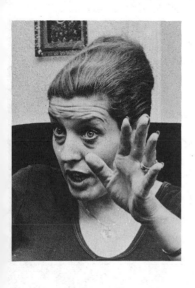

The **EUROPEAN ECONOMIC COMMUNITY**, or Common Market, originated in a new spirit of co-operation after the Second World War. The countries of Western Europe wanted closer economic ties, in the hope of creating greater prosperity and reducing the risk of future wars.

1951 The European Coal and Steel Community (ECSC) was established, removing barriers to trade in these vital industries in six countries – West Germany, France, Italy, the Netherlands, Belgium and Luxembourg. In the next three years there was a 25 per cent increase in European steel production.

1957 The European Economic Community (EEC) was set up by the Treaty of Rome on 25 March. The same six countries agreed on a timetable of changes to achieve, in future years, (i) abolition of all tariffs between the Six, and a common external tariff on trade with other countries (ii) the *harmonisation* (blending together) of tax systems, social policies, control of agriculture, and so on.

The European Atomic Energy Community (EURATOM) was set up by a second treaty signed on the same day. It provided for the coordinated development by the Six of atomic energy for peaceful purposes.

Britain's trade with the Community

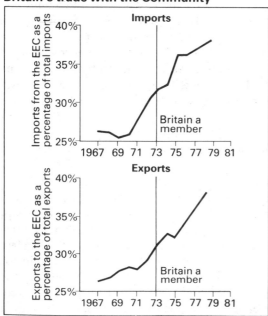

1961 Britain, having declined to be a 'founder member' of the EEC, now applied to join. French opposition led to the failure of the first application in 1963, and of a further attempt in 1967–8.

1968 The EEC achieved its first objective – the completion of a customs union by the removal of all tariffs between the Six.

1973 After fresh negotiations (1969–71) the **United Kingdom, Ireland and Denmark joined the EEC and EURATOM on 1 January.**

1975 After 're-negotiation' of the UK terms of entry into the EEC, Parliament voted for continued UK membership. In a national **referendum** 67.2 per cent of the votes supported this decision.

1977 The *transitional* (changeover) period ended and the UK , Ireland and Denmark became full EEC members.

1979 All citizens of the Community voted for their first directly elected members of the **European Parliament.**

1981 Greece joined the EEC.

Edward Heath, Britain's chief representative in the first unsuccessful bid to join the EEC. He became Prime Minister in 1970, and his Government negotiated British entry in the following year

However the other five members of the EEC were broadly in favour of British entry. Their continued support, together with a growing envy in Britain of the prosperity enjoyed by the Six, encouraged Harold Wilson's Labour Government to re-apply for membership in 1967 – even though his party was deeply divided on the issue. De Gaulle again proved a stumbling block, and little progress could be made until his fall from power in 1969. Talks began in earnest following the election of Edward Heath's Conservative Government (June 1970) and by the autumn of 1971 terms of membership had been agreed. The **United Kingdom** finally turned the tide of history and 'went into Europe', along with the **Irish Republic** and **Denmark**, on 1 January 1973.

Britain in the EEC

Firework displays and other official celebrations of British entry into the EEC failed to stir much enthusiasm among the people. The public mood soon seemed justified, as it became clear that Britain had joined at almost the worst possible time. The long post-war period of rapid industrial expansion in the Western world was ending. Massive increases in oil prices in 1973–4 (see page 346) pushed up fuel costs and hit manufacturers hard. British producers struggled harder and harder for customers against keen foreign competition.

The majority of Labour MPs had opposed Britain's entry into the EEC on the terms accepted by the Conservatives. They also claimed that the British people had not been consulted properly. So after the election of a Labour Government under Harold Wilson in 1974, the terms were 're-negotiated'. Better terms were obtained, notably on the amount of money Britain had to pay to the Community, but there was little fundamental change. The question of whether Britain should stay in the EEC on the new terms was then put to the people in a *referendum* (a ballot in which voters are asked to answer 'yes' or 'no' to a specific question). After a campaign in which the main political parties were divided amongst themselves, the **EEC Referendum** (5 June 1975) produced a two-thirds majority in favour of continued membership. Many voters were puzzled and bored by the complicated arguments on both sides. Probably many of them simply thought it was too late to go back.

With a combined population of almost 270 million (in 1981), the EEC offers a valuable market to efficient British producers. But its organisation works to Britain's disadvantage. Members' annual contributions to the **Community Budget** are calculated in such a way that big importers of food and other goods from outside the Community, like Britain, pay most. When Britain, only the third richest member, far behind West Germany and France, became the largest contributor to the Budget in 1979, the Prime Minister, Margaret Thatcher, protested strongly. She managed to get a sizeable refund – much of it in the form of extra EEC spending in the UK – but no basic change in Community policy.

In 1980 the EEC spent well over 70 per cent of its total Budget on

the **Common Agricultural Policy (CAP)**. This is a system of farm price subsidies or grants paid to farmers to encourage the production of certain foodstuffs and to make the Community self-sufficient in food. Britain, with her relatively small but efficient farming industry, wants to see less spent on the CAP, especially as it has often led to big food surpluses which have been disposed of at give-away prices. For instance, surplus butter has been sold to the USSR at a third of the EEC price. However some other EEC members, especially France, which have much larger and less efficient farming industries than Britain, are less concerned about the cost of the CAP. If it did not exist they would still have to spend a lot of money on propping up their own agriculture.

It would be better for Britain if much more EEC money were spent on regional, industrial and social policies, which in 1980 took altogether only just over 10 per cent of the Budget. Britain has paid a price for her late entry into a Community shaped by the interests of its original members. If she had been a founder member, involved in the early negotiations, she could have secured much more favourable arrangements.

The British public's lack of enthusiasm for the EEC was shown in the elections to the **European Parliament** in 1979. Less than a third of the electorate bothered to vote – a much smaller proportion than in the other member countries. The Conservatives won 60 of Britain's 81 seats (allocated out of a Community total at that time of 410). By then further enlargement of the EEC was planned. **Greece** became the tenth member in 1981, and **Spain** and **Portugal** were busily negotiating to join. All three countries have similar farm surpluses to existing members such as Italy. This will not make it any easier to reform the CAP and redistribute Community spending in ways which

The European Parliament in Strasbourg, France. It meets on average once a month for sessions lasting up to a week, to advise the EEC's Council of Ministers and, with them, to decide on the Community Budget. It was originally made up of existing MPs from each member country, who performed a dual role. Since 1979, however, separate elections have been held

would benefit Britain. In the early 1980s it still seemed to the British that the Empire sunset had been followed by a somewhat murky and uncertain European dawn.

Timeline

1931	Statute of Westminster.
1947	Independence of India and Pakistan.
1952–6	Mau Mau troubles in Kenya.
1953–63	Central African Federation.
1957	Ghana becomes the first black African state to gain independence from Britain. Treaty of Rome – EEC created.
1960	European Free Trade Association (EFTA).
1961	South Africa leaves the Commonwealth.
1965	UDI in Rhodesia.
1968	Riot in Londonderry sparks off the 'troubles' in Northern Ireland.
1972	Northern Ireland Parliament dissolved – direct rule from Westminster.
1973	Britain a member of the EEC.
1974	General Strike in Northern Ireland – collapse of 'power-sharing' Assembly – direct rule reimposed.
1975	EEC Referendum in Britain.
1979	Direct elections to the European Parliament.
1980	Zimbabwe independent – end of British rule in Africa.

Questions

1. 'India in March 1947 was a ship on fire in mid-ocean with ammunition in the hold. By then it was a question of putting the fire out before it actually reached the ammunition. There was in fact no option before us but to do what we did.'
   (A. Campbell-Johnson, Lord Mountbatten's Chief-of-Staff)

   a) Name the leader of Indian opposition to British rule. What methods of protest did he use?
   b) Why was India like 'a ship on fire' in 1947? What was the 'ammunition' in the hold?
   c) What did the British feel they had 'no option' but to do?
   d) How far is it true to say that the 'fire' later reached some, but not all, of the 'ammunition'? Give reasons for your answer.

2. 'Such Africans by reason of their contacts with other peoples, including Europeans, had developed a political and national consciousness. The fact that they were disappointed with conditions on their return . . . made them the natural focal point for any general movement against authority.' (Report of a Commission enquiring into riots in the Gold Coast, 1948)

   a) What sorts of Africans is the Report referring to? Why had many of them recently 'returned'?

b) Why were they 'disappointed with conditions on their return'?

c) What was 'authority' and why was it being resisted?

d) The Gold Coast was the first black African state to gain independence from Britain. When and under what name?

e) Who was its first President and why was he overthrown?

3. 'Parliament will...be invited to pass before Easter a Measure transferring all...powers now vested in the Northern Ireland Parliament and Government to the United Kingdom Parliament.'
(Edward Heath, Prime Minister, March 1972)

a) How did preceding events in Northern Ireland influence Britain's decision to dissolve the Parliament at Stormont?

b) What earlier action had the British Government taken (in August 1969) to maintain law and order in Ireland?

c) What attempt was made to set up a new Assembly in the North?

d) Why did it fail, and with what result?

4. a) Look at the picture below of the EEC Referendum ballot paper.

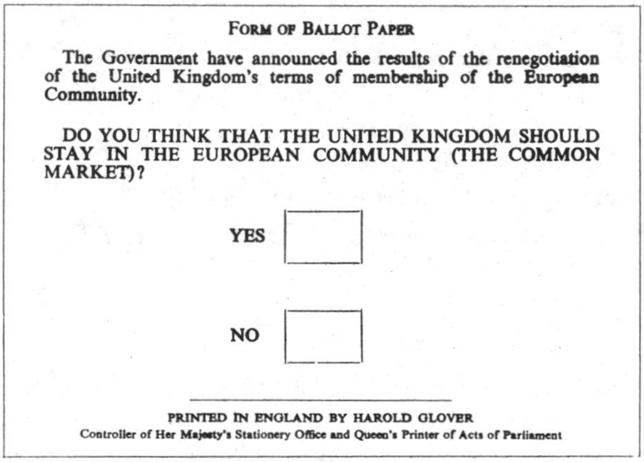

FORM OF BALLOT PAPER

The Government have announced the results of the renegotiation of the United Kingdom's terms of membership of the European Community.

DO YOU THINK THAT THE UNITED KINGDOM SHOULD STAY IN THE EUROPEAN COMMUNITY (THE COMMON MARKET)?

YES

NO

PRINTED IN ENGLAND BY HAROLD GLOVER
Controller of Her Majesty's Stationery Office and Queen's Printer of Acts of Parliament

i) What was the 'renegotiation' referred to?

ii) Why did the Labour Government hold the referendum?

iii) What was the result?

b) Write brief notes on
   i) EEC tariff policy
   ii) the Common Agricultural Policy
   iii) the European Parliament

5. Write a paragraph on each of the following:
   a) the Statute of Westminster   b) UDI in Rhodesia
   c) Apartheid   d) the 'New' Commonwealth

26

Towards Automation
Modern Industry, Agriculture, Transport and Communications

During the Second World War the Government controlled almost every aspect of national life, including industry and agriculture. Factories were converted to produce shells, bombs and guns, uniforms and parachutes, tanks and military aircraft. Farmers were paid to plough up grassland and grow more grain crops. In these and many other ways, state control was more far-reaching than it had been in 1914–18. When the war ended the Government could hardly withdraw its guiding hand. Reconstruction after the bombing and the return to peacetime industrial production had to be carefully planned and directed.

Public ownership

A sudden ending of state controls was even less likely after Labour's victory in the 1945 election. The Labour Party favoured **nationalisation** – the transfer of industries from private ownership to boards of managers appointed by the government. In particular, Labour believed that the basic industries – fuel, power and transport – should not be run for private profit. Under public ownership they could be reorganised and fitted into an overall plan for supplying the needs of manufacturers and the public.

Nationalisation of the coal industry had been recommended by a Royal Commission in 1919. If its advice had been taken, the General Strike might have been avoided (see page 276). There had been a history of bitter disputes between miners and their employers, so Labour's Coal Nationalisation Act (1946) was enthusiastically received by the National Union of Mineworkers. Compensation amounting to £164,660,000 was awarded to the mine-owners, and on 1 January 1947 the **National Coal Board** took over the industry and began a vast modernisation scheme. Exactly a year later, the **British Transport Commission** was set up. It took control of the four railway companies (merged into *British Rail*) along with the canals, docks and steamers they owned, London's buses and underground trains, and long-distance road haulage (which became *British Road Services*). Shortly afterwards, the production and distribution of **electricity** was nationalised (1948) and, in the following year, all **gas-works** were purchased by the state.

So far there was little strong opposition to the policy of nationalisation. The Government was clearly in a better position than private owners to provide the huge sums of money needed to modernise these industries. But the nationalisation of the major **iron and steel** firms (1951) was strongly resisted by the Conservative Party, the company owners and even the leaders of the steelworkers' trade unions. Steel was a manufacturing industry, unlike the others, and the owners had recently invested a lot of money in it. The Conservatives, who got back into power in 1951, returned iron and steel to private ownership (1953) and also most road haulage business. But the steel industry remained a political football and 90 per cent of it was re-nationalised in 1967 by the next Labour Government.

Meanwhile, the political parties' views of public ownership were changing and, to some extent, drawing closer together. The Conservatives came to accept a **mixed economy** – one in which some industries, mainly those providing services, were publicly owned, while the remainder stayed in private hands. On the Labour side, many supporters showed less enthusiasm for nationalisation. It had originally been hoped that profits from public corporations would help finance, among other things, better social services. But in fact there were many heavy losses, partly because of the high cost of re-equipping the public industries. Although there was some further nationalisation of manufacturing, including the **aerospace** and **shipbuilding** industries (1977), generally governments found other ways of providing aid to industry and stopped short of public ownership. For instance the **National Enterprise Board**, set up by Labour in 1975, was given power to invest taxpayers' money in industries without taking control of them.

The revival of agriculture

In 1939 two-thirds of Britain's food was imported. So when German U-boats began sinking British merchant shipping urgent efforts were made to increase home food production. The Government paid a subsidy of £2 per acre (approximately 80p per hectare) to farmers who ploughed up grassland and sowed grain crops. As a result the total area of arable land increased by a half. In the emergency, wasteland was cleared, many playing fields ploughed up and even roadside verges planted with potatoes. To make room for more crops farmers reduced stocks of poultry, sheep and pigs – but not cattle, because of the need to maintain milk supplies.

In peacetime, governments went on giving financial support to agriculture. Wartime subsidies were continued, and additional grants paid to farmers for such things as improved land drainage and the reconstruction of farm buildings and workers' cottages. An **Agriculture Act (1947)** set the pattern for the future. It gave farmers greater security by laying down guaranteed prices for about three-quarters of all farm products. In the 1950s more state marketing boards were set up, to control the sale of wool, cheese, eggs, fatstock and tomatoes. Meanwhile farmers' incomes rose rapidly, especially among the larger employers. The wage rates of labourers also improved, although they failed to catch up with the earnings of factory workers.

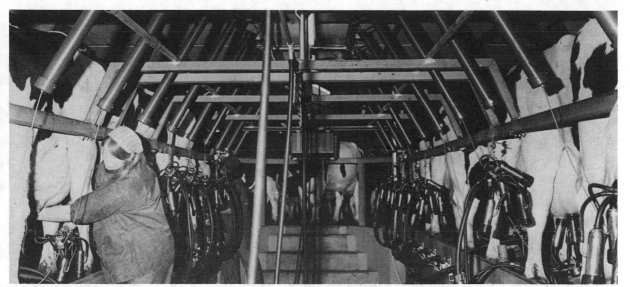

Milking Friesian cows on a Sussex farm. All milk consumed in Britain is home produced, so this is a vitally important part of the farming industry. Milking machines are installed on all but the very smallest dairy farms nowadays

British farming now became the most highly mechanised in the world. In 1939 there were 50,000 tractors in use; fifteen years later the total had risen to 400,000, and it passed the half million mark in 1978. Numbers of combine harvesters and milking machines rose in even greater proportions. Better fertilizers and improved varieties of seeds both helped to raise crop yields. By 1957 the average dairy cow was producing 30 per cent more milk than in pre-war years. As farming became more scientific, 'broiler houses' greatly increased the output of chicken and made it one of the cheapest meats available.

Not since the days of Robert Bakewell and Thomas Coke (see Chapter 5) had there been such rapid progress in British farming. Total agricultural output nearly doubled between 1938 and 1970, even though the land area devoted to farming was reduced slightly and the labour force cut by 60 per cent. The proportion of the total working population engaged in agriculture continued to fall. It was under 3 per cent in 1980. Yet Britain was producing just over half her total food requirements. This was possible with fewer workers because modern farming methods and the merging of many smaller farms into larger, more efficient units made *productivity* (output per worker) among the highest in the world.

Energy resources – old and new

Britain's large reserves of coal, petroleum and natural gas give her the richest energy resources of any EEC country. Of these, **coal** remains the most abundant. In the first ten years after the war coal production increased, but then a gradual decline set in. Unprofitable pits were closed, and the total workforce fell from 700,000 in 1957 to 235,000 in 1979 – although output *per man* increased because of more labour-saving machinery. The use of coal for domestic heating and for driving steam locomotives and ships declined rapidly from the 1950s, but it remained a vital fuel in the production of electricity. In

A modern coal-cutting 'shearer' in operation at Bentinck Colliery, Nottinghamsh[...]

1980 more than two-thirds of Britain's coal output was consumed by power stations. Most of the remainder was used in steel-making and as a source of chemicals for such products as artificial fibres, plastics and fertilizers. Britain's workable coal reserves will last at least 300 years at present production levels.

British coal output

1945	178 million tonnes
1954	227 million tonnes
1969	163 million tonnes
1981	124 million tonnes

As coal consumption fell, the use of **petroleum** increased rapidly. Different kinds and grades are required as fuel for aircraft, road vehicles, railway engines, ships and furnaces; and a wide range of lubricating oils is used for engines of all sizes. Petroleum by-products are used in making such goods as paint, synthetic rubber and plastics (together known as 'petro-chemicals'). By 1959 oil had become cheaper than coal as an industrial fuel – even though all but a tiny fraction was then imported, mainly from countries around the Persian Gulf. Until its price rocketed in 1973 (see page 346), petroleum remained cheaper than coal, and this encouraged the Electricity Board to build a number of oil-fired power stations. As a result Britain became even more dependent upon overseas supplies.

Imports of crude petroleum, which reached a peak of 113 million tonnes in 1973, became by far the most costly item in Britain's trading account. So there was great excitement when the first

A drilling platform – searching for oil in the North Sea in the 1960s

Bradwell nuclear power station, on the Essex coast, pictured soon after its opening in 1962. Like many of the older nuclear reactors, it later developed technical problems and proved less efficient than had been hoped. There were lengthy shutdowns for repairs

discoveries of **North Sea oil** were made in 1969–70, off the north-east coast of Scotland. Early hopes were fulfilled, as drilling by the oil companies revealed several rich deposits – including two of the world's largest offshore oilfields: Brent and Forties. The first oil from the British sector of the North Sea was brought ashore in June 1975. In the following year the **British National Oil Corporation** was formed by the Government, to invest in North Sea exploration and development and share in the profitable oil trade.

By 1980 the output from British oilfields was equivalent to the country's total crude oil requirements. In theory, Britain was 'self-sufficient' in oil; but because of the need to mix the light, high quality UK oil with heavier types from the Middle East, petroleum continued to be imported and a proportion of Britain's output was sold abroad. New discoveries are still being made in the North Sea, so it is difficult to estimate the size of Britain's oil reserves. However most experts do not expect them to last much beyond the end of the century.

The bed of the North Sea is also bountiful in **natural gas**. Commercial production began in 1967, from large gasfields located mainly off the coasts of Norfolk and Lincolnshire. Output grew rapidly, and natural gas was soon sufficiently plentiful to replace town gas (mainly produced from coal) in all parts of the UK except Northern Ireland. All gas appliances in homes and places of work had to be converted to use the new fuel – a task which the British Gas Corporation completed in 1977. Large reserves of offshore natural gas remain, and a growing quantity is being produced along with the petroleum in the oilfields further north.

Resources of coal, oil and gas will run out in the foreseeable future. This explains the big investment in **nuclear power** – a

development in which Britain led the world in the 1950s. Through the *fission* (splitting) of atoms of uranium, immense heat is released which can be used to produce steam for driving the turbines of electricity generators. The world's first large-scale nuclear power station, at **Calder Hall** on the Cumbria coast, began producing electricity in 1956. There followed an expensive development programme, although it was slowed down in the 1960s and early 70s by technical problems and the relative cheapness of oil fuel.

In 1979 Britain had sixteen nuclear power generating sites, which together provided about 13 per cent of the public electricity supply. Nuclear energy was by this time cheaper than that generated by coal or oil, and several new nuclear power stations were under construction. But because of the ever-present risk of polluting the environment with deadly radio-active waste many politicians had serious doubts about committing Britain to a nuclear-powered future. Indeed, in the 1970s governments began to encourage more research into 'cleaner', **renewable sources of energy** – sea-wave, wind and tidal power, and solar heating (harnessing the sun's rays). However, many technical problems will have to be solved before such renewable sources can make a significant contribution to Britain's energy supplies.

The decline of British manufacturing

The decline of Britain's old-established industries, which began in earnest with the First World War, continued after 1945. For instance **textiles**, especially cotton, met severe competition from the cheaper products of developing countries in Asia, where wages were much lower. During the 1970s alone, over 400 British textile mills were closed – mainly in Lancashire and West Yorkshire. **Shipbuilding** is another example. Like the coal industry, it increased production immediately after the war but then declined from the mid 1950s. Newly equipped foreign shipyards, notably in Japan, captured many of Britain's former export markets. British yards were slow to respond to the growing demand for oil-tankers and other types of freighter.

Falling production in many older industries was for a time more than balanced by expansion in a newer range of manufactures, including motor vehicles, aircraft, electronic equipment and plastics. However these industries developed mainly in the Midlands and south-east of England – already the most prosperous regions (see Chapter 22). New jobs were needed urgently in northern England, Wales and Scotland, which still depended heavily upon declining industries. Successive governments tried, with mixed success, to encourage expanding firms to set up factories in these areas by offering special grants and tax allowances.

Meanwhile there was a trend towards much **larger companies**. The 1950s and 60s saw numerous *mergers* (where two firms agree to join together) and *take-overs* (where one company buys sufficient shares in another to gain control of it). Huge concerns like British Leyland

Decline of textile employme

UK cotton industry	UK wool industry
710,000 workers — 1914	216,0 work (170,0 W Yorksh — 1951
200,630 — 1960	202,0 (145,0 — 1961
109,600 — 1970	145, (77,0 — 1971
66,800 — 1979	73, (43,0 — 1979

Automation in the motor industry: robot arms at work on the body shell of a BL Mini-Metro (1980)

Motors and the General Electric Company replaced a number of smaller firms – just as in the average High Street supermarkets and chain stores captured much of the trade of small family businesses. Big firms can afford large-scale research and buy materials and components in bulk at reduced prices. Many are **multi-national corporations**, with factories in a number of countries. Foreign-owned multi-nationals such as the American Esso, Ford Motors and Hoover provide many jobs in Britain.

Britain's fastest growing industry after the war was **motor vehicles**. Output increased from 350,000 cars and commercial vehicles in 1946 to well over 2 million in 1973. During this period car sales abroad were Britain's greatest source of income. However in the later 1970s the world demand for cars grew more slowly and there was more competition from foreign producers. British-based manufacturers, often hampered by outdated models, frequent strikes and low productivity per worker, could not compete effectively in the home market, let alone abroad. In 1965 British factories supplied 95 per cent of all cars sold in the UK. By 1980 the figure was down to 43 per cent. One in every eight cars sold in Britain in 1980 was Japanese. Overseas it was the same story. Britain's share of total world sales slumped from 11 per cent in 1964 to 4 per cent in 1980.

Following several big mergers, over 95 per cent of British motor production came from four companies by the late 1960s: British Leyland, Ford, Vauxhall and Chrysler (renamed Talbot). Of these, only **British Leyland (BL)** was British-owned. It was formed in 1968 when the old Austin and Morris plants, already amalgamated, joined with Leyland, mainly a producer of buses and trucks. But BL's sixty factories were never welded into an efficient unit. By 1975 massive government aid was needed, and BL became 95 per cent state-owned. Despite factory closures and big reductions in its labour force, BL still struggled to get customers and required further injections of public money to stay in business. Its decline had a ripple

Notice that output went up in this period in all the major car-producing countries except the UK

Car production – international comparisons

Figures in thousands

	1969	1979
UK	1,717	1,070
France	2,168	3,220
W. Germany	3,313	3,933
Italy	1,477	1,481
Japan	2,611	6,176
USA	8,224	8,434

effect on scores of other firms supplying components such as batteries, tyres, electrical equipment and upholstery. With fewer orders, these smaller firms also had to lay off workers.

Like motor vehicles, the manufacture of **aircraft and aero-engines** was a fast-growing export industry after the war. For a brief period in the early 1950s Britain led the world in jet aircraft production. Rolls-Royce jet engines also gained a high reputation abroad. But in the 1960s the industry suffered a serious falling off in sales. The development costs of several advanced military aircraft were badly misjudged, and enormous losses were later made on the 'Concorde' supersonic airliner (see page 341). The aero-engines branch of the industry also became over-ambitious. Rolls-Royce went bankrupt and had to be taken over by the Government in 1971. The UK aerospace industry was nevertheless still the largest in Western Europe in 1980. As well as aircraft and aero-engines, it produced helicopters, guided weapons, hovercraft and space satellites.

Aerospace developments were aided by rapid advances in **electronics**. The electronics industry began with the production of radio valves before the First World War. Much later came the cathode ray tube, used in TV sets, and transistors (developed in the USA) which, like valves, control the flow of electrons but take up much less space. British companies are among the leading producers of telecommunications systems (including automatic telephone exchanges), radar and navigational aids, and many types of control, measuring and testing equipment. But the mass market for household goods such as radios, TVs and 'hi-fi' audio equipment came to be dominated by Japanese and American firms from the 1960s.

The most advanced electronic devices are **computers**, which can store and recall vast amounts of information, perform routine tasks and make complicated calculations at high speeds. The first computer was made in the USA in 1944. By the 1950s smaller and cheaper types, made with transistors instead of valves, were being introduced into offices to handle orders and compile payslips by the thousand. Computers then spread to factories, where they were used to control and check manufacturing processes automatically. Such replacement of human labour by machines is called *automation*. By the 1970s there was widespread automation in industries such as petroleum refining, chemicals, engineering, printing and processed foods, as well as in weather forecasting and financial services such as banking.

American-owned companies dominate computer development in the UK. However Britain maintained her own industry when, in 1968, the Government persuaded rival firms to pool their resources in **International Computers Ltd (ICL)**. Despite government financial backing, ICL still found it difficult to compete with American giants like International Business Machines (IBM). The possibilities of automation were greatly increased from the late 1970s by the development of **micro-electronics**, especially what are called *micro-processors*. These are miniature wafers or 'chips' of silicon about 5 millimetres square which can carry electronic circuits equivalent to those found in the central processing unit of a computer.

'n addition to large computer ystems of the kind shown on he right, models of desk-top ize are now available through he development of micro-'lectronics (see above)

Modern scientific research has brought changes not only in manufacturing processes but also in the materials industry uses. For instance many new metal alloys have been created and a growing range of **plastics**. Made by complicated chemical processes, plastics provide cheap, strong and flexible alternatives to wood and metal. Many basic discoveries in plastics, including *polyethylene* (used in coverings and packaging) were made in Britain. Research in the **chemical industry** also led to the production of **artificial fibres**. The first fully synthetic fibre, nylon, was developed in the USA and first made in Britain in 1941. Terylene, developed in Britain at about the same time, is similarly light, strong and hardwearing. The chemical industry in general was one of Britain's most successful after the war – producing medicines, fertilizers, paint, dyestuffs, soap and detergents, as well as industrial acids, oxides and so forth. But from the 1950s West Germany and other trading rivals moved ahead in the use of new technology. Britain's share of world trade in chemicals fell from 16 per cent in 1954 to 9 per cent in 1979.

Steel remains the most important raw material in manufacturing industry. Between 1945 and 1960 Britain's output of steel doubled – almost half of it produced in two areas, South Wales and north-east England. But then a decline set in. Despite big investment in new plant and equipment, output per worker fell – especially after re-nationalisation (1967). In the late 1970s the British Steel Corporation (BSC) began to close steelworks and cut its labour force drastically. As a basic supplier to the motor and shipbuilding industries, BSC was caught up in their decline. Between 1975 and 1980 the steel industry lost over £1,500 million and shed nearly half its workforce.

This once great steelworks at Consett in County Durham was closed down in 1980 as a result of the slump in sales of British steel

'De-industrialisation'

The unhappy truth from the British point of view was that her industries were falling behind those of her leading competitors. Industrial production expanded three times faster in Western Europe than in Britain in the period 1955–60. At about this time what is called **'de-industrialisation'** began in Britain. Her share of world trade in manufactured goods started to fall sharply (it roughly halved between 1960 and 1980) and fewer people were employed in manufacturing. Between 1955 and 1973 the number of workers in manufacturing industry fell by 13 per cent in Britain, while it rose in rival countries – by 18 per cent in West Germany, 31 per cent in France, 57 per cent in Italy and a staggering 155 per cent in Japan. The loss of jobs in British manufacturing continued unchecked into the 1980s.

Britain's industrial production rose by an average of 3 per cent a year during the 1950s and 60s. This was one of the fastest growth rates in British history, yet it was far behind that achieved in Western Europe, the USA and Japan. The British were getting richer year by year, but *other industrial countries were getting richer much faster*. Among the many **causes of Britain's decline**, relative to other countries, were the following factors:

1. Britain suffered from having been the first highly industrialised country. Many firms had outdated plant and equipment, and old ways were often deeply rooted among the workforce, at all levels. Managers were slow to invest in new designs, and trade unions

Industrial disputes arising from the introduction of new technology have cost many millions of pounds in lost production. Here we see a mass meeting of one of the printing trade unions in 1978 to protest at plans by the Times Newspaper Group to use new machines and employ fewer workers. This dispute stopped publication of 'The Times' and 'Sunday Times' for ten months

frequently blocked the introduction of new technology and working practices – fearing that there would be fewer jobs for their members.

2. The end of the Empire (see Chapter 25) meant the loss of many guaranteed customers overseas. Britain had previously been able to send large quantities of exports into relatively easy and secure colonial markets. Meanwhile her rivals (all with fewer colonies, if any) had been forced to trade in the more competitive markets of the developed world. This made them more efficient. Britain's decline relative to other industrial countries really began around 1870 (see Chapter 15). But her colonies acted as layers of warm clothing round an ailing body. When the padding was removed after the Second World War, British industry felt the chill wind of competition more keenly.

3. The British actually spent more on industrial research than their European and Japanese rivals after the war, but this was not reflected in sales of goods. For example, in the mid 1960s the aerospace industry took nearly 40 per cent of all British spending on research and development, yet supplied only 4 per cent of total exports. Britain went in for too many costly 'prestige projects' like the Concorde airliner. Japan, West Germany and other trading rivals preferred to concentrate on less risky 'consumer' goods such as television and 'hi-fi' equipment, kitchen appliances, cameras and watches, which sold to millions.

So Britain entered the 1980s rich in energy resources but poorly equipped to make the best use of them in manufacturing industry. Just as the Empire cushioned Britain's fall for nearly a century, so now North Sea oil and gas are helping to bolster the national income. But Britain cannot afford to drop out of the 'big league' of manufacturing countries. Manufacturing industry provided roughly a third of all jobs in the UK and two-thirds of export earnings in 1980. If 'de-industrialisation' is not checked, living standards in Britain will fall further behind those of many Continental countries.

British Rail, roads and shipping

After the **railways** were nationalised (1948) vast sums of public money were spent on re-equipping them. Locomotives and rolling stock had deteriorated through lack of maintenance during the war, and many bridges, stations and sections of track were in poor condition. A new series of BR Standard steam locomotives was introduced in 1951. But by the time the last one was built – a goods engine named *Evening Star* (1960) – **diesel and electric locomotives** were taking over from steam. In 1955 there were 19,000 steam engines in operation, yet eight years later the number had dropped below 7,000. Many that were scrapped had years of useful life left in them. However diesel and electric trains were cleaner, more efficient and required less servicing between runs. The busy Southern Region suburban services to London had been largely electrified by 1939. But there was little electrification in other regions until well after the war.

A costly **Modernisation Plan** was introduced in 1954. More routes were to be electrified; the building of diesel and electric engines was speeded up, and stations and marshalling yards were remodelled. Nevertheless the railways continued to lose traffic to both road haulage and the private motor car. Many local passenger services which did not pay had to be reduced or withdrawn. Britain's rail network, which reached a peak of nearly 33,000 kilometres in 1930, had come down to 27,500 kilometres by 1963. In that year further, drastic cuts were proposed by a Committee of Enquiry under **Reginald Beeching**. To reduce British Rail's big losses, Beeching advised that a further 14,000 kilometres of unprofitable lines should be closed. At the same time, traffic would be built up on well loaded routes: mainly long distance freight and passenger runs and city suburban services.

The Government stopped the full swing of the 'Beeching Axe', in the interest of country areas where railways were an important link with the outside world. Even so, the railway network was down to 18,000 kilometres in 1980, of which just over 20 per cent was electrified. By this time British Rail was carrying only 15 per cent of the country's inland freight tonnage – and losing even more money. But it did better on the passenger side. Higher standards of track and signalling made possible faster and more comfortable Inter-City services. The world's fastest diesel rail service was introduced in 1976 on the route from London to Bristol and South Wales. A similar service began between London and Edinburgh in 1978. These routes used **High Speed Trains (HSTs)**, travelling at a maximum sustained speed of 200 kph. While HSTs were being introduced on other routes, the electric **Advanced Passenger Train (APT)**, capable of over 240 kph, was being developed for the early 1980s.

One of British Rail's prototype Advanced Passenger Trains on a test run between London and Glasgow in 1980

Meanwhile the rapid growth of **motor traffic** caused serious congestion on many roads. The number of private motor vehicles in the UK increased by two and a half times between 1951 and 1961 (from 2,433,000 to 6,114,000) and doubled in the next ten years (to 12,361,000 in 1971). The total increased by a further 2 million in the 1970s – a much slower rate of growth, partly explained by the rising cost of petrol after 1973 (see page 346). The difficulty of finding parking spaces in busy towns, together with ever increasing running costs, led to a growing demand for **small cars**. The 'bubble car' appeared in the early 1950s, and the popular 'Mini, with its engine mounted sideways to occupy less space, in 1959. However British manufacturers failed to follow up this success, until the appearance of the 'Mini-Metro' in 1980. Consequently most of the popular small cars of the 1970s were imported.

The increase in traffic outpaced the improvement of the roads. Not until 1959 was the first of Britain's **motorways** opened – the six-lane M1 between London and Birmingham. By 1978 over 2,500 kilometres of motorway had been completed in the UK. But Britain was still well behind countries like the USA and Germany, where roads of this kind had been built since the 1920s. While motorways improved long-distance travel, **traffic congestion in towns** remained a serious problem. Simply knocking down buildings and widening streets tears the heart out of towns. Other ways had to be found to regulate traffic flow, such as one-way systems, more traffic lights and the introduction of traffic-free shopping precincts. Coin meters discouraged motorists from parking in towns for long periods, 'No

Waiting' signs multiplied, and multi-storey car parks were built to take stationary vehicles off the roads altogether.

The number of **road accidents** remained at a high level, despite improved pedestrian crossings, the fitting of seat-belts in cars and the compulsory wearing of crash helmets by motor cyclists. In 1966 road deaths numbered 7,985 – Britain's highest recorded figure. Hoping to reduce the appalling slaughter, the Government introduced laws against drunken drivers (1967) involving the use of 'breathalyser' tests. There was an immediate reduction in road deaths, to 6,810 in 1968. Overall, this improvement in road safety was maintained in the next ten years. Seat-belts were more widely used, tougher speed limits imposed on some roads and more searching tests carried out on cars over three years old (which require an MOT roadworthiness certificate). Britain's accident record compares favourably with that of most other countries.

In the late 1970s Britain's **merchant fleet** (much of it built overseas) was the world's fourth largest, after those of Liberia, Japan and Greece. A third of its tonnage was under five years old in 1979, making it one of the most modern afloat. Giant oil tankers began to dwarf passenger liners. They became too big for the Suez Canal (which was closed in any case from 1967 to 1975) and had to sail from the Persian Gulf via the Cape. While the value of freight carried by sea has increased steadily since the war, passenger services have suffered in competition with airlines. A shortage of customers on transatlantic crossings led to the sale of the *Queen Mary* and *Queen Elizabeth* and their withdrawal from service (1967–8). The Cunard Company introduced the smaller **Queen Elizabeth 2** in 1969, but this was used for luxury cruises rather than inter-continental travel.

Motorways often require major traffic intersections, with a complicated arrangement of bridges. This one, at Gravelly Hill, Birmingham, was opened in 1972 – and nicknamed 'Spaghetti Junction'

*This enlarged version of the
SR-N4 hovercraft carries
416 passengers and 60 cars*

An outstanding technical advance was the invention of the
hovercraft by a British engineer, **Christopher Cockerell**. It hovers
over water or land on a cushion of compressed air. The first
experimental model, the SR-N1, crossed the Channel in 1959 at an
average speed of 40 kilometres per hour. Regular passenger services
began in 1965, to the Isle of Wight, and in 1966 across the Channel
to France. By 1980 hovercraft were carrying about a quarter of all
traffic on the short sea crossings to the Continent – in about a third
of the time taken by ships.

Flight in the Jet Age

The Second World War, like the First, brought rapid developments in
aviation. Radar navigational aids led to greater safety and regularity,
and aero-engines were improved – particularly with the introduction
of the gas-turbine or **jet engine**, invented by **Frank Whittle**, an RAF
officer. Air was sucked in at one end and compressed by a rotating
fan before passing into a combustion chamber, where liquid fuel was
sprayed in and the mixture ignited. The resulting gases expanded
violently and were forced out of a rear nozzle with such power that
the aircraft was driven forward. Although very expensive on fuel, its
continuous rotary motion caused less rubbing and vibration than
pistons in cylinders, so it could run for much longer without overhaul.

Whittle had taken out his first patent in 1930, being already
convinced that piston-engines and propellers could not provide flight
at much greater speeds. But the difficulty of finding metal alloys
capable of withstanding immense heat held up progress and
prevented the Air Ministry from giving its official backing until 1939.
An experimental aircraft, the **Gloster E28**, was fitted with Whittle's
turbo-jet engine and successfully completed its trials in May 1941,
reaching a speed of 600 kilometres per hour (faster than the Spitfire
then in service). By the end of the war, jets had fought on both sides

Sir Frank Whittle's first jet engine in its original 1937 form

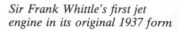

– the Gloster Meteor, designed by Whittle, and the German ME 262. Both proved deadly in air combat.

BEA (British European Airways) was set up by the government in 1946, to operate routes at home and to the Continent. By 1949 all regular British routes were controlled by two state corporations, BEA and BOAC (formed in 1940 – see Chapter 21). The two were later merged as **British Airways** in 1972, while a few much smaller privately-owned airlines were allowed to operate alongside the nationalised giant. After the war British airlines were the first to take advantage of Britain's lead in jet propulsion. The world's first turbo-jet airliner, the De Havilland **Comet**, went into service with BOAC in 1952. It was followed, a year later, by the Vickers Viscount, fitted with turbo-prop engines (gas turbines drove ordinary propellers). Around this time jet-powered military aircraft such as the Hawker Hunter were reaching the speed of sound (about 1,200 kilometres per hour at sea level). Swept-back delta (triangular) wings helped reduce wind resistance.

However just as Britain seemed set to win massive export orders for her jets, serious technical problems showed up in the Comet. Two mysterious crashes in the Mediterranean early in 1954 led to all Comets being grounded. By the time structural weaknesses had been found and a new, larger version produced, Britain's lead in jets had gone. From 1955, US manufacturers such as Boeing and Douglas were producing bigger jet aircraft of greater capability. Boeing later pioneered the wide-bodied airliner with its 747 'jumbo jet', which went into service in 1970. The original 747 carried 370 passengers; later models could seat approximately 500. Throughout the 1970s the world's airlines built up fleets of American wide-bodied jets, including the Macdonnel-Douglas DC10, the Lockheed TriStar and the 747. Britain joined some of her EEC partners in producing the rival European Airbus. Laker Airways, a private concern owned by Sir Freddie Laker, flew Britain's first Airbuses (with British-made wings) in 1981. However these planes had to be sold off when Laker's business collapsed in the following year.

Britain made an earlier bid to get back into the forefront of aircraft design – but with disastrous results. In 1962 the British and French Governments agreed to share the cost of producing the world's first supersonic airliner, **Concorde**. The delta-winged Concorde was designed to fly at speeds of up to 2,350 kilometres per hour (almost twice the speed of sound). The original estimate of research and development costs was £160 million. But unforeseen technical problems delayed progress and put up costs. By 1969, when the first prototype made its maiden test flight, estimated development costs had soared to £730 million. Four years later, while the plane was still being tested, the eventual outlay was expected to be £1,065 million.

Mounting development costs made the selling price of Concorde unattractive to possible buyers. Moreover its heavy fuel consumption and limited seating capacity made the chance of operating it at a profit very slender indeed. These factors, together with concern about its noise at ground level, led most foreign airlines to withdraw their advance orders even before Concorde went into service, with British Airways and Air France, in 1976. Once again Britain was involved in a great technical achievement which proved a miserable failure commercially. In the end only four prototype and sixteen production Concordes were built – at a final cost of £1,400 million. By 1980 only eleven were in regular service – from London and Paris to New York and Washington. The other nine were either laid up, being used for test programmes, or in museums.

Britain's airlines fared better than her plane-makers. British Airways, serving 180 destinations in 80 countries, was carrying more international passengers than any other airline in the world.

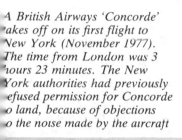

A British Airways 'Concorde' takes off on its first flight to New York (November 1977). The time from London was 3 hours 23 minutes. The New York authorities had previously refused permission for Concorde to land, because of objections to the noise made by the aircraft

Meanwhile Laker Airways pioneered a low cost **Skytrain** service. Instead of booking in advance, passengers were allocated seats on a first come, first served basis. This cut operating costs and reduced fares. The first Skytrain services, from London to New York (1977) and Los Angeles (1978), led to a 'price war' between airlines, with the result that transatlantic air fares tumbled. More passengers had been entering or leaving Britain by air than by sea since 1962. In 1980 overseas air passengers were double the number travelling by sea. Lower fares encouraged millions to fly every year, mainly on cheap 'package' holidays or to visit friends and relations abroad. Air travel, once confined to the rich and to businessmen, had come within the reach of ordinary families.

Sir Freddie Laker entertains photographers at Gatwick Airport (September 1977) before joining the passengers on his first low cost 'Skytrain' service to New York. Rival airlines soon hit back by cutting their own fares, and the resulting fierce competition for customers led to the bankruptcy and collapse of Laker Airways in 1982

Timeline

1941	Successful trials of Whittle's jet-powered 'Gloster E28'.
1946–9	Nationalisation of coal, transport, electricity and gas.
1947	Agriculture Act.
1952	De Havilland 'Comet' – the world's first jet airliner.
1954	Railways Modernisation Plan.
1956	First nuclear power station opened at Calder Hall.
1959	Ml opened – Britain's first motorway.
	Christopher Cockerell's SR-N1 hovercraft.
1967	Production of North Sea natural gas begins.
1968	British Leyland Motor Corporation and International Computers Ltd. formed.
1969	*Queen Elizabeth 2* introduced into service.
1975	First North Sea oil brought ashore.
1976	High Speed Train (HST) introduced.
	Concorde supersonic airliner begins service.
1980	Britain 'self-sufficient' in oil.

Questions

1. 'The British coal industry reached its peak of production in 1885. For every man employed in the coalfields in that year 319 tons [324 tonnes] of coal were brought to the surface. Last year, after 64 years of technical development... only 282 tons [286 tonnes] of coal were raised for every man employed.' (*Manchester Guardian*, 1950)

   a) Why do you think it was harder to maintain high *productivity* (output per man) in 1950 than in 1885?

   b) Since 1950 many unprofitable pits have been closed. How has this affected productivity?

   c) Name *three* ways in which coal has been replaced, wholly or partly, by oil fuel since the Second World War.

   d) Apart from oil, what other new energy resources has Britain developed since the last war?

   e) What are the main uses of coal today?

2.

UK PRODUCTION OF STEEL, CARS AND SHIPS			
	1969	*1974*	*1979*
Steel (millions of tonnes)	26.8	22.3	21.4
Motor cars (thousands)	1,717	1,534	1,070
Merchant ships (thousands of gross tonnes)	1,617	1,951	691

a) Give reasons for the sharp decline in the production of
   i) motor cars   ii) merchant ships.
b) What is the link between the three sets of figures?
c) What changes were made in the steel industry in the late 1970s?
d) How did the fortunes of British Leyland in this period reflect the general situation in the British car industry?
e) Which regions of Britain were most affected by the decline in the output of steel, cars and ships in this period?

3. 'Since 1945 Britain has had one of the fastest rates of economic growth in its history. But it has not been as fast as those in other manufacturing countries. In particular, our rate of growth of industrial production has been lower and our share of world trade has declined.' (*The Industrial Strategy*, published by the Treasury, 1979)

a) What was the average yearly increase in Britain's industrial production in the 1950s and 60s?
b) Name any *four* 'other manufacturing countries' which did better.
c) By how much did Britain's share of world trade in manufactured goods decline between 1960 and 1980?
d) What is 'de-industrialisation'? What effect has it had in Britain on (i) jobs, and (ii) living standards compared with other countries?

4. 'The project is much further advanced than any other known design for a supersonic aircraft . . . and . . . thus has every chance, if we press on with it now, of securing a substantial part of the world market for supersonic airliners.' (Julian Amery, UK Minister of Aviation, November 1962)

a) What was the aircraft referred to here?
b) How was it different from other passenger aircraft?
c) Which country co-operated with Britain in its development?
d) When did it go into regular service? Why was there a delay before it flew to New York?
e) Give reasons for its commercial failure.

5. Write a paragraph on each of the following:
   a) public ownership of industry
   b) post-war modernisation of agriculture
   c) the 'Beeching Axe'
   d) attempts to reduce motor traffic congestion and accidents

27

Elizabethan Britain
Social and Political Changes from the 1950s

On 3 May 1951, King George VI declared the **Festival of Britain** open. To mark the centenary of the Great Exhibition of 1851 (see page 163) special displays and activities were held all over Britain. the centrepiece was a big exhibition in the heart of London, on the south bank of the Thames by Waterloo Bridge. A pleasure gardens, known as 'Battersea Funfair', was also built 5 kilometres up the River. The Festival celebrated 'British contributions to world civilisation in the arts of peace'. It was also intended to give the people what a government minister, Herbert Morrison, called 'a pat on the back' for the sacrifices they had made during the difficult post-war years.

To pay massive debts resulting from the war, Britain had to export as much as possible. Overseas customers came first, so many goods were not available in the shops and **rationing** of basic necessities continued. Clothing was rationed until 1949, milk and eggs until 1950, and ration books were still needed for meat up to 1954. Moreover the country had to rearm for a **war in Korea**, in the Far East (1950–3), where Britain fought along with the USA against Communist China and North Korea. This led to higher taxes and diverted resources from the production of 'consumer goods' such as cars and TV sets. The Festival of Britain gave the people hope of easier times ahead and a glimpse of the kinds of goods that would be available once the export drive could be eased. Some saw the Festival differently. They asked how many houses could have been built with the materials used for the South Bank Exhibition. Nevertheless it attracted 8 million visitors before closing on 7 October.

The end of the Festival coincided with defeat at the polls for Attlee's Labour Government, and the return of the Conservatives under Churchill. Four months later the King died (February 1952) and his elder daughter became **Elizabeth II**. With a new government and monarch, the ending of the Korean War, and the gradual removal of post-war controls and shortages, the early 1950s saw the start of a new era. Thirty years of industrial depression, war and painful reconstruction were over. The radiant young Queen symbolised a new national mood of confidence and hope for the future.

The political scene

Churchill's election victory in 1951 ushered in thirteen years of Conservative government. Many voters were attracted by Conservative promises of greater freedom and prosperity. Helped by a steady expansion of international trade, Britain did, indeed, enjoy rapidly

Princess Elizabeth (destined to be Queen nine months later) with her husband, the Duke of Edinburgh, on the steps of St Paul's Cathedral for the opening ceremony of the Festival of Britain

The House of Commons, 1945-79 (the party forming the government is shaded)

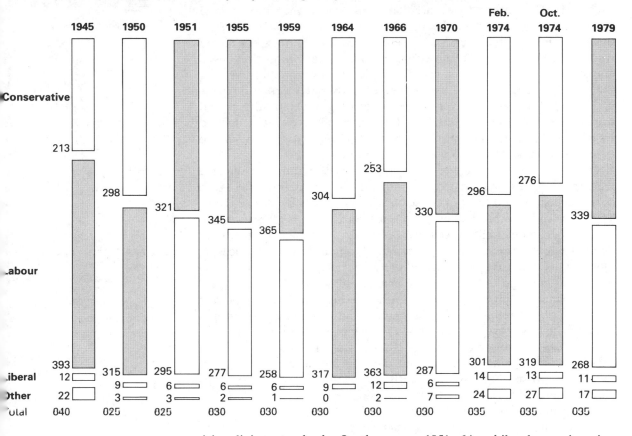

Harold Wilson. During his thirteen years as leader of the Labour Party he won four general elections out of five

rising living standards. In the years 1951–64, while shop prices increased by a half, average weekly earnings more than doubled. 'They have never had it so good', said the Prime Minister, **Harold Macmillan**, of the British people in 1957. But by the early 1960s it was clear that Continental workers were forging ahead, with higher wages, longer holidays and better social welfare schemes. **Harold Wilson**, the Labour leader from 1963, promised a 'technological revolution' and 'planned industrial growth'. Labour won the 1964 election and governed for all but four of the next fifteen years. Although living standards rose, the gap between Britain and her industrial rivals continued to widen.

Both main political parties were pledged to try to maintain **'full' employment** with policies of the kind recommended by John Maynard Keynes (see pages 272 and 302). If business activity slackened and unemployment began to rise, governments normally borrowed to increase their spending and so created extra jobs. At first the task of curbing unemployment proved easier than expected, as the graph on page 346 shows. Many jobs were created by the post-war reconstruction of industry and transport, and expanding world trade kept exporters busy. Indeed, there were usually plenty of job *vacancies*, especially in the public services, in the 1950s and 60s.

Getting to grips with one problem often creates another. Instead of there not being enough spending, 'full' employment meant there was too much. The outcome was **inflation**. This occurs when the demand for goods is greater than the supply and *prices go up* as a result. Once inflation starts, it tends to feed on itself. Workers expect bigger wage increases, firms put up prices to cover higher production costs, and wages and prices chase each other in an upward spiral. As the graph shows, between 1951 and 1968 the yearly rate of inflation averaged 3 to 4 per cent. Overall the purchasing value of the pound roughly halved in these years. But then inflation accelerated, fuelled by higher prices for imported food and raw materials. In 1978 the pound was worth only a third of its 1968 value.

The peak inflation rate of 27 per cent in 1975 followed massive rises in oil prices. Within three months at the end of 1973 the Arab oil producers put up their prices to the oil companies by 300 per cent. They also reduced production. The resulting **Oil Crisis** in Britain and most other industrialised countries showed how heavily they depended upon Arab supplies. Higher fuel costs affected the prices of most goods and gave a further twist to the spiral of inflation. Furthermore the huge extra outflow of money to the Arab states meant there was less to invest in industry at home. So production slackened and **unemployment** increased. The number out of work in Britain was already rising because of the decline of many manufacturing industries.

Governments now had to try to reduce *both* inflation *and* unemployment at the same time. But remedies for one sickness often made the other worse. For instance, cutting government spending might damp down inflation but cause more unemployment – and higher spending might have the reverse effects. In 1979 a new Conservative Government under **Margaret Thatcher** concentrated on attacking inflation. However it did not fix limits on wage and price increases, as many other post-war governments had done (see page 349). Instead it tried to limit the total supply of money and also cut government spending. Unemployment rose, unchecked, and passed the 3 million mark in 1982. This was a clear departure from policies which had been followed since the war.

Failure to solve Britain's problems led to falling support for the main parties in elections. In 1951 nearly 97 per cent voted either

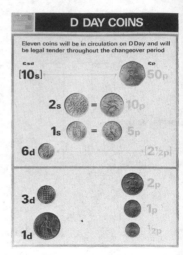

Poster issued by the Decimal Currency Board before the replacement of the old shillings and pence with decimal currency in 1971. The change coincided with rising inflation. Indeed, many people believed it contributed to price rises, because shoppers expected unfamiliar prices and often did not bother to compare them with the old ones

The graph on the left shows the falling value of the pound since 1951. Not all prices go up by the same amount. The 'inflation rate' is the average figure for all goods and services. Compare the graph on the right with the one on page 266

Price inflation in the UK – percentage annual increase in prices

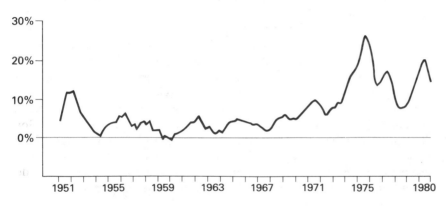

Unemployment 1940–81

Percentage of working population unemployed

Conservative or Labour. By 1974 this figure was down to 75 per cent, although it went up again, to 81 per cent, in 1979. Nevertheless smaller parties found it difficult to break down the **two-party system**. Ever since the Liberal decline in the 1920s (see page 280) there had been no strong third party in British politics. The method of electing MPs was one important reason for this. Only the candidate with most votes in each *constituency* (voting area) is elected. All votes cast for losing candidates count for nothing. So a party like the Liberals could get millions of votes in the country as a whole (over 6 million in February 1974, compared with under 12 million for each of the main parties) yet win only a handful of seats.

Critics of Britain's electoral system pointed out that every government since the war had been elected on less than 50 per cent of the total votes. They called for some form of *proportional representation* (PR). This gives a much closer relationship between the total votes cast for a party and the number of seats it wins. PR is favoured by the **Social Democratic Party (SDP)**, formed in 1981 by a group of ex-Labour politicians who opposed certain changes of policy and attitude within their old party. The SDP and Liberals formed an 'electoral alliance' and quickly gained some striking successes in by-elections.

Two important changes in the political system in this period were the lowering of the voting age to eighteen (1969) and the **reform of local government**. The system of local government set up in 1888 (see page 182) contained many small counties and county boroughs. Rutland for example, with 30,000 people, provided the same range of services as Lancashire, with 2¼ million. Services generally work out cheaper per head if they are run on a large scale. Another problem was caused by people travelling to work in cities from homes outside their boundaries. Such people did not pay rates in the city even though they used its amenities. City councils wanted extended boundaries to bring in these *commuters*. This was done in London in 1963, when a new **Greater London Council (GLC)** took in the outer suburbs. The rest of England and Wales was reorganised by a **Local Government Act (1972)**, which took effect in 1974 (see map overleaf). Six big Metropolitan Counties were created in heavily populated areas, county boroughs disappeared, some thinly populated counties were merged, and district councils, within the counties, were made bigger.

A political reform that failed was an attempt to give Scotland and Wales greater control over their own affairs – known as **devolution**. In the mid 1960s nationalist parties seeking full independence – **Plaid Cymru** in Wales and the **Scottish National Party (SNP)** – began to win parliamentary seats. The SNP built up a particularly large following. In the October 1974 election its candidates received 30 per cent of all votes in Scotland and won 11 of the 71 seats. The Labour Government eventually produced proposals in 1978 which would have given limited powers to new assemblies in Edinburgh and Cardiff. Referenda were held in 1979 and the proposals were decisively defeated in Wales and narrowly agreed in Scotland.

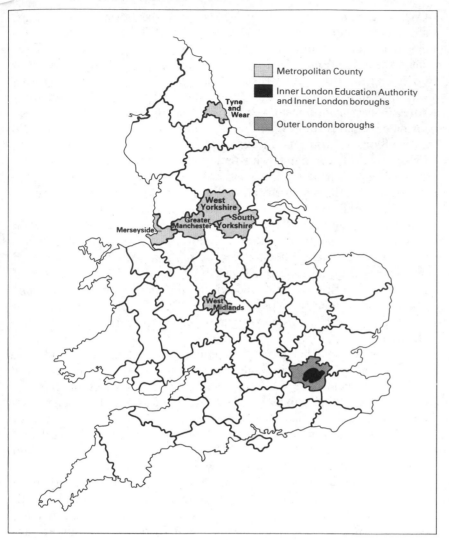

Local government reforms in 1963 and 1972. The new metropolitan counties were not given boundaries as wide as they would have liked. There are still many people who work in these areas yet live outside them. The metropolitan counties are sub-divided into thirty-six metropolitan district councils which have some of the powers of full county councils, notably control of education and social services

Results of the referenda on 'devolution', 1979

	In favour	Against
Scotland	1,230,937	1,153,502
Wales	243,048	956,330

Before anything more could be done, the 1979 election brought to power the Conservatives who were against devolution.

The power of the unions

A new relationship between the trade unions and the government grew out of the Second World War. During the war union leaders sat on various councils which advised Churchill's Coalition Government, and **Ernest Bevin**, leader of the giant Transport and General Workers' Union (see page 275), was invited to be Minister of Labour. Bevin's Ministry could direct people into jobs defined as 'essential' to

Clive Jenkins, General Secretary of the Association of Scientific, Technical and Managerial Staffs (ASTMS) – one of Britain's fastest growing unions in the 1970s. Its membership doubled, from 220,000 to 441,000, between 1971 and 1977

the war effort, and their wages were fixed by the Government. Never before had a trade unionist been given such power. After the war, leaders of the Trades Union Congress (TUC) were regularly consulted by governments of either party – along with the equivalent employers' organisation, the Confederation of British Industry (CBI). Trade unionists were no longer 'outsiders' but accepted as the rightful representatives of the working millions.

Trade union membership, already at a record 7½ million in 1945, went on increasing. Many of the extra recruits in the 1960s and 70s were 'white collar' workers. In the past few technicians, junior managers and clerical workers had belonged to unions. But they had fallen behind many less skilled workers in the wages league and felt the need of some union 'muscle' to recover their former position. New unions like the Association of Scientific, Technical and Managerial Staffs (ASTMS) attracted large numbers of well-qualified and highly-skilled workers. By the late 1970s, half the total working population belonged to a union.

Total trade union membership

1951	9.5 million
1961	9.9 million
1971	11.1 million
1979	13.2 million

Industrial stoppages were still frequent, although **Britain's strike record** in this period was not as bad as many people believed. Simply counting strikes can be misleading. A more useful guide is the number of *working days lost* (if fifty workers were on strike for ten days, 500 working days would be lost). Before the war strikes were generally fewer but they lasted longer. Unions then were fighting to establish their position, often against hostile employers. Now long disputes are rare. In 1921 there were 763 strikes costing altogether 86 million working days. In 1970 there were 3,906 strikes (then the highest post-war total) but only 11 million working days lost. Most modern strikes are *unofficial* (called without approval from union headquarters by *shop stewards*, elected in the workshop or factory). They are often more like demonstrations than strikes – drawing attention to grievances – and are mostly over before official union approval can be gained.

When workers are scarce their 'price' goes up – as happens with goods. Shortages of labour in the years of 'full' employment meant employers had to offer more money to attract suitable recruits, and unions were able to drive a hard bargain. So wage demands accelerated. Union pay claims were often based on both past and expected *future price rises*. This pushed inflation higher and led to growing resentment of trade union power among some sections of the public. Successive governments tried various kinds of **incomes policies** to restrict pay and price rises. But the unions did not always co-operate. They dislike giving up their right to bargain freely with employers – the main reason for their existence. In 1948–50 the trade unions

Strikes – how the UK compares

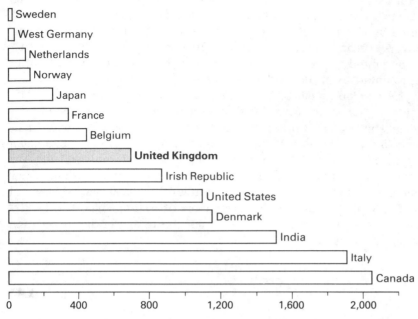

Annual average number of working days lost per thousand employees, 1973–77

Recent statistics put Britain about half way down the international table of working days lost. They do not confirm the widely held belief that Britain's industrial decline is mainly the result of having a far worse strike record than other countries

supported a Labour Government's attempt to control incomes. But they refused to co-operate when the Conservatives tried, in 1961, to get a temporary standstill, or *pay pause*. They objected that profits and prices were not controlled along with wages.

Harold Wilson's Labour Government set up a **Prices and Incomes Board** (PIB) in 1965, to act as a watchdog on profits and rents as well as pay and prices. Meanwhile the TUC agreed to help by discouraging 'excessive' wage demands. But when these schemes failed to produce quick results the Government ordered a year's complete wages standstill, or *freeze* (1966–7). Edward Heath's Conservative Government abolished the PIB. It hoped to reduce inflation partly through curbing the legal powers of trade unions with an **Industrial Relations Act (1971)**. This was bitterly resented by the unions, especially when five dockers ignored a court ruling under the Act and found themselves in prison (1972). The Heath Government changed course and introduced wage and price controls backed by law – the *Counter Inflation Policy*, 1972–4. Again, the unions refused to accept a Conservative incomes policy. A miners' strike eventually forced a showdown with the Government which ended with its defeat in the February 1974 election.

The incoming Labour Government repealed the Industrial Relations Act and made a voluntary agreement with the unions called the **Social Contract**. Unions agreed to limit wage demands in return for Government action to safeguard jobs, restrict price rises and give special help to the low paid. By mid 1978 the annual inflation rate

Miners in Mansfield, Nottinghamshire, march through the town at the end of a month's strike in 1974. Their Union had rejected a wage award under the Conservative Government's Counter Inflation Policy. The Government held an election and campaigned on the slogan 'Who Governs Britain?' It lost, and the new Labour Government made a generous settlement of the miners' claim

was down to 7½ per cent. But the unions were growing restless. Many refused to accept the Government's 5 per cent 'guideline' for pay rises in 1978–9, and numerous strikes led to higher settlements. This contributed to Margaret Thatcher's election victory (1979). She said incomes policies had failed. Her Government tried to control inflation by other means (see page 346) but unemployment soared. Many firms were laying off workers or going out of business altogether, and this reduced trade union power. Unions were reluctant to take a tough line on wages with firms which were struggling to survive.

Population growth and movement

The rapid increase in population in the last century (see page 179) slowed down after the First World War. The average size of families fell from six children in the 1860s to just over two from the 1920s onwards. This reflected the growing use of **birth control** devices. Various kinds of sheath were widely used in the early twentieth century, as were 'solubles' (chemical tablets placed inside the female). However in the 1960s more reliable birth control methods became readily available: the oral contraceptive or 'Pill' and the 'coil' or intra-uterine device (IUD), which fits inside the womb. In 1974 contraceptives were made available free on the National Health Service.

The termination of an unwanted pregnancy by **abortion** became legal in 1968. There were still restrictions – abortion was not provided

Changes in life expectancy at birth – Great Britain (excluding Northern Ireland)

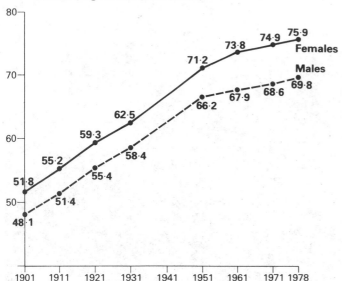

Population growth in the UK since 1901 (in millions)

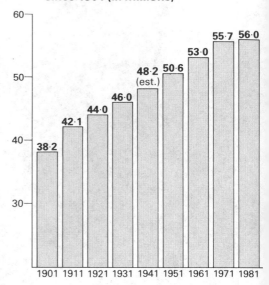

'on demand' as some reformers had urged. Nevertheless from a total of 60,000 legal abortions in 1969, the annual figure rose above 100,000 from 1971 onwards. About 40 per cent of all known pregnancies outside marriage were being terminated by the late 1970s. The widespread use of modern birth control methods and abortion contributed to a further slowing down of the rate of population growth. Indeed, during the 1970s the UK population remained almost static, as the graph shows.

The average UK family size has varied only slightly (between 2.0 and 2.4 children) since the 1920s. How, then, did the population increase steadily up to the 1970s? There are two main reasons: increasing life expectancy and **more marriages**. Since the early twentieth century a growing proportion of the population has been getting married. In 1911 only 55 per cent of women in the 20 to 39 age group were married. Today the figure is above 80 per cent. More marriages mean more families, so the population increased without any marked rise in average family size. At the same time, the **expectation of life** has increased steadily (see graph). This reflects improvements in nutrition, living conditions and medicine in the twentieth century.

Very old age is not much more common now in Britain than it was a century ago. But in all other age groups life expectancy has improved. There has been a particularly dramatic fall in the **infant mortality rate**. Medical advances such as immunisation against diphtheria and the use of penicillin played a big part in this improvement during and after the Second World War. Increased life expectancy means the present population is an ageing one. The proportion of retired people doubled (from 9 to 18 per cent) between 1931 and 1981. So the 'working population', in the 16 to 64 age group, has to support a larger 'dependent' population.

INFANT MORTALITY RATE IN THE UK

Deaths of infants under one year old per 1,000 live births

1911	1931	1951	1971	1980
110	67	31	18	13

Britain's population would have grown more rapidly since the early nineteenth century if it had not been for **emigration** overseas – mainly to Canada, Australia and the USA (see page 214). For a century and a half more people have been leaving Britain than entering it, apart from two brief periods when the trend was reversed. The first was in the 1930s, when many political refugees entered Britain, mainly from Nazi Germany, and the world depression made it difficult to get jobs abroad. The second was in 1958–63, when **immigration from the 'New' Commonwealth** was at its height.

The people of Britain's colonies were granted legal equality with UK citizens by the British Nationality Act of 1948. This entitled them to a British passport, with the right to enter Britain freely. Soon many new UK passport holders were seeking work in Britain, where there were plenty of vacancies in lower-paid jobs. London Transport and the National Health Service even set up offices in the West Indies

The 'Empire Windrush' brought the first post-war black immigrants to Britain from the West Indies in 1948. The 492 people on board were mainly men from Jamaica, a number of them ex-RAF servicemen

in the 1950s to recruit bus crews and nurses. Between 1955 and 1962, over 400,000 immigrants arrived in Britain from India, Pakistan and the West Indies alone. In their search for cheap accommodation, they crowded together in the poorer, decaying areas of cities. Over half settled in Greater London and the remainder in places such as Birmingham, Wolverhampton, Bradford and Leeds.

Black immigration declined after the first **Commonwealth Immigration Act (1962)**. This withdrew the automatic right of entry from the New Commonwealth and based future entry on various kinds of work vouchers. Critics condemned this and later restrictive Acts in 1968 and 1971 because they treated black people differently from white. However governments argued that controlled numbers would make it easier for the white British to adjust to a multi-racial society. Despite the restrictions, an average of 40,000–50,000 black immigrants continued to be accepted for settlement each year. Most were the wives, children and other dependents of men already working in Britain. Black citizens accounted for 4 per cent of the UK population in 1981.

As well as movements in and out of Britain, there were important shifts in the **distribution of population** within the country. The 'drift to the South' (see page 268) continued, because of the decline of the old-established industries in the coalfield areas. Newer industries grew mainly in the South-East and Midlands – close to the largest number of customers at home and on the Continent. The distribution of population is gradually returning to the pattern before the Industrial Revolution, when a third of the people of England and Wales lived in the South-East.

Meanwhile increasing numbers of people have moved out of inner-city areas to the outer fringes or *suburbs*, and beyond. The spread of car ownership since the 1950s has encouraged such **urban dispersal**. It is no longer necessary for people to live near places of work and entertainment, so they can choose more desirable residential areas. Greater London's population fell by over 1½ million between 1951 and 1981, and there were similar movements out of other towns and cities. The resulting 'urban sprawl' has blurred the division between town and countryside in many areas. Despite attempts to check it (see page 305) new housing estates went on eating up fields and woodland. The built-up area of Britain has more than doubled since 1901, from 4 per cent of the land area to over 8 per cent.

Laws against race and sex discrimination

Black immigrants were often resented and treated as outsiders by their white neighbours. Open hostility between the races was rare, but there were frequent attempts to *discriminate* against blacks, by keeping them out of clubs, jobs or good housing. So Parliament gave legal protection to black citizens in a series of **Race Relations Acts**. The first, in 1965, made it unlawful for any public place such as a hotel, restaurant or dance hall to discriminate against anyone on grounds of race or colour. It also became an offence to publish or

Notices like this were common in Britain until the Race Relations Act of 1968 made them illegal

say in public anything intended to stir up racial hatred. The 1965 Act set up a Race Relations Board to deal with complaints.

However racial discrimination continued, especially in housing and employment. Whites often refused to rent or sell property to blacks, and black applicants for jobs were frequently told lies about the post already having been filled. A second Race Relations Act (1968) outlawed such forms of discrimination. It also set up a Community Relations Commission, to work for good race relations and advise the government on future policy. But both the Community Relations Commission and the Race Relations Board had insufficient power. They were replaced by a stronger, unified body – the **Commission for Racial Equality (CRE)** – in a further Race Relations Act (1976).

Instead of just receiving complaints, the CRE can *seek out* discrimination, in firms, public services and elsewhere. It can demand information and call witnesses to give evidence. The 1976 Act covered *indirect* forms of discrimination. For example, an employer could not make conditions, such as the need to have attended school in Britain, which might have the effect of keeping out black people. The Act also allowed individuals to take their own cases of alleged discrimination direct to a court or *tribunal* (industrial court). Nevertheless disguised forms of discrimination continued unchecked. The law can give a moral lead, but it cannot change people's basic prejudices.

Racial discrimination is of course different in many ways from discrimination on the basis of a person's sex (usually to the disadvantage of women). Nevertheless in the 1970s the thinking behind the Race Relations Acts was directly applied to laws affecting the position of women. We saw in Chapter 20 how women won the basic rights of property ownership, higher education and voting. However these measures were only a start on the long road to equality. Women were still discriminated against in jobs, education, family law and services such as housing. In the 1960s a **Women's Liberation Movement** ('Women's Lib') spread to Britain from the USA. Its supporters drew attention to forms of discrimination that had long been taken for granted. They argued forcibly that many women were regarded as possessions, household 'drudges' or 'sex objects' in a male-dominated world.

With new, safer contraceptives, women had more control over the size and spacing of their families. Meanwhile labour-saving devices like washing machines made housework easier and allowed women to lead a fuller life outside the home. They increasingly demanded the right to work and to follow a career. Most jobs could now be done by either sex, as machines replaced muscle power. In 1951 less than 3 million married women had jobs. By 1975 the figure was 6½ million, and married women made up a quarter of the labour force. However, women usually earned less than men, and few reached the top of their trade or profession.

Parliament saw the need for new laws to enlarge women's rights.

A woman working at a blacksmith's forge. Today few jobs are done exclusively by men

Margaret Thatcher became Britain's first woman Prime Minister after the 1979 election. But in other ways the election was a setback to the advance of women in public life. Only 19 of the 635 MPs were women – the lowest number in any election since 1951

Under the **Equal Pay Act, 1970** (effective in 1975) men and women were entitled to equal pay and conditions when doing the same or broadly similar work. Taking effect at the same time was the **Sex Discrimination Act (1975)**. It made discrimination on grounds of sex unlawful in employment, housing and education (although single sex schools continued). The provision of goods and services was covered too. For instance banks, building societies or hire purchase companies could not refuse loans to women on terms that would be applied to men. Like the race law, the Act prohibited *indirect* as well as direct discrimination. A firm, for example, could not impose requirements which would have the effect of putting one sex at a disadvantage.

To help enforce both the Equal Pay and Sex Discrimination Acts, an **Equal Opportunities Commission** was set up in 1975. It works like the Commission for Racial Equality, advising people of their rights and investigating alleged cases of discrimination. Another important measure, the **Employment Protection Act (1975)**, removed some of the disadvantage felt by women at work who have babies. Dismissal because of pregnancy became illegal, and women were given the right to six weeks' paid maternity leave. More important, from 1977 women could return to their jobs for up to twenty-nine weeks after giving birth. This gave them time to adjust to motherhood before deciding finally whether or not to continue working.

Another legal change important for women was the **Divorce Reform Act 1969** (effective from 1971). Divorce was granted upon 'irretrievable breakdown of marriage', including separation of the partners for two years when both sides are agreeable and five years at the request of one side only. In 1977 the procedure for agreed divorce became largely a matter of form-filling. As divorce became easier, the number of dissolved marriages soared. This reflected the changing attitudes of

Divorce in England and Wales: petitions filed (Figures in thousands)

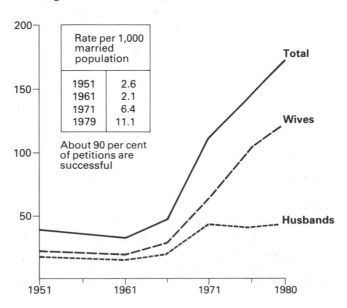

Rate per 1,000 married population	
1951	2.6
1961	2.1
1971	6.4
1979	11.1

About 90 per cent of petitions are successful

women because, throughout the 1970s, about 70 per cent of all divorce petitions were filed by women. Women in particular now have higher expectations of married life. As more got jobs and became self-supporting, they were less prepared to make the best of an unsatisfactory marriage.

There is more 'partnership' and sharing of tasks in modern marriages. Married women, especially if they go out to work, have good reason to expect their husbands to help with the children and the 'chores' and give them an equal say in the spending of money. But greater equality *within the family* has not been matched by similar progress in other directions, especially at *work*. Britain's working married women (7 million by 1979) are still at a disadvantage in competing with men. Only a very small number hold top jobs. So, despite the Equal Pay Act, women working full-time only earned on average just over two-thirds of the wages and salaries of men in 1980.

Widening educational opportunity

The selection of pupils for different types of secondary school at **'eleven plus'** (see page 300) was soon criticised as being unfair. For example, in some LEAs (local education authorities) a third of all pupils went to grammar schools, whereas in others the proportion was as low as 10 per cent. When newspapers began to carry stories of eleven plus 'failures' obtaining university degrees, it seemed that the actual methods of selection could be a lottery. Studies by *sociologists* showed that children of middle-class parents generally received more help with their schooling than those of manual workers. They were more ambitious to succeed, and did better in examinations and interviews than most working-class children of *equal* ability. This gave the middle classes a built-in advantage at eleven plus.

Some LEAs began to scrap the eleven plus in favour of **comprehensive schools**, which took pupils of all abilities. London County Council opened its first new, purpose-built comprehensive school, Kidbrooke, in 1954. Not long afterwards, LEAs such as Leicestershire and Croydon experimented with smaller, two-stage comprehensives in an attempt to reorganise within existing buildings. Meanwhile the number of pupils staying on beyond the minimum leaving age of fifteen doubled between 1945 and 1960. Secondary modern schools developed extended courses to sixteen, entering their brightest pupils for the **GCE** (General Certificate of Education) which replaced the old School Certificate in 1951 at both 'O' and 'A' Levels. Here was further evidence of the ability of some eleven plus 'failures', for the GCE was designed for grammar schools. As numbers staying on in the modern schools continued to increase, the **CSE** (Certificate of Secondary Education) was introduced in 1965 for the majority.

Comprehensive schools were made official policy by a Labour Government in 1965. Its **Circular 10/65** asked (it did not compel) LEAs to submit plans for ending eleven plus selection. Reorganisation schemes began in many areas. However some Conservative-controlled LEAs disagreed with the policy and did not co-operate. A later

Part of the first page of the Labour Government's Circular 10/65, which requested local education authorities to reorganise secondary schools on comprehensive lines. Only 9 per cent of UK secondary schools were comprehensive at the time. Some Conservative-controlled authorities took no action. The Conservatives were not in favour of the wholesale abolition of selective schools, although they later came to accept the comprehensive principle in nearly all areas

To Local Education Authorities
and the Governors of Direct Grant,
Voluntary Aided and Special Agreement Schools

Circular 10/65
12th July, 1965

DEPARTMENT OF EDUCATION AND SCIENCE, CURZON STREET, LONDON, W.1.

All communications should be addressed to The Permanent Under-Secretary of State.

THE ORGANISATION OF SECONDARY EDUCATION

I INTRODUCTION

1. It is the Government's declared objective to end selection at eleven plus and to eliminate separatism in secondary education. The Government's policy has been endorsed by the House of Commons in a motion passed on 21st January, 1965 :

> "That this House, conscious of the need to raise educational standards at all levels, and regretting that the realisation of this objective is impeded by the separation of children into different types of secondary schools, notes with approval the efforts of local authorities to reorganise secondary education on comprehensive lines which will preserve all that is valuable in grammar school education for those children who now receive it and make it available to more children; recognises that the method and timing of such reorganisation should vary to meet local needs; and believes that the time is now ripe for a declaration of national policy."

The Secretary of State accordingly requests local education authorities, if they have not already done so, to prepare and submit to him plans for reorganising secondary education in their areas on comprehensive lines. The purpose of this Circular is to provide some central guidance on the methods by which this can be achieved.

Labour Government took a tougher line in 1976 and tried to compel the few remaining LEAs with selective schools to 'go comprehensive'. When the Conservatives returned to power in 1979 this compulsion was removed. Labour also abolished the 'direct grant' grammar schools (see page 299) in 1976. The Conservatives did not restore them (most had turned into independent fee-paying schools). Instead they began an **Assisted Places Scheme** in 1981, whereby selected clever pupils whose parents could not afford the fees of independent schools would have them paid by the state.

Over 90 per cent of UK state secondary school pupils attended comprehensives by 1980 – more than double the proportion ten years earlier. The change was not achieved without some fierce opposition from those who claimed standards would fall and bright children suffer from being taught with slower ones. Official reports seemed to deny these claims, yet employers often complained about the educational standards of school leavers. For their part, teachers protested that they were starved of the resources they needed. Lack of money had delayed the raising of the school leaving age to sixteen (nicknamed **ROSLA**) until 1973 – nearly thirty years after the 1944 Act had given it high priority. Spending cuts also affected **milk and meals** (see page 297). Free milk was restricted to primary schools in 1968 and to infants in 1971. From 1980, LEAs no longer had to provide milk at all, and government control over school meal prices was removed – to allow LEAs to charge more.

Students at Sussex University, shortly after its opening in 1961. The number of full-time university students in the UK more than doubled in the 1960s

However there were massive increases in spending on **higher education**. In 1945 the UK had seventeen universities – fewer in proportion to the population than in any other major European country. By 1979 there were forty-five. Some, in historic centres such as York, Canterbury and Stirling, were wholly new. Others grew out of *colleges of advanced technology* (CATs), created in the 1950s to meet Britain's need for applied scientists. From the 1960s, *polytechnics* developed a wide range of degree courses, and teacher training colleges (renamed *colleges of education*) increased in number and size. A new B. Ed. (Bachelor of Education) degree course was offered to student-teachers from the late 1960s. But the number of pupils in schools began to fall sharply after 1977. This meant fewer teaching jobs. Many colleges of education had to close down or run courses for students other than intending teachers.

For those unable to study full-time for a degree, the **Open University (OU)** was launched in 1971. Based on the new town of Milton Keynes, it runs correspondence courses backed by TV and radio programmes, residential summer schools and a team of regional tutors. Its degrees are of the same standard as those of other universities, yet no formal academic qualifications are needed to apply to be an OU student. So the OU offers a 'second chance' to mature people who had limited educational opportunities in their youth. In practice, however, the OU has difficulty in recruiting as many unqualified people as it would like. Many of its students are teachers and other professional people. In 1980 over 75,000 undergraduate students were following Open University courses and the OU was awarding one in fourteen of all degrees in Britain.

New directions in the Welfare State

'There aren't any poor now ... Just a few ... in London.' So said a resident in a new town to a researcher in 1959. Many people believed at this time that Britain's Welfare State was 'the best in the world' and that it was 'abolishing poverty'. The truth was different. As Britain's industrial rivals grew richer faster (see Chapter 26) they provided superior social services; and though the Welfare State did much to raise living standards overall, millions still suffered hardship. In 1954 it was estimated that 8 per cent of the population were living below the official 'poverty line' – and the figure was increasing.

From the start of the National Insurance scheme (1948) cash benefits were lower than recommended in the Beveridge Report (see Chapter 24). Moreover they failed to keep pace with inflation. Pensioners especially applied in growing numbers for additional National Assistance – renamed **Supplementary Benefits** in 1966. By 1979, four people out of ten receiving National Insurance benefits were getting Supplementary Benefits too. Some people do not claim the extra money because they consider it 'charity'. To make it easier for them, the organisation of National Insurance and Supplementary Benefits was merged, along with the Health Service, in 1968 in a unified **Department of Health and Social Security (DHSS)**. Enquiries about the whole range of benefits could now be made in one office. It was hoped that those who had been reluctant to advertise their poverty by going to the old Assistance Board would now seek help. But more than half a million pensioners *still* did not claim the Supplementary Pensions to which they were entitled.

Meanwhile, some lower paid workers with large families found they were better off giving up their jobs. Their National Insurance and Supplementary Benefits, which included allowances for children, were more than they could earn. To encourage them to keep working, the **Family Income Supplement (FIS)** was introduced in 1971. Low paid workers, including single parents, with at least one child, can claim weekly cash allowances on top of their wages the amount depending on their income and the size of their family. They can also claim

An applicant for National Assistance (1955). The need to give details of one's income discouraged many people from applying for cash to which they were entitled

free school meals for their children, free dental treatment, spectacles and medical prescriptions, and other benefits including free welfare milk and vitamins for the under-fives. Critics of the scheme called it a 'poverty trap' because its benefits can be lost if the wage-earner gets a rise taking him or her above FIS levels.

Family Income Supplement and Supplementary Benefits concentrate help where it is most needed. However both go against the basic principles of Lord Beveridge, on which the Welfare State was founded. They are paid out of general taxes not insurance contributions, and they are *selective* (only available to those who can give evidence of exceptional need). Equal treatment for all had been abandoned in favour of schemes which reflect inequalities in society.

Similar changes were made in National Insurance. Instead of everyone paying the same flat-rate contributions and receiving equal cash benefits, the better-paid made higher contributions for higher benefits. This **wage-related principle** was applied to retirement pensions in 1961 and sickness and unemployment benefits in 1966. The idea was taken further with the Earnings Related Scheme of 1975. National Insurance contributions became a *percentage of earnings* up to a certain limit (8.75 per cent of up to £220 per week in 1982–3). At first, higher contributions earned higher benefits, but, as the jobless total mounted (see page 346), the cost of unemployment benefits soared. From 1982, only flat-rate benefits were paid to all claimants. Pensions were reorganised differently because two-thirds of all employees belonged to private or *occupational* schemes run by employers. In 1978 a **two-tier pensions scheme** was introduced, consisting of a *basic* pension equivalent to the old flat-rate one and an *additional* pension related to earnings. Those in satisfactory occupational schemes could opt out of the 'additional' state pension.

A new scheme of **Child Benefit** replaced Family Allowances in 1977. Until this date, the Inland Revenue had given an allowance for each dependent child when calculating the income tax of the head of the family. But the poorest families do not normally qualify for income tax, so they gained nothing. From 1977 these tax allowances for children were gradually withdrawn and the money saved used to pay enlarged Child Benefits – for *every* dependent child (the first child was excluded in the original Family Allowance scheme). All parents qualify for Child Benefit, and single parents get an extra allowance.

There were important changes, too, in **housing** policy. Between 1945 and 1955 three-quarters of all new dwellings were built for renting – by councils or new town corporations, with the aid of government subsidies. From 1956 subsidies were only available for houses built as part of slum clearance schemes. More resources could now go into **private house building**. Growing numbers of people borrowed money from building societies to buy their own homes. Many of these new 'owner-occupiers' were manual workers. However the need to find a deposit of at least 5 per cent of the cost of a house to qualify for a *mortgage* (loan) put home ownership beyond the reach of millions of families. Some councils therefore provided 100 per cent (no

Notice the increase in owner-occupied homes. Governments encourage home ownership by allowing house purchasers off some of their income tax (on the part of their earnings that goes to pay the interest on the mortgage)

Types of householder in Britain

Rented from local authorities or new town corporations

Owner-occupied

Rented from private owners and other tenures

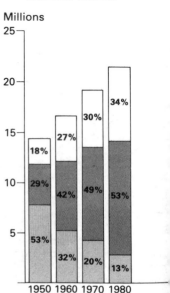

Millions

○ The original twelve new
towns designated before
1950

deposit) mortgages for people of limited means, and various government schemes helped 'first time buyers' – especially young newly-weds. For example, a scheme called *Homeloan* (1980) gave cash bonuses and loans to those saving a deposit for their first house.

Council houses were originally intended for poorer families. But by the 1950s and 60s some tenants were well off and it seemed unfair that their rents should be subsidised. In 1972 a Conservative Government substantially increased council rents, but allowed poorer families to claim some money back – another example of the *selective* approach. The Conservatives also favour selling council houses to their occupants. In 1980 councils were obliged to sell dwellings to tenants of at least three years' standing who wanted to buy them. Labour opposed this policy, saying that there were too few council houses for those who needed them. A million families were on council

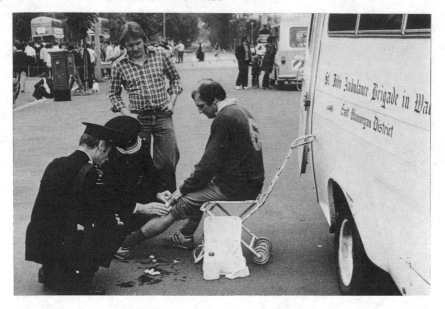

The St John Ambulance Brigade in action. Voluntary services of this kind, financed by private gifts and collections, help to fill some of the 'gaps' in the Welfare State

waiting lists at that time. Many lived in slums. There were still half a million homes classed as unfit for habitation in 1980, despite massive **slum clearance** schemes. Over 3 million people in England and Wales alone were rehoused following such clearances between 1956 and 1974. Some moved to **new towns**, which went on increasing in size and number (see map on page 363).

Meanwhile the **National Health Service (NHS)** remained short of facilities and equipment through lack of money. Long-awaited health centres were set up in most areas by the 1970s, but hospital waiting lists lengthened by a third in the years 1966–78. **Charges** on prescriptions, dental treatment and spectacles did little to offset the cost of the NHS. They covered only 2 per cent of total expenditure in 1979–80 – partly because many people were exempted, including children, pensioners and those receiving FIS and Supplementary Benefits. Many better-off people became **private patients**, often covering the cost with medical insurance. Membership of private medical insurance schemes increased from half a million in 1955 to over 3 million in 1980. A private patient can usually have a routine operation almost immediately, whereas a NHS patient might wait a year or more.

Some people receiving health care, such as the elderly and handicapped, also require **personal social services**. These include domestic help, delivery of cooked meals, day centres and luncheon clubs. The aim is to help the old and infirm to live at home if possible, but special residential homes have to be provided for a small minority. Since 1971 the whole range of personal social services has been organised by the **Social Services Department** of each local council, staffed mainly with social workers. Others helped include 'problem families', young offenders, the mentally disordered and children deprived of a normal home life. All children under seventeen whose parents are unable or unwilling to provide for them must be taken into the care of the local authority. Where possible, they are 'boarded out' with

**Weekly hours of work in the UK
(full-time adult male manual workers)**

Actual hours
of work

Basic working
week

1950 1954 1958 1962 1966 1970 1974 1979

*Alongside the decline in the
basic or 'normal' working
week, there has been an
increase in the number of hours
of overtime worked by adult
male manual workers*

*These 'Teddy Boys' of the
1950s are wearing the first
fashion styles to be designed
just for the young. The
increased spending power of
young people led designers to
produce clothes, shoes,
make-up and hairstyles
specially for them. Some
youthful fashions, such as the
'mini-skirt' of the 1960s, spread
to older age groups*

foster parents, who receive a maintenance allowance. Alternatively
they are placed in children's homes, some run by voluntary organisations like Dr Barnardo's in co-operation with the state.

The Age of Leisure

The British were, on average, 50 per cent better off in 1980 than in
1960, after allowing for inflation. The unemployed still struggled to
make ends meet, as did many pensioners, single parents and low paid
workers with large families. But the great majority of people enjoyed living standards which had risen faster since the 1950s than in
any equivalent period. As the number of working married women increased, millions of households were living on two or more incomes.

When the post-war shortages finally disappeared, the nation went
on a spending spree. With the aid of **hire purchase(HP)**, vacuum
cleaners, refrigerators, TV sets, washing machines and so forth came
within the reach of most families. Luxuries became 'necessities' when
all that was needed was a small deposit, followed by monthly instalments. Britain's total HP debt increased by 75 per cent between 1955
and 1959. Cars accounted for an increasing proportion of the total,
and many new owners were manual workers. The introduction of
credit cards in the 1960s and 70s further encouraged people to obtain
goods without having to pay for them immediately. By 1980 almost
two-thirds of all households had a car, nearly all had a TV set and a
refrigerator, more than three-quarters had a washing machine and
two-thirds a telephone.

As well as more money, most people had more free time. They
worked fewer hours per week and had longer paid holidays. A minimum of two weeks' paid holiday became usual in the 1950s. By 1980,
well over 90 per cent of manual workers had more than three weeks.
Most families could afford to take holidays away from home. At first,
seaside resorts were by far the most popular destinations. Later,
families increasingly took to camping, caravanning and **foreign holidays**. In 1980 over 9 million British people took holidays abroad,
compared with 2 million in 1951. The majority were 'package' holidays, with fares and accommodation included in the overall cost.
Many were as cheap as holidays of the same duration in Britain.

Among the foreign holidaymakers were many teenagers, enjoying a
new freedom from parental restraint. Before the war young people
earned a fraction of full adult wages. But the scarcity of workers after
the war led firms to offer more money to attract school leavers.
Advertisers encouraged teenagers to think of themselves as a separate
group, with their own styles of clothing and a taste for cosmetics,
motor cycles, 'pop' records and magazines. By the late 1950s the
teenage market had become big business, accounting for 5 per cent of
all personal spending. The **record industry** in particular received a
boost. The *Beatles* alone sold 225 million records in 1963–5 – the
peak period for sales of 'singles'. From then on LP sales grew. The
LP was invented (1950) with the idea of putting a whole symphony on
one disc. But before long most LPs were made by 'pop' performers.

Meanwhile young and old alike became addicted to **television**. The BBC's Alexandra Palace service (see page 256) re-opened in 1946. When regional transmitters were provided, starting with Sutton Coldfield in the West Midlands (1950), the rush to buy sets became nationwide. In 1949 two-thirds of the population had never seen a TV programme. Ten years later 70 per cent of households had a set. **Commercial television** began in 1955, financed by advertising, and soon captured a majority of viewers. There were two important technical advances in the 1960s. Transatlantic TV pictures reached British screens in 1962, via *Telstar*, the first in a series of communications satellites in space. Five years later **colour transmissions** began on BBC 2, a new channel opened in 1964. All channels had colour by 1969.

Television led to the decline of both sound radio and the cinema. The average **radio** audience fell from 9 million in 1954 to 3½ million only three years later. Interest in sound broadcasting revived in the mid 1960s with the appearance round Britain's coasts of 'pirate' popular radio stations, illegally financed by advertising. Parliament banned the 'pirates' (1967) but a BBC 'pop' channel – Radio 1 – was provided instead. Commercial radio was later legalised. Meanwhile the **cinema** was even harder hit by competition from television. In the 1950s and 60s hundreds of cinemas were closed or converted into bowling alleys or bingo halls. Weekly cinema audiences fell from 26 million in 1951 to 2 million in 1977. However a slight recovery began in the following year, reflecting the efforts of film makers to recapture customers with lots of thrills, sex and violence.

Increasing leisure time and car ownership encouraged more people to get out and about. Growing numbers visited *National Parks* (preserved areas of natural beauty), stately homes, castles and other historical sites. Attendances at most professional sports declined –

Sales of popular daily newspapers

soccer crowds, for instance, shrank by 15 per cent in the 1970s. But **outdoor pursuits** gained in popularity. Organisations such as the British Sub-Aqua Club and the Caravan Club more than doubled their membership in the 1970s. The less energetic who preferred **reading** bought increasing numbers of books and magazines. However newspaper sales declined from a peak in the 1960s. At that time half of all households took either the *Daily Mirror* or *Daily Express*, and the British bought more newspapers per head than any other nation. In the late 1970s the *Sun*, featuring nude 'pin-ups', became the biggest selling daily newspaper.

Nudity and frankness about sex were already common in films and the theatre by the late 1960s – one sign of more *permissive* (freer or less restricted) attitudes in society. Greater freedom had its drawbacks. Venereal disease, pregnancies among the unmarried, drug abuse and vandalism were all on the increase. Violent crime doubled in the 1970s, and the prisons became seriously overcrowded. But despite its darker side modern Britain is **a caring society** – showing concern for the poor, sick and oppressed both at home and abroad. It is more tolerant and merciful too. People are rarely persecuted for behaviour out of the ordinary, and punishments are less severe. Legal flogging was abolished in 1948 and the death penalty

Until recent times a person's social position was apparent from his or her clothes. But nowadays people from all walks of life buy mass-produced clothes from chain stores and dress in broadly similar ways

in 1965. It is a very different world from the harsh, brutal and much more unequal Britain of 1700.

Since the eighteenth century the gulf in living standards between rich and poor has greatly narrowed. People are on average taller, heavier and healthier. They are better fed, housed, clothed and educated than ever before. But a doubt remains. How much longer will the resources to maintain these standards last? As the twenty-first century approaches, this question becomes increasingly urgent.

Timeline

1951   Festival of Britain.
1952   Elizabeth 11 succeeds George VI.
1955   Commercial television introduced.
1962   First Commonwealth Immigration Act.
1965   Circular 10/65 – comprehensive schools become official policy.
        First Race Relations Act.
1968   Abortion available on the National Health Service.
1969   Divorce Reform Act.
        Voting age lowered to eighteen.
1970   Equal Pay Act.
1971   Family Income Supplement introduced.
        Open University launched.
1972   Local Government Act reorganises local government.
1973   School leaving age raised to sixteen.
        Oil crisis.
1975   Sex Discrimination Act.
        Employment Protection Act.
        Earnings Related National Insurance.
        Annual inflation rate reaches 27 per cent.
1977   Child Benefit replaces Family Allowances.
1978   Two-tier National Insurance Pensions Scheme.
1979   Referenda on Scottish and Welsh Devolution.
1982   Unemployment passes 3 million mark.

Questions

1. 'This month we shall probably get about 85 tons of oil for every 100 tons we expected . . . We must hope that the shortage of supplies will be reversed before long. We cannot expect the sharp rise in oil *prices* to be reversed. This is bound to have a very damaging effect.' (Edward Heath, Prime Minister, December 1973)

   a) Why was there a 'shortage of supplies' of oil at this time?
   b) This would have caused fewer problems by the late 1970s. Why?
   c) By how much did the cost of petroleum to the oil companies increase in the last quarter of 1973?
   d) In what ways did the price increase have a 'damaging effect'?
   e) An additional threat to Britain's energy supplies led to the fall of the Government early in 1974. Explain what happened.

2.

STRIKES AND WORKING DAYS LOST IN BRITAIN					
	1912	*1921*	*1926*	*1972*	*1979*
Number of strikes	834	763	323	2497	2598
Working days lost (thousands)	40,890	85,872	162,233	24,000	29,474

a) The table shows the three years before and the two years after the Second World War when the largest number of 'working days' were lost by strikes. How are such figures calculated?

b) 1926 was an exceptional year. Why?

c) Why would it be misleading to judge Britain's strike record purely on the total number of stoppages each year?

d) Strikes generally lasted longer before the war. Why?

e) What is an *unofficial* strike? How is the tendency for most modern strikes to be unofficial reflected in the figures?

3. Look at the picture of the front of *Circular 10/65* (page 359).

a) How did 'selection at eleven plus' lead to 'separatism'?

b) Why and how was the Labour Government aiming to end such separatism?

c) How are comprehensive schools different from earlier types of secondary school? Give *three* examples of local education authorities (LEAs) which had already experimented with them.

d) Did all LEAs co-operate with the Government after 1965? If not, why not?

e) What percentage of UK secondary pupils attended comprehensives by 1980? Can you explain the big increase in the 1970s?

4. 'The spirit of Beveridge is dead...One look at the financial figures...from the Supplementary Benefits Commission... demonstrates how far away Beveridge's goal of providing "security against want without a means test" has become...Far from declining, the number on Supplementary Benefit has continued to swell.' (*The Guardian*, June 1979)

a) Why are the large numbers receiving Supplementary Benefit against the 'spirit of Beveridge'?

b) What was Supplementary Benefit originally called? Which group in the population has needed it most ever since 1948?

c) The total amount paid in Supplementary Benefit should be even greater than it is each year. Can you explain why?

d) What would be needed to restore the 'spirit of Beveridge'?

e) What are the obstacles in the way of such a policy?

5. Write a paragraph on each of the following:

a) the Festival of Britain

b) immigration from the 'New' Commonwealth

c) laws against sex discrimination

d) the growth of the 'leisure industries'

Index

Page numbers in **bold** type refer to illustrations

Acknowledgements

For permission to reproduce photographs we are grateful to the following:

Aerofilms Ltd., pages 40, 159, 268, 304, 329 (below), 334, 338; Amalgamated Union of Engineering Workers, page 190; Associated Press, page 312; Barnaby's Picture Library, pages 339, 360, 364; BBC Hulton Picture Library, pages 3, 4, 7, 17, 19, 22, 28, 31, 35, 45, 50, 51, 59, 63, 74, 100, 103, 110, 113, 115 (above and below), 116, 119 (below), 120, 122, 126, 127, 130, 131, 135, 145, 146, 147 (above), 151, 152, 154, 156, 157, 161, 162, 168, 172, 178, 180, 181, 186, 198, 199, 201, 202 (above and below), 205, 207, 209, 211, 217, 218, 222, 224, 227, 228, 231, 235, 237, 238, 239, 241, 242, 252, 255, 256 (above and below), 264, 265, 272, 275, 276, 278, 279, 282, 285, 286, 289, 290, 297, 300 (above), 344, 361; British Airways, page 341; BL Cars Limited, pages 249, 331; Courtesy of the Trustees of the British Museum, page 105; BP Photograph, page 329 (above); British Rail London Midland, page 337; British Rail Western Region, page 143; Camera Press, pages 301, 309 (below), 311; Canada House, page 308; Canadian Pacific, page 215; Decimal Currency Board, page 346; Eric de Maré, pages 54, 64, 89 (below), 96, 144 (above), 167; Department of Education and Science by courtesy of the Controller of Her Britannic Majesty's Stationery Office, page 359; Department of Medical Illustration University Medical Buildings, Aberdeen, page 187; Fotomas Index, London, pages 55, 56, 66, 70, 75, 81, 87, 94; Fox Photos Ltd., page 270; Courtesy John Frost Newspaper Library, page 210; The Greater London Council Photograph Library, page 212; James Hall, page 128; John Hillelson Agency Ltd. (Photo: Capa/Magnum), page 295; ICL Photo Library, page 333 (right); Imperial War Museum, London, pages 291, 293; Keystone Press Agency, pages 277 (left), 299, 300 (below), 302, 321, 353; Mansell Collection, pages 2, 6, 8, 11, 12, 14, 21, 25, 26 (above and below), 29, 33, 36, 46, 82, 85, 89 (above), 90, 91, 106, 109, 114, 119 (above), 121, 124, 138, 148, 169, 184, 193, 194, 197, 203, 208, 220, 221, 233, 240, 251, 254, 262, 271; Mitchell Library, Glasgow, page 15; National Coal Board, page 328; National Portrait Gallery, London, pages 44, 52, 99, 259; Pacemaker Press Agency Ltd., pages 318 (above and below), 319; Popperfoto, pages 267, 303, 315, 317, 335, 342, 365; Post Office Copyright Reserved, page 92; Press Association, page 351; Punch, pages 102, 155, 170, 277 (right); Rex Features Ltd., pages 309(above), 313, 322, 345, 349, 355, 356, 357; Rolls-Royce Motors Limited, page 247; Ann Ronan Picture Library, pages 57, 72; Science Museum, London, pages 41, 53, 67, 77, 78, 79, 137, 139, 140, 144 (below), 147 (below), 165, 173, 246, 248; Society for Promoting Christian Knowledge, page 34; Topham, pages 296, 306, 327; Trades Union Congress, page 192; University of Reading, Institute of Agricultural History and Museum of English Rural Life, pages 42, 43 (above and below), 86, 232; Victoria and Albert Museum. Crown Copyright, page 107; Josiah Wedgwood & Sons, page 80; Courtesy of The Wellcome Trustees, pages 175, 177, 182, 183, 185, 188, 204; Sir Frank Whittle via Brian Johnson page 340; York City Engineers Office, pages 253, 284; Reproduced by Gracious Permission of Her Majesty the Queen, page 132.

We have been unable to trace the copyright owners of the following photographs and apologise for any infringement of copyright: pages 69, 129, 164, 191, 280.

Cover: *Steam Hammer at Work*, James Nasmyth 1871. Science Museum, London.